Originally published 1857

GORDON PRESS
P. O. Box 459
Bowling Green Station
New York, N.Y. 10004

Library of Congress Catalog Card Number 72-88301

International Standard Book Number 0-87968-025-3

Printed in the United States of America

TWO VOLUMES IN ONE

THE

SOCIAL DESTINY OF MAN,

OR

THEORY OF THE FOUR MOVEMENTS,

BY

CHARLES FOURIER.

TRANSLATED BY HENRY CLAPP, JR.

WITH A

TREATISE ON THE FUNCTIONS OF THE HUMAN PASSIONS.

AND

AN OUTLINE OF FOURIER'S SYSTEM OF SOCIAL SCIENCE.

BY

ALBERT BRISBANE.

GORDON PRESS
New York
1972

CONTENTS.

THEORY

OF THE

FUNCTIONS OF THE HUMAN PASSIONS.

PRELIMINARY.

IT has been recognised in all ages that the most important of studies is the STUDY OF MAN. In him is the ACTIVE PRINCIPLE, the GENERATING POWER in which all social phenomena have their origin. In him is the Creative Force which has evolved the Arts, the Sciences, Industry, and Political, Social and Religious Institutions. These are Effects of which he is the Cause. His Ear has given rise to the art of Music, his Eye to Painting, Sculpture, and Architecture; his Intellect has created the Sciences; his social Affections have founded Laws and Institutions.

It is of primary importance, then, to understand the nature of the Active, Creative Principle which thus originates Art, Science, Government, and Religion. Moreover, if we would comprehend the social Destiny of the Human Race, the end for which it was created and placed on the Planet it inhabits, the functions assigned to it in the Scheme of the Universe by that Creative Wisdom which called it into existence, the future social changes which are to take place on our Globe, we must first of all study MAN, — must discover and comprehend the nature of that passional and intellectual Motor in him, called the SOUL.

Metaphysicians, the class particularly occupied with the study of Man, have confined their attention chiefly to the study of mental phenomena — the nature of Reason, the origin of Ideas, and other questions of secondary importance. They have not gone to the bottom of the subject; they have made no study — at least no impartial, integral, systematic study — of those active Forces, those motor Powers, those Springs of Action in Man, of which all his acts and deeds, his works and creations are but

2

the *External Manifestation*, and of which the Social Movement is the *Effect*.

To know according to what "categories" the Mind thinks, whether our ideas are derived through the Senses, or whether a portion of them are intuitive, are matters of secondary interest. What we need to understand is the nature of the Passions or Motors of the Soul—of Love, of Ambition, of Friendship—so that we may comprehend their natural action, their tendencies, their requirements, the institutions which should govern them, the system of Society adapted to them. As social Order and Happiness depend on the natural development and action of these Forces, a knowledge of them is of primary importance.

Metaphysicians, seeing the Passional Forces misdirected or perverted under the influence of false Social Systems, and mistaking the effects which they produce under these systems for their true and legitimate action, have become imbued with prejudices against Human Nature, have assumed the Passions to be imperfect and vicious Motors, so that instead of making a careful and impartial study of them, they have fallen into the error of reviling and denouncing them. The Passions can be harmoniously developed, and act legitimately only on condition that they operate in a Social Order adapted to their nature and requirements.

It may be laid down as a Law, that forces can operate naturally and rightly only in mechanisms which are suited to them. This is as true of the Passions as it is of all other forces in Nature—of Steam, for example, which can not produce its legitimate effects in Mechanics, except on condition that it operates in an engine perfectly fitted to it. Metaphysicians have not understood this simple law in its application to the Forces of the Soul. They have not understood that the Social Organization—the external Mechanism of the Passions—should be conformed to them; on the contrary, they have supposed that the Passions should be conformed to the Social Organization—to its laws and institutions. But the Passions rebel against all attempts to adapt them to a Mechanism not in unity with them; in such a Mechanism, their action is misdirected or perverted, and they engender as a consequence, social discord and evil. Instead of condemning the false Social Systems which pervert and denaturalize the Passions, the world condemns the Passions themselves; hence the doctrine of the Depravity of Human Nature and its corollary, the permanent reign of Evil on Earth, have become the general belief of mankind. It has misled the metaphysicians, who have fallen into the common prejudice against human nature and have consequently failed entirely in the study of Man.

A new school of Mental Philosophy has sprung up in our day, founded by GALL, the doctrines of which are much more satisfactory than the old metaphysical theories. It does something more than treat of the origin of Ideas, the phenomena of Conscience, and the operations of Reason. It treats of the real living Springs of action in the Soul, and of their functions in the individual sphere, of their modes of operation and their uses in that sphere, and explains their nature as they manifest themselves in present Society. It does not, however, furnish an integral and systematic analysis of human nature; it does not explain the nature and essence of the Passions, nor the developments of which they are susceptible; it does not explain their relation to the terrestrial Destiny of Man, to the Globe of which he is the Overseer, nor to the Universe, in the scheme of which he has an important work to perform.

In the brief Treatise which follows, we shall endeavor to explain the functions of the Passions, both in the Individual and the Universal sphere, the Destiny to which they impel and guide Man, and their relation to Nature, to Humanity, and to the Universe. We shall present a synthetical view of their Individual and Collective action, of the objects or foci to which they tend, the ends for which they were created, so that the reader may have a general idea of the nature and destiny of the Passions of the Soul. We shall not enter into a detailed analysis of the divisions and subdivisions of the Passions, nor of the special functions which their minor ramifications fulfil, neither shall we explain the Scale and Gamut of each Passion, the degrees of development of which it is susceptible, nor the accords and dissonances it furnishes in Social Harmony. These and many other details we omit, because we are not writing a full Treatise. Our object is simply to present a general analysis of the twelve Radical Passions, and to give an idea of their functions in directing Man in the fulfilment of his Social Destiny on Earth.

I.

GENERAL VIEW OF MAN.

MAN is a COMPOUND BEING, composed of two principles—one ACTIVE, the other PASSIVE. The Active Principle is what is called the MIND, the SOUL; the Passive Principle is the BODY. The latter is the Material Instrument of the former, the means by which it inhabits the planet, acts upon matter, and arrives at a state of positive and practical existence.

The Soul, or Active Principle in Man, is a WHOLE, composed of a certain number of Forces or Motors, which we shall call the PASSIONS; by the Metaphysicians, these Forces are variously termed—sentiments, affections, feelings, faculties, impulses, instincts.

The Passions are spontaneously active and self-determining Forces; they are the thinking, feeling, creating principle in Man—the source of his acts and works in all spheres, material and spiritual. They are the agents of Supreme Wisdom, the Motors implanted in him by that Wisdom to impel him to fulfil his Destiny on Earth.

The Human Passions were not created at random, were not called into existence without functions and employments having been assigned to them; on the contrary, their functions and uses have been calculated with mathematical precision.

Misdirected, smothered, or perverted in our false Social Organizations, no correct or adequate idea can be formed of them in their present phase of development. They are in a state of conflict, confusion, and chaos, and engender the wild disorder, the universal antagonism, the vices and crimes, which now desolate Society, and lead the world to look upon Human Nature as inherently vicious and depraved. Men will not be able to understand the true nature of the Passions, the end for which they were created, until they shall see them naturally and rightly developed in a Social Order perfectly adapted to them. The Passions will then produce as much Order and Harmony as they now produce Disorder and Discord, and in fact far more, for, according to a law in Universal Movement, the order and harmony which reign in any sphere in a state of accord, are much greater than the disorder and duplicity which reign in the same sphere in a state of discord; in Music, for example, the ratio is as seven to one.

In studying the nature and action of the Passions—their distribution, arrangement, classification, and the laws which govern them—a knowledge of the order which reigns in the Material World is an invaluable analogical guide. On the principle of Unity of System, the laws which govern the one, govern the other, and as a consequence, the order and distribution which reign in the one, reign in the other. Let us explain:—

The Universe, like Man, is composed of two principles—the one Active, the other Passive—called in common language, MIND and MATTER; the former is the creative, forming principle, the latter the plastic principle which is acted upon. The order that reigns in the Material World, and the laws which govern it, emanate from the Active Principle or Mind; as a consequence, the Material World is an image, a mirror of the Spiritual World; there is correspondence, analogy, unity, between the two; comprehending the laws which govern Matter, we can comprehend the laws which govern Mind; comprehending the order, distribution, and classification which reign in the kingdoms and creations of Nature, we can comprehend the order, distribution, and classification which reign in the Passions; the knowledge of the one is a key to the knowledge of the other. As we can study Nature more easily than we can Mind, being aided by the Senses, it is important that we should be guided in the study of Passional Phenomena by the study of Material Phenomena.

From the principle of Unity of System here laid down, we infer that the Passions are governed by the laws which we observe in the Material World, that they are distributed in Series like the kingdoms of Nature—are like them divided into classes, orders, genera, species, and varieties, and are capable of harmonies like the Planetary or Musical.

With these explanations, the reader will be able to understand many of the following statements which might otherwise appear obscure or arbitrary; he will have the clue to the analogical study of the whole subject. He has only to remember that the Laws which govern Matter govern Mind, that they have their source in the Supreme or Divine Intelligence, and that all the effects which he sees in the Material World have their correspondence in the Spiritual or Passional World.

The Human Soul, as we stated, is a WHOLE, composed of a certain number of constituent parts or elements, which we call the PASSIONS.

The 1st division of the Soul, or its analysis in the first degree, gives three PRIMARY PASSIONS as follows :—

THE SOUL.
{
1. THE SENSUOUS OR MATERIAL PASSION. . . . Attraction to Matter and its phenomena.
2. THE SOCIAL OR PSYCHICAL PASSION. . . . . Attraction to Spirit and its phenomena.
3. THE INTELLECTUAL OR SERIAL PASSION. . . Attraction to Order and its phenomena.
}

These three Passions place Man in relation and association with the three great departments of the Universe.

The Universe is ONE—a great Organic Whole, which, like the Soul, is composed in its 1st division or first degree of analysis, of three principles which are self-existent, eternal, indestructible :—

THE UNIVERSE.
{
1. THE ACTIVE PRINCIPLE. . . . . MIND.
2. THE PASSIVE PRINCIPLE. . . . . MATTER.
3. THE REGULATIVE PRINCIPLE. . . . . LAW.
}

(In general analysis, we may speak of two principles, an Active and a Passive, united by a third principle, Law.)

Man, standing at the head of the Terrestrial World which he inhabits, and having a function to perform in it analogous to that which the supreme central Mind, GOD, performs in the Universe—that of establishing the reign of material and spiritual Order and Harmony—is a UNIVERSAL BEING, is endowed with a complete Scale of Passions, and stands in relation to and is associated with the three great principles of the Universe above mentioned. The three primary Passions with which he is endowed establish this relation and association.

The first, the Sensuous or Material, places him in relation with Matter, its attributes, phenomena, and harmonies.

The second, the Social or Spiritual, places him in relation with Mind, its attributes, phenomena, and harmonies.

The third, the Intellectual or Serial, places him in relation with the Laws of Universal Order by which the other two are regulated.

We find this threefold division in various other departments of Nature: in Sound, for example, the unity of which, in its first division, gives three sounds—Do, Mi, Sol; and in Color, the unity of which, in its first division, gives three colors—Red, Blue, and Yellow. Nature herself is a unity or whole, divided into three great departments—the Animal, Vegetable, and Mineral.

The three Primary Passions are divided into twelve SECONDARY PASSIONS, which constitute the 2d division or the analysis in the second degree of the spiritual unity in Man—the Soul.

The first Primary Passion branches out or ramifies into five Secondary Passions:—

1st PRIMARY PASSION, divided into five Senses:

1. THE SAPOROUS SENSE, OR TASTE—Perception of and attraction to Flavors.
2. THE ODORIFEROUS SENSE, OR SMELL—Perception of and attraction to Odors.
3. THE OPTICAL SENSE, OR SIGHT—Perception of and attraction to Forms and Colors.
4. THE AURICULAR SENSE, OR HEARING—Perception of and attraction to Sounds.
5. THE TACTILE SENSE, OR TOUCH—Perception of and attraction to Tactile qualities.

These Faculties place Man in relation to the five great departments of Nature on which he is to operate, attract him to and guide him in their regulation, and in establishing Order and Harmony in their domain.

The second Primary Passion branches out or ramifies into four Secondary Passions:—

2d PRIMARY PASSION, divided into four Affections:

1. AMICISM, OR FRIENDSHIP—the benevolent and fraternal sentiment; Sympathy for kind.
2. AMORISM, OR LOVE—the amatory sentiment; Sympathy for Sex.
3. HONORISM, OR AMBITION—the aspiring sentiment; Sympathy for Co-operators.
4. FAMILISM, OR PARENTALISM—the family sentiment; Sympathy for the Young.

These four Affections preside over and govern the four primary modes of Social Relations possible between human beings, and regulate their intercourse with each other. They are the Motors that guide Man in his acts and deeds as a Social Being, and establish Order and Harmony in the Social World.

The third Primary Passion branches out or ramifies into **three Secondary Passions:**—

3d PRIMARY PASSION, divided into three Faculties:	1. ANALYSISM—tending to Division, Individuality, Dissonance. 2. ALTERNATISM—tending to Change, Alternation, and Modulation. 3. SYNTHESISM—tendency to Combination, Collectivism, Accord.

These three Faculties or Forces serialize the play and action of the other Motors of the Soul, and the elements and phenomena of the Material World over which Man presides and in which it is his function to establish Order and Harmony.

Thus the analysis of the Soul in the 2d degree furnishes 12 Secondary Passions; these elements of the Soul, distributed in a consecutive Series, form the *Passional Scale or Gamut.*

The number 12 is that employed in all the higher harmonies of the Universe, and analogy points it out as that employed in Passional Mechanics, which is the highest of all harmonies. Observation, so far as it can be relied upon in the analysis of a sphere so intangible as that of Mind, proves this number to be correct.

It is evident, for example, that there are but five Senses; this requires no demonstration.

A close analysis will show that but four *primary* modes of Social Relations can exist between human beings, and, as a consequence, that there can be but four Social Passions to regulate these four Cardinal modes of relations; Nature never employs more Motors or Forces than there are effects to be produced.

In the Regulative sphere, or that of Law and Order, three *primary* processes or operations produce all the effects of distribution and classification, that is, of Serialization. Viewed in their simplest and most radical action, these are Separation or Division, Combination or Reunion, and Alternation between the two—that is, Analysis, Synthesis, and Comparison. Three Faculties correspond to and perform these three processes.

The 12 Passions of the Soul form the Passional Scale or Series, or, to borrow a technical term from the Musical System, the Passional Gamut. In the higher harmonies of the Universe, the number 12 appears to be universally employed; the elements of each sphere of harmony are distributed in Series or Gamuts of 12.

In Music, for example, we have the Gamut of 12 Sounds — 7 diatonic or full tones, and 5 semi-tones. In Color, we have the Gamut of 12 colors — 7 principal colors as shown by the prism, and 5 intermediate tints, which the prism does not show, but which exist nevertheless in the White ray, though not brought out by the ordinary or prismatic mode of refraction. In the human body, which is a mechanism of high harmony, and a beautiful model of harmonic Serial Distribution, the bones are distributed in Series or Gamuts of 12.

[The system which exists in the distribution of the bones must, however, be understood. In the Series called the Skeleton, there are, as in all Series regularly constituted, *Pivotal elements*, and *Ambiguous* or *Transitional elements*; these are not classed among the *regular* elements of the Series or Gamut, and are not counted as such. In Color, for example, White, the pivotal or central color, is not counted as one; Instinct has governed Observation rightly in this instance. Pivots and Transitions exist throughout Creation, and in all the works of Man which are regularly organized. These, we repeat, are not to be counted among the *regular elements* of the Series; they do not belong, so to say, to the *rank and file*, but are officers and supernumeraries. A few examples will explain what we mean by Pivots. The Sun is the Pivot of the Solar System; Man is the Pivot of the Kingdoms of Nature; the Pope is the Pivot of the Catholic Hierarchy; the General is the Pivot of an army; the heart is the Pivot of the sanguiferous system; the brain is the Pivot of the nervous system; the thumb is the Pivot of the hand; the lion and the eagle are the Pivots of the feline and falcon species; the hub is the Pivot of the wheel, etc.

Mixed, Ambiguous or Transitional elements exist in like manner in all regularly constituted Series, but are not classed among the regular elements of the Series of which they possess in part the characteristics. The bat, for example, is an ambiguous animal, a link between the bird and the mouse; it cannot however be considered as a mouse or a bird, or classed in either species. The quince is a fruit of an ambiguous or mixed character and forms a link or transition between the two series — the apple and the pear — with neither of which it can be classed. The cat is a transition in the feline species. These transitions exist throughout Creation; there are transitional planets in the solar system, transitional bones in the skeleton, transitional sounds, colors, etc. Naturalists have not properly analyzed and classified Pivots and Transitions, and the theory of them is little understood; this gives rise to much confusion, and many mistakes in distribution and classification.]

If there is Unity of System in Nature, unity between the Material and Spiritual spheres, we are led to infer from analogy, that the Soul, divided into its constituent elements, furnishes a

Series of 12 Passions, with its Pivots and Transitions. The Sociologist, with a knowledge of this Series, and comprehending the Laws of Passional Harmony, will be able in the Future, to create Social Harmony, as the Musician, with the Gamut of Sounds, now creates Musical Harmony.

Out of the 12 Secondary Passions spring the Passions of the 3d division, which may be called the TERTIARY PASSIONS; these in turn furnish those of the 4th degree or division—and so on. All shades of developments of the Passions—the tastes, inclinations, desires, in a word the attractions of human beings—are but divisions or subdivisions of the original 12. The perception and sensation of form and color, and secondary perceptions and sensations, like those of proportion and distance, spring, for example, from the Sense of Sight. In like manner, the perception and sensation of weight, density, heat, and the qualities of surfaces, spring from the Sense of Touch. The sentiments of benevolence, fraternity, cordiality, charitableness, etc., spring from Friendship. The sentiments of pride, self-esteem, love of approbation, love of distinction, and the sentiments of dignity and justice, spring from Ambition. All perceptions and sensations, all sentiments and feelings, are shades of development or subdivisions of the 12 Secondary or Radical Passions.

These 12 Passions form the basis of TWELVE DISTINCT CHARACTERS in men, or the great Series of Primary Human Characters. (A character is the result or effect of the predominant activity of some one of the 12 Passions, the others being developed in lesser degrees, and acting in subordination to it. In a MOZART or a BEETHOVEN, the Sense of Hearing is the predominant Passion; in a RAPHAEL or a TITIAN, the Sense of Sight; in a NEWTON or a CUVIER, Analysis and Synthesis. The Poet has combination, imagination, that is Synthesism, in predominance: his poetry receives its coloring from the sub-predominance of other Passions; if the senses are strong, it is full of material beauty and imagery; if the Affections, it is full of sentiment. The Mathematician has Analysism predominant. Thus a Passion developed in predominance over all the others gives rise to a corresponding character which is impassioned for the function to which the Passion tends. Characters of a false or subversive type are based upon the preponderance of the same Passions in their inverse development. The character of the Tyrant, for example, is based upon some shade of Ambition in its inverted or thwarted action ; the scheming, crafty character, upon the low action of the Regulative Faculties, governed by or ministering to selfishness or perverted ambition ; the party-politician is a type of this character.)

The 12 primary Characters are divided into two classes, Male and Female, forming a Series or Gamut of 12 Masculine and 12 Feminine Characters, or the 24 radical Characters of the Human Species. To these 24 Characters, which are the *regular elements* of this Double or Compound Series, are to be added the Pivotal and Transitional Characters, making in all 32 radical Characters.

The 3d division of the Soul, or its analysis in the third degree, furnishes the 32 *Characterial* Passions, forming the basis of these 32 Characters. This is not a regular division, or a division of the 12 Secondary into shades of Passions, but a separation of the 12 Secondary Passions into two gamuts, Male and Female, in which each Passion becomes the Pivot of a Masculine or a Feminine Character.

It is at this 2d stage of Analysis, that the Passions become sufficiently individualized to attract human beings to general functions, and thus decide the predominant capacity in each individual, and his Character. The Sense of Sight, for example, when preponderant, creates the Painter ; here is a general function. The sense developed in its Species and Varieties, gives rise to specific functions, and creates the Draughtsman, the Colorist, the Painter of landscapes, of marine views, of animals, of the human figure, etc.

The 24 Functional or Characterial Passions constitute the *Regular Elements* of the 3d division or analysis of the Soul — or what we may call the *Series of Passions of the 3d Power*. (The Series of the 1st Power is formed of the 3 Primary Passions ; that of the 2d Power, of the 12 Secondary or Radical Passions.)

As Pivots and Transitions are not included among the Regular Elements of a division, it is the 24 Elements or Passions, and not the 32, which form the basis of the 4th division. It is the division of these 24 Passions into their constituent parts which furnishes the Passions of the 4th division ; the number of these

Quaternary Passions is 96; adding Pivots and Transitions, 132. The 5th division of the soul, or its analysis in the fifth degree, furnishes 288 Regular Elements or Passions, and with Pivots and Transitions, 405. In the 5th degree of analysis, the constituent elements of the soul become VARIETIES of Passions, that is— tastes and inclinations, or special capacities and attractions.

The distributive system of the Human Passions into 5 degrees is analogous to the distributive system that reigns in Nature— that is, the division into Classes, Orders, Genera, Species, and Varieties.

CLASSES.	ORDERS.	GENERA.	SPECIES.	VARIETIES.
3 Primary Passions.	12 Radical Passions.	32 Characterial Passions.	132 Passions of the 4th degree.	405 Passions of the 5th degree.

These Classes, Orders, Genera, etc., are so many Series divided and subdivided into Powers, as follows:—

SERIES OF THE 1ST POWER.— 3 Passions plus the Pivot, ... 4
SERIES OF THE 2ND POWER.— 12 Passions plus the Pivot and Transitions, 15
SERIES OF THE 3RD POWER.— 24 Passions plus Pivots and Transitions, 32
SERIES OF THE 4TH POWER.— 96 Passions plus Pivots and Transitions, 132
SERIES OF THE 5TH POWER.— 288 Passions plus Pivots and Transitions, 405

It will be remarked that the number of Regular Elements in each Series is fixed and invariable; the number of Pivots, and particularly of Transitions, is subject to variation, according as the Series is more or less regularly organized; the numbers given above are those which are found in a Series with its full contingent of Elements.

The Passions of the 3d degree from the basis of the 32 Fundamental Characters; those of the 5th degree, or Varieties of Passions, form the basis of the Complete Scale of Human Characters, and direct human beings in the performance of all the varied functions which are required in Social Harmony, and in regulating the distributive system of Order that reigns on our planet.

The 405 Characters, duplicated as Male and Female, form a total of 810 Characters, constituting the Grand Scale, masculine and feminine, of Human Characters. In this Scale or Series each Individual is a note, represents a Character, and fulfils the destiny to which his Attraction directs him. The 810 Characters, united, constitute the INTEGRAL MAN, that is, the COMPLETE SOUL, developed fully in all its degrees.

In this General View of Man, the distributive system that reigns in Nature—that is to say, the Plan of Order and Harmony existing in the Material World—is taken as guide. We proceed from the Known to the Unknown, from the visible and tangible sphere of Matter, to the invisible and intangible sphere of Mind. We believe that this is the only method by which Reason can arrive at a true theory of the Passions. If the Laws which govern Nature or the Passive Principle, emanate from Mind, the Active Principle, it follows, as a consequence, that the order reigning in the former must be a reflex, an image of the order reigning in the latter. Proceeding on this principle of Unity between the Material and the Spiritual, we are safe in affirming that the system of distribution and classification in the Natural World is a sure analogical guide in studying the system existing in the World of the Passions.

As imperfect observations and errors of analysis are easily made, we give what is stated above on the analysis of the Passions, at least after the 2d degree, as purely conjectural ; up to this point, the theory is confirmed by observation. This analogical guide is indispensable to the discovery of a natural classification of the Passions—of a Positive Science of Man.

When we consider the utter ignorance that prevails in relation to the Passions—an ignorance so complete that they are held to be inherently vicious and depraved, incapable of any Order or Harmony—we may say that a SCIENCE OF THE PASSIONS, however elementary or incomplete it may be, provided the basis on which it rests is true, would be an invaluable acquisition ; it would direct the human mind rightly in the study of the most important of all problems, namely, the Nature of Man and the possibility of establishing the reign of Social Harmony on Earth.

The Table that follows presents a general outline of the subject we are treating. It gives the analysis of the Soul in its 2d degree of division, defines the twelve Radical Passions composing the Passional Gamut, explains their nature, and points out their Functions in the Great Scheme of Human Destiny.

The three articles on the Functions of the Senses, the Affections, and the Intellectual Faculties, are intended merely as explanations of the Table, and should be read in the order indicated in the central column.

II.

FUNCTIONS OF THE FIVE SENSUOUS PASSIONS.

THE PRIMARY FUNCTION of the five Senses is to establish relation and connection between the ACTIVE and PASSIVE Principles, between Mind and Matter, between Man and Nature, and to attract man to and guide him in an important work in the Economy of the Universe, namely, the Supervision of the Planet which he inhabits, and its Vegetable and Animal Kingdoms.

Man is the OVERSEER of the Globe, charged by divine Wisdom with the cultivation and embellishment of its surface, with the improvement of its animal and vegetable creations, and with the realization upon it of material beauty, order, and harmony.

The execution of this great work is of supreme importance in carrying out the Divine Plan of Harmony in Creation :—

I. Because it would place the Globe in its natural condition of Order, that is to say, of Health, and thus enable it to perform all its functions in the Sidereal System to which it belongs.

II. Because it would furnish the basis of the Social Elevation of Man ; for a harmonized Globe, on which material order, beauty, and unity reign, is the primary condition of the moral and intellectual elevation of its inhabitants.

To attract man to the cultivation and embellishment of the Earth, the five Senses, or the five modes of perceiving the attributes and relations of Matter, have been given to him by God, who distributes to all his creatures ATTRACTIONS PROPORTIONAL TO DESTINIES.

On every Globe, the supervision, the regulative action of a superior Intelligence is necessary, for Matter degenerates without the supervising and controlling influence of Mind. On the Earth, this superior Intelligence is Man. He is its OVERSEER, its intellectual Sovereign. He is the Science and Reason of Nature ; in other words, he alone possesses the knowledge necessary for the development and improvement of her creatures ; he alone can establish Order and Harmony in her Domain. The animal and vegetable creations are active, living Forces, but they do not possess the Reason necessary for regulating their development, their distribution, their relations, and for attaining to perfection. The fruit-tree, for example, can not graft nor transplant itself, nor can the animals cross their breeds or otherwise improve their species. This must be done for them by Man; hence, as we have stated, he is the Reason, the Science of Nature—the Regulator of her Vegetative and Instinctual Forces.

The five Senses have each a special Function to perform in attracting and impelling Man to fulfil his destiny of Overseer and Harmonist of the Globe.

The SENSE OF TASTE, which finds its gratification and delight in agreeable Flavors, attracts Man to the cultivation and improvement of the fruits, grains, vegetables, spices, wines, oils, and other products which please his palate and serve him as food. He can not possess these products without cultivating them, and in cultivating them he is led of necessity to the improvement and embellishment of the Earth. Man is omnivorous; his palate harmonizes with nearly all the flavors of Nature, and not with one or two like that of the animal. This universality of Taste in Man was given him to secure the cultivation of all the various edible and condimentary products of the Earth, from the fruits and spices of the Tropics to the grains and vegetables of the Temperate Zone. Had Man been created moniverous—that is, to live like the animal, on one or two products—he would have cultivated those products only, and have covered the Earth with them. If he had attraction for bread alone, he would make of the earth one vast wheat-field; if for the potato, one great potato-patch. Without this universality in the Sense of Taste, the Globe would present in its culture one unbroken scene of monotony and uniformity; most of the creations in the vegetable and many in the animal kingdom would be neglected, and finally become extinct.

The SENSE OF SMELL, which finds its delight in agreeable perfumes, attracts Man to the cultivation of the flowers, plants, shrubs, gums, etc., which yield fragrant perfumes. Taste having no affinity for these products, another Sense intervenes to establish the relation between them and Man, and to secure at the hand of the Terrestrial Overseer, their cultivation and development.

The SENSE OF SIGHT, which finds its gratification in harmony of Form, Color, and Proportion, attracts Man to beauty of rural scenery, and induces him to cultivate the ornamental trees, shrubs, vines, flowers, etc., necessary to the embellishment of the landscape. It attracts him to splendor and elegance in architecture, and leads him to work the marbles, woods, metals, and other materials necessary to the construction and to the beauty of his edifices. It attracts him to elegance in dress, in furniture, and in personal appearance, and leads him to grow and cultivate the silks, the fine fleeces, the rich dyes necessary to the interior decoration of his abode, and to the embellishment of his person.

The SENSE OF TOUCH finds its delight in agreeable Tactile Sensations; spread over the entire body, it places the nervous sensibility of Man in contact with Matter, and compels him for its protection and gratification to provide himself with comfortable dwellings, to invent comfortable means of locomotion, and to adapt to its requirements all material objects which come in contact with his body. The demands of this Sense impel Man to grow the cottons, the wools, the flax, etc., with which the other Senses—Taste, Sight, Smell, Hearing—have no affinity. Were it not for the Sense of Touch, a wide range of products in the three kingdoms would be neglected, leaving so many blanks in the great field of Nature. The Tactile Sense is destined also to exercise a powerful influence upon the general Cultivation of the Globe by inducing Man to improve the Climate — to temper the Atmosphere, which is the great external Dress of all animated Nature, and upon the state of which his comfort and well-being so much depend. Man can perfect the Climatic System, which is a department of Nature under his control, by an integral and scientific Cultivation of the Globe; and in future ages, this important work will enter largely into the industrial policy of nations.

The SENSE OF HEARING; this Sense exercises the least direct influence in attracting Man to Industry, and to the Cultivation of the Globe. Nevertheless, in requiring instruments of Music, concert-halls, opera-houses, etc., the construction of which involves the growing of the choicest woods, the preparation of metals and other substances, it is not without some influence in the great work of terrestrial Cultivation and Embellishment. The Sense of Hearing is the only one of the five Senses which has evolved a complete system of Art and Harmony. The four other Senses are destined to evolve similar systems of Harmony in their respective spheres; the Sense of Sight, for example, Geometrical and Chromatic Harmony, or Harmony of Form and Color—already partially developed in Painting, Sculpture, and Architecture; the Sense of Smell, Odoriferous Harmony or Harmony of Odors; the Sense of Taste, Saporous Harmony or Harmony of Savors; the Sense of Touch, Tactile Harmony or Harmony of Sensations.

Each Sense has, like that of Hearing, its Scale or Gamut of Elements upon which to operate, and from which to evolve its corresponding Art and Harmony. As the Sense of Hearing has its Scale or Gamut of Sounds, which can be so distributed and arranged as to furnish the elements of Musical Harmony—namely, Accord, Dissonance, Measure, Rhythm, etc.—so each of the other Senses has its Scale or Gamut of Elements from which so many systems of Art and Harmony are to be evolved; Taste, its Gamut of Flavors; Sight, its Gamut of Forms and Colors; Smell, its Gamut of Odors; Touch, its Gamut of Sensations.

When each of the five Senses shall have led to the discovery and creation of its corresponding Harmony, Man will realize upon the Earth the reign of UNIVERSAL ART; he will harmonize the Globe and the Kingdoms of Nature under his supervision, elevate the Natural World to Unity with the Spiritual World, and make of this Planet a grand Concert of Material Harmonies.

Thus the Senses, which have been looked upon by Moralists and Philosophers as Passions of a low order, ministering merely to the wants of the body, engendering often sensuality, brutality, and vice, and always at war with the higher nature of Man, are in truth noble and sublime Faculties—agents employed by Supreme Wisdom in attracting Man to the cultivation and embellishment of the Material World over which he presides.

It is true that the Senses do not at present fulfil their natural or legitimate functions. Undeveloped or falsely developed, misdirected or perverted in Social Organizations unsuited to their nature and action, they perform only their lower or animal functions, ministering simply to the physical wants of the body, and leading often to selfishness, sensuality, and debauchery. It is only in a true Social Order, in which they will be fully and harmoniously developed and properly directed, that they will per-

3

form their higher and Artistic functions; they will then be found to be noble Faculties, Interpreters of the designs of God in respect to Man's relations with the Material world—Harmonic Forces, attracting him to make of this Globe a terrestrial Paradise, in which to develop the higher Spiritual nature with which he is endowed, and to erect a magnificent Superstructure of Social Harmony on the Substructure of Material Harmony, prepared by the Senses.

The present neglected, uncultivated, or devastated condition of the Earth—covered as three fourths of it are with vast deserts, marshes, wastes, and wildernesses—is not its true and is not to be its permanent condition. It is a false and subversive state, the result of Man's neglect to fulfil his destiny of Overseer of the Globe. The effects of the maladministration of his Terrestrial Domain are terrible upon himself and upon all animated Nature. The Climate is everywhere deranged, as is seen by the sudden and violent fluctuations of temperature, by droughts and prolonged rains, by hurricanes and tornadoes, and other atmospheric excesses which are constantly recurring. The magnetic system of the Planet is vitiated, and the effect of this vitiation, combined with the emanations from morasses, swamps, bogs, etc., is to engender epidemic diseases—the plague, the cholera, the yellow fever, etc.—which scourge the race alternately on every part of the Globe. The Equatorial Regions are covered with great deserts and burned by intense and unnatural heats, while the vast regions of the North are chilled by perpetual frosts, and both are rendered uninhabitable to Man, and unfit for fields of Industrial activity.

These evils, the result of Man's malsupervision of the Globe, gigantic and irremediable though they appear, may be extirpated by the systematic and integral cultivation of the Earth's surface, which will be effected when the combined Labor and Talent of the Human Race, under the influence of Universal Association and Attractive Industry, shall be directed to this great end. The deserts will then be reclaimed, the marshes and morasses drained, the waste lands fertilized, the vast forests cleared, the waters diked and regulated in their course—in a word, the Earth's entire surface brought under scientific and artistic cultivation.

Having now explained the Primary Function of the five Senses, that of impelling and directing Man in the fulfilment of his Industrial Destiny of Overseer of the Globe, we will touch briefly upon some of their subordinate functions.

I. They enable the Soul to communicate with the external world; the Soul, embodied in a material frame, must have material instruments by which to hold intercourse with the world around it; the Senses—the physical faculties of the Soul—perform this function. The Ear, for example, hears sounds, caused by the human voice, the cries of animals, the vibrations of bodies, and conveys to the mind the ideas of intelligent beings and the knowledge of the motions of material objects. The Eye sees signs, gestures, written and printed characters, and the movements of bodies, and thus in another way conveys to the mind a knowledge of the phenomena of mental and physical existence; and so with the other Senses, in their respective spheres.

II. They form the basis for the development of the seven higher or Spiritual Faculties of the Soul, and strengthen and exalt their action. These faculties, the four Social and the three Intellectual, see themselves represented and mirrored in material forms, and this image of themselves impressed on Matter gives to them a full and practical consciousness of their existence.

In the Soul of the Painter float the conceptions of beauty, love, dignity, tenderness, justice, which he would represent; but it is only when these conceptions are embodied in a material shape, in a work of Art, and are presented in form and color—in tangible reality—through the eye back to the Soul, that the latter fully feels itself, fully enjoys its own ideal.

In like manner, in the Soul of the Musician exists the ideal of the harmonies he would create, but they are without form and void of reality. It is only their artistic execution on material instruments and by the human voice, which gives to him the real sentiment of his ideal, exalting the Soul by presenting to it an external image of itself. The ideal, without its external and material embodiment or correspondence, is vague, void, and unsatisfactory. The delight of God himself is to behold in the material creations of the Universe the Types and Images of the ideas and sentiments which prompted him to their creation.

III. They furnish the elements or materials for the creation of the Fine Arts. The Ear hears sounds, the Eye perceives forms and colors, which they communicate to the Mind. These elements are distributed, classified, arranged, in a word, *serialized* by the three Intellectual Faculties, and the Arts of Painting, Sculpture, Music, etc. are the result. The other three Senses—Taste, Smell, Touch—furnish the elements of three other branches of Art, not yet discovered, but which at some future day will be scientifically developed, as the Musical Art now is.

IV. They furnish Man with ideas of a Material Order. He possesses three classes of ideas—first, Material ideas, derived from the perceptions of the Senses; second, Immaterial or Spiritual Ideas, derived from the intuitions of the Social Affections; third, Abstract or Complex ideas, or ideas of Laws and Principles, derived from the reflection of the Intellectual Faculties. The Senses furnish the first of these three classes of ideas; they perceive Material facts and phenomena which they communicate to the Mind, and which, by a certain process of intellectualization that may be called analysis, synthesis, and comparison, become Ideas.

V. They form the basis of the Positive Sciences. In furnishing observations and ideas of Material things to the mind, they supply the elements with which the Intellectual Faculties create these Sciences. The Eye, for example, in observing the phenomena of the heavens, furnishes Reason with the data from which it creates the Science of Astronomy; and so with Chemistry, Physiology, and the other Physical Sciences.

The other functions of the Senses are summed up in the Table, under the proper head, and will be understood without further explanation.

III.

FUNCTIONS OF THE FOUR SOCIAL OR PSYCHICAL PASSIONS.

THESE Passions perform functions in the Social World analogous to the functions which the Senses perform in the Material World. They are the means of sympathetic or affectional communication between Souls, as the Senses are the means of communication between the Soul and Matter. They establish the Unity of Man with Man, as the Senses establish the Unity of Man with Nature. They impel him to fulfil his Social Destiny on Earth, as the Senses impel him to fulfil his Industrial Destiny.

The Social Passions constitute in their unity but one Passion or Love, namely, Love for the great Collective Being inhabiting the Planet, and variously called Mankind, Humanity, the Human Race. This Collective Love, when resolved into its constituent elements, contains in its 1st division four Primary Loves or Modes of Sympathy, imperfectly defined under the names of Friendship, Love, Ambition, and Parentalism. These four Affections govern the four primary modes of Social Relations between Human Beings, as the five Senses govern the five primary departments or spheres in the Material World.

The first of the four Psychical Passions — FRIENDSHIP — presides over and governs the Social Relations of Human Beings in their capacity as individuals of the same Species, members of the same Race, without regard to distinctions of age, sex, rank, color, or fortune, and regulates their intercourse on the basis of Equality. It associates them as friends, comrades, companions, and equals, leveling for the time ranks, grades, and other distinctions, and establishing between them the Spirit and Tone of familiarity, equality, and fraternity. It is the most general in its action of the four Social Passions, and the most independent of external distinctions; it is the benevolent, fraternizing, equalizing Sentiment of the Soul. This Passion establishes frankness, candor, sincerity, cordiality, benevolence, and charitableness in the Social relations of men.

The Human Race is ONE. It is a great Collective Being, with the Globe for its field of Operations, and having certain Functions to perform in the Scheme of Creation. This Collective Being is composed of innumerable Individualities, which must be associated and united in their operations, so that through perfect co-operation and unity of action, they may fulfil their Function or Destiny.

As Man is a Compound Being, composed of an Active and a Passive Principle, of Spirit and Matter, and as the former acts through the latter, each of the four Social Passions manifests itself Materially as well as Spiritually, and is excited to action by material as well as spiritual affinities.

The two affinities which call out the action of the Passion of Friendship are :—

1. Spiritual—Affinity of Character.
2. Material—Affinity of Pursuits.

Thus the individual is drawn to his Race,

1. By Sympathy of Species, or Identity of Nature.
2. By Unity of Function, or Identity of Destiny;

and is drawn to Individuals,

1. By Spiritual Affinity of Character.
2 By Material Affinity of Industrial, Artistic, and Scientific Pursuits.

Thus is established the first link between the members of the Species—the first degree of Sociality and Social Unity among Men.

The Second Social Passion—Love—presides over and governs the relations between the Sexes. It attracts beings of opposite sex to each other, and associates them by Spiritual and Material ties—by the Spiritual tie of the Soul, and the Material tie of the Body—and thus establishes the unity of the Male and Female elements or principles in the Race. It inspires deference, devotion, admiration on the part of the stronger for the weaker sex, subordinates the principle of Force to that of Charm and Beauty, and thus furnishes an important element of Harmony in the Social Movement.

This Passion establishes the second degree of Sociality and Social Unity on earth.

The Race, as we have stated, is One, divided into Individualities; these Individualities, again, are divided into two parts or

Sexes— the MALE and the FEMALE. The Passion of Love brings together and associates the Sexes, and establishes between them the closest, the most intimate, the most tender and romantic ties. It gives to the Social relations it forms a poetry, a charm, which exalts the beings whom it animates, idealizes them in each other's eyes, fills the Soul with enthusiasm, and thus neutralizes and absorbs the selfish tendency of the Senses and the cold calculations of Reason.

We speak, now, of the influence of Love in its Spiritual action, (which should govern the Material as the mind governs the body,) and in a Social Order adapted to its free, full, and natural development. The stimulants which excite this Passion to action are :—

1. SPIRITUAL —Affinity of Soul, or Platonic Love.
2. MATERIAL —Affinity of Sense, or Sensuous Love.

The latter is the body of the former ; it gives to it individuality, intensity, and definiteness ; it should, however, always be kept under the control and regulation of the former, by which it is elevated and idealized. Let us add that this Passion, enslaved, thwarted, or misdirected in the present Social Order by poverty, by defective domestic arrangements, by moral prejudices, and false Social Institutions, can neither receive its legitimate development nor fulfil its natural functions. Of all the Passions, it is the least understood and appreciated, and the one upon which the most erroneous judgments are passed.

The Third Social Passion — AMBITION — presides over and regulates the relations of men in their capacity as coöperators, colleagues, united in the prosecution of the various departments of Industry, Art, and Science — that is, of all the functions and labors of life. It draws individuals together who have a common purpose in view, a common end to attain, and unites and associates them for the realization of their plans. It arouses emulation, excites aspiration, stimulates to the execution of great works by the desire of the approval of coöperators, and assigns ranks, honors, rewards, position, according to Genius, Devotion, and Services. It establishes rank, grade, distinction in human relations, determined by services and merit, as Friendship establishes fraternity, equality, and companionship. The action of Ambition is consequently the inverse of that of Friendship, and it is by the operation of these contrasted influences that Harmony is established in Society.

In its individual action, it is the desire on the one hand of leadership, with the love of direction, command, and dominion, and on the other, the desire of following capable and experienced leaders, with the sentiment of deference, respect, reverence for recognised genius, capacity, and merit. In its essence, it is the aspiring, exalting Sentiment, the love of grandeur and power, the desire of accomplishing great ends, of achieving great works, — the passion for elevation and distinction. It prompts Man to acts of Devotion and Heroism, by the stimulus of these various motives.

The Individualities of which the Race is composed possess different degrees and varieties of capacity, and stand to each other in the relation of Superiors and Inferiors in genius, talent, knowledge, and skill. Ambition associates them on this basis, that is to say, as leaders and followers, instructors and instructed, directors and directed, organizers and executors, coöperating together for the accomplishment of a common work. It creates sympathies founded on admiration for genius, merit, and executive power. In its ascending scale of development, it is, as we have said, the desire of Leadership, and in its descending scale, reverence for capacity of Leadership. It ranks and classifies diversified talents and capacities, establishes hierarchy in them, and creates sympathies between individualities based on genius and merit.

Ambition thus establishes the third degree of Sociality and SOCIAL UNITY between human beings, founded on the accord of diversified capacities, necessary to each other and to the execution of works connected with Human Destiny. The two elements of this Passion are : —

1. SPIRITUAL — Love of Grandeur, Distinction, Fame.
2. MATERIAL — Love of Power and Wealth.

The Fourth Social Passion — PARENTALISM or the Family Sentiment — presides over and regulates the relations of parents and children, and, in its more general action, of the old and the young, the strong and the weak, the capable and the helpless, exciting sympathy for childhood, and extending its action to all the weak, unprotected, and dependent members of the human family. It associates Age and Infancy, forms the tie between Generations, and governs their relations and interests; it is the protective, guardian, tutelary, providential Sentiment.

The Individualities composing the Race are divided into different ages, distributed in an ascending and descending Series, extending from infancy to old age. These individualities appear and disappear on the stage of life, and establish the succession of ages and generations. Parentalism creates sympathy between the successive generations and the different ages, associates them, and thus renders Humanity a continuous Whole, united in all its various stages of development. It excites in the older, stronger, and more experienced individualities of the Race, regard, love, and watchful supervision for the younger, weaker and less experienced, and by their protection, and education, secures first the care of the Species, and second, the intellectual progress and development of Mankind. This Passion thus establishes the fourth degree of Sociality or SOCIAL UNITY among the members of the Human Family. Its elements are : —

1. SPIRITUAL — Adoptive Paternity, from sympathy of character.
2. MATERIAL — Natural Paternity, from the tie of consanguinity.

All forms of Social Relations which can exist among human beings, all modes of intercourse between them, are but branches of some one of these four Cardinal Relations, and are presided over and regulated by the four Social Passions.

All subversive Social Relations — those of an oppressive, tyrannical, treacherous, and generally of an antagonistic character — are Inversions of some one or more natural or harmonious relations, produced by the clashing of interests, compulsory association of antipathetic characters, and conflicts of plans, thwarting the affections, and engendering antipathies, disappointment, and despair. These false relations are governed by the Social Passions in their inverted or subversive development. The Tyrant who oppresses and spoliates his subjects for his own aggrandizement, is governed by false or inverted Ambition. The Calumniator who slanders and injures his fellow-man, is governed by inverse Friendship, or Friendship perverted in its action.

All forms of hatred and cruelty are but inversions of good and noble sentiments; for example, Antipathy is the inversion of Sympathy, Misanthropy of Philanthropy, Malevolence of Benevolence, Jealousy of Confidence, Calumny of Charity, Baseness of Dignity, Cruelty of Compassion, and so on through the whole scale of the developments of the Passions, in their direct and inverse, their harmonious and discordant action.

All direct and harmonious sentiments, such as benevolence, kindness, justice, philanthropy, etc. are *spontaneously active in the Soul*—that is, act naturally and of themselves—while the same sentiments, inversely developed and engendering hatred, jealousy, revenge, malevolence, antipathy, are *not spontaneously active;* these subversive emotions are aroused by false and unnatural circumstances, thwarting and outraging the true and harmonious affections corresponding to them.

The four Social Affections, developed in their lower degrees, manifest themselves in the form of sympathy between individuals —affection for one's friends, one's children, the desire of personal elevation. Developed in their higher degrees, and transcending the sphere of individual sympathy, they manifest themselves in the form of Collective or General sentiments, such as Love of Country or Patriotism, Love of Mankind or Philanthropy. Developed in their supreme or super-terrestrial degrees, and transcending the sphere of Humanity, they generate the Religious Sentiment, or Love of God.

The love of Man for Man is the same in nature and essence as the Love of Man for God; they are the two extreme links in the great chain of sympathies extending from the Finite to the Infinite—the two extremes in the grand Series of Sympathetic Accords of which the Soul is capable. Thus the Religious Sentiment is nothing but the Humanitary Sentiment universalized. The Love of Man is the basis of the Love of God, and the latter can not exist in its fullness till the former is developed and exercised in all its degrees.

The four Social Passions, falsely or subversively developed, do not now perform their function of impelling Man to fulfil his social Destiny on Earth. The same discord which we pointed out as existing in the Material world, exists in the Social world.

Instead of the Social Unity of the Human Race, instead of the reign of Social Order and Harmony on Earth, we see Mankind divided into hostile nations, with different forms of society, religion, and government, waging wars against each other, and alienated by social, religious, and political prejudices and hatreds. We find each nation, again, divided into antagonistic sects, parties, and classes, with conflicting interests and opinions, which engender injustice, oppression, feud, and discord, throughout all ranks and among all the members of society. This state of social incoherence and discord is not the true and permanent destiny of the Human Race. It is the result of the subversive action and play of the Passions, operating in false social oganizations which thwart their natural and harmonious development.

Having now explained the primary function of the four Social Passions—namely, the establishment of UNIVERSAL ASSOCIATION and SOCIAL HARMONY on Earth—let us glance briefly at some of their secondary or subordinate functions.

I. They are the means of communication between Soul and Soul, as the Senses are the means of communication between Soul and Matter. As the five senses perceive the attributes of Matter—form, color, perfume, flavor, etc.—so the four Social Passions perceive, through sympathy, the attributes of Soul, namely, benevolence, love, mercy, justice, dignity, veneration, honor, rectitude, equity, and the whole range of Spiritual attributes.

II. They are the exalting, idealizing, harmonizing Forces, which, through the industrial action of their instrument the Body, mould and fashion Matter, stamp upon it their own image, bring it into correspondence with their attributes, and elevate it to their standard of beauty and perfection. While Matter furnishes the basis for the action and development of the Soul, giving to it finite and positive existence, the Soul, on the other hand, permeates, animates, and ennobles Matter, bringing it into unity with itself. In the sphere of Sounds, for example, the four Social Affections, which form the central principle of the Soul, impart to Music their own character, stamp upon it the impress of their own harmonics; thus Music becomes the expression of the emotions of the Soul, and is made to represent the various shades of the four Cardinal Passions; hence we have the music of Love, of Ambition, of Religion, according as these emotions predominate in the soul of the Composer. The same remarks apply to the other Fine Arts—Painting, Sculpture, Architecture, etc.; all true and great creations in Art must body forth one or more of the four cardinal Loves of the Soul. Thus, we repeat, the Soul impresses its own image upon the Material World, informs it with its own innate harmonies, and elevates it, so to say to a level with itself.

III. The Social Passions furnish Man with the second class of Ideas which he possesses, namely, those of an Immaterial or Spiritual nature, as the Senses furnish him with those of a Material or Sensuous nature. Every Sentiment or Emotion of the Soul gives birth to a corresponding Idea. All our ideas of moral attributes and qualities—of right and duty, of justice, equality, dignity, in a word, of spiritual phenomena which the Senses do not perceive or take cognizance of, are derived from the four Social Passions—from their spontaneous emotions. They *first feel* these spiritual attributes or phenomena; the Feeling or Sentiment is then transmitted to and taken cognizance of by the three Intellectual Faculties, subjected to their action, compared with images or ideas furnished by the Senses, associated with them and clothed in form, so that it becomes intelligible to the Mind in its unity, and can be expressed in words: it is thus converted into what is called an Idea.

The Passion of Friendship, for example, generates among other ideas that of Equality; it first *feels* the equality, the identity of nature of Man with Man; this Feeling is then received and analyzed by the Intellectual Faculties, compared with the ideas of objects, attributes, and principles which they have previously examined, associated with the ideas already existing in the mind, and thus becomes known to the Consciousness or the Unity of the Intellect, after which it is clothed in language and expressed as an Idea.

Men in whom the Social Passions are intense and powerful, feel deeply certain emotions and the moral truths corresponding to them. CHRIST, for example, in whom the sentiment of the unity of the Human Race was so profound, so sublime, proclaims the Brotherhood, the Oneness of Mankind, the natural and inherent Equality of all men; this sentiment, grasped by the intellect and subjected to the processes of analysis, comparison, and synthesis, becomes an Idea, and is expressed in words; it is thus rendered intelligible to other minds, is transmitted from man to man, from generation to generation, and becomes the common property of the Human Race. The Idea is permanent and universal, while the Feeling in which it originated is individual and transitory, and passes away with the life of him who experiences it. By means of ideas ·recorded and rendered permanent in language, the intuitive conceptions of the individual Soul are spread before the world, which is enlightened by the truth which they reveal. The Idea may be compared to Light, and the feeling which generates it to Heat. The light of the idea shines into the souls of men in whom the feeling corresponding to that which originally generated it, is inert and dormant. This feeling perceives the truth of the idea which it had not strength enough to generate, and is aroused and quickened by its influence into life and activity. Thus the function of ideas is to enable the great souls of Humanity to arouse the torpid masses of mankind, to instruct and enlighten them, and thus secure the progressive improvement and elevation of the race.

As the various sentiments constituting Friendship, generate the ideas of equality, fraternity, the unity of the race, so the sentiments which branch out of Ambition generate the ideas of justice, dignity, federation, hierarchy. Thus, as we said, every sentiment or emotion of the Soul gives birth to a corresponding idea. The emotion is the original active Force, the idea, the Passive resultant or Effect. Ideas are the fixed and permanent representatives of fleeting emotions.

IV. The Social Passions furnish the elements of the Moral or Ethical Sciences; they generate the ideas which enter into these Sciences, and which, analyzed, compared, and synthesized by the three Intellectual Faculties, are reduced to Moral Theories and Systems.

V. They lead to the establishment of Social Laws and Institutions, as the five Senses lead to the creation of Art and Industry.

VI. They give rise to the Art of Politeness, which may be called the Fine Art of the Social Passions, as the Senses give rise to the Material Fine Arts. The Social Passions, developed and exercised artistically and harmoniously, produce those amenities of Social life, termed urbanity, civility, courtesy, deference, kindness, etc., which are the elements of Politeness.

IV.

FUNCTIONS OF THE THREE INTELLECTUAL OR SERIAL FACULTIES.

THE Primary FUNCTION of these three Passions or Forces of the Soul is to discover the Laws of Order and Harmony by which the Universe is governed, and to apply them to the regulation of the Moral and Material phenomena connected with Humanity and the Globe — that is, to the Organization of Society and to the establishment of Order in the kingdoms of Nature.

Man must establish order,

1. IN THE SOCIAL WORLD — that is, in the play and action of the Passions in the Social Mechanism;

2. IN THE MATERIAL WORLD — that is, in the kingdoms of Nature, of which he is the Overseer.

This he can do only by discovering and applying to these two departments the Laws of Universal Harmony.

As the five Senses perceive the attributes of Matter, and place Man in relations with the Material World; as the four Social Affections feel the attributes of Spirit, and place him in relations with the Social World; so the three Intellectual Faculties comprehend Laws and Principles, and place him in relation with the Divine Plan of Universal Order and Harmony. They guide him in all his works and operations which require invention, combination, classification, and arrangement — that is, in the organization of Industry and of his Social relations, and in the harmonious distribution of the creations of Nature over which he presides.

By comprehending the Laws of Universal Harmony and applying these laws to the Material World and to himself, Man enters into unity with the general Order of Creation, and conforms in his labors and social life to that Order, which is the manifestation of Divine Reason in the Universe.

This is the External or Universal function of the three Intellectual Faculties.

Their Internal or Individual function is to establish order in the action or play of the other nine Passions of the Soul; that is, to regulate, balance, methodize, in a word *mechanize* their developments, producing as result Passional Equilibrium and Harmony in the individual.

These faculties in their Unity constitute what is called REASON, and correspond to similar Faculties or Forces in the Universe, which in their Unity constitute the REASON OF GOD.

There is thus identity of Nature between Human Reason and Divine Reason; the same Faculties exist in the one as in the other; and this explains why Man can discover the Laws and comprehend the Scheme of that Order and Harmony which reign in Creation, and which are the revelation and embodiment of Divine Wisdom.

These Forces, acting in the Divine Mind, are the source of the Order, Harmony, and Unity that reign in the Universe; they regulate the movements of Worlds and Systems of Worlds; they regulate the distribution and arrangement of all the creations on the different Planets; they regulate the distribution of the Passions; in a word, they distribute, classify, coördinate, and systematize, that is, regulate all the elements and phenomena of the Universe, from the lowest to the highest, from molecules in the mineral to Planets in the Sidereal Systems.

The same Faculties or Forces acting in the mind of Man, guide him in the performance of similar functions in the spheres in which he operates and over which he presides. In the sphere of Ideas, for example, they distribute, classify, and systematize the perceptions and observations of the Senses, and the intuitive or spontaneous conceptions of the Social Passions, and thus create the Positive and Moral Sciences. They operate on the Sensuous and Social Passions in their various shades of development as they operate on Ideas; they distribute, classify, arrange, and mechanize them, and produce as result, Social or Passional Order and Harmony.

These three Faculties or Forces of the Soul, considered in their simplest and most radical action, may be called:—

1. The Separating, Analyzing, Individualizing.. ⎫
2. The Modulating, Alternating, Comparing........ ⎬ Faculties.
3. The Combining, According, Synthesizing..... ⎭

The First separates, divides, analyzes, and individualizes; the Second alternates, compares, modulates, and equilibrates; the Third combines, coördinates, unites, and synthesizes.

All operations of distribution, classification, combination, systematization, arrangement, and organization, from the most simple to the most complex, are the result of the action of these Forces or Faculties.

To express the joint, collective action of these three Faculties, we shall use the word *Serialize* and its derivatives; we employ this term because the most striking effect of the action of these Forces in Nature is the distribution of her Creations in SERIES.

Let us add a few words in regard to the Series and its properties, in order to convey a more complete idea of the meaning of the term.

A Series is a natural, graduated, and consecutive distribution of the elements of which any Unity or Whole is composed.

For example, the seven notes of music distributed in their natural order, as follows,

Do,   Re,   Mi,   Fa,   Sol,   La,   Si,

are a Series of Sounds.

The Unity of Color — White — divided into its seven elementary colors by the prism and distributed in the following order,

Violet,   Indigo,   Blue,   Green,   Yellow,   Orange,   Red,

forms the Series of Colors.

Thus, every Unity or Whole in the Universe, divided into its constituent elements or parts, and these parts distributed in their natural order, furnishes a Series. The skeleton, for example, is a Series of bones, the body a Series of organs, the Soul a Series of Passions, the Solar System a Series of Planets.

Whenever the elements of any Whole are arranged in their natural order, in a graduated succession, that is to say, in a SERIES, we find in their distribution some or all of the following effects:—two Wings and a Centre; an Ascending and a Descending movement; a Pivot at the centre; Transitions at the extremes; Contact of extremes; Dissonance between contiguous elements, as between Do–Re in Music, Violet–Indigo in Color; Accord between all non-contiguous elements; Modulation from one group of elements to another; regularly graduated Intervals between elements, etc. These are effects or results of Serial Distribution, and are necessary to the creation of Harmony in all spheres; they may be considered as the elements of Universal Order and Harmony.

Let us now state briefly the primary functions of the three Regulative or Serializing Faculties.

I. THE SEPARATIVE FACULTY. —This faculty divides or disintegrates any Whole upon which it operates, resolving it into its constituent parts or elements. This division gives rise to the principle of VARIETY IN UNITY; the principle of Variety gives rise in turn to INDIVIDUALITY, and Individuality to DISSONANCE, which latter is necessary to prevent the fusion of contiguous Individualities. It also calls out Rivalry and its various effects between these individualities. The tendency of this Faculty to division or analysis gives rise further to CAUSALITY, that is, to the desire of penetrating into the Unknown—into undivided, unanalyzed Unities. It performs one of the three primary processes of Classification, as it separates and brings out the elements to be classified, sees the differences between them, and assigns positions according to Dissimilarity or Difference. In its more intense action, it leads to minute subdivisions and analyses, and distinguishes the most delicate shades of difference ; in this operation, it is one of the sources of universal Refinement and Perfection. In its more complex action, operating upon a variety of elements and in conjunction with other Passions —particularly with Ambition and Parentalism—it gives rise to management, planning, scheming, manœuvring, tactics, policy, diplomacy, intrigue. In Science, it originates the Deductive Method.

II. THE ALTERNATING FACULTY. —This Faculty produces change, alternation, and modulation in all elements and forces upon which it operates, and thus gives rise to Vibration, to Movement, which in turn gives rise to Balance or EQUILIBRIUM in the action of Forces. It alternates between the Combining and Separating Faculties, varying their action from Individuality to Collectivity, from Accord to Dissonance, and thus establishes the principle of MODULATION and TRANSITION. It develops in the Soul the love of Variety, Change, Novelty. The action of this faculty in producing alternation and modulation, gives rise to COMPARISON, that is, to the alternate perception of similarities and dissimilarities, resemblances and differences. It performs one of the three primary processes of Classification, as it perceives Relations and establishes Comparisons. In its more intense action, it leads to rapid alternation and modulation, making the nicest distinctions and establishing gradations and suc-

4

cessions the most exact; it thus contributes in its way toward universal Refinement and Perfection.

III. THE COMBINING FACULTY.—This Faculty operates in an inverse order to the Separative. It combines, groups, synthesizes different elements which are in affinity, uniting them in Wholes, and thus gives rise to the principle of UNITY IN VARIETY. This principle gives rise in turn to that of COLLECTIVITY, which leads to ACCORD—the basis of Harmony. It awakens in the Soul enthusiasm, and produces concord and its various effects. The tendency of this Faculty is to Combination and Synthesis; it is the basis of Constructiveness and Ideality, that is, the desire of combining, bringing together, adjusting different elements, ideas, and passions, and establishing in them concert of action. It performs one of the three primary processes of Classification, as it unites the elements to be classified, perceives the resemblances between them, and assigns position according to Similarity or Affinity. In its more intense action, it leads to ever-widening combinations and syntheses, opens a broader and broader range to the mental vision, leads to exaltation and sublimity, and thus contributes in the third way to the attainment of universal Perfection. In its more complex action, operating upon a variety of elements, it is the source of Combination and Constructiveness, and acting in conjunction with other passions—particularly with Friendship and Love—it generates Zeal, Enthusiasm, Exaltation, Ideality. In Science, it originates the Inductive Method.

A few illustrations in the Human and Divine Spheres will show the practical operation of these three Faculties or Forces. In Man, they serialize the facts and phenomena of the world in which he lives; in the Divine Mind, they serialize the facts and phenomena of the Universe.

Acting in a BEETHOVEN, a MOZART, they distribute, classify, that is, serialize Sounds, and create Musical Harmony. Acting in a CUVIER, a LINNÆUS, they discover the system of serialization in the Kingdoms of Nature; they classify the animal, vegetable, and mineral creations, reproduce the order established in them by Divine Wisdom, and evolve the Science of Natural History. Acting in a KEPLER, a NEWTON, they discover the laws which regulate the movements of the heavenly bodies, and create the Science of Astronomy. Acting in a CÆSAR, a NAPOLEON, they combine, distribute, and marshal masses in an army, that is, they serialize the movements and operations of vast bodies of men, and create the Art of War. Acting in a HOMER, a DANTE, a SHAKESPEARE, they serialize the perceptions, ideas, and images furnished by the other Passions of the Soul, and distribute the language in which they are clothed in number, measure, and rhythm, and thus create the Poetic Art. Acting in a WATT, an ARKWRIGHT, a FULTON, they serialize mechanical elements and forces, construct machinery, and create the Mechanic Arts. Acting in FOURIER, they discover the Laws of Order and Harmony by which the Universe is governed, and by the knowledge of these Laws enable him to penetrate the mystery of the Human Passions, to see through their incoherent and subversive action, comprehend their natural mode of development, explain their nature, functions, and Destiny, and determine the Social Organization to which they are adapted.

Ascending from Man to the supreme Source of Order and Harmony, these serializing Forces in the DIVINE MIND regulate the distribution, classification, and arrangement of the elements and phenomena of the Universe. They serialize Worlds and Systems of Worlds, and create Sidereal Harmony. They serialize the Intelligences inhabiting these Worlds, and assign to them functions and Destinies, according to the part they are to take in the scheme of Universal Harmony. They serialize the Passions, assigning to them modes of development and action which in a true Social Order would produce Concord and Unity. They serialize the animal, vegetable, and mineral kingdoms on the different planets, distributing them in classes, orders, genera, species, and varieties, and establishing Order and Unity in the animate and inanimate creation.

Thus from the highest to the lowest, in the Spiritual and Material worlds, these Forces serialize all elements, phenomena, and movements, combining and uniting them in one great, harmonious, organic WHOLE, called the UNIVERSE.

The unity of system, the concert of action, the order and harmony which pervade this vast ORGANIC WHOLE, result from the fact that the laws which govern it, emanate from one Centre, from one System of Regulative Forces: the laws which govern one department govern every other, and if we can comprehend their action and effects in one sphere, we have the key to their action and effects in all spheres.

The SUPREME HARMONIST has created for and adapted to Harmony the elements of all departments of Creation, and has left to intelligent beings to establish Harmony in those spheres over which it is their function to preside.

Man on the Earth harmonizes, for example, Sounds, Forms, Colors; he must also harmonize his own Passions and social Relations, and the Creations in the animal and vegetable kingdoms; he will thus establish ORDER IN NATURE AND IN HIMSELF.

The only complete system of Harmony which Man has as yet discovered is the Musical — the Harmony of Sounds. This Harmony, a type and measure of all others, is an invaluable guide which enables him, by going from the Known to the Unknown, to discover other and higher branches of Harmony. If he had followed this guide, if he had studied universal Analogy, he would have discovered that the Planets in the Solar System are the elements or notes of a Sidereal Harmony, as Sounds are the elements or notes of Musical Harmony; that the Passions of the Soul are the elements or notes of Social Harmony; that the bones in the skeleton are the elements or notes of an Osseal Harmony; that the colors of the Prism are the elements or notes of Chromatic Harmony; that lines and curves are the elements or notes of Geometrical Harmony; that the animal, vegetable, and mineral creations are the elements or notes of Nature's great Organic Harmony; he would have discovered that the same Laws which establish Order and Harmony in one department establish it in all others, so that if we discover these laws in one Sphere of Creation, we have the Key to their discovery in all other spheres.

Having now explained the primary functions of the three Intellectual Faculties, we will touch briefly upon some of their subordinate functions.

1. They are the means of communication of the Soul with Laws and Principles, as the Senses are the means of its communication with Matter, and the Affectional Passions with other Souls. As laws and principles can not be perceived by the Senses, nor

felt by the Affectional Passions, a third class of Faculties is necessary to their perception and comprehension. Man, who is not a *simple* being like the animal, which is guided by Instinct, but a *compound* being, whose actions and functions are varied and complex, must regulate his operations by fixed laws and principles, which it is the work of the three Intellectual Faculties to discover and apply. Man can not establish Order in his multifarious relations and labors except by the application to them of Principles which regulate, on a unitary plan, generalities the most comprehensive and details the most minute.

II. They are the source of political Laws and Institutions of a general nature, and hence of Administration or Government. Their function in this sphere is to regulate on one plan the general interests of States and Nations. In future ages, they will lead to the ADMINISTRATIVE UNITY OF THE GLOBE, or to a uniform system of government throughout the Earth. The result will be UNIVERSAL ASSOCIATION—that is to say, the harmonious combination of the labors, operations, and interests of Mankind, and universal coöperation and concert of action in executing the great Works of which this Earth is to be the theatre. The Administrative Unity of the Globe is nothing more nor less than the SERIALIZATION of the general interests, operations, and relations of the Human Race. The Intellectual Faculties in their more universal action, perform this function of Serialization as they perform the same function in the most restricted spheres.

III. They are the source of the third class of Ideas which Man possesses, namely, ideas of an abstract and complex nature, or ideas of Laws and Principles. They analyze, compare, and synthesize perceptions and intuitions, that is, the ideas furnished by the Senses and the Social Passions, and deduce from them Generalizations or complex ideas—that is, Laws and Principles. A KEPLER, for example, arrives at the discovery that the planets move in their orbits, direct as masses and inverse of the square of distances. He deduces this truth from a great variety of special observations made by the Senses—or, in other words, he resolves, by the processes of analysis, comparison and synthesis, a multitude of observations into one Generalization; this Generalization is grasped, conceived by the Intellect as an IDEA, and proclaimed as a Law. This furnishes an example of the generation of Complex Ideas, or Ideas of Laws and Principles, deduced from the observation of individual facts and phenomena.

IV. They distribute, classify, and arrange—that is, serialize the ideas furnished by the Senses and the Social Passions, reduce them to a regular system, and thus create SCIENCE; the Sciences are but methodical Generalizations of special observations and ideas. They serialize, in like manner, the elements of Material Harmonics—sound, form, color, etc.—furnished by the Senses, and create the Fine Arts.

The other functions of the three Intellectual Faculties will be understood by reference to the Table.

V.

DUAL ACTION OF THE PASSIONS.—THEIR DISCORDANT AND HAR-MONIOUS DEVELOPMENT.—CAUSES OF MORAL EVIL IN SOCIETY.

THE PASSIONS, as we have sufficiently explained, are the Springs of Action, the Motor-Powers, the impelling and directing Forces in Man; they are the source of all his acts; they are, in fact, the Man himself; his Life with all its phenomena is but their external, concrete manifestation; they are, as a consequence, the source of all his good as of all his bad deeds, of all his virtues as of all his crimes—in a word, the source of GOOD and EVIL in his Social career. If, therefore, we would determine the CAUSES OF MORAL EVIL in Society, we must seek for them in the operation of the Passions.

The Passions are liable, like all the other Forces of Nature, to be misdirected, thwarted, or perverted in their development and action; when thus falsely developed, they produce evil effects which are the opposite of the good effects they would produce in their true, natural, and legitimate action. This law is of universal application to all active Forces.

The Passions, acting in the false Social Organizations existing on the Earth, which are wholly unsuited to their nature, are subject to four modes of imperfect or deranged development, constituting what may be called the Subversive Development of the Passions, or the state of *Passional Counter-Movement.*

I. DEVELOPMENT OF THE PASSIONS IN THEIR LOWER DEGREES. —The five Material Passions—the Senses—developed in their *lower Degrees*, uncultivated and unrefined, give rise to coarseness, grossness, vulgarity, and brutality. The Sense of TASTE, for example, leads to coarseness of appetite, to gluttony, to gormandism, and is one of the causes of drunkenness. The Sense of HEARING when unrefined is pleased with noise, racket, hubbub; the Sense of SIGHT, with tawdry forms and colors. The Sense of TOUCH is indifferent to personal cleanliness, texture of clothing, etc. The same Senses developed in their higher degrees and harmoniously disciplined and refined in their action, excite in Man a love of material elegance, beauty, refinement, splendor, and harmony; they guard him against coarseness, vulgarity, slovenliness, uncleanliness, and sensual discords generally, stimulate him to refined tastes and habits, and awaken in him the sentiment of Universal Art. Thus the same Senses produce opposite effects, according as they are developed in their lower or higher Degrees.

The four SOCIAL PASSIONS developed in their lower Degrees, that is, restricted to Individual Sympathies, lead to the formation of exclusive ties, leaving no room for Collective Sympathies, for the nobler and more universal emotions, and producing indifference to the welfare of the masses, and to general interests. The Passion of PARENTALISM, for example, when restricted to an exclusive and absorbing affection for one's own offspring, begets an indifference to Collective Sympathies of the same character, and often excludes liberal and comprehensive sentiments; it leads the parent to disregard the welfare of his fellow-men, and to prey upon them in order to promote the prosperity of his own family. In like manner, the sentiment of FRIENDSHIP, when individual or exclusive in its action, leads to generosity toward the few and to indifference toward the mass. In the Passion of LOVE, what can be more exclusive or more selfish, indirectly, than the affection of two Lovers, wholly absorbed by their individual relation? Of all the Social Passions, however, AMBITION, when developed in its lower or individual Degrees, produces the worst results; it prompts to the desire of personal aggrandizement, and grasps at the possession of individual power and wealth, regardless of the rights, interests, and welfare of others.

The Social Passions developed in their *higher Degrees*, extending to and embracing in their sympathetic action masses of men, become the source of every social virtue—of benevolence, courtesy, urbanity, hospitality, chivalry, justice, honor, magnanimity, fraternity, philanthropy, etc.—The three Intellectual Faculties follow the lead of the Sensuous and Social Passions, and aid them in obtaining their ends.

Thus the first cause of Moral Evil is to be found in the development of the Passions in their *lower Degrees.*

II. MISDIRECTION OF THE PASSIONS — or their tendency toward ends divergent with the interests of the Masses and Human Destiny. A single illustration will explain this false mode of Passional action and development; we will select it from AMBITION. This Passion in a NAPOLEON, for example, is directed to Conquest and War; these are the means by which it attains its ends, namely, Glory and Power. Thus misdirected, it produces as result the slaughter of millions of men on the battle-field, and the financial exhaustion of nations. The effects of this Passion, when falsely directed, are terrible, and yet Ambition in itself is a most useful and noble Force. What would Man be without it? He would be a creature devoid of aspiration, without high or noble aims, without self-respect, dignity, or magnanimity. Had the ambition of NAPOLEON been directed to good and noble ends, to internal improvements and the industrial development of his Empire, for example, he would have covered France with splendid works and monuments of Industry, and elevated the people to a state of universal prosperity. His gigantic Ambition which, directed to War, enabled him to communicate fire and enthusiasm to the prosecution of his vast works of destruction, and to inspire the people with a passion for Military Glory, would, had it been directed to Industry, have communicated the same enthusiasm to the prosecution of great and useful enterprises, and inspired the people with a passion for Industrial Glory. Thus the *effects* of a Passion may vary, but the Passion itself remains unchanged; in studying Forces, we must distinguish between Causes and Effects, that is, between the mode of action of Forces and the Forces themselves.

III. PERVERTED OR INVERSE DEVELOPMENT OF THE PASSIONS; THEIR COUNTER-MOVEMENT.—We have given in the TABLE the Scale or Gamut of the twelve natural or Harmonic Passions which impel Man to fulfil his Functions and Destiny on Earth.

Whenever any of these Passions are thwarted in their action—are disappointed, violated, outraged, repressed—they act inversely, and engender emotions opposite in their character and effects. We may lay it down as a Law, that the SYMPATHIES of the Soul when thwarted or violated in their action, become or give rise to exactly corresponding ANTIPATHIES. Philanthropy, for example, when outraged and disappointed, and driven back upon itself, turns into its Counter-Passion, Misanthropy. In like manner, Benevolence gives rise to Malevolence, Confidence to Distrust, Kindness to Harshness, Compassion to Cruelty; these emotions belong to the Scale or Gamut of Friendship, which thus may be developed directly or inversely, harmoniously or discordantly. [Each of the twelve Passions is a Unity or Whole having its Scale or Gamut of Emotions, which are shades of the primary Passions, as the Soul itself is a Unity or Whole having its Scale or Gamut which is composed of the twelve radical Passions.]

In the present Social Order, the Passion most active is AMBITION; the emotions of which it is composed, when violated, thwarted, and outraged, produce as a consequence the greatest Passional Subversion, that is, the most intense discord and disorder, and the greatest crimes. The thwarting of the sub-passions or emotions of which Ambition is composed—such as vanity, pride, self-esteem, love of approbation—gives rise to various shades of envy, jealousy, revenge, etc., the intensity of which is in proportion to the strength of the Passion; the sentiments of dignity and honor, which generate respect and esteem, give rise, when thwarted, to contempt and scorn—and thus throughout the Gamut of the Passion; when thwarted in all its aims and aspirations, as is frequently the case, it turns to the deepest hatred—to rage, fury, frenzy, malignity, and other subversive emotions.

It may be laid down as a principle, that Man under the influence of the Passions in their inverse development or the antagonist emotions, is impelled to the commission of wrong and unjust acts, of deeds of violence—called Crimes—as under the influence of the Passions in their Natural or Harmonic development, he is impelled to the performance of deeds of kindness and justice—called Virtues. Thus we have a *dual development* of the Passions, giving rise to a dual series of effects, the one good, the other bad, and producing the reign of Good or of Evil in the social world.

The Senses, like the Social Passions, are subject to perversion and inverse development. When repressed or outraged, they engender a multitude of eccentric, unnatural, and vicious tastes and inclinations, and lead to extravagance, sensuality, and brutality. The Sense of TASTE, for example, in certain perverted and diseased states, creates an appetite for substances wholly unsuited to the natural palate; such is the hankering for chalk, lime, charcoal, slate, and other deleterious substances repulsive to Taste in a healthy condition; we may include to a certain extent among the perversions of this Sense, the chewing of tobacco, flag-root, camomile, etc. The Sense of SIGHT when perverted takes delight in uncouth and hideous objects; the Sense of HEARING, in discordant noises, such as the shrieks and yells so often heard at brutal carousings and assemblies of desperadoes. As regards the Intellectual Faculties and Social Passions, their perverted action consists in devising ways and means to enable the latter to attain their subversive ends.

When we consider the infinite variety of false and unnatural circumstances in present Society which thwart and outrage the Passions, developing them in *Counter-march* to their true nature and destiny, we ought not to be surprised at the multitude and variety of passional eccentricities and excesses, of depraved tastes and inclinations, of antipathies and hatreds which we see around us, nor at the vices and crimes to which they give rise. The Social World is a great *Passional Charivari*, and the only wonder is that the discord and confusion are not greater; we want no better proof of the inherent goodness of Human Nature, than that it resists to the extent it does the continual pressure of so many perverting influences. To condemn the Passions as vicious and depraved because, when perverted or misdirected, they produce evil effects, is as absurd as it would be to condemn steam, fire, and other Forces, because under bad regulation they produce so many accidents and disasters.

An important principle which we have before stated, and which we here repeat, is that the antagonist Passions or subversive Emotions *are not spontaneously active*—that is, do not act of themselves or without external provocation; it is only when the

natural or harmonic Passions are thwarted and outraged, and
thrust inwardly upon themselves, that the corresponding subversive Passions appear; the latter are dormant, passive, latent,
incapable of self-action, while the former are spontaneously active, self-determining, positive, requiring no external stimulants
to call them out. Thus man is naturally, positively GOOD —
artificially, negatively BAD; he tends to Good *spontaneously;*
he is impelled to Evil *circumstantially.* In a Social Order perfectly adapted to Human Nature, and giving free scope to the
natural action and development of the Passions, the subversive
Emotions would remain quiescent, and we should then behold the
reign of Good — of PASSIONAL HARMONY on Earth.

IV. THE CONFLICT OF THE PASSIONS WITH EACH OTHER AND
THEIR UNBALANCED DEVELOPMENT. — The Passions are distinct individualities in the Soul, as Men are distinct individualities in
Society, and Nations in the Race. Each Passion has its attractions, and seeks to satisfy them as best it can. In the present
Social Order, in which the Passions are without harmonious development and discipline, and unbalanced in their action, they
are *in conflict,* like the greater individualities above mentioned.
The Sense of TASTE, for example, seeks the pleasures of the table, and impels the individual in whom it dominates to extravagance in order to secure its gratification; this does not suit the
sentiments of Economy or Avarice (shades of Ambition); they
accordingly wage a war upon it, and thus is established the Conflict, the Battle of the Passions in the Soul. The same Sense
may violate health by its excesses, and in so doing rouse the ire
of the other Passions which require for their action a sound physical organization. It may prompt also to drunkenness, and by
causing the individual to lose the esteem of his fellow-men,
his social position, his respectability, outrage the sentiments of
pride, of self-esteem, of dignity; this occasions conflicts often
so terrible that the Soul, torn by them and rendered desperate,
turns upon itself and breaks violently the thread of its finite existence. How often do we find men committing suicide because
they can not resist the action of some dominant Passion which
hurries them into vices and excesses! The passion for Gambling,
a branch of Ambition and Intrigue, furnishes perhaps the most
frequent example of this.

Thus is established the Conflict of the Passions, which places Man in a state of warfare with himself.

To sum up; the Passions are subject to the four following modes of imperfect or false development:—

1. Development in their Lower Degrees;
2. Misdirection;
3. Inverse or Counter-Development;
4. Conflict and Unbalanced Action.

These are the four CAUSES of Moral Evil—the causes of the discords, vices, and crimes which we see in Society, out of which has sprung the doctrine of Human Depravity, a doctrine based on a profound ignorance of the nature of Man, and essentially Atheistic.

The Passions being Forces can not *remain at rest*, but *must act;* acting, they must act either truly or falsely, directly or inversely, naturally or subversively, harmoniously or discordantly. In their false, subversive, or discordant action, they engender EVIL and give rise to the reign of SOCIAL DISCORD; in their natural, direct, or harmonious action, they engender GOOD and give rise to the reign of SOCIAL HARMONY.

There is one more explanation to be given on the subject of Human Depravity and Moral Evil, which we believe will cover the whole ground, and furnish a solution of the *direct* or *immediate* cause of these phenomena; the *indirect* cause is to be found in the false Organization of Society—in the conflict of all interests, in the poverty and ignorance which reign, in the imperfect systems of Education, in the false system of Industry, etc., which pervert or derange the action of the Passions, and also in Natural circumstances, such as climatic excesses, resulting from the absence of a scientific and integral cultivation of the Globe.

The additional cause of Moral Evil which we will proceed to explain, will be found in the unbalanced or excessive development of the Senses, and their preponderance over the Social Affections.

These two classes of Passions tend in two opposite directions; their action is the inverse of each other. The Senses tend *inwardly*—to Self; they consequently give rise to SELFISHNESS, SELFISM. The Social Affections tend *outwardly*—to Others; they generate the LOVE OF MAN, SELF-DENIAL, SELF-SACRIFICE.

The Senses minister to the body—to its growth, health, wants, and comforts; they are *introactive*; the individual impelled or attracted by them to act, does so for his own interest or pleasure —to attain ends which come home to himself alone. The pleasure they procure can not be felt or shared by others. If he enjoys the pleasures of the table, the gratification which his palate experiences, he alone can feel. If he sees beautiful sights, no one can feel with him the sensations which his visual organs experience, that is, no one can share the visual pleasure which he enjoys. The pleasures of the Senses are thus restricted to the individual—are exclusive, that is, selfish.

The Social Affections, on the other hand, tend to Others; they minister to the wants, comforts, and happiness of those whom we love; their action is *outward* (except in the case of Ambition, developed in its lower degrees). Acting under their impulse, we must act for the good of others; they find their gratification only in promoting the welfare and happiness of the objects of their sympathy; they can not be enjoyed alone, in isolation like the Senses, but only in the society of other beings. To enjoy Friendship, Love, Parentalism, Ambition, we must have friends, lovers, children, colleagues; and we can gratify these sentiments or affections toward them only by acts of kindness, benevolence, generosity, devotion, loyalty, justice, etc.

Thus the action of these two classes of Passions is the inverse of each other. The first tends *inwardly*, to Self—and takes care of the Individual; the second tends *outwardly*, to Others—and takes care of the Masses. These two tendencies or modes of action of the Sensuous and Social Passions are equally necessary and important, for it is as indispensable to take care of the Individual as of the Mass, and of the Mass as of the Individual.

When the Senses are developed in predominance over the Social Affections, they lead to Selfishness and its effects—to indifference to the interests and rights of others, to cold-heartedness, etc. When the Social Affections are developed in preponderance over the Senses, they lead to Love of the Neighbor—to devotion to others, to disinterestedness, self-denial, self-sacrifice, etc.

From what precedes, we deduce the conclusion that Selfishness, which is looked upon as an insuperable obstacle to the establishment of Social Harmony on Earth, to the reign of Justice and Philanthropy among men, is simply the result of *the excessive or unbalanced development of the Senses — their predominance over the Social Affections.*

Now the mind that penetrates below the surface of things will see that Selfishness is not inherent to Human Nature, not a positive attribute of Man and therefore irremediable, incurable; he will see that it is not *essential* but *accidental* — the result of the over-action or the unbalanced action of one class of Passions, and that it can be remedied by fully developing another class of Passions — the Social Affections — and thus establishing balance, equilibrium in the Forces of the Soul. As this end can be easily attained in a true order of Society, in which unity of interests and general prosperity and refinement reign, the obstacle to social improvement and human elevation which Selfishness presents, is not so terrible, so insurmountable, as superficial thinkers represent.

In conclusion, we would call the attention of impartial and sincere minds to one more fact, namely, the Social Condition of Man in present Society. When we consider that Poverty is almost universal, that the immense majority of men find the greatest difficulty in satisfying their physical wants — that is, in meeting the demands of the Senses, which must first be gratified, or the individual perishes — that they are harassed by cares and anxieties, obliged to undergo hard and continuous toil to obtain food, raiment, and shelter — that even the Rich are steeped in Relative Poverty as the Poor are steeped in Positive Poverty, finding the greatest difficulty in maintaining their position and satisfying their more complex wants — should we be surprised that the Senses are developed in preponderance, in excess, that they sink the Social Affections under the weight of their imperative demands, and that they reign supreme in the Soul?

We here close this brief treatise on the Human Passions. In the Table, and in the accompanying articles, we have explained the natural or legitimate action of the Motor-forces of the Soul, the functions they have to perform in a true Social Order, and the Destiny which they impel man to fulfil on Earth. Our aim has been to show what Man is in essence and nature — what he will be in the Future when all the forces and faculties of the Soul are fully and harmoniously developed. He is now but a chrysalis, in a state of torpor and non-development in the night and winter of a false Social atmosphere; we have endeavored to describe the magnificent Being which is to be born from this chrysalis under the influence of the genial light and warmth of Social Harmony.

In the short article on the Dual Development of the Passions, we have pointed out the different modes in which these Forces may be deranged, thwarted, and perverted in their action; how they give rise under such circumstances to the excesses, vices and crimes, which we behold in the Social World, and thus make Man appear a depraved and vicious Being.

Our object has been to vindicate Human Nature, to show the fitness of Man for Social Harmony and for fulfilling a noble Destiny on Earth. If we have proved this point, our faith in the Future, our hope in the Elevation of Man and his social Redemption from the Evils which scourge and degrade his terrestrial existence, are based on a sure and solid foundation.

FUNDAMENTAL PRINCIPLES

OF

FOURIER'S SYSTEM OF SOCIAL ORGANIZATION.

I.

GENERAL SURVEY OF THE SCOPE AND CHARACTER OF FOURIER'S LABORS.

It is supposed by those who who have but a superficial idea of FOURIER'S Theory, that he did nothing more than elaborate a plan of Social Organization, more or less arbitrary and imaginative in its character, like the Republic of Plato or the Utopia of Sir THOMAS MORE, and that he was visionary enough to propose this plan—the creation of his own fancy—in the place of the present system of Society, which appears to the world as the fixed, immutable, and natural order of things.

To correct these and other erroneous ideas which prevail in respect to the great Pioneer in Social Science, we will point out briefly the real nature and scope of his labors, and the vast problems which he solved.

FOURIER was eminently qualified by Nature for the great work which he undertook; he was impelled to it by the very character of his genius; it was consequently no impulse of vanity, no influence of other minds, that led him to grapple with the new and intricate problem of social Organization and the social Destiny of Man.

With a high-toned nervous organization, joined to great capacity of endurance, which formed the basis of his mental constitution, he possessed the keenest observation, and immense powers of analysis and synthesis; he could with equal facility descend to the minutest details and dissections, or rise to the broadest and most complex generalizations; his intellectual capacity in

5

this respect may be compared to the physical capacity of the trunk of the elephant, which, while it can pick up the lightest straw, can wield the most ponderous beam. The social Affections of FOURIER were equally strong; he combined a profound sentiment of justice with a wise and comprehensive benevolence; this gave to his intellect a high humanitary direction, and determined the character of his scientific career. The admirable balance of his Faculties and Affections, and the lucidity which resulted from a finely-organized nervous system, gave to him a natural instinct of Truth, an intuitive perception of the Relation and Fitness of things, which constituted in him, as it were, a sublime Common Sense, that may be called the balance and equilibrium of Genius.

As he appeared to us in our personal intercourse with him, he seemed like a being endowed with an extraordinary, almost superhuman *power of mental Vision.* He seemed to penetrate by means of some internal faculty into and through those intricate and complex problems — such as that of the Human Passions, of the terrestrial Destiny of man, of the Order of Creation — which have baffled the human mind for so many ages.

FOURIER, beholding the discord, disorder, and misery, prevailing on the Earth, witnessing the terrible scenes of the French Revolution, and seeing, engaged as he was in commercial pursuits, the reign of fraud, selfishness, and duplicity in the details of everyday life, came early to the conclusion that there was something artificial, false, unnatural, in the general Order of things on our globe — that there was some derangement or perversion of Nature's plan, that Man was out of the path, off of the track of his Destiny.

Pursued by this idea, he undertook, unaided and alone, to penetrate and solve the mystery of this Disorder — of the reign of EVIL on the Earth. While occupied with this general investigation, his commercial pursuits gave a practical direction to his mind; they led him to a careful study of mercantile abuses and corruptions, and to speculate upon the possibility of a commercial Reform which would relieve productive Industry from the frauds, extortions, and spoliations of Commerce. By the joint influence of these circumstances, he was led on gradually to conceive the possibility of an INTEGRAL SOCIAL REFORM — the possibility of establishing an entirely new Order of things, which would do away with the reign of Discord and Misery on the Earth. His instinct of Order and Unity led him to believe that our Globe and Humanity upon it were created for Harmony, that some method existed for establishing its reign in Nature and in Man—in the Material and in the Social world. His strong and methodical mind could not long remain in a vague middle state of apathy and doubt—in a state of indifference to the reign of Good or Evil. He was forced to believe, either that Order and Harmony could be established on the Earth, or that it was created and presided over by some malignant and diabolical power. He did not long hesitate between these two alternatives, but decided that the reign of EVIL was to be supplanted by the reign of GOOD, and that our Globe was destined to become a scene of Social Unity, Harmony, and Happiness.

When FOURIER had conceived and become convinced of the possibility of a new state of things on the Earth, he saw that the primary condition necessary for its realization, was the discovery and establishment of a NEW ORDER OF SOCIETY, in which the labors of mankind would be properly, wisely directed, their social relations harmoniously regulated, and UNITY established in all the great interests and affairs of the Race.

FOURIER saw that the human mind, in order to solve the intricate and complex problem of a true Social Order, must possess *Positive Laws, Fixed Principles,* to guide it in its researches; that it was impossible for human Reason, by its own theorizing, its own speculations, to construct so complicated a mechanism as that of Society; he felt that there must be Natural Laws for the organization of Society as there are for all other organizations in the Universe, and that the same Laws which produce order and harmony in Creation generally, would, if discovered and applied to Society, produce order and harmony in the Social World.

Proceeding on this basis, and speculating on the principles of Universal Harmony in Creation, FOURIER arrived at the conclusion:—

I. That the Universe is governed by FIXED AND MATHEMATICAL LAWS, which distribute, coördinate, classify, in a word, regulate its phenomena, and establish in it the reign of Unity and Order.

II. That by discovering these laws, he would have an *infalli-ble Guide* to direct him in the construction of a true Social Mech-anism; for he believed that these Laws would reveal the means of regulating harmoniously human relations and the human pas-sions, as they regulate harmoniously the other elements of Crea-tion.

The first study, therefore, upon which FOURIER entered, was the discovery of the Laws of Order and Harmony by which the Universe is governed; he devoted the first years of his investiga-tions to this great and important work, which he successfully achieved. Had he done nothing more, had he stopped here and simply announced the following propositions, he would have been entitled to the admiration and gratitude of posterity :—

1. That the reign of Order, Harmony, and Happiness can be established on this Earth;

2. That to attain this great end, a true System of Society must be discovered and organized in the place of the present false and incoherent systems;

3. That this true System must be based upon the Laws which govern Creation, and which produce Order and Harmony in its various departments.

This general conception was but the initial idea of FOURIER, the starting point of his labors. The first work he accomplished, as we said, was the discovery of the principles of Distribution, Classification, and Organization in the Universe—that is to say, the Laws of universal Order and Harmony, which in their unity, he calls in his works the LAW OF THE SERIES.

Possessing a knowledge of this Law, it opened to him branches of Science which had remained unexplored, and ushered him into regions of thought which the human mind had never pen-etrated.

Having now explained the basis upon which FOURIER pro-ceeded, the means he employed in his explorations, we will point out the nature of his labors and the results to which he arrived.

The most important of these results was the discovery and elaboration of the Plan of Social Organization which he has given to the world; he devoted the main part of his life to this great work, as he believed it to be the first in importance and necessity—the only means of eradicating the social evils which afflict Humanity. This plan of Social Organization he deduced in all its parts from the Laws of Universal Order which he had discovered. The various branches of which it is composed—such as its System of Industry, of Education, of Social Relations, of Government, and even its Architectural arrangements, are rigorous deductions from, or applications of these Laws. He has not, therefore, brought forward a Social System of his own devising —a mere creation of his own fancy. " I do not propose," he says in a hundred places, " any plan or system of my own ; I give the System of Nature, that is, the NATURAL ORDER OF HUMAN SOCIETY, based on the Laws of Universal Order and Harmony ; if my plan is defective or false, in details or as a whole, let those interested in the welfare of mankind correct it by studying Nature's Laws, and deducing from them the true plan of Social Organization."

This is a sufficient answer to the multitude of superficial or prejudiced minds, who suppose that FOURIER has merely wrought out of his imagination a system of Society, which is arbitrary, impracticable, immoral, etc., etc. So far from this, he has solved the greatest problem which can engage the attention of the human mind, namely, the discovery of the NATURAL ORDER OF SOCIETY, which is destined to replace the incoherent and absurd Social Systems existing on the Earth, and to extirpate the evils which they entail upon the human race.

If we examine FOURIER's Plan of Social Organization in detail, we shall find parts of it, which are in themselves wonders of analysis and construction, creations which alone would immortalize a man. Among these, for example, is his System of ATTRACTIVE INDUSTRY. He elaborated a plan for the Organization of Industry, based on the Law of the Series—a plan by which Agriculture and other productive pursuits will be conducted with so much elegance and refinement, in so artistic and scientific a manner, with so many accompaniments of material beauty and even splendor, will afford scope and delight to so many of the passions of the Soul, that Labor will be prosecuted with energy and enthusiasm, will be dignified and rendered honorable and Attractive, and will lead all mankind to engage voluntarily in its pursuits and thus create the two great elements of Human Happiness,

UNIVERSAL WEALTH,   UNIVERSAL HEALTH.

Another magnificent creation of FOURIER's genius is his system of NATURAL EDUCATION. It is a system which is at the same time practical and theoretical—that is, INDUSTRIAL and SCIENTIFIC—developing and forming conjointly the body and the mind; it is based, like all natural or harmonious systems, on ATTRACTION, and will lead the child, by the various inducements it holds out, to take as much delight in industrial and scientific exercises, as it now takes in infantile sports.

Another important problem, and one of a most abstruse nature, which FOURIER solved, was the discovery of a system of PASSIONAL EQUILIBRIA AND RALLIANCES—a system by which the Passions will be harmoniously balanced and equilibrated, in their play and action, and will produce, as result PASSIONAL UNITY.

Even the system of ARCHITECTURE which FOURIER proposes, and which he deduces from the same Laws, is equally remarkable in its way; it is not of artistic details that we speak, but of its general plans and arrangements; he traced out the plan of an integral, unitary Habitation for Man, a habitation that would be the external or architectural expression of all his wants, material and moral. Nature's plan of UNITARY ARCHITECTURE remained to be discovered, and FOURIER accomplished the task.

The discovery of the Laws of Universal Order furnished FOURIER, as we have stated, with the guide by which to penetrate new regions of thought. He explored these regions, discovered several new Sciences, and pointed out a new basis for others which had been imperfectly developed.

The most general and comprehensive problem which FOURIER solved, and the one which we will mention first in order, was THE UNITY OF THE UNIVERSE, or UNITY OF SYSTEM IN CREATION. As ONE system of Laws governs universal Creation, these laws must produce as a consequence ONE system of Effects—that is, ONE system of Distribution, Classification, and Organization in all the departments and details of the Universe, and ONE system of Order and Harmony in all the spheres of Life and Movement.

On this basis, FOURIER establishes THE UNITY OF MAN WITH THE UNIVERSE. This Unity he divides into three

Primary UNITIES, each composed of an internal and an external branch—in all, six UNITIES.

TABLE OF THE SIX BRANCHES OF UNIVERSAL UNITY.

1. INTERNAL UNITY OF MAN WITH HIMSELF in true Society, by the Unity of the Passions with each other in the Individual, and by the unity of the Individual with the Race, extending to unity between Communities, Peoples, and Nations.—Social and Political Unity of Mankind.

2. EXTERNAL UNITY OF MAN WITH HIMSELF in Creative Art and Industry, by the unitary cultivation and artistic embellishment of the Globe, securing the unity of the Soul with Nature, which is its great external body, the individual body being merely the medium of sensation.—Unity of Humanity with the Planet.

3. INTERNAL UNITY OF MAN WITH GOD, by the full development of Passional Attraction, which is the Interpreter to Man of the Divine Will.

4. EXTERNAL UNITY OF MAN WITH GOD, by the Immortality of the Soul.

5. INTERNAL UNITY OF MAN WITH THE UNIVERSE, by the analogy existing between the phenomena of the Mind, or ideas and sentiments—and the phenomena of Matter, or the creations in the animal, vegetable, and mineral kingdoms.

6. EXTERNAL UNITY OF MAN WITH THE UNIVERSE, by the influence which the scientific and integral cultivation of the Globe would exert upon the aromal or magnetic communications and relations between our Globe and the other Planets.

The Destiny of the Human Race is to establish Unity with itself, with God, and with the Universe under these six forms. The Sciences which FOURIER discovered or to which he gave a new basis, have for their object the explanation or realization of these Unities. We will now point out the principal sciences which he has indicated or developed in his works.

I. SCIENCE OF MAN, OR THEORY OF THE HUMAN PASSIONS. This Science he developed with more detail than any other, as it was the basis of his SCIENCE OF SOCIETY. It is one of the most important and valuable branches of FOURIER's discoveries, for in furnishing a true theory of Human Nature, that is, in explaining the functions and destiny of the Passions, the ends for which they were created, their uses in Social mechanics, he has explained MAN; and in so doing he has exploded the old, absurd, and degrading doctrine of Human Depravity, of the unfitness of the Passions for Social Order and Harmony, and the corollary of this doctrine, that the Earth must forever remain an abode of misery, a scene of discord, vice, and crime. FOURIER has demonstrated that the Soul is a beautiful and perfect Mechanism, the crowning work of Supreme Wisdom, and that the elements or parts of which it is composed — the twelve Passions and the Scale of Characters—are, in his own language, " the springs and levers of a brilliant system of Social Harmony and Universal Unity." The Science of Man and the Science of Society explain the means of realizing the first two branches of UNIVERSAL UNITY.

II. SCIENCE OF PASSIONAL ATTRACTION, or Theory of the Laws which govern the Moral World and its Phenomena. — This Science FOURIER discovered and elaborated quite fully; it is the continuation and counterpart of KEPLER'S AND NEWTON'S theory of Material Attraction, or theory of the Laws which govern the material Universe and its phenomena. As the latter explains the Laws which regulate the movements of the Heavenly Bodies and of Matter generally, so the former explains the Laws which regulate the movements of the Soul, and of the moral or spiritual universe of which the Soul forms a part. This new Science which FOURIER discovered is as deeply interesting as it is original. It throws a flood of light on a multitude of problems which the Moralists and Philosophers have never been able to solve, and their ignorance of which has led them to put forth superficial and absurd doctrines on the necessity of " *repressing, compressing, and suppressing*" the Passions, in order to adapt them to our incoherent Social Systems and their arbitrary and capricious laws and institutions. In deducing their moral theories of Man from the study of Human Nature, perverted in its development by our false social institutions, and without any true Science of the Passions to guide them, they have committed as many absurd errors as the Physiologists would have committed, had they formed their physical theories of Man from the study of deformed and diseased bodies, without being guided by a knowledge of the natural functions and structure of the human frame.—The Science of Passional Attraction explains the third branch of UNIVERSAL UNITY.

III. IMMORTALITY OF THE SOUL.— FOURIER undertakes to demonstrate scientifically the truth of this great problem by proofs and analogies deduced from his general principles. He treats the subject, however, too briefly for us to pronounce upon the validity of his deductions. We think that he has demonstrated the fact of the continued existence of the Soul, but his views and explanations of the future world we consider as hypothetical, and class them among his poetic creations. He is however the only man who has written anything satisfactory upon the subject, and his treatise will be read with profound interest. He gives it in his works as the explanation of the fourth branch of UNIVERSAL UNITY.

IV. COMPARATIVE PSYCHOLOGY AND UNIVERSAL ANALOGY.— FOURIER has sketched out the principles of this new Science, and made some practical deductions from them; it explains the relations between Mind and Matter, or the analogy, the correspondence existing between the phenomena of Mind—that is, ideas and sentiments—and the phenomena of Matter, or the creations in the animal, vegetable, and mineral kingdoms. Many of the applications which he makes of these principles, that is, many of the analogies which he institutes between the material and spiritual worlds, appear to us arbitrary and defective, while there are others which seem to us as true and beautiful as they are poetic. In any case, the principles upon which his Science of Analogy is based, are true beyond all question. — This Science explains the fifth branch of UNIVERSAL UNITY.

V. COSMOLOGY, OR THE SCIENCE OF THE UNIVERSE, that is, of the relations, distribution, classification, functions, origin, etc., of the planetary bodies in the Universe. The same laws that govern these great bodies and the phenomena connected with them, govern the creations on our own planet, so that by discovering the order that reigns in the latter—which are visible and tangible to us—we have the Key to the order that reigns in the former which are beyond the reach of practical study and observation. This is the basis upon which FOURIER builds his Cosmical Theory.　He proceeds from the *known* to the *unknown*, having implicit faith that as there is UNITY OF SYSTEM in the Universe, a knowledge of the distribution and order which exist in one sphere, reveals the order and distribution which exist in all other spheres. — The Cosmical Theory explains the sixth branch of UNIVERSAL UNITY.

FOURIER'S Cosmogony is one of the most curious and original of his productions.　It is characterized by the boldest and most wonderful speculation, and considered merely as a poetic, imaginative creation, it excels in magnificence of conception any poem ever written by man.　In this Science as in all others which FOURIER has treated, the basis upon which he proceeds, the principles which guide him, are unquestionably true; the deductions which he makes from these principles, the conclusions at which he arrives, being the result of his own reasoning, may be defective or erroneous.　We must therefore distinguish between the former and the latter, that is, between the *basis on which he builds*, and his *inferences and deductions*.　In justice to the great Pioneer in these new regions of thought, the intelligent reader will make this distinction, and not condemn the theory of UNIVERSAL UNITY because some details may appear to him erroneous or absurd.

In connection with this subject we may remark that a knowledge of the Laws of Nature is to Reason what the possession of tools and implements is to the hand, furnishing it with aids which immeasurably increase its power and efficiency in the exploration and study of truth.　BACON, in his *Novum Organum*, treating of the value and importance of Method to the mind in its scientific investigations, and of the necessity of not leaving it to itself, unassisted as it were by mechanical aid, says:—

" If men, for instance, had attempted mechanical labors with
" their hands alone, and without the power and aid of instru-
" ments, as they have not hesitated to carry on the labors of
" their understanding with the unaided efforts of their mind, they
" would have been able to move and overcome but little, though
" they had exerted their utmost and united powers.　And just to
" pause a while on this comparison, and look into it as a mirror;
" let us ask, if any obelisk of a remarkable size were perchance
" required to be removed, for the purpose of gracing a triumph or

" any similar pageant, and men were to attempt it with their bare
" hands, would not any sober spectator avow it to be an act of
" the greatest madness? And if they should increase the num-
" ber of workmen, and imagine that they could thus succeed,
" would he not think so still more? Nay, if not content with
" this, they were to determine on consulting the athletic art, and
" were to give orders for all to appear with their hands, arms,
" and muscles, regularly oiled and prepared, would he not ex-
" claim that they were taking pains to rave by method and de-
" sign? Yet men are hurried on with the same senseless energy
" and useless combination in intellectual matters, as long as they
" expect great results either from the number and agreement, or
" the excellence and acuteness of their wits; or even strengthen
" their minds with logic, which may be considered as an athletic
" preparation, but yet do not desist (if we rightly consider the
" matter) from applying their own understandings merely with
" all this zeal and effort. Whilst nothing is more clear, than
" that in every great work executed by the hand of Man without
" machines or implements, it is impossible for the strength of indi-
" viduals to be increased, or for that of the multitude to combine."

BACON hoped by his Inductive Method to be able to furnish the
mind with the tools and implements necessary to work out all the
intricate problems of Science. He was right as far as he went;
but his method is only a part, a branch of the integral method;
it is but a single tool or instrument, competent only to a specific
work, that of assisting and guiding the mind in the systematic
observation and classification of facts and phenomena. The Laws
of Order and Harmony are the complete tools and implements,
the great machinery necessary to Reason—the complementary
means and powers requisite for the successful investigation of the
System of Nature, or of Universal Truth. With the aid of this
intellectual machinery, it can work out problems which would
appal the Mind left to its unaided powers; we repeat, then, that
Laws and Principles are to the Mind what implements and
machinery are to the Hand, increasing its power a hundred, a
thousand fold. The advantage which FOURIER possessed over
preceding explorers in the labyrinthan regions of the Passions
and of Social Organization, was that at the commencement of his
labors, *he created the tools and implements with which he was*

to work; that is to say, he discovered the laws and principles of universal distribution and organization. *He did not trust to the researches and speculations of his own Reason; he did not undertake to build up the Edifice of Universal Unity with his unaided Intellect.* He first secured the necessary implements and machinery, and with their aid accomplished the Herculean labor which he undertook. In all his discoveries and plans of organization, from the simplest to the most complex, from the details of his architectural arrangements and his system of Education, to the grandest generalizations in his Cosmical Theory, he uses the same instrumentalities, he follows and applies the same Laws and Principles, makes all his deductions from them, and takes them exclusively as his Guide.

If many of his discoveries appear grand and magnificent, almost beyond the power of the human intellect, it is because he employed means which are new and unknown. If by a careful study of the laws and principles with which he worked, we obtain the Key to his method of exploration, everything will then appear easy and natural, and the mystery of his great discoveries will be explained.

We will close this general Survey of the scope and character of FOURIER's labors with the following brief recapitulation of what he has accomplished:—

1. Discovery of Nature's Laws of Distribution, Classification, and Organization—that is, the LAWS OF UNIVERSAL ORDER AND HARMONY.

2. Discovery of the THEORY OF UNIVERSAL UNITY, or determination of the General Plan of Creation.

3. Discovery of the NATURAL ORDER OF HUMAN SOCIETY, deduced from the Laws of Universal Harmony; that is, determination of the SCIENCE OF SOCIETY, necessary to guide Man in his Social Career.

4. Discovery of the SCIENCE OF MAN, or THEORY OF THE HUMAN PASSIONS; determination of the terrestrial Destiny of the Human Race.

5. Discovery of the SCIENCE OF PASSIONAL ATTRACTION, or Theory of the Laws which govern the Moral Universe.

6. Treatise on the IMMORTALITY OF THE SOUL.

7. Treatise on UNIVERSAL ANALOGY AND COMPARATIVE PSY-

CHOLOGY; determination of the principles which lie at the basis of this Science.

8. Treatise on COSMOLOGY; determination of the guide which the Human Mind is to follow in studying the great phenomena of the Universe lying beyond the scope of observation.

II.

FUNDAMENTAL PROPOSITIONS.

LET us now state more categorically the fundamental propositions upon which FOURIER bases his System.

The first Proposition is :—

That the Universe is governed by LAWS; that these Laws, fixed and immutable in their action, are the source of Order and Harmony in Creation; that it is according to them that all the elements and phenomena of the Universe, from the highest to the lowest, from worlds and systems of worlds to plants and insects, are distributed, classified, and regulated; and that wherever Harmony reigns, it is the result of the application of these Laws.

The second Proposition is :—

That MAN, endowed with Reason, can discover these Laws, which may be called the LAWS OF UNIVERSAL ORDER AND HARMONY; that it is his function as an intelligent being to discover them, and to apply them to those spheres over which he presides, and which it devolves upon him to organize and regulate.

The third Proposition is :—

That when Man has discovered these Laws and applied them to the ORGANIZATION OF SOCIETY—that is, to the regulation of his Passions and of his Social Relations—he will establish the reign of SOCIAL HARMONY on Earth, and realize upon it an order of things in unity with the DIVINE PLAN OF ORDER which reigns throughout Creation.

FOURIER claims to have discovered the Laws of Universal Order and Harmony, which he calls, in their unity, the LAW OF THE SERIES. He also claims to have deduced from these Laws a Plan of Social Organization, which he affirms to be the NATURAL OR DIVINE ORDER OF HUMAN SOCIETY.

MAN, endowed with the power of discovering and applying Laws and Principles, has a function to perform on Earth of the highest importance. This function is to establish Order and Harmony in the Terrestrial Sphere at the head of which he is placed and over which he presides; this he can do only by discovering the Laws of Divine Order, and applying them to the regulation of its elements and phenomena.

Among the departments over which Man presides and the control of which is delegated to him, are :—

1. The regulation of the development and action of his Passions ;

2. The creation of the Arts and Sciences, and the organization of Industry ;

3. The establishment of social and political Laws and Institutions ;

4. The development and perfection of the creations in the animal and vegetable kingdoms, their proper regulation and distribution, and the establishment of order in the material world.

The supervision and control of these and other departments are left to MAN, and he can establish Order and Unity in them only by taking as his guide those principles which are the basis of Order and Unity throughout Creation.

GOD has created all the elements of the Universe with the capacity of Harmony ; he has left to Man the task of establishing harmony in those which are within his domain and come under his control. HE HAS CREATED MAN THE HARMONIST ON THIS PLANET, AS HE HIMSELF IS THE HARMONIST OF THE UNIVERSE.

Let us illustrate this by a few examples. God has so created Sounds that they are susceptible of Harmony, and has delegated to Man the function of harmonizing them; this man has done by applying to them a branch of the laws of Universal Order. FOURIER affirms that the Human Passions have also been created with the capacity of Harmony, and that the function of regulating harmoniously their play and action is left to Man, as in the case of Sounds, so that he can establish PASSIONAL HARMONY as he has established Musical Harmony. In like manner, God has created forms and colors with the capacity of harmonic arrangement, and has delegated to Man the function of establishing harmony in them, as in the other spheres we have mentioned. In fact, the Earth and all the creations in its animal and vegetable kingdoms are destined by God for a vast Concert of Material Harmonies, and he has assigned to Man their harmonic regulation, distribution, and arrangement. So far as Man has established Order and Harmony in any sphere upon which he operates—in Art, Science, Industry—he has done so by applying to it those regulative Principles which govern the Universe.

This truth can not be too often repeated; Man must learn that his province as an inventor, a regulator, an organizer in every sphere of Art, Science, and Industry, is not to devise Laws and Principles, but to discover and apply them; not to create arbitrary theories and systems, but to study and follow the Laws of Nature; this is his great function on Earth.

In higher spheres, order and harmony are established by a Power superior to Man; in some of these spheres order now reigns, as, for instance, in the Solar System and in the physical organization of the planet and its creations. The human body, for example, is a perfect and harmonious organism; the same is true of the plants and animals; they may be improved by human skill, but without changing their organic structure, which remains the same.

Man, we insist, must discover the Laws of Nature and apply them progressively to the departments within his province, and which he is delegated to organize. He has discovered and applied the Laws which govern Sounds, and created the Art of Music; he has partially discovered those which regulate the Solar System, and created the Science of Astronomy; he has also arrived at a knowledge of a portion of those which form the basis of Geology, Chemistry, and some other sciences. It remains for him to discover the Laws of Universal Order in their integrality, and to apply them to all the spheres or departments which he has to organize—the passional, social, political, artistic, scientific, industrial, etc. In respect to the Passional or Social, we may affirm that unless the Human Passions are out of the pale of Universal Order, are incapable of harmonious development and action, are, in a word, exceptions to the divine Scheme of Harmony, and inherently discordant, it is evident that they must have been created according to and must be regulated by the eternal laws and principles which govern the Universe.

The basis on which FOURIER proceeds is beyond all question true. That the Universe is governed by fixed Laws and Principles is a truth not only confirmed by the spontaneous intuitions of the human Soul, but demonstrated by Science and accepted at the present day by all scientific men. In fact, no progress is made in any department of knowledge or in any sphere of organization, except by proceeding on this basis. These Laws and Principles explain to us the Plan of the distribution and organization of the Universe, for it is according to them that all its details are ordered and arranged, and that all created things are made.

Now is it not self-evident that if Human Reason can discover the system of Laws and Principles by which Creation is governed, that it will have the Key, the guide to the establishment of absolute Order and perfect Organization in every sphere the ordering and organization of which devolve upon Man?

If the plan of Social Organization discovered by FOURIER, or any of its details, be found erroneous, it can only be shown at most that he has made wrong deductions from his premises, for the basis upon which he builds is positive and absolute.

Let moralists, theologians, political economists, and all others who condemn FOURIER, if they take any real interest in the welfare and elevation of mankind, adopt this basis and deduce from it a Social Order which shall supplant the present absurd and incoherent system of Society, and deliver the Human Race from the horrible discord and misery which now reign upon the Earth.

We shall enter into no details respecting the Laws of Universal Order; this is a subject which would require an elaborate treatise by itself. Our object in the preceding remarks has been simply to state the following propositions:—

1. That the Universe is governed by a system of Laws which are mathematical and invariable in their operation.

2. That human reason can and must discover these Laws and apply them to the Organization of Society.

3. That FOURIER claims to have discovered, and we believe has discovered them.

4. That the Plan of Social Organization which FOURIER proposes is a deduction from these Laws, and is not therefore an ar-

bitrary, capricious creation of his intellect, but a scientific theory based upon the principles which govern the Universe.

The Laws by which the various departments and phenomena of Creation are distributed and regulated, we have called the Laws of *Order and Harmony*, because they produce these effects in the Universe.

FOURIER, considering these Laws in their unity or as one supreme Law, calls them, as we have before stated, the LAW OF THE SERIES ; he does this because the distribution in Series is the basis of Order and Harmony in Creation. We will now make a short extract or two from his writings, which will present a general view of the subject :—

" The Series of Groups is the order adopted by God in the dis-
" tribution of the Kingdoms of Nature and of all created things.
" The Naturalists in their theories and classifications have unani-
" mously adopted this mode of distribution ; they could not have
" departed from it without placing themselves in contradiction with
" Nature, and falling into confusion. The three Kingdoms —
" animal, vegetable, and mineral — present to us only Series of
" Groups. The Planets themselves are distributed in Series, but
" of a higher and more perfect order than the Kingdoms ; the
" latter are distributed in *simple* or *free* Series ; (the term sim-
" ple or free signifies that the number of groups is not fixed,
" but may vary ;) the former are distributed in *compound* or
" *measured* Series ; this order, more perfect than the simple,
" is unknown to the astronomers and geometers ; it is for this
" reason that they can not explain the cause of the distributive
" system existing in the planetary worlds — explain why God has
" given a greater or less number of satellites to certain planets,
" why a ring to one and not to another, and other similar prob-
" lems.

" If the Human Passions and Characters were not subject
" to distribution in Series, like the material kingdoms and
" the planetary worlds, Man would be out of Unity with the
" Universe ; there would be duplicity of system and incohe-
" rence between its Material and Passional elements. If Man
" would attain to Social Unity, he should seek for the means in
" this Serial order which God has established throughout Crea-
" tion.

" The Series is the Lever which regulates the whole Move-
" ment of Social harmony; the discovery of this process is the
" means by which Man is to attain to his social Destiny; the
" knowledge of it is the condition of Harmony on all globes.
" The Social world can not on any Planet attain to Unity, nor
" rise to a happy destiny, till it has discovered the mechanism
" of the PASSIONAL SERIES, the discovery of which is the essential
" task of genius."

FOURIER divides the Series into three kinds.

1. *The Simple or Free Series.*—The number of component
parts or elements in this Series is not fixed but may vary. The
Kingdoms of Nature are distributed according to this order;
hence we find in one genus or family of animals or plants, ten species; in another, fifteen; another, twenty—and so on.

2. *The Compound or Measured Series.*—In this Series, the
number of component parts or elements is fixed and invariable.
In Music, for example, which is of the Measured Order, the number of notes in the Gamut—which are the parts or elements of
the Series—is fixed and unchangeable; in the Diatonic gamut,
they are seven—in the Chromatic, twelve. In like manner,
measure, rhythm, etc. in this Harmony are regulated by fixed
numbers.

3. *The Mixed Series.*—This Series is a compound of, or a
cross between the Free and the Measured Series.

A good illustration of this subject is found in literary composition; Prose represents the Simple or Free Series, Poetry the
Measured Series, and Blank-verse the Mixed Series.

The Passions of the Soul with their effects—the characters,
tastes, and inclinations of men—are, like all the higher creations
of God, distributed in Measured Series, and are regulated in their
play and action by this order; hence they tend instinctively to
the Measured Order in the external world, as it corresponds to
their natural mode of activity, to their wants and attractions.
" The Passional System is an echo of all the accords established
" in Nature; or, rather, Nature is the echo and emblem of the
" Passions, for GOD, in order to create the Universe according to
" the laws of eternal justice, must have depicted Himself in Cre-
" ation, and consequently have depicted in it the twelve Passions,

" which are his essence, and the play of those Passions in all
" their possible developments."

We quote in this connection the following striking passage
from FOURIER in which he shows the intuitive tendency of the
Soul to Measured Harmonies, and the employment of the Measured Order in the government of the Universe.

" Whence comes the universal taste in all nations and among
" all races for whatever is regulated by the Measured Series —
" for poetry, for music, for the dance — which are measured har-
" monies applied to language, to sound, and to movement? These
" measured harmonies are found even among the most savage
" tribes; they spring up as by instinct in regions where the in-
" clemency of the climate would seem calculated to destroy all
" the illusions of art. Among the ices of the North, we find the
" native bards cultivating poetry, music, and the dance, and in
" our own time the Ossianic Muse still gives delight to the most
" polished nations. The rude Savages of Northern Siberia,
" people more like brutes than men, have also their imperfect
" verse, their coarse music, and their grotesque dances; the
" art of measured harmonies is on a level with their Social con-
" dition, but it still exists, and is everywhere an accompaniment
" and support of religion. Among Savages, the rude tribute of
" measured art is offered in homage to the Divinity, while in
" Civilized nations, harmonies, poetic, vocal, and instrumental,
" contribute to the lustre of all religious solemnities. The dance,
" which was formerly admitted among the rites of Religion, fig-
" ures among them no longer. Is not this omission the effect of
" corruption rather than of reverence? The Psalmist danced
" before the Ark of the Covenant; DAVID, then, thought the
" dance an homage worthy of the Creator. If DAVID was de-
" ceived as to the honors which should be rendered to the
" Deity, how is it that our modern religions address to God no
" other praises than those which come from the muse of this
" Poet-King, who thought that, in the offerings of holy joy and
" pious fervor, the dance should be united before the altar with
" music and poetry. Everything connected with measured har-
" mony becomes worthy of our respect as an act of union with
" Divinity. It is already said that poetry is the language of the
" gods; this is a truth of sentiment as well as of reason. The

" Lyric bard is looked upon by us as a being in communion with
" Divinity; we would have him address the gods as one with
" them — would have him act upon and move the most inflexible
" of deities, as we read in the following noble strophe of the
" French Pindar :—

> " C'est ainsi qu' au-delà de la fatale barque
> Ma voix adoucirait de l'orgueilleuse parque
> L'impitoyable loi ;
> Lachésis apprendrait à devenir sensible,
> Et le double ciseau de sa sœur inflexible
> Tomberait devant moi."

" This privilege of the Divine language, this power of commu-
" nion with the gods which is given to us by ·Poetry and Music,
" a power which belongs to all measured harmonics, is truly an
" inspiration of God, who manifests himself especially in meas-
" ured harmonics, in which he delights — as we see in his most
" sublime work, in the harmony of the planets, which despite the
" inconceivable rapidity of their movement, are so regular in their
" gravitation that our globe traverses every year more than two
" hundred millions of leagues within a given minute.

" The principal measured harmonics known to man are the
" Mathematical and the Musical. Hence these are preëminently
" the Divine language; Mathematics, by exactness, Music by
" harmony. Now if the Human Passions were excluded from
" this system of measured harmony, which in our eyes is the seal
" of Divine Order in the material world, where would be the
" Unity of system in the Universe ? So long as we fail to recog-
" nise the spirit of God in Material harmonics, we are unworthy
" of knowing his designs in respect to Passional harmonics, in
" which the Measured Order should especially reign since the Pas-
" sions are the portion of the Universe most identified with God.

" We should have foreseen the destiny of the Passional World
" from observing the rigorous exactitude which God observes in
" all measured movements. Measure must have been of great
" value in his eyes for him to have restricted the planets to rota-
" tions and orbits so exact that they traverse thousands of mil-
" lions of leagues within a given minute. And from this regu-
" larity in the sidereal system we may judge how impassioned
" God must be for precision of movement and for the general

" combination of motors and their effects. We have scarcely a
" finer example of this, after the harmony of the Planets, than is
" found in the harmony of Sounds.

" Music is for Man an abridgment of the system of Universal
" Harmony, a faithful picture of the play of the Measured Series,
" which operate only by masses of groups, arranged in octaves,
" like musical sounds. Men should have perceived long ago,
" that there was some divine revelation, some speaking analogy
" in Music—the true language of collective harmony in the ma-
" terial world—and that if Man is destined to discover the
" laws of Passional Harmony, he should seek its emblems and
" rules in the harmonics of music, which must coincide with all
" the harmonies, Material and Passional, of the Universe; if this
" were not so, we could not conceive unity of system in the Uni-
" verse, or in the designs of God."

III.

SOCIAL INFANCY OF THE RACE.—THE LAW OF CAREERS.

EVERY created thing in the Universe, from the least to the
greatest, from the plant or insect to worlds or systems of worlds,
passes through a CAREER—that is to say, through certain stages
of existence, which constitute the course of its finite life. This
is a self-evident proposition, requiring no demonstration; for a
created thing is necessarily a *finite* thing, and that which is finite
must have a beginning, a middle, and an end, and these imply
necessarily a *Career*, with an ascending and a descending movement, or ascending and descending phases of life.

The three great stages of a Career, namely, the

BEGINNING,   MIDDLE,   END,

are analogous in living organisms to

BIRTH AND INFANCY,   MATURITY,   DECLINE AND DEATH.

This Law of Careers is of universal application. It is true,
in the first place, of all the creations we see around us on the
planet—mineral, vegetable, and animal. Geology shows that
it must also be true of the Globe itself, demonstrating that it
has gone through a great epoch of primitive formation, and that
it must consequently have had a Beginning; having had a begin-

ning, it must have an End, for a beginning implies finiteness, and finiteness implies termination. The observations of astronomy indicate that certain stars have disappeared—that is, have had an end—that different nebulæ are in different stages of development or formation, and that comets are probably embryonic stellar bodies; all these facts go to the support of the proposition that every created, Finite Thing goes through a Career, and passes successively — unless some accident interrupts its course —through the phases of infancy, growth, maturity, decline, and dissolution.

Life is Movement and Development. Every created thing is endowed with a spark of the universal active Principle, called Life ; even the mineral exists by virtue of some magnetic force which binds its particles together. Life, engendering movement, gives rise to Careers, and in passing through careers develops itself in the concrete, that is to say, unfolds or manifests its qualities, attributes, and phenomena, in positive existence.

As it is important that the reader should have have a clear idea of what constitutes a Career, and of the phases of life which enter into it, we will take the career of some one finite creation as a pattern or model of careers in general, for according to the law of Unity of System in the Universe, the same principles lie at the basis of all organizations. As the Career of Man is the most familiar to us, we will take that as our model.

CAREER OF MAN.

	Primitive or Embryonic Development	Formation in the Womb.
ASCENDING MOVEMENT.	1st or *Ascending Transition*	*Birth and Infancy.*
	1st Phase of Life . . . Growth	Childhood and Youth.
	2d *Transition*	*Puberty.*
	2d Phase of Life . . . Development	Adolescence.
	APOGEE OF LIFE—Full Development . . .	MANHOOD.
DESCENDING MOVEMENT.	3d Phase of Life . . . Decline	Mature Age.
	3d *Transition*	*Loss of Virility.*
	4th Phase of Life . . . Decrepitude	Senility.
	4th or *Descending Transition*	*Decay and Death.*
	Decomposition of the Body.	Dissolution.

By studying these Phases in the Career of Man, the reader will have a type or model of all careers in the Universe; they may vary somewhat in their characteristics, as, for example, in the number and duration of phases and transitions, but the principles on which they are based are the same, as are also the principal stages of development which are, 1st, Embryonic Formation; 2d, Infancy; 3d, Maturity; 4th, Decline and Decay; 5th, Death and Dissolution. An example or two will illustrate the analogy existing between the above Model and other careers. The formation of the chicken in the egg, requiring twenty-one days, is the period of embryonic development; the breaking of the egg and the appearance of the chicken are the first Transition — birth. For the plant or tree, the sprouting of the seed in the earth and the formation of the root, constitute the period of its embryonic development; the shooting of the sprout above ground into the air, is the first Transition or birth; the epoch at which it first begins to flower or bear fruit is the period of its second ascending Transition, corresponding to puberty in man; that at which it ceases to flower or bear fruit corresponds to the third Transition in his career.

Proceeding from the known to the unknown, from that which lies within the scope of our observation to that which lies beyond it, let us apply the Law of Careers to our Globe. We shall find in so doing that the great geological period which preceded the creation of the species now inhabiting the Earth, was the period of embryonic formation and development; the epoch at which the present creation took place marked a Transition for the Globe corresponding to birth in man, while the period that has elapsed since this creation, is the period of Infancy and Childhood.

This Law of Careers applies to collective Beings like the Human Race, as to single Beings like the individual Man.

Now the important points we wish to establish are:—

1. *That the Human Race must pass through a Social Career corresponding to the Organic career of the Individual, and that it has its Social infancy, growth, maturity, decline, and old age, corresponding to these periods in the life of Man; and*

2. *That the Human Race is now in the phase of its Social Infancy and Childhood.*

The Human Race is a collective, continuous, progressive WHOLE, multiplying from a few couples, spreading over the Globe, developing its powers, and acquiring and accumulating knowledge, experience, and resources, from generation to generation, as it progresses in time and expands in space.

That the Race is a Collective Being, is ONE, is proved by the fact that the association of all the members composing it, that their united intelligence and power, their coöperation and concert of action, are necessary to the fulfilment of the functions which it has to perform on the Earth. That it is a Progressive Being is proved by the fact that the inventions, discoveries, creations and experience of one age or epoch are transmitted to succeeding ages or epochs, that the Race thus grows in knowledge and power, and that the knowledge and experience it possesses at any one period are the fruit of all its past labors.

The individuals composing the Race appear and disappear by birth and death on the scene of life, but the Race remains and advances in its unity through successive ages; its onward movement gives rise to the great Humanitary Career of which we are speaking.

Let us now point out some of the analogies existing between the Career of the Individual and that of the Race, and deduce from them the present stage or phase of development of the latter, or the part of its career through which it is now passing. (The reader will observe that in the above Table we have given the physical career of the Individual, and it is with that that we compare the Social Career of the Race.)   The career of the Individual is one of Organic growth and development; that of the Race is one of Social growth and development; the former consists in creating, developing and perfecting a Physical organization; the latter, in creating, developing, and perfecting a Social organization. This consists in creating the elements of Society—that is to say, in discovering and perfecting the processes of Industry and the Arts and Sciences, which are necessary to the material power and the enlightenment of the Race—and in organizing social, political, and religious institutions, which are necessary to the regulation of its collective interests, labors, and social life.

We make our comparison between the Career of the Race in developing and perfecting a Social Organization and the Career of the Individual in developing and perfecting a Physical Organization, because there is analogy or unity of process between the discovery and establishment of true institutions—industrial, educational, political, social, religious, etc.—and the formation and development of the various parts of the body; social institutions are the instrumentalities, the means of the Social development of the Race, as physical organs are the instrumentalities, the means of the mental development of the Individual. The Intellect and Passion of the Race invent and create Industry, Art, Science, Laws and Institutions, which are parts of the Social Machine, as the vital force of the Individual, or the principle of life, forms organs, members, etc., which are parts of the physical machine.

Let us now proceed to point out the indications we have of the Social Infancy and Childhood of the Race; they are,

1. The condition of Industry and Science.

2. Reign of Social Incoherence.

3. Reign of Evil on Earth.

4. Development of the Passions in their lower Degrees.

5. Absence of historical records and monuments of great antiquity.

I. CONDITION OF INDUSTRY AND SCIENCE.—Before entering upon this subject, a few preliminary explanations are necessary.

Two characteristics of the phase of Infancy and Childhood in the career of all beings, individual and collective, are WEAKNESS and IGNORANCE. In the career of the individual Man, the *Weakness* attendant upon this phase is a consequence of the undeveloped condition of the body and the inability of the will to manage and control it; in the career of the collective being called the Human Race, it is a consequence of the undeveloped condition of Industry, that is to say, of the non-possession of tools, implements, and machinery, and a knowledge of the processes of agriculture, manufactures, etc. A fully-developed and well-organized system of Industry is to the Human Race what a fully-developed and well-organized physical frame is to the Individual Soul; when the Race has a complete and perfect Industrial Organization through which to operate on Nature and create material wealth, it will be in the same position as the Soul which has a complete and perfect Physical Organization through which to act and fulfil its material destiny; the absence of such an organization in either case indicates that the being is in the phase of Childhood, in the early period of its Career.

The *Ignorance* of the Race results from its not having discovered the Sciences, which are necessary to guide and enlighten it in its Social Career and to explain to it the plans and phenomena of Creation. Science constitutes the intelligence and wisdom of the Race as Industrial Machinery constitutes its physical power and efficiency; the former is for it, so to say, a Second Reason, created by the combined intellectual labor of all the members of the Race, and multiplying immensely the powers of the Individual Reason, as the latter, in the same sense, is a Second Physical Organization, multiplying indefinitely the powers of the Individual Organization.

It follows from the above that by studying and determining the degree of development which Industry and Science have attained, we can determine the phase of the Social Career of the Race.

Four different Societies, so far as History preserves the record, have been established on our Globe, namely, the Nomadic or Savage, the Patriarchal, the Barbaric, and the Civilized. The advanced Nations of the Earth are now living in the fourth Society, called Civilization. These four Social Periods enter into and form a part of the Social Infancy and Childhood of the Race, as a glance at the State of Industry and Science in each will show.

STATE OF INDUSTRY AND SCIENCE IN THE FOUR SOCIAL PERIODS.

1. NOMADIC OR SAVAGE.—Inertia, Repugnance to Labor and Mental Exertion. Refusal to engage in Industry and Science; non-development of both. Hunting and Fishing the only means of livelihood. Reign of Poverty and Ignorance. Complete Intellectual Night.

2. THE PATRIARCHAL.—Dawn of Industry and of Mental Activity. Exercise of Pastoral Industry; raising of flocks and herds. Prosecution of a few elementary branches of mechanics, without machinery. Reign of Poverty and Superstition.

3. THE BARBARIC.—Primary development of Agriculture and Manufactures. Dawn of Science. General prosecution of Industry by the masses, and their initiation into Labor through physical coercion, that is, Slavery. Commencement of the use of tools, implements, and machinery. First exercise of the Reason-

ing Faculties. Study of some of the phenomena of Nature, and of a few of the elementary Sciences. Reign of Poverty, Superstition, Fanaticism, and Brutality.

4. THE CIVILIZED.—Development of Industry on a large scale ; its prosecution through Poverty or indirect Coercion. Invention of machinery and its application to Manufactures. Employment of one of the forces of Nature—Steam—in Industry. Discovery of the Art of Navigation ; creation of the means of rapid transportation. Commencement of analytical thought and observation. Empirical development of the Physical Sciences. Reign of Poverty and Ignorance among the masses. Tolerance in Religious and Scientific matters.

Leaving aside the first three Societies, let us examine the condition of Industry and Science in the present Social Order, called Civilization, which is the most advanced. The majority of men in this Order, struck with the inventions and discoveries that have been made in Mechanics, the means of Locomotion, and the Sciences, and dazzled by comparing the progress of Civilization with the stagnation existing in the other Societies, imagine that the Human Race has arrived at a high degree of perfection in all departments, has reached all but the climax of Industrial and Scientific perfection, and that it is consequently in its maturity or period of full development. This superficial idea is not peculiar to the present epoch, but has been entertained in every age. The great majority of men have always supposed that the degree of perfection attained was the highest degree of perfection possible. This prejudice was as prevalent before the great improvements in Industry and Science had been made, before the invention of machinery, of printing ; before the application of steam · before railroads, telegraphs, etc., and before the discoveries in Astronomy, Chemistry, and other sciences, as it is at the present day.

Having made these preliminary explanations, let us now point out the present imperfect condition of Industry and Science as a proof that the Race is in the early phase of its Social Career.

I. INDUSTRY.—It is but a century since the really great improvements which now exist in machinery began to be made, and it is only to Manufactures that mechanical power has been applied to any extent. In Agriculture—the basis of the whole

Industrial System—it is almost unknown, and this primary branch of Human Industry is prosecuted in nearly as rude and imperfect a manner as it was ages since. In Locomotion, the steamboat and railroad are inventions of our own day, showing that up to a very recent date this department was in a state of complete infancy.

A peremptory proof that Industry is in an imperfect and undeveloped state, is that it does not produce enough to secure the physical well-being of all the members of Society. The masses are poor, are badly housed, badly clothed, and badly fed. It can not be replied to this, that the rich absorb so large a portion of the wealth created by Industry that there is very little left for the masses, for if the total product of the three most advanced Civilized Nations—France, England, and the United States— were divided equally among the population of these countries, it would average for each individual, in the first-named country but about thirteen cents a day; in the second, eighteen; and in the third, twenty-five. This shows the meagre results of Industry in the present Social Order; production should be increased at least tenfold to secure a degree of prosperity proportional to the legitimate wants of Man.

Ascending to considerations of a more comprehensive character, we find that *Industry is not organized;* that is to say, that no general order and method, no general unity of plan exist in its prosecution; there is no concerted action, no association (with the exception of a few Joint-Stock Companies), no direct communication, no unity of interest between its different branches—Agriculture, Manufacturers, Commerce, and Banking; on the contrary, opposition of interests and general antagonism exist between them, and they wage against each other a war of speculation, spoliation, and fraud, giving rise to the reign of universal anarchy in the great field of Industrial activity. The various departments of Labor, and business operations generally, are prosecuted incoherently, fragmentarily, wastefully, and often ignorantly and blindly by individuals, while selfishness, distrust, and duplicity of action animate all parties and add to the general confusion. These facts, which are notorious, demonstrate that Industry is in an incoherent, unorganized state, and that the productive powers of the Race are not directed with wisdom, order, and unity of purpose to their legitimate ends, namely the creation of the means of its collective prosperity, its material happiness and grandeur, and to the execution of the great works which devolve upon Man as Overseer of the Globe. This imperfect and incoherent state of Industry furnishes us with the first proof that the Human Race is in the Phase of its Social Childhood.

SCIENCE. — Science, still more than Industry, is in an imperfect, undeveloped state. The branches most advanced — the Positive or Physical Sciences — are, with the exception to a certain extent of Mathematics and Astronomy, in the purely empirical phase — that is, are but collections of facts, observations, experiments, and special analyses, presenting mere systems of external classification, without any theory of general laws and principles; in a word, they explain *Effects* without giving any theory of *Causes*. On the other hand, the abstract and ethical Sciences, those relating to the Universe, to Man, to Society — such as Cosmogony, Theology, Anthropology, Moral Philosophy — are mere speculative, arbitrary theories, that is, mere generalizations, evolved for the most part by the Imagination, and unsupported by any positive data, by any careful observation or close analysis. They are in a vague and purely speculative state, and are characterized by puerile and infantine conceptions which bring them into discredit among scientific men.

There are many new Sciences that remain to be discovered, and the existence of which is hardly suspected. The Science most important to Man — namely, SOCIOLOGY or the Science of Society — has been mooted only in the present century; it is consequently in its early stage of development, and it has been associated with so many absurd schemes and visionary plans that it is looked upon with distrust by all classes.

There is no UNITY in the Sciences; the chain that binds them together, the common basis upon which they all rest, is unknown to the scientific world. This basis is to be found in the laws of Universal Order, which underlie the varied phenomena of Creation — laws which, in distributing, coördinating, classifying these phenomena, and regulating their movement, succession, and development, explain the UNITY OF THE UNIVERSE, and as a consequence the Unity of the Sciences which treat of its various departments or branches.

Not only the Sciences themselves, but the methods by which they are prosecuted, are in an imperfect and infantine state ; for when we observe the mode of action of the mind in studying the Positive or Physical Sciences on the one hand, and the Abstract or Speculative Sciences on the other, we find that it operates in two opposite directions, that it is engaged in two one-sided and exclusive processes of thought. In the first case, it occupies itself exclusively with minute analyses and the observation of material facts and phenomena, aiming at nothing but an experimental knowledge of the subject of which it treats, and leaving aside Laws and Principles : in the second case, it engages in mere generalizations, in systematizing imperfect observations, and in speculating on vague ideas and intuitions. Thus we have empirical observation and minute analysis of facts on the one hand, and vague generalizations without facts or analytic observation on the other.

The imperfect state of the known Sciences, the absence of Unity in them, the number of sciences still undiscovered, and the one-sided development and activity of the human mind, furnish another demonstration of the Social Childhood of the Race.

II. REIGN OF SOCIAL INCOHERENCE ON THE EARTH, or existence of different systems of Society, with conflicting customs, laws, and institutions, giving rise to national antipathies, jealousies, enmities, and wars. This Incoherence is the result of the Social Ignorance and Inexperience of the Race, and as Ignorance and Inexperience are accompaniments of Infancy and Childhood, they furnish another proof that Mankind is in the early phase of its Social Career. If this be not so, if Social discord and incoherence are the natural and permanent state of Mankind, are to last through all time, what idea must we form of the wisdom of the Author of this world, and of the order of things that he has established in it ? We can find no satisfactory explanation of the cause of the Social Evils that exist on our Globe except in the fact that the Human Race is in the early period of its Social Career — that it is, like all beings in the state of Infancy and Childhood, without knowledge and experience, and *that it is subject in consequence to Error ;* — the poverty, ignorance, discord, and war, which now fill the Earth are the fruits of this Error.

The Human Race can not establish a true Social Order on Earth, securing the reign of political, social, and religious Unity, except on condition —

1. OF CREATING THE ELEMENTS OF SOCIETY; these elements are Industry, the Arts and Sciences: Humanity can no more construct a true Social Order without these elements than the individual Man can construct an edifice without the requisite building materials.

2. OF DISCOVERING THE SCIENCE OF SOCIETY; this science is necessary to guide Humanity in the complex work of Social Organization, and in fulfilling the important functions which devolve upon it on the Earth. On every Globe, as on ours, Social discord and incoherence must necessarily reign until these two conditions are fulfilled, that is to say until the elements of the Social Organization are created, and the Science of that Organization is discovered.

The different systems of Society which the Human Race has established on Earth — the Nomadic or Savage, the Patriarchal, the Barbaric, and the Civilized — are so many experiments which it has made in Social Organization, so many steps in the path of Social progress. Notwithstanding the rise and fall of Nations, which appear to the world like so many advance and retrograde movements in the Social Career, so many temporary successes and failures — leading to the belief that the Race is to move forever in a Circle — there has been a continued and unbroken progress from the earliest period down to the present day. Even the Middle Ages, which appear dark and confused in comparison with the period of Greek and Roman Civilization, adorned by Art and Literature, were in advance of that period by a higher development of the sentiments of justice and philanthropy, and by the transformation of Slavery into the more lenient and humane system of Serfdom.

Thus the Human Race, continually progressing, advances through the ages toward a state of social Unity, Order, and Harmony; but to arrive at this state, it must pass through certain periods of social experiment, apprenticeship, and initiation; it must study and learn, as the individual Man must study and learn, and acquire knowledge and experience as he must acquire knowledge and experience. The history of the past is the history of the social initiation and apprenticeship of the Race. When it has acquired the necessary resources and experience, it will establish a true and unitary system of Society on the globe, and inaugurate the reign of Social Order and Harmony; this will mark the transition of the Race from the period of Social Childhood to that of Social Adolescence.

The Social Mechanism being a Whole, composed of parts or branches—the Industrial, the Administrative, the Religious, etc.—if incoherence reigns in the whole, it must reign as a consequence in the parts; having spoken of the incoherence which prevails in two of the branches, we will add a few remarks upon the incoherence which reigns in the third branch—Religion.

Leaving aside the rude religions of the Savage, Patriarchal, and Barbaric Societies, which require no criticism, is it not evident that the multitude of Sects into which the most advanced religion, Christianity, is divided, with their incoherent and antagonist doctrines and dogmas, is a demonstration that no Criterion of Certainty, no Standard of absolute Truth in religious matters exists—that is, no POSITIVE SCIENCE OF GOD and of his scheme of Providence? Had the Human Mind discovered the laws and principles which govern Creation and, by their aid, penetrated the theory of Universal Unity and the Plan of Divine Providence, it would have arrived at a SCIENCE OF THE ABSOLUTE, at a POSITIVE THEOLOGY. As a consequence, all incoherent, conflicting, and antagonist theories and opinions in the domain of Religion would have disappeared, as they have in the sciences which have arrived at a Positive state, such as Mathematics and Astronomy. In these Sciences—which are called Positive, because they are based on certain branches of the Laws of Universal Order—we do not find opposite opinions and theories upheld by different learned bodies—one, for example, maintaining the theory of the rotation of the Sun round the Earth, and another that of the rotation of the Earth round the Sun, as was the case within less than three centuries, when men like Galileo and Bacon held opposite opinions on this subject. There is absolute unity of opinion on the fundamental problems of these two sciences; Catholic and Protestant, and the Pagan with them, believe alike in the sphericity of the Earth and its rotation round the sun; they accept with the same unanimity the theorems of

Mathematics; two and two make four, the world over. When Human Reason more advanced, shall have discovered a Positive Theology, based like the Positive Sciences on the laws of Universal Order, the Human Race will accept it unanimously as they now accept the fundamental principles of Mathematics and Astronomy; it will then establish on the Earth ONE RELIGION, with the reign of Religious Unity, as, by the discovery of a Positive Social Science, it will establish One Social System with the reign of Social Unity.

III. Reign of Evil on Earth.—In offering this third proof of the Social Childhood of the Race, we shall enter at the same time upon an examination of the Cause of Evil, and explain the reason of its existence on earth.

This important and intricate problem is one which has occupied and bewildered the human mind for ages, and has given rise to endless controversies and to the most contradictory theories and opinions. The problem is as far from being solved as ever, for men are still discussing it—still seeking new theories for its solution.

The main reason why the human mind has been so much misled on this question, is that it has committed the error of supposing that the past and present false state of things on the Earth is the true, natural, and permanent condition of the Race; that Poverty, Ignorance, Oppression, War, are to be forever the lot of Man; holding this belief, men have been obliged logically to seek for some explanation that would reconcile the reign of Order, of Good in the general scheme of Creation, with the reign of Disorder, of Evil on our globe—reconcile the goodness and wisdom of God, of the Creative Power which called Man and the Planet into existence, with the reign of social misery and discord on Earth. Had Human Reason discovered and applied the Law of Careers, had it risen to the conception that the past few thousand years of human existence on the Planet form but a part, a fragment of the great Social Career of Mankind—a conception not so very difficult—it would have been led to study and determine through what portion of its Social Career the Human Race has been passing up to the present time; and would have discovered that it was the initial or transitional Phase, and that

7

the Evil which has existed during this Phase is a natural and unavoidable result of the social imperfection and non-development attendant upon it.

Among the theories of the cause of Evil which have been put forth, the one most commonly accepted is that of the primitive Disobedience and Fall of Man. Man, this theory assumes, was created *Good*, but using his free will, he disobeyed the commands of God, fell from his original state, incurred the Divine wrath, entailed upon his Race imperfection and sin, and thus ushered into the world the reign of Evil. With this doctrine is coupled the idea that this Earth is a place of trial and probation, and that the final solution of the mystery of the present life with all its sufferings, is adjourned to another world.

On the other hand, the Skeptic, who believes that the Universe is governed by Chance, holds that Man is an essentially imperfect creation (as well might be the case with so complex a being if he were created without system) and that the cause of Evil is to be found in the inherent imperfection of Human Nature.

Others, again, of a stern and ascetic character, believe that life is a combat, that Man is to be developed and disciplined only in the battle of life, that his greatness and dignity consist in achieving victories over adverse circumstances, that without the existence of Evil, Man would have no opportunity to develop his powers or to exercise his virtues.

A fourth party hold that Evil is Perversion—that Man is depraved but not inherently, that he is progressing through trials and experiments to a higher and better state. This opinion prevails among the more liberal religious sects, and is an approximation to the truth.

Various other theories of a similar character exist, but it is unnecessary to describe them, as our object is simply to present to the mind of the reader the most current opinions, that he may compare them with the solution which we shall offer of this great problem.

In studying the Laws of Nature, and particularly the Law of Careers—the Law which governs the course and development of the Life and Movement of finite creations — we arrive at once at a simple, natural, conclusive explanation of the great problem of evil ; this explanation is :—

That Evil is inherent and unavoidable in the two transitional Phases which exist at the Beginning and End of Careers, and that it is an effect of the incomplete and imperfect development attendant upon the First of these two Phases, and of the decay and dissolution attendant upon the Second.

These two Phases are in a state of Divergence with the great Central or Organic Period, which occupies the main portion of the Career; Evil is natural, is essential to these transitional stages, and as a general rule is restricted to them.

During the course of the transitional Phases at the Beginning and End of every created thing, the natural Organism not being formed on the one hand, or being in the course of decay and dissolution on the other, the Law which governs the Organism, and which is the Source of Order, of Good, is in the one case not yet in force, and in the other interrupted or suspended.

Let us illustrate this by a practical example drawn from the Career of the Individual Man.

In the Career of Man, Infancy and Childhood constitute the first or ascending transitional Phase of life—the period of formation and early development. Old age and decrepitude constitute the last or descending transitional Phase—the period of decay and dissolution. It is in these two phases or periods that we find, as a necessary consequence of the imperfect condition of the organism, physical and mental debility, helplessness, disease, suffering, etc., which constitute for the Individual a state of evil. In the first transitional phase, he is subject to many physical derangements and maladies—such as teething, hooping-cough, and other infantile diseases—from which mature age is exempt; he is also weak, helpless, ignorant, and subject to accidents and errors of all kinds.

As the individual grows up, the body and mind are developed, and he acquires strength and intelligence; his body becomes accustomed to the elements of Nature around it, to the air which it is to breathe, the food on which it is to live, the climate which it is to inhabit, etc.; he outgrows the diseases of Infancy, and acquires a vigor which enables him to resist the antagonist influences of the outward world; his will drills the physical organism and renders it the pliant and obedient instrument of the mind; the intellect is developed, and he enters upon a career of health, strength, and knowledge, which is the true and natural state of Man — the state of Good. The physical and mental development thus acquired renders him an independent, self-acting, self-determining being, capable of fulfilling his function and destiny on the Earth.

The first transitional phase — that of Infancy — passed through, the Individual enters upon a relatively long career of existence, extending from Childhood to Old Age, which is a period of full and harmonious development — of complete organization; he passes through this period possessing health, vigor, and intelligence (provided he does not violate the laws of his nature) until he reaches old age, when the physical frame worn out by long exercise, begins to decay; it then loses its power, its vital force of reaction, and becomes liable again, at the close of the career, to debility, disease and suffering; the mind, also exhausted, loses its vigor and its capacity of consecutive reasoning. This last stage of life, which is one of decrepitude and decay, forms the descending Transitional Phase in the career of the Individual.

Now, in studying the question of Good and Evil in the Career of Man — who is a little world within himself, to which the laws of Nature apply as to the great Universe of which he is a part — we shall find that Evil — that is weakness, ignorance, incapacity, disease, pain, suffering — reigns during the two transitional Phases of life, is a consequence of and natural and essential to them, while Good — that is, health, vigor, intelligence, capacity — reigns during the long intermediate or middle period of life. This intermediate period, provided life has its natural course, occupies from seven-eighths to fifteen-sixteenths of the Career. If Evil is found in this long period, in the natural, harmonic phase of the Career, it is accidental, unnatural, unessential, and therefore avoidable; it is a result either of the violation of the laws of his being, or of his living in a social world which is in a transitional state, and which reacts upon him, deranges the course of his organic career, and as a consequence involves him in its disorders and evils.

Now if God would do away with Evil, he would have to do away with Transitions — that is, with the Phases of Formation and Dissolution; he would have to do away in the Career of Man with Infancy and Old Age — would have to abolish Birth and

Death. To save Man from the imperfection and suffering attendant upon the first and last periods of life, he would have to create him fully developed, in a state of maturity, with a complete physical and mental organization, possessing vigor and intelligence, and maintain him forever in that state. To abolish Evil *universally*, the same course would have to be pursued with all finite creations; the consequence would be that Change, Variety, Movement, and as a consequence the Process of Creation would have to cease — that in fact Life in the Universe would become fixed and stationary, and the Universe itself a great petrifaction.

Let us now state the principle in its abstract form, after which we will examine it in its application to the Race.

Every Created thing being Finite, living in time and space, must have a Beginning, a Middle, and an End; having a Beginning, a Middle, and an End, it must go through a Career. At the Beginning of the Career there must be a period of formation and primary development; at the End there must be a period of decay and dissolution. The central portion of the Career is one of full development and organization; this we will call the natural, organic, or harmonic phase of the Career — the true and natural state of the finite Creation. The process of formation and early development precedes the Organic Phase; the period of decay and dissolution follows it. The two transitional epochs of formation and dissolution, differing from and being in opposition, in many respects, to the Organic Period, it follows that if Good — that is perfection, order, harmony — reigns in the one, Evil — that is, imperfection, disorder, discord — must reign to a greater or less extent in the other. God admits of no contradictions in his system — no violation of mathematical laws. If he has connected health, strength, and happiness with the state of full development and complete organization, he could not, according to inviolable mathematical laws, connect the same phenomena with the opposite state of decay and dissolution. He could no more do this than he could reconcile absolute contradictions — no more than he could make two and two four and at the same time five : he could not do it without violating all his laws of order, falling into duplicity of system, and establishing incoherence in his own action and in the universe.

Evil, in some mode, is connected directly or indirectly, posi-

tively or relatively, with all finite creations. Those below Man
—the animal, vegetable, and mineral—are to be judged of according to their usefulness or perniciousness to Man, and their
good or evil character are to be determined by this standard. The
tiger, the rattlesnake, the scorpion, are evils in Nature because
they are at war with man and injurious to him, although their
existence may be very agreeable to themselves. So also, though
in a different way, the young fruit-tree, not bearing fruit, is relatively in a state of Evil, for it requires labor at the hand of Man
without requiting him for it. It enters upon its career of Good
only when it bears fruit, and rewards him for his care and at-
attention. The green and unripe fruit is also, relatively, in a
state of Evil ; its acrid or sour juices render it unfit for food and
injurious to the health. This stage of greenness, however, is
temporary, as the fruit is destined to ripen and furnish a delicious
and healthy nutriment.

Life and Movement repeat themselves in all spheres. Let us
pause a moment and compare this fruit in its unripe state with a
Globe during its period of Social Infancy. Let us suppose the
fruit to be an apple, and that it is the world of some little
ephemera, living upon it but for a day, and obliged to suck its
acrid or sour juices, which excoriate and derange its tiny stomach,
and entail upon it great suffering. Would not our little insect
exclaim : " What an imperfect world I live in ! Misery and Evil
are certainly the Destiny, the law of my race. What terrible
sin have we committed to be placed on such a Globe ?" The
poor insect does not know that its little world is in its Transitional Phase, that the fruit is to ripen, to lose all its imperfect
and disagreeable qualities, and become a delightful abode, a
happy world, on a summer's day for future ephemerae. Its existence is too short for it to discover and determine this fact ; it
believes that it lives in a world of Evil, and would, had it intelligence, compose theories on the cause of Evil, similar to those
which men now compose who live, without knowing it, in a world
which is in the stage of Social Infancy—*in a green and unripe
state.*

Let us now pass to the consideration of the question of Evil
and its causes in the career of the Human Race. The same law
that applies to the individual Man or to any other Finite crea-

tion applies to this great Collective Being; and the same cause that produces evil in the career of the one, produces evil in the career of the other.

The Collective being, Humanity, must pass through a Career, as we have explained, like the Individual being, Man, and is subject to the same law of progressive development. The former must evolve, create a Social Organism, with all the elements which enter into it — the Arts, Sciences, Industry, Laws, and Institutions — as the latter must develop a Physical Organism, with elements of another character which enter into that; the former must acquire knowledge and experience, and obtain dominion over Nature, as the latter must develop its intellect and acquire skill and capacity in the more restricted sphere in which it lives and operates.

Now the Human Race can no more accomplish this great work, no more create the various elements of society and attain to a true Social Order, at once, at a single bound so to say, than the infant can spring in an instant into a state of manhood. The Race must pass through a transitional phase of social initiation before it can attain its destiny, as the individual must pass through a transitional phase of growth and development before it can attain to adolescence.

The Human Race begins its Career on earth at 0; it is created naked and ignorant, without Industry, Art, or Science, without laws and institutions, without a knowledge of its Destiny. Commencing at this point, it must discover the processes of Industry; it must invent and create tools, implements, and machinery, discover the sciences and the laws of social organization, and establish a true Social Order for the regulation of its life and Career. This is a great and complex work, requiring a succession of ages with their accumulated and transmitted labors, discoveries, and knowledge. (We estimate that on our Earth a period of somewhere between five and ten thousand years is necessary for the accomplishment of this work.) This great period of Initiation, during which the Social Mechanism is in process of formation, constitutes the Social Infancy and Childhood of the Race — the ascending transitional Phase of its social development; it is the Period when Poverty, Ignorance, Discord, and Social Incoherence reign on the Globe.

As it is important to convey a clear idea of the extent of the labors, mental and physical, which the Race must accomplish before it can arrive at a true Social State, and of the time which is required for their execution, let us glance briefly at the wants, moral and material, of Man. Man is not a *simple* being, like the animal, satisfied with simple Nature, and with the resources she spontaneously offers him ; he is a *compound* being who has compound wants that can be satisfied only by all the creations and resources which a fully developed system of Industry, Art, and Science offers him, and whose complex social relations and life require to be regulated, like all complex movements, by universal Laws.

He is not supplied like the animal with natural clothing, but is born naked, and must clothe himself by artificial means ; this renders it necessary for him to rear flocks and herds, to cultivate flax, cotton, and other products, to invent mechanical processes, and to manufacture the covering which he requires for the protection of his body. He is not supplied with a natural abode ; he can not live in the open fields or forests, in the trunks of trees, or burrow in the ground, but must dwell in houses ; to construct these, he must understand the mechanic arts, some branches of the sciences, the use of metals, etc. His stomach is not adapted to raw or unprepared food — to grains, vegetables, etc., as they come from Nature ; he must prepare his nutriment by artificial means, and this requires the knowledge of various mechanical and scientific processes. He is a social being and must live in Society ; he requires in consequence laws and institutions to regulate his social relations, which are too varied and complex to be regulated by instinct alone, like the simple relations of the animal. His mind requires knowledge, and aspires and craves to comprehend the mystery of Creation around him ; he must discover the Sciences to satisfy this want of his mental nature, and to guide him in his Career. His Senses and Imagination require beauty and harmony, and he must create the Fine Arts. He is a universal and migratory being, a citizen of the Globe, and requires means of rapid locomotion ; he must invent the carriage, the railroad, the steamboat, to meet this want.

Without all these means and resources, which Industry, Art, and Science alone can furnish him, he can not lead what is to him a true and natural life : he can not develop his physical, moral, and intellectual nature ; he can not fulfil his function on earth ; he can not attain his Destiny. More than this, without these resources, he suffers privations of all kinds, which degrade his moral and physical nature, and sink him into compound poverty, ignorance, and error—into a condition below that of the animal, which is a *simple* being and is satisfied with the simple resources of Nature.

Now, is it not a self-evident truth, as obvious as any axiom in mathematics, that the Human Race can not discover, develop, and perfect the means and instrumentalities above described—industrial, scientific, artistic, and social—*at once ;* that it must do so by degrees and progressively ; that it requires the labors of a series of Generations to accomplish this work, transmitting their knowledge and experience from age to age ? During the period while the Race is thus employed in creating the elements of a true Social Order, it must of necessity be deprived of all the benefits, of all the good, which such an Order would confer, and suffer as a consequence all the corresponding privations and evils ; it must suffer physical privation from the want of good houses, good food and clothing ; be exposed to ignorance and error from the want of the sciences and of proper intellectual development ; it must undergo severe toil and drudgery from the want of proper machinery, and a proper organization of Industry ; it must be deprived of the refining and elevating influences of beauty and harmony from the want of the Fine Arts ; it must live in unnatural and uncongenial social relations from the want of true and natural Social Laws and Institutions.

This being the case, being a consequence of INVIOLABLE LAW, it explains the reason why the Human Race must undergo the privations and sufferings to which it is now subjected, and furnishes us with a simple, natural solution of the CAUSE OF EVIL on Earth.

If God would abolish Evil, he would have to resort to one of the three following alternatives ; he would have :—

1. To create the Race with the capacity and power necessary to discover and perfect, *at once,* Machinery, the processes of Industry, the Arts and Sciences, and to establish at the very outset of its Career, a true Social Order on Earth ;

2. To do all this for Man — furnish him with dwellings, clothing, implements, and machinery, communicate to him by instinct or revelation a knowledge of the Arts and Sciences, and place him in a State of Society every way prepared for his reception, and thus leave him nothing to do;

3. Or to Create Man a *simple* being, without complex wants, without independent, self-determining, intelligent action, without free-will, and without being subject to the necessity of progressive development — which would be equivalent to the suppression of the creation of intelligent beings.

Neither of these alternatives is admissible. Supreme Wisdom, as is evident by the fact, has deemed it best that the Race should pass through a transitional phase of Social Infancy, and endure the sufferings consequent thereupon, as the Individual must endure the sufferings, for example, of teething and other physical derangements during the infantile period of his career. The temporary suffering attendant upon the imperfect development of the transitional phase of Infancy, is compensated for a thousand-fold by the long period of Happiness which follows. Besides, if man had not himself to execute the great works we have pointed out, if he were not to be the author of his own Destiny, he would possess no independent action, no individuality, no merit, no dignity, no grandeur, in a word no attributes of an intelligent being.

Let us now point out some of the principal evils which exist in Society, and indicate the special reason of each, so that the reader may trace the connection between the Cause and the Effect; we speak of collective or generic evils which extend to the whole Race.

I. POVERTY — caused by the imperfect development of Industry and its processes, and the false Economical laws that regulate the distribution of its products.

II. IGNORANCE — caused by the imperfect development of the Sciences which are collective Reason of the Race.

III. EXCESSIVE AND BRUTALIZING TOIL — caused by the non-organization of Industry, and the want of labor-saving machinery.

IV. WAR AND SOCIAL DISCORD — caused by false political and social institutions and the perversion of the human Passions through their influence.

V. GENERAL CONFLICT OF INTERESTS, with the reign of fraud, falsehood, deception, and universal duplicity of action—caused by the false system of Industrial and Commercial Relations.

VI. SLAVERY AND SERVITUDE—caused by a repulsive System of Industry, which impels man to avoid productive labor.

VII. DISEASE—caused by privation, ignorance, over-work, false habits and customs, etc., and by the imperfect state of the climate and atmosphere of the Globe, which is a result of the incoherent and fragmentary cultivation of its surface.

VIII. PASSIONAL SUBVERSION in the four modes described in the Treatise—caused by the above false conditions combined, and leading to the reign of Social Discord and Incoherence on Earth.

All these EVILS will disappear in a true Order of society and give place to their opposite GOODS; in the future ages of Social Harmony we shall see the reign of:—

1. Universal Wealth and Prosperity.
2. Universal Knowledge and Intelligence.
3. Attractive Industry.
4. Permanent Peace and Social Concord.
5. Unity of all Interests and Universal Coöperation and Association.
6. Practical Liberty in all relations, and Social Equality of the Race.
7. Universal Health and Vigor.
8. Passional Harmony and Social Unity.

After the preceding explanations, we may lay down the following Law which will now be understood:—

That there is *Duality in the Social Movement;* that two great Orders of Society must exist in turn on the Globe, the one Discordant and Incoherent, the other Harmonious and Unitary; the first exists at the commencement and close of the Career of the Race, the second during the long intermediate or central portion. The former we may term technically the Subversive Order, as in it there is a subversion or inversion of the principles of Order and Harmony; the latter, the Harmonic Order, in which these principles receive their natural or legitimate development: the Subversive Order gives rise to the reign of EVIL, the Harmonic to the reign of GOOD.

This dual development—Subversive and Harmonic—in the movement of Society is analogous to the dual action or development of the Passions, which we have explained; Social Subversion and Passional Subversion accompany each other and act and react upon each other, though the former is primary and determines to a great extent the latter.

FOURIER, in his *Theory of Universal Unity*, admirably sums up and contrasts in two Tables the permanent EVILS which characterize the course of the Subversive Societies, and the opposite GOODS which accompany the Harmonic Societies ; we give these two tables :—

TABLE OF THE SEVEN PERMANENT EVILS OF THE SUBVERSIVE SOCIETIES.	TABLE OF THE SEVEN PERMANENT GOODS OF THE HARMONIC SOCIETIES.
1. Poverty.	1. General and graduated Wealth.
2. Fraud.	2. Practical Truth in all relations.
3. Oppression.	3. Reign of Justice, and real Liberty.
4. Carnage.	4. Permanent Peace.
5. Climatic and atmospheric derangement.	5. Equilibrium of climate and purity of atmosphere.
6. Epidemic and factitious diseases.	6. Reign of Universal Health and Vigor.
7. Circle of Error, with the reign of Prejudice and Intolerance.	7. Opening for all Improvements, with the reign of Universal Tolerance.
PIVOTAL EVILS. { *Collective and Individual Selfishness.* *Conflict of the Individual with the Collective Interest.*	PIVOTAL GOODS. { *Collective and Individual Philanthropy.* *Unity of the Individual with the Collective Interest.*

In a later work, FOURIER gives the following more complete Table of the Evils of the Subversive Societies :—

CONFLICT OF MAN WITH NATURE, WITH GOD, AND WITH HIMSELF, DURING THE REIGN OF SOCIAL SUBVERSION.

Combat of Reason with the Passions.
War of Violence, Murder, and Pillage.
War of Craft and Cunning — one half of the world cheating the other.
War of the Poor against the Rich.
War of Commerce against Productive Industry.
Schism with God by doubt of the Universality of his Providence.

Compulsory exposure to unhealthy labors.
Population exceeding the product.
Anarchical and fraudulent Competition.
Circle of Error in theory and practice.
Compound misfortune for the multitude
Strife of Instinct against Industry.
Immense majority of Poor and Non-producers.

Political Partisans and Non-producers contending for the spoils of Industry.
A minority of armed Slaves repressing the majority of unarmed Slaves.

Incompatibility between the four Subversive Societies.
Heterogeneous and incongruous, languages, customs, and religions.
Incompatible castes, classes, and morals.
Unjust and antagonist relations between Labor and Capital.
Contradictory Laws and Conflicting Administrative Powers.

Progress of Contagious diseases — cholera, yellow-fever, etc.
Derangement of the Climate by fragmentary cultivation.
Inverse distribution of Health and Vigor.
Fragmentary, partial, and illusive Reforms.
Repressive Laws and imaginary remedies, aggravating Social disorders.
Indirect Slavery from the want of fortune.
Slavery spreading by the slave-trade and its increase on the new continents.

It follows from the arguments which we have presented in the course of this Article, that the reign of Evil in the existence of all created things, is confined to the two extremes — that is, to the ascending and descending transitional phases — of the Career; this Law applies to great Collective Beings like the Human Race as well as to Individual Beings.

As Evil in all the various forms above described now reigns on earth, it follows, according to the Law of Transitions, that the Human Race must be either in its Social Childhood, in the ascending transitional Phase of its Social Career, or in its Old Age, the descending transitional Phase; and as we have no historical records, no knowledge of a long period of Harmony, of Happiness, through which the Race has passed, it follows that it must be in the first Transitional Phase, or the Infantile Period of its social existence on the Planet.

The reign of Evil on Earth is the third demonstration, then, of the Social Childhood of the Race.

If we go back of the explanation of the Cause of Evil which we have given in the preceding pages, and seek for a more radical solution, we may state, generally :—

I. That Matter being FINITE, it exists in TIME and SPACE; all material Creations must, as a consequence, take place in Time and Space, which renders the creative process, that is, the process of formation and development, and the phenomena attendant upon it, perceptible and measurable. Among these phenomena are imperfection, incompleteness, incoherence, disorder, etc., which must exist *for a Time,* and this Time constitutes the period of the reign of Evil.

II. That Matter being PASSIVE, and offering the resistance of inertia to the Forces which operate upon it, these Forces, or the Active Principle which moulds, forms, and fashions Matter, can not perfect and develop *instantaneously* the organizations it creates out of it; a transitional process of formation and development is therefore necessary — is inherent in and determined by the passive, inert nature of Matter.

The Active Principle is the source of all Order and Harmony in the Universe; it can not, however, when connected with Matter, produce this Order and Harmony until it has perfected the material Organism through which it is to act and operate. The period during which it is forming a material Organism or Instrument for its manifestation and action, is one during which its natural or harmonic action is thwarted; this period is consequently to a greater or less extent a period of incoherent and discordant action — a period of Evil. Let us illustrate this principle by an example.

The Sense of Hearing is the Source of Harmony in the sphere of Sound; it is the Active Principle in this Sphere, but it can not produce Sonorous or Musical Harmony until it has : —

1. A Physical Organism, a Body, sufficiently developed to serve as the instrument or medium of its action.

2. A drilled, disciplined, and educated voice or hand, which are its immediate instruments in producing Harmony, and which must be accustomed to obey the most delicate promptings of its will.

3. Instruments properly constructed and adapted to the requirements of the Musical Art.

Until these conditions are fulfilled, the Musical Sense produces discords or at least very imperfect music; the Active Principle can not control and bring into unity with itself the material elements on which it operates. The same is true of all the other Forces in the Soul, and of the Active Principle in the Universe generally.

To sum up : When Matter — the Inert, Passive Principle — is not under the control and regulation of the Active, Creative Principle and the Laws of Order and Harmony inherent in it, it is in an incoherent, discordant, and chaotic state. When in this state, it is in antagonism to the Active Principle, which tends naturally, spontaneously to Order and Harmony—that is to say, it is in a state of EVIL.

Evil, then, is the negation of Order and Harmony; it exists during the period of the formation and early development of material Creations or Organisms, and during their period of decay and dissolution. In these two periods, the Material Principle is not under the control and regulation of the Active Principle and its Laws; in the one case, it is not yet brought under its control and fully organized and disciplined by it, and in the other, it is escaping from its control and falling into disorder, incoherence, and chaos.

GOOD is an attendant upon, is a consequence of mature Organization, of the reign of Law, of the subjection of the Passive to the Active Principle.

EVIL is an attendant upon, is a consequence of Non-organization and Dissolution, of the violation of Law, of the non-subjection of the Passive to the Active Principle.

In closing, let us lay down a principle which will furnish a standard by which to judge the degree of Harmony, of GOOD, possible in any department, sphere, or system, by studying *inversely* the Discord or EVIL we find existing in it: this principle may be called the *Law of Inversion.* It demonstrates that Good and Evil are not two essentially distinct things—that the latter is the inversion of the former, and is an effect attendant upon the play and action of elements in a false or inverted state of development, as Good is an effect of the same elements in their true and harmonic state of development.

The greater the number and variety of elements which enter into any organism, department, or sphere, the greater the Disorder and Discord which may be produced in it on the one hand, and the greater the Order and Harmony on the other. A hundred instruments produce more discord when unskilfully played upon than a single instrument; on the other hand if skilfully played upon, they produce a much higher degree of harmony.

A highly organized body like that of a man or an animal, gives rise in a state of decay to a much fouler degree of corruption than a simply organized body, like a tree or a plant.

Hence we may say that the Discord and Disorder possible in

any department or sphere—in the Passions, in Society, in Organized Bodies—are in ratio to the Order and Harmony of which the same sphere or department is capable. We do not say in exact or direct ratio, for the degree of Harmony is always greater than the degree of Discord; in Music for example the Accords exceed in number the Discords, and a fine musical composition has more elements of beauty, variety, and harmony than a charivari or clatter of sounds has of discord, disorder, and confusion. With a knowledge of this Law—that Discord is an Inversion of Harmony, and that there is a certain relative proportion between the two—we can by studying the Discords of any sphere in a state of disorder, determine proximately the Harmonies of which it is susceptible in a state of order.

Applying this Law to the study of Society and its phenomena, we arrive at the conclusion, that the Discords and Evils which reign in the four Subversive Societies—such as poverty, ignorance, oppression, injustice, duplicity of action, conflict of interests, passional perversion and discord, vice and crime—offer an inverted image of the Harmony, the Good, which is to reign in the long Organic or Harmonic Period that is to follow—that is to say, the wealth, intelligence, justice, liberty, unity of action and interests, the passional concord, the social virtues, and the philanthropy which will exist in the true Social Order of the Future.

The Law of Inversion is then an invaluable aid and guide to the Human Mind in studying Harmony through Discord; it teaches how, by inverting the EVILS which we find in any sphere or organism in a subversive state, and replacing them by the opposite GOODS, to understand the true nature of the same sphere or organism in its harmonic state.

Let us now pass to the fourth proof of the Social Childhood of the Race.

IV. DEVELOPMENT OF THE PASSIONS IN THEIR LOWER DEGREES, and the preponderance of the Sensuous Passions.—It is a characteristic, a law of Childhood, applicable to the Race as to the Individual, that the Passions in this phase are undeveloped, or developed in their lower degrees, and that the Senses alone are really active; in the Individual, the material appetites are, as we know, predominant, while the social Affections, particularly those of a more universal character like Benevolence and Philanthropy, are dormant, and the intellectual Faculties slumber or are occupied merely with trifles. We will remark in this connection that the life of the Race being more complex than that of the Individual, a much more complicated degree of disorder exists in the childhood of the former than in that of the latter.

The low or undeveloped state of the Passions and the preponderance of the Senses, explain why we find so much materialism and selfishness in the Social World, even among the Rich who are exempt from poverty, its privations, and its perverting influences; explain why the aims, the pursuits of men are of a low or purely individual nature, their pleasures as a general rule material and sensual, their friendships exclusive, rarely rising to the higher degrees of Philanthropy and collective Sympathy, their ambitions personal and restricted to self-aggrandizement, their family-sentiment limited to the child or two of their own, with no collective interest in childhood, their loves undeveloped or developed only in the sensuous degrees, and their intellectual faculties occupied with schemes and plans, combinations and manœuvres of a narrow and trifling character.

This is at present the prevailing passional state of Mankind, and it demonstrates that the Race is in the early stage of passional development—in the Phase of Childhood. In the Future, when the Race shall have entered upon the Harmonic Phases of its Social Career, and the Passions shall be developed in their higher degrees and properly cultivated, disciplined and refined, we shall see them producing the magnificent results which we have described briefly in the Treatise upon the Functions of the Passions.

V. ABSENCE OF AUTHENTIC HISTORICAL RECORDS, OF MONUMENTS AND OF INDUSTRIAL WORKS, dating back to any very great antiquity, that is, to a period of more than four or five thousand years.—If we study the progress of nations, their advance toward Art, Science, and Industry, we find that the intelligent races arrive in the course of twenty or thirty centuries at some degree of intellectual development, that they discover the art of Writing so that they can record their History, and that

S

they develop Industry sufficiently to be able to erect some permanent monuments. This appears to have been the case with the ancient Hindoos, the Egyptians, and the races inhabiting Asia Minor, Greece, and Italy. Now if the Human Race had existed on the Earth for a long Period, say thirty or forty thousand years, we should have positive historical records extending back at least twenty or thirty thousand years, and monuments of this antiquity would now be seen on the Earth ; but such is not the case ; the oldest temples of India and the pyramids of Egypt do not date back more than four or five thousand years.

If the Human Race were in its Manhood, if it had passed some thousands of years in the Organic or Harmonic Phases of its Career, we should see magnificent monuments existing everywhere upon the earth, and stupendous industrial works covering its surface, whereas in fact we find but very few, and those of a comparatively recent date, which are the initial experiments of an Infant Humanity in the first or transitional Phase of its social existence.

We here close our proofs of the Social Childhood of the Race ; we could adduce others, and some of a detailed character, if we were to enter into a minute analysis of the development of Industry, the Arts and Sciences, Laws and Institutions, that is, of the creation and formation of the elements which constitute the Social Organism ; but this would only tire the reader by a multiplicity of minute analyses.

IV.

THE NATURAL ORDER OF SOCIETY—THE DIVINE SOCIAL CODE.

WE have shown in the preceding article, that the Human Race is in the period of Social Infancy and Childhood, or the Ascending Transition of its Social Career on Earth ; that this Phase is one of invention, discovery, experiment, and initiation ; that it is, so to say, the SOCIAL APPRENTICESHIP of the Race. During this period, it establishes successively different systems of Society, all of which are necessarily imperfect for the reason that the elements which go to form a true Social Organization — Industry, the Arts and Sciences, Laws and Institutions — are undeveloped or developed only in their elementary degrees. These preliminary and temporary Societies dissolve and disappear when they have fulfilled their mission, when they have evolved some principle or element necessary to the Social Organism which is finally to be established on the Earth.

The special mission of the Barbaric Society, for example, has been to initiate the Masses, who, in the Savage and Patriarchal States, are given to a life of idleness and inertia, into habits of Labor, and thus to develop or create Industry ; this it effects through Slavery, but Slavery being a false institution, the Social System based upon it languishes after a time and goes to decay.

The chief mission of Civilized Society is to create and perfect the Arts and Sciences ; when it has accomplished this work, it possesses the means of passing to a higher social state, which it must do or fall into decline, as was the case with Greek and Roman Civilization, and as will be the case with Modern Civilization, unless it organizes a superior Social Order.

Each of these preliminary Societies agglomerates, combines, and unites in a body politic a certain mass of population, and founds what are called Nations. The nations thus founded rise and fall with the rise and fall, the development and decay of the Systems of Society upon which they are based.

The Human Race is now passing through these preliminary, infantine Societies, and is advancing toward the true, natural, and permanent Social Order which it is destined to realize on Earth when it shall have evolved and perfected all the elements necessary to it, and discovered the Science of their organization.

That there is such a Social Order, that there is a true, natural, and harmonious system of Society in reserve for the Human Race, can no more be doubted by the mind which understands the laws of Nature and of Universal Movement, than that the child after passing through the phases of physical growth and incipient mental development, is destined to arrive at the state of permanent vigor and intelligence which characterize manhood.

FOURIER in his works demonstrates that such a Social Order as we have described, is destined, is in reserve for the Human Race on this Planet ; he shows that the elements for organizing it are prepared, that the world is ready for the commencement of the great work of Social transformation, and he calls the attention of minds capable of great and comprehensive ideas to the importance and grandeur, the necessity and philanthropy of the work, and explains the means for its realization.

This natural and harmonious system of Society, FOURIER terms the Divine Social Order, as he affirms and proves by analogical reasoning that God before creating Man and placing him on this Earth, must have precalculated and planned a Social Mechanism adapted to his nature — a Mechanism that would employ usefully and regulate harmoniously all the Passions he has implanted in the Human Soul. The existence of a NATURAL or DIVINE ORDER OF SOCIETY is one of the fundamental conceptions of his Theory ; it is the general basis of his idea of a Social Reform.

We will make a quotation or two from the *Theory of Universal Unity* in which FOURIER himself explains this sublime conception of a Social Order preëxisting in the Divine Mind before the Creation of Man.

" The idea of a preëstablished Destiny for Man, existing in the
" Divine Mind before his creation, of a pre-determined mathemat-
" ical theory of Social Organization adapted to the play and ac-
" tion of the Passions, will be ridiculed by the world as visionary
" and absurd. Nevertheless, how can we conceive that a Being
" infinitely wise could have created the Passions without first
" having determined upon a plan for their employment ?

" How could GOD, with the experience of an eternity in crea-
" ting and organizing worlds, have been ignorant that the first
" Collective Want of their inhabitants is that of a Code for the
" regulation of their Passions and their Social Relations ?

" Left to the direction of our pretended Sages, the Passions
" engender Scourges which might well lead us to doubt whether
" they are the work of an Evil Spirit or of Divinity. If we ex-
" amine successively the laws of Legislators the most revered —
" of Solon and of Draco, of Lycurgus and of Minos — we shall
" find that they reproduce constantly the nine Permanent Scourges
" which result from the subversive action of the Passions. Must
" not God have foreseen this shameful result of Human Legisla-
" tion ? He must have observed its effects in the myriads of
" Globes created anterior to our own ; he must have known, be-
" fore creating Man and giving him Passions, that his Reason

" would be incapable of harmonizing them, and that Humanity
" would require a Legislator more enlightened than itself.

" As a consequence, God, unless we suppose that his Provi-
" dence is insufficient and limited, and that he is indifferent to
" our happiness, must have composed for us a Passional Code, or
" system of Domestic and Social Organization applicable to the
" whole Human Race, which has everywhere the same Passions;
" and he must have interpreted this Code to us in a way which
" would leave no doubt as to its excellence and its origin.

" There exists, then, for Man a Unitary Destiny or Divine So-
" cial Order to be established on the Earth for the regulation
" of the Social and Domestic Relations of the Human Race. The
" task of Genius was to discover it, and, preliminarily, to de-
" termine upon the method by which the investigation should
" be pursued: this method can be no other than the *Analytic*
" *and Synthetic calculation of Passional Attraction*, since Attrac-
" tion is the only known interpreter between God and the Uni-
" verse.

" Again: how can we suppose God more inconsiderate than the
" merest novice among men? When a man collects together ma-
" terials for building, does he neglect to prepare or to have pre-
" pared a plan for their employment? What should we think of a
" person who, having purchased the stone, brick, framework, etc.
" for the construction of a vast edifice, had no idea what kind of
" a structure he would erect, and confessed that he had collected
" his materials without having decided how to employ them?
" Such a man would be considered insane.

" Such, nevertheless, is the degree of folly which our Sophists
" attribute to God in supposing that he could have created the
" Passions, Attractions, Characters, Instincts, and other mate-
" rials for the Social Edifice, without having determined upon
" any plan for their employment.

" GOD, then, according to the sophists, did not know how to
" frame for Man a Social Code—must have been obliged to
" leave to the wisdom of the Solons and Dracos the work of de-
" termining the Domestic and Industrial Mechanism of Society.
" Common Sense revolts at the idea of suspecting Divinity of this
" excess of incapacity. We must believe, then, despite the So-
" phists, that there exists for our Social Relations a preëstab-

" lished Destiny—a Destiny regulated by Divine Law anterior to
" the creation of our Globe, a Mechanism of Social and Indus-
" trial Unity, the plan of which human Reason should have en-
" deavored to discover, instead of playing the part of a Titan and
" wresting from God his highest function, which is the direction
" of the Social or Passional Movement.

" Of all impieties the worst is the impertinent prejudice
" which suspects God of having created Man, created the Pas-
" sions and the elements of Society, without having determined
" upon any plan for their organization. To believe this is to at-
" tribute to the Creator a want of reason at which even man
" would blush ; it is to fall into an irreligion worse than atheism ;
" for the atheist, though he denies God, does not dishonor him ;
" he dishonors himself alone by an opinion bordering on mad-
" ness. But our legislators despoil the Supreme Being of his
" noblest prerogative ; they pretend, by implication, that God is
" incompetent in legislation. And so he would be if, after the
" experience acquired during a past eternity in the material and
" passional distribution of worlds, he had neglected to provide
" for the most urgent of their collective wants—that of a Uni-
" tary Passional Code, and of a permanent revelation of that
" Code.

" So long as we have not discovered the Divine Code, we do
" not know Man, since we are ignorant of the uses and end as-
" signed by God to the Motor-forces of the Soul—to its Pas-
" sions, Attractions, etc.—and to human Societies directed by
" these Forces.

" Now since God must have composed a Social Code for the
" regulation of our Passions and of our Domestic, Industrial,
" and Social Relations, how can we presume that he would wish
" to conceal it from us to whom the knowledge of it is of abso-
" lute necessity ? He has not concealed a branch of the Laws
" of Movement much less important to us—that of Material
" Gravitation or Sidereal Harmony ; he has initiated us, since
" NEWTON, into these mysteries of the equilibrium of the Uni-
" verse, held in previous ages to be impenetrable. Why pre-
" sume, then, that he would refuse to us an initiation into the sys-
" tem he must have composed for the Mechanism of the Passions
" and of Human Societies—refuse to us the Science most impor-

" tant for us to know, most essential to our Industrial Relations?

* * * * *

" Whenever a branch of study is neglected by the Exact Sci-
" ences, we see rise in its place some scientific charlatanry. Be-
" fore Experimental Chemistry, we had the reign of the Alche-
" mists ; before Natural Philosophy, we saw the reign of the
" Magicians ; before Mathematical Astronomy, that of the As-
" trologists, who are still believed in by the common people ; be-
" fore the discovery of quinine, we had Sorcerers, who pretended
" to conjure away a fever. Thus the human mind, whenever it
" departs from the Exact Sciences, is doomed to fall under the
" yoke of quacks and impostors ; it is for this reason that Civili-
" zation has from the beginning been misled by several classes
" of Sophists who would persuade us that there is no such thing
" as a Social Destiny for Man because they have never thought
" of studying its theory in the calculation of Passional Attrac-
" tion, and because they find it easier to fabricate systems than
" to trouble themselves with the thorny problem of Social Har-
" mony. If an error may last three years with an individual,
" thirty years with a family, three hundred years with a corpo-
" ration, following the same proportion, it may last three thou-
" sand years with the Human Race, especially when the error is
" propagated by the learned bodies, all of which agree in uphold-
" ing the prejudice that God has created the Passions without
" first composing a Code for their regulation.

" I have already observed that in committing such a blunder,
" God would have shown himself less wise than the least of mor-
" tals ; do I claim too much for Divine wisdom when I suppose
" it equal to the wisdom of Man ? Our Sophists will reply that
" Divine wisdom is a million times superior, but to confound
" them we only ask that they accord to God as much reason as
" is found among men—as much judgment in the Material and
" Passional Distribution of Worlds, and especially in that of this
" world, so justly criticised by King Alphonso of Castile who
" said :—' If God had consulted me as to the creation of the
" world, I would have given him some good advice.' Doubtless
" Alphonso would have recommended the exact opposite of the
" nine scourges which we see reigning up to the present time in
" the Social World ; but are these nine scourges accidental

" vices, or essential and irremediable ?   Ought we not to pre-
" sume that a wise Providence has reserved for us a Social Des-
" tiny diametrically opposite to the present—a Destiny, the theory
" of which should be sought in a systematic study of Attraction,
" the sole interpreter between God and Man ?

    *   *   *   *   *

   " If we were making our first Social Experiment, were in
" the first ages of Civilization, we should perhaps be excusable
" for founding some hope of Social Happiness on our own intel-
" ligence, on the legislation of Man, without the intervention of a
" Divine Code ; but we have been fully undeceived by a long ex-
" perience ; we have evidently nothing to hope from Human
" Laws.   Twenty-five centuries' trial of them has proved that so
" far from fulfilling any of their promises, they increase and ag-
" gravate all the social scourges they would remedy.

   " What is the result, for example, of the most vaunted of po-
" litical Constitutions—that of England ?   Its great capital con-
" tains over a hundred thousand thieves, beggars, and vagabonds;
" while an annual poor-tax of over thirty millions does not pre-
" vent the country from swarming with destitute laborers without
" bread, without work, emigrating to other lands by the thousand.
" How the spectacle of these results should inspire us with dis-
" trust of the theories and constitutions of legislators and con-
" querors, and stimulate us to make researches for the Divine
" Social Code, and for an issue from our disastrous Civiliza-
" tion !"

   The question may now be asked : If there is a natural Order
of Society, predestined for Man by Supreme Wisdom, why was
it not established from the beginning—why is it not now in existence on the Earth ?

   We have answered this question in a previous Article in treating of the Social Childhood of the Race, but as it presents a difficulty which may perplex some minds, we will answer it again
very briefly.

   1. Man must himself discover the plan or Mechanism of the
Natural or Divine Order of Society ; Supreme Wisdom in endowing him with REASON has left to him this task as it has left to
him, for example, the task of discovering the Sciences, inventing
machinery, etc.   As God creates no useless agents, he would not

have endowed Man with Reason, had he judged it proper to reveal to him at once or to communicate to him by instinct the Social Order predestined for him. In suppressing Reason in Man, he would have reduced him to the condition of a creature of instinct — to a level with the beaver, the bee, and the ant, which organize by instinct their simple communities. The same principle applies to the discovery of the Divine Code or the Science of Society that applies, as we have said, to the discovery of the other Sciences, of the Arts, of the processes of Industry, etc. Man was destined, as is evident, to possess a knowledge of the Sciences, but Supreme Wisdom has not revealed them to him, nor communicated them by instinct; it has left him to discover them himself and meanwhile he must suffer all the evils attendant upon an ignorance of them. Man was destined in like manner, to possess the railroad, and the steamboat, those immense facilities for locomotion, but railroads and steamboats were not established for him by Nature; he had to invent and construct them himself; Nature furnishes him with all the necessary resources and materials, but her action stops there.

Take another illustration; there exists in Nature a system of Music, all the elements of which are provided and prepared for Man. The atmosphere or sonorous medium in Nature produces in its vibratory action twelve radical sounds which form the complete musical scale or gamut. The human ear is so constructed as to hear and distinguish these twelve sounds and all the combinations and effects of which they are susceptible. The human hand is so constructed as to produce these sounds on musical instruments; the fingers, for example, are divided by twelve joints into twelve divisions, corresponding to the twelve notes in the musical gamut, while the thumb, in like manner, corresponds to the thirteenth note which sounded with the Tonic forms the Pivotal Accord, or Accord of the octave. One joint less in the fingers would have destroyed the capacity of the hand to produce perfect music, as one note less in the gamut would derange the whole system of musical harmony. There is thus unity running through the physical organization of the hand, of the ear, and the sonorous qualities of the atmosphere, showing that the conditions necessary to the Musical Art have been prepared by and exist in Nature. She has not, however, established the Art; she did not teach it to Man by instinct or any other means, but left him to discover it himself. Had some bold Genius, before the discovery of the Musical Art, conceived and proclaimed the idea of its existence in its integrality, as FOURIER conceived and proclaimed the existence of a Natural Order of Society, his less-gifted cotemporaries would probably have said to him, "If such an Art has been predestined for Man, why is it that it does not exist, why is man deprived of it, why did not Nature adopt means to communicate it to him at once." The reply would have been the same as that which we make to the inquiry, why the Divine Social Code was not established at once.

2. The Human Race must create the elements that enter into the Social Organization before it can establish a true and complete Order of Society on the Earth. It would be impossible, it is evident, to establish anything like a complete or perfect Order of Society in the Nomadic or Savage State, in which there is no knowledge of agriculture, manufactures, of the use of metals and machinery, of the arts and sciences, of Human Nature and Human Destiny, or of the laws which govern the Universe. The Race must first discover or create these elements; this is an indispensable preliminary—a work which can be accomplished only by a long period of observation, study, and experiment. It can not as a consequence establish the Natural or Divine Order of Society reserved for it, until it has accomplished this preparatory work—a work which requires, as we have explained, a few thousand years of labor and experience on each Planet; this period is that of the Social Infancy and Childhood of Races, and is accompanied by the reign of Social Incoherence and Evil.

We could adduce other reasons why the Divine Order of Society could not have been established at once on the Earth, but those which we have presented are sufficient.

In conclusion, we would ask whether it is not probable that Nature which has adapted our lungs to the air we are to breathe, our stomachs to the edible products upon which we are to live, our whole physical organization to the external world that surrounds us, has adapted the passions, characters, tastes, and inclinations of the Soul to some Social Mechanism in which they will be usefully employed, and in which they will act naturally and freely, and produce Order, Unity, and Harmony? The common sense

of Humanity will answer that Nature could not have done otherwise, and a scientific investigation of the subject demonstrates the
truth of this intuitive conviction.

From what precedes, then, we may affirm that there must exist a Natural or Divine Order of Society, precalculated and predestined for Man by Divine Wisdom, and that the function of
Human Reason is to discover and establish it.

Let us now proceed to inquire what is the basis of the Natural
or Divine Order of Society, and what are its essential conditions.

The basis, as we have explained, is the LAW OF THE SERIES,
which is the Law of all Organization and Harmony in Creation.
Let this law be discovered, let a Social Order be organized in
conformity with it, and we shall see on earth the reign of Social
Harmony—the reign of what is called, in the language of Religion, the Kingdom of God.*

The essential conditions which a true Social Order must fulfil,
may be summed up under two general heads.

1. It must be adapted to the nature of Man—that is, to the
demands and requirements of the twelve Radical Passions.

2. It must conform to the primary attributes of God, or the
principles of Order and Unity in the Universe.

I. The Passions—the impelling, directing Forces in Man—
are the work of God; like all Forces, they must express the
will of their Author; they may do this *directly* or *inversely*, according as they are truly or falsely developed. They point to
the ends to which the Creator would direct us; they impel us to
fulfil the Functions or Destiny he has assigned to us; they are
his Voice speaking through us, his Will acting in us.

* In like manner, the harmonious play and action of the twelve Radical Passions
in the Divine Social Order, will be the fulfilment of what is termed the WILL OF
GOD. The advent of a future state of Harmony on Earth has been intuitively felt
by many great minds, particularly by the Prophets, in whom UNITYISM or the Religious Sentiment was predominant, and above all by ISAIAH, who proclaimed in the
fervor of his enthusiasm, that the time would come — "when the wilderness and the
"solitary place should be made glad, and the desert should rejoice and blossom as the
"rose," when men should "beat their swords into ploughshares and their spears into
"pruning-hooks, and nation should not lift up sword against nation, neither learn
"war any more."

This advent of a future Social Harmony on Earth is the MILLENNIUM which has
been prophesied in all ages, and is the realization of the great prayer of Christianity:
"Thy Kingdom come, thy will be done on Earth as it is in Heaven."

The Passions, we assert—and the whole scheme of Social Harmony and Human Destiny rests on this basis—are a manifestation of the Divine Will that called them into existence, and are an infallible Revelation and Interpretation of that Will to Man. Being the agents of Supreme Wisdom, the Forces that impel Man to fulfil his Destiny, the Social Mechanism must be adapted to them; they are the standard, the Model according to which all its laws and institutions should be formed, and it is only by the study of their nature and tendencies, that we can arrive at a knowledge of the form of Society which should be established on earth; they are our only guide in the intricate work of Social Organization.

We will now point out briefly the tendencies and requirements of the Passions, which, as we have explained, are divided into three classes—namely, five Sensuous, four Social, and three Serial, constituting the scale or gamut of the twelve Radical Passions.

The first Class, the Material Passions, tend to beauty, elegance, and refinement in all material arrangements—in architecture, scenery, dress, food, etc.—to splendor and luxury, and to the five branches of material Art and Harmony. A true Social Order must meet and satisfy these demands and attractions of the Material or Sensuous Passions; all ascetic notions of denying and mortifying them, all theories in favor of mediocrity, of poverty, of abstemiousness, self-denial, etc., however well adapted to a poor and necessitous Social Order like the present, are false in principle and in conflict with the nature and Destiny of Man.

The second Class, the Social Passions, tend to the formation of social ties and relations of all kinds, to sympathetic unions, to association in all degrees, and to universal politeness, urbanity, and philanthropy. A true Order of Society must conform to these requirements of the Social Affections, and secure to them full development and satisfaction.

The third Class, the Serial Passions, tend to individuality, rivalry, alternation, variety, enthusiasm, ideality, and to general Unity and Order; a true Social Mechanism must satisfy these requirements of the Soul; its organization in all departments must be in Series, corresponding to the natural action of the three Serial Faculties.

Let us explain more in detail the necessity of adapting the Social Mechanism to Human Nature, by two illustrations drawn from GOVERNMENT and MARRIAGE.

The Hierarchical element in Government must be adapted to the Passion of Ambition and regulated in conformity with its nature and requirements. By the Hierarchical element, we mean the system of ranks, grades, promotions, honorary distinctions, rewards, etc., and the laws by which they are regulated.

The Passion of Ambition, when fully developed, and balanced in its action by the influence of the other Passions, tends to a natural and just system of Hierarchical Organization, upon which all true Government must be based. In establishing Order and Hierarchy in Society, we must take this Passion as our Guide, consult it as our Oracle, follow its indications and model on it the Hierarchical organization of Industry, Government and all other departments in which the labors of men, acting together as Coöperators, require to be systematized and regulated.

The Passion of Love is, in like manner, the guide we are to take in the discovery and establishment of a true system for the regulation of the relations of the sexes. The System must be adapted to the Passion and not the Passion to the System. LOVE, a creation of Divine Wisdom, interprets to Man the intentions of its author; in studying its wants and requirements, we have a divine and absolutely certain revelation of the nature of the Institution and the laws which should govern it. This, we admit, is in direct opposition to the old moral theories, but we assert nevertheless that Love, like the other Passions of the Soul, being the work of God, he must have calculated with mathematical precision its action and uses, its functions and effects, and, as a consequence, an external Mechanism suited to it; this external Mechanism, whatever it may be, is the true or natural system of Marriage.

As a wise physiologist, in devising a true or natural system of food, would take the Sense of Taste and the requirements of the stomach for his guide, so a wise legislator, in devising social Institutions should be guided by the corresponding Passions and their requirements. But human legislators act on an entirely different principle; they set up arbitrary laws and institutions, and then seek to compel the Passions to conform to them. This is especially true with the Passion of LOVE, which with the Passion of Ambition, has given the most trouble to legislators.

In respect to Love, what a mass of arbitrary and conflicting systems have existed and still exist for the regulation of the relations to which it gives rise! Among Barbaric and Patriarchal nations (composing more than half of the Human Race) Polygamy, or plurality of wives, is the law; in Civilized nations, Monogamy, or the union of a single couple for life. In China, a man of wealth must have several wives and a separate establishment for each, otherwise he passes for a mean and parsimonious spirit, and loses caste; while in Civilized countries, he is condemned as a criminal and held up to scorn as an immoral and licentious character, if he takes more than one wife. The Catholic church does not permit divorce on any ground, while the Protestant church allows it on various grounds, and sanctions many marriages which the former condemns as immoral. These few examples will suffice to show the absence of a standard which commands universal acquiescence.

Now, if a truly impartial observer, setting aside the influence of all preconceived ideas and prevailing opinions, wished to discover the true or natural law for the regulation of the sexual relation, what course should he pursue? We answer that he should study the nature and requirements of the Passion of LOVE; that he should take it as the standard of truth, the criterion of certainty in his investigations; that he should analyse carefully its wants, its revelations, and the conditions of its natural and harmonious development; it is only by a scientific analysis of the Passion itself that the true Institution corresponding to it, can be determined with that certainty which the positive mind requires.

The Institution, whatever its form may be, is the external mechanism in which the Passion is to act, and must be adapted to it as the musical instrument, for example, is adapted to the ear. As Reason has discovered and perfected musical instruments by a careful study of the indications and requirements of the Sense of Hearing, so it must discover and perfect a true system of Marriage by a careful study of the indications and requirements of the Passion of Love.

There exists a system of Laws for the regulation of the action and development of each Passion of the Soul. These laws constitute what we will call the Science of the Passion, its external Form or Body; they correspond to and express the mode of its activity. The Sense of Hearing is the only Passion the Science of which has been discovered. The laws of Musical Harmony constitute this Science; they are the expression of the natural and harmonious mode of action of the Sense, the regulative principle of its development; they furnish the standard to which it should be raised in each individual, and the means by which it should be brought up to and maintained on a level with its highest capacity of harmony. The great musical Composers discover and perfect the Art and Science of Music and the means of imparting it to others; in so doing, they create and furnish the means of developing, educating, and perfecting the Musical Sense in the masses of mankind, and thus of elevating them in this respect to their own standard.

Let us remark that in present Society, the means do not exist for educating, disciplining, and harmoniously developing any other Passion in the Soul. There exists, however, for every Passion, as for the Sense of Hearing, a system of Laws for the regulation of its action and development; the great problem in Social Mechanics is to discover these laws in each instance and apply them; the result will be the harmonious development of each Passion, and the creation of harmony in the sphere over which it presides, analogous to the harmony evolved by the Sense of Hearing.

Let us now recur to the Passions of AMBITION and LOVE, and apply to them what we have here said.

If we would establish a true system of Government, or Hierarchical Harmony in Society, we must discover the system of Laws which regulate the action and development of AMBITION. On these Laws we must base the whole system of authority—of ranks, grades, distinctions, preferment, and everything pertaining to hierarchical order and arrangement. The governmental institution will then be the external expression and correspondence of the natural mode of action of this Passion—of its tendencies and requirements, and of the play and development of its Forces. It will furnish a fixed and permanent standard for its true and harmonious action, and Ambition in each member of the Social Body will be led to conform to this standard, will be educated, disciplined and harmonized by it, as the Sense of Hearing is now educated, disciplined and harmonized by the teachings and influence of the Art and Science of Music.

In like manner, if we would establish a true system for the regulation of the sexual relations, we must discover the laws which regulate the action of the Passion of Love, and base upon them the Institution that is to govern these relations. An institution based upon such a foundation, will correspond perfectly to the natural mode of action of the Passion, to its tendencies and requirements, and will fully satisfy all its wants; it will be the true and natural system of Marriage—the system precalculated and predestined for the Passion by its Author; it will be to it what the musical system is to the Ear, and will develop, refine, and satisfy Love, as that system develops, refines, and satisfies the Sense of Hearing.

Thus, as Music with its laws is the external Mechanism, the Form or Body of the Sense of Hearing, so Government with its laws and hierarchical organization, is the external Mechanism, the Form or Body of the Passion of Ambition, and Marriage, the external Mechanism, the Form or Body of the Passion of Love. In like manner, the whole system of Society with the laws on which it is based, and all its arrangements—industrial, artistic, scientific, political, religious, etc.—is the external Mechanism, the Form or Body of the Soul, or Unity of the twelve Passions.

From what precedes, we may now lay down the principle, that the Human Passions are the standard or criterion by which Social Institutions should be organized; that on them they should be modelled, and that by them they must be judged. The Passions, it cannot be too often repeated, are the work of Divine Wisdom; they reveal, in their direct or natural action, the will of that Wisdom, and its calculations in regard to them and to Human Destiny—they are the only Guide, the only permanent revelation which human Reason can follow in discovering and establishing a true Social Order. Could Reason have discovered a true System of Music, except by studying the mode of action, the tendencies and requirements of the Sense of Hearing? Evidently not—and what is true of this Passion is true of all the Passions; they alone reveal the external mechanism corresponding to them

—that is, the Institutions adapted to their nature, their wants, their action, and their development.

In this connection, let us make use of an illustration which will be easily understood.

Machines must be adapted to the Forces that are to act in them; the steam-engine, for example, must be adapted to steam, and not steam to the engine. When men construct machines in which this motor-power is to be used, they calculate its nature, action, properties, and requirements, and plan the machine accordingly; they do not construct machines according to their own fancy and imagination, to suit their own preconceived ideas, and then undertake to make steam adapt itself to their arbitrary contrivances; were they to do this, they would only derange the action of this Force, and produce disastrous effects at every step.

Now the Passions implanted in Man by Creative Wisdom to impel him to act, are FORCES—as much so as steam, electricity, or any of the active agents in Nature. Social Institutions are to these passional Forces what Machinery is to material Forces. They are the mechanisms in which the Passions are to act, and by which their play and development are to be regulated. This being so—and it is too evident to require further demonstration—is it not as certain as any law in Mechanics, that Social Institutions must be adapted to the Passions—must be so planned, so organized as to conform in every way to their nature, their mode of action, and their demands and requirements? This appears almost too evident to need any argument, and yet such is the degree of ignorance and prejudice prevailing in respect to the Passions, that it is universally believed they must be made to conform and adapt themselves to the arbitrary Laws and Institutions which it may please legislators, moralists, theologians, etc., to devise and establish. If the Passions rebel against these laws and institutions, the doctrine is at once laid down, that they must be forced into obedience by compulsory means. It is this doctrine which has led to the establishment of the whole system of constraint and repression which exist in Society—to penal codes, prisons, scaffolds, police organizations, to fear of future punishment, of excommunication, etc.; these and other instrumentalities have been employed to subdue and keep in check the rebellious Passions, and force them to conform to our incoherent and

9

conflicting systems of Society—to laws devised by legislators and moralists.

Thus the Passions, the work of God, are judged by Institutions, the work of Man ; the former are made subservient to the latter, and are declared good or bad, according as they conform to the standard of right and wrong set up by human Reason ; and Reason, while constantly condemning the Passions, the work of Divine Wisdom, never questions the goodness of its own Institutions. The attempt to make the Passions obey the arbitrary prescriptions of Human Legislation, and adapt themselves to its artificial, unnatural, or false standards, has resulted in their general derangement and subversion. They have been either dwarfed, smothered, or developed in their lower degrees ; they have been misdirected, forced into false channels, and compelled to seek unnatural or subversive means of satisfaction ; they have been perverted or inversely developed ; and finally they have been plunged into strife and conflict with each other and with Reason.

The Passions in this state of subversive development and action, give rise to so many disorders, that a complete Table of them could not find place in a Summary like the present. We will mention, by way of example, the most striking of those engendered by the two Passions of which we have spoken in the present Article—AMBITION and LOVE.

AMBITION, in its subversive action, engenders in the field of Politics, tyranny, oppression, usurpation, revolutions, conspiracies, plots, cabals, class-legislation, party-divisions, strifes, and intrigues ; in the business-world, it engenders rapacity, avarice, venality, fraud, extortion, injustice, and duplicity of action ; in the sphere of social relations, cruelty, inhumanity, malignity, assumption, arrogance, insolence, and an overbearing and domineering spirit.

LOVE, in its subversive action, gives rise to prostitution, sexual excesses, adultery, rape, seduction, infanticide, jealousy, despair, insanity, and other disorders and crimes which can not well be mentioned.

The other Passions are liable to perversion in the same manner ; but as we have not space to enter into details, we will sum up in the following Table the general effects produced on them by our false Social Systems, with their false laws, customs, and institutions.

1. Undeveloped state of each Passion.
2. Want of balance and equilibrium of each Passion with the others.
3. Internal conflict of the Passions, resulting from this want of balance and equilibrium.
4. External conflict of individual with individual, family with family, class with class, state with state, nation with nation.
5. General discontent and dissatisfaction of the individual with himself, with his pursuits, with his social position, with his circumstances generally, and with Society.
6. Constant violation, secret or open, of established laws and customs, in order to satisfy some thwarted or outraged Attraction.
7. Reign of Universal Selfism and Duplicity of Action, in the individual, the family, the class, the corporation, the state, the nation.

Such are the results of our false systems of Society, and of the attempt to compel the Passions to adapt themselves to arbitrary and capricious laws and institutions which are unsuited to them. Now would it not be worth while, in view of the complete failure of human legislation to meet the wants of Man's nature, in view of the innumerable evils which have resulted from the attempt to suppress and smother the Passions by violence and constraint, to seek for some system of Society more in conformity with the Attractions implanted in the human Soul, and better adapted to secure their free play and action?

Is it not probable, we again ask, that Supreme Wisdom in creating Man, and in creating him a Social Being, devised some social Mechanism, some plan of social organization adapted to his nature—to the natural or harmonious development of his Passions? And if so—and how can we suppose that God has devised laws for all other branches of Movement and not for the Social?—is it not the part of wisdom to seek for the Divine plan of Social Organization, for the Divine Social Code, and to substitute it in the place of the false and incoherent systems devised by human legislation?

The first essential condition, then, of a true Social Order is that it should be adapted to Human nature—to the demands and requirements of Passional Attraction.

II. The second essential condition of a true Social Order is that it must be based on the Attributes of Divine Wisdom. FOURIER has given a clear and concise summary of these Attributes in the following Table :—

Radical Attributes. { Supreme Direction of Movement.
{ Integral Distribution of Attraction.

Primary Attributes. { 1. Economy of Means.
{ 2. Distributive Justice.
{ 3. Universality of Providence.

Pivotal Attribute.—UNITY OF SYSTEM.

We will not enter into any detailed explanation of the mode in which the Social Order is to be made to conform to these attributes or principles of Unity in the Universe, for this would render it necessary to give a description of the details of the Social Mechanism, which would be out of place here. We will merely give a few illustrations, and leave the reader to pursue the subject.

The first Primary Attribute—ECONOMY OF MEANS—implies that a true Social Order must be based on the principle of Association, which is the source of all Economy, and that a general system of coöperation, of concert of action, of combination in all departments of human affairs, and a scientific and methodical direction of Forces, together with perfect order in all works and enterprises, must exist in a Social System based on this Attribute.

The second Primary Attribute—DISTRIBUTIVE JUSTICE—implies among other conditions that equal opportunities and privileges in all spheres of life—in education, in the pursuits of Industry, Art, and Science, in the acquisition of fortune, of social position, etc.—must be secured to every individual without exception.

The third Primary Attribute—UNIVERSALITY OF PROVIDENCE—implies that a wise, just, and benevolent protection and guardianship—that is, Unitary Social Charity—must be extended to the young and helpless, to the sick, the infirm, the unfortunate, and to all who require encouragement, aid, assistance, or protection.

The Pivotal Attribute—UNITY OF SYSTEM—implies that a Unitary Social Order should be established throughout the Earth, with unity in all departments—in Religion, in Politics, in Industry, and even in the most minute details, such as weights and measures, typographical signs, language, etc.

The two Radical Attributes— SUPREME DISTRIBUTION OF MOVEMENT, AND INTEGRAL DISTRIBUTION OF ATTRACTION—imply that Human Society must be based on the Laws of Universal Harmony by which the organization and movement of all departments of creation are directed and governed, and that its mechanism must be made to conform to the Attractions which Divine Wisdom has seen fit to implant in the human Soul.

V.

PASSIONAL ATTRACTION.

PASSIONAL ATTRACTION is that Force implanted by God in Man, which impels or attracts him to the external objects, relations, principles, and functions to which the Passions—the particular forces of the Soul—tend, and in which they find their gratification; it is the active principle, the original motor-power in Man existing prior to reflection, and persisting in its demands despite the opposition of conventional theories of right and wrong, of moral precepts, of laws and customs, of reigning prejudices, etc. Coming from God, it is the interpreter of his Will and the Oracle of his decrees. In its collective action, it impels Man to fulfil his Destiny on Earth.

In a general sense, Passional Attraction may be defined as the power that governs the Moral or Spiritual World as gravitation is the power that governs the Material World; the one governs the movements of intelligent beings, the other the movements of material bodies.

We will explain this subject by giving a few examples of special Attractions.

The Sense of Taste, for example, which tends to and finds its delight in agreeable Flavors, is the SAPOROUS ATTRACTION in Man ; it draws him to the various products of the vegetable and animal kingdoms — to the fruits, grains, spices, wines, viands, etc. — which contain agreeable flavors ; it imparts to him a love for food, and thus leads him to nourish the body and secure its health and vigor

The Sense of SMELL, which tends to and finds its delight in agreeable Odors, is the ODORIFEROUS ATTRACTION in Man ; it imparts to him a love for perfumes, and for purity and fragrance in the atmosphere, and leads him to cultivate the flowers, plants, etc. which yield agreeable odors, and to execute whatever works are necessary to maintain a state of atmospheric purity.

The Sense of HEARING, which finds its delight in agreeable Sounds, is the MUSICAL or SONOROUS ATTRACTION in Man ; it imparts to him a love for Musical Harmony, impels him to create Music, and to enliven his festivities and labors with its charms.

The Passion of FRIENDSHIP, which draws man to man, is the AMICAL or BENEVOLENT ATTRACTION in the Soul ; it imparts a desire for social ties and relations of a friendly character with other beings, for amical sympathy with them, and establishes the Social Unity of the Race.

LOVE, which draws beings of opposite sex to each other, is the AMATORY ATTRACTION in Man. It imparts a desire to form ties and relations of an Amatory character, and leads to the Sexual Unity of the Race, and to the procreation and continuation of the species.

Each of the other Passions is in like manner a special Attraction for some external object, relation, or principle to which it tends, for which it has an affinity, and in which it finds its gratification.

Passional Attraction is the generic term which expresses the tendencies or Attractions of the Passions collectively ; it is the power, the influence which they exercise upon Man in inducing him to seek for the means of their gratification. Being spontaneously active Forces or Motors, they gravitate toward their external affinities or correspondences, and in so doing determine the action of Man ; this *Gravitation of the Passions toward their Centres or Foci* is what we call *Passional Attraction*.

Having given these preliminary explanations, we will now lay down a law which is of universal application.

God, in requiring of any of his creatures the performance of a work or function, employs no other lever or agent than Attraction; he never resorts to coercion, constraint, or violence in any form; he governs the Universe by this power alone; he impels all beings to fulfil their Destiny from the pleasure, the charm, the delight he connects with it, and not from fear of pain or punishment.

God in wishing for example the continuance of the various Species which he creates, does not resort to compulsory means to secure this end; he does not force his creatures by violence or constraint to propagate their kind; he simply imparts to them the sexual Attraction, and the function is performed voluntarily and with delight: he secures his end by Attraction, by connecting pleasure with the fulfilment of the function. Again, he requires that every creature should nourish its body in order to maintain itself in health and vigor; he does not force it to eat by compulsory means; he imparts Attraction for agreeable flavors and the food in which they are contained, and the nutritive function is performed with alacrity and delight.

These two examples are sufficient to demonstrate the Law above laid down, that God employs ATTRACTION alone in inducing his creatures to act, and that he leads them to fulfil the functions, the Destiny he assigns to them, by the charms, the pleasures, and the happiness which he connects with the performance of the function, or the fulfilment of the Destiny.

In studying Man in the light of the above Law, we shall find that God has implanted in him the Attractions necessary to impel and guide him in fulfilling the various functions which constitute his Destiny.

Man, as we have explained in the Treatise on the Passions, has a three-fold Destiny to fulfil, namely :—

1. AN INDUSTRIAL DESTINY—that of Overseer of the Globe, or Harmonist of the Material World.

2. A SOCIAL DESTINY—that of Founder of Social Harmony, or Harmonist of the Passional or Moral World.

3. AN INTELLECTUAL DESTINY — that of Discoverer of the Laws of Universal Order and Harmony, and their application to his social and industrial relations.

God, in accordance with his general plan of Attraction, leads man to fulfil this three-fold Destiny by means of three classes of Attractions.

The first Class comprises the five MATERIAL or SENSUOUS ATTRACTIONS; they excite in man a desire for material elegance, beauty, refinement, splendor, luxury, art, and harmony; they attract him, for example, to beauty in scenery and cultures, to splendor in architecture, to elegance in dress and furniture, to delicacy in his food and mode of living, and to artistic refinement in all the material details of life. Man can satisfy these Attractions only by establishing material Unity and Harmony on the Globe—that is, by fulfilling the first branch of his Destiny.

The second Class comprises the four SOCIAL or SPIRITUAL ATTRACTIONS; they excite in Man a desire for Unity with his Species, individually and collectively, that is, a desire for social ties and relations, for sympathetic unions, for concord and sociality, and for association of all kinds and in all degrees with his fellow-beings. Man can satisfy these Attractions only by establishing UNIVERSAL ASSOCIATION, and the Social Unity of the Race—that is, by fulfilling the second branch of his Destiny.

The third Class comprises the three INTELLECTUAL or SERIAL ATTRACTIONS; they excite in Man a desire for Serial distribution, classification, and arrangement in all departments of Nature and of Society, for Knowledge and Science, for the reign of Order on Earth, and for coördinating his finite life, his labors and creations with universal laws and principles. Man can satisfy these Attractions only by discovering the Laws of Universal Order and Harmony, and applying them to the organization and regulation of his social and industrial relations—that is, by fulfilling the third branch of his Destiny.

Thus Divine Wisdom, in delegating to Man the function of HARMONIST on the Globe, that is, of realizing upon it the reign of Material, Moral, and Intellectual Harmony—so that the Planet associated with Humanity may form a harmonious note in the great Concert of the Universe—implants in him the Attractions necessary to guide him in the fulfilment of this function.

[The intelligent reader will understand that our remarks on

Destiny and Attraction apply to the great central, organic, or harmonious period in the Social Career of the Human Race, and not to the preliminary and incoherent Societies which have existed on the Earth up to the present time, in which Man neither fulfils his Destiny nor obeys Attraction.]

The Material Universe in all its departments and details, from the affinities of molecules to the movements of the planets, is governed by ATTRACTION. Kepler and Newton discovered and calculated in part the laws of Material Attraction; FOURIER, proceeding on the principle that there is Unity of System in the Universe, discovered and proclaimed that the Passional or Moral World is governed like the Material World by Attraction. He calculated its Laws and its effects in the Social Movement, and took the ground that, in evolving the Science of Passional Attraction, he continued the work of Kepler and Newton, and extended their calculations from the Material to the Spiritual Sphere.

We will make a quotation or two from his works in which he explains briefly his conception of Passional Attraction. After giving a concise definition of Attraction, pointing out its three primary tendencies, and the Pivotal, which tendencies are to:—

1. LUXURY.*   2. GROUPS.   3. SERIES.   *Pivot*, UNITY.
   Riches.   Affections.   Association.   Harmony.

and after defining the twelve essential or radical Attractions which impel Man to the above centres or foci, namely:—

5 Material or Sensuous, tending to LUXURY,	1st Focus.
4 Social or Affectional, tending to GROUPS,	2d "
3 Serial or Regulative, tending to SERIES,	3d "
PIVOTAL ATTRACTION, tending to UNITY;	

he gives a familiar illustration of the nature and influence of Attraction.

"ATTRACTION is, in the hands of God, an enchanted Wand which "enables him to obtain results by the allurements of Love and

---

* Collective term, signifying material elegance, beauty, refinement, sumptuousness, splendor.

" Pleasure which Man knows how to obtain only by coercion and
" violence. It transforms functions the most repugnant in them-
" selves into positive pleasures. What can be more repulsive,
" for example, than the uncleanly offices incident to the care of
" a new-born infant? What does God do to transform these re-
" pulsive functions into pleasures? He gives to the mother Pas-
" sional Attraction for them; he simply uses his magic preroga-
" tive of Imparting Attraction. From that moment duties in
" themselves most repulsive are transformed into pleasures.

" To estimate the value of this exclusive prerogative of God,
" let us suppose it bestowed upon some ambitious Monarch. Such
" a Monarch, once invested with the power of Imparting Attrac-
" tion, would have no need either of tribunals or armies to cause
" his laws to be executed, and to bring the whole world under
" his empire. It would suffice him to give to all nations an At-
" traction for the system he would establish—for example, for
" our delectable Civilization with its policy of spoliation and
" war; as soon as he had imparted Attraction for this fortunate
" regime, the people would hasten to carry all their savings to
" the tax-gatherer; the young men would vie with each other
" in their ardor to enlist in his service; the Savage tribes would
" engage with delight in the Industry which they now abhor; the
" Barbarians would disperse their seraglios, etc., etc. In addi-
" tion, such a Monarch would impart to all other sovereigns, far
" or near, an *Attraction for recognising his supremacy;* they
" would hasten to anticipate each other in sending Ambassadors
" to give in their adherence to him, and proclaim him Arch-
" Monarch of the Globe. And since every sovereign and people
" would find their happiness in the measures which this Monarch
" had invested with the charm of Attraction, it must be admitted
" that the Ruler who should be the exclusive possessor of the
" talisman for imparting it, would be foolish indeed if he em-
" ployed any other means, such as coercion, punishment, or war;
" such a course would imply wilful malignity and unparalleled
" stupidity in him, for in addition to inflicting misery upon his
" subjects and upon neighboring states, he would fail in his plan
" of universal supremacy, through the resistance and despair of
" nations—whereas by employing the magic lever of Attraction
" alone, he would at the end of a few years be in peaceful pos-

" session of the entire Globe, without having incurred the least
" expense, run any risk, or dissatisfied any individual.

" Such is the position of God in respect to his creatures ; ex-
" clusive Possessor of the most powerful of Motors, of the talis-
" man of Attraction, would he not be both oppressive and absurd
" if, neglecting so brilliant an instrumentality, he should have
" recourse to any other lever than Attraction for ruling the Uni-
" verse, and coördinating on a general plan all departments of
" creation."

Having shown that Attraction is the agent or Motor by which
God governs the Universe, FOURIER lays down the following important law :—

THE ATTRACTIONS OF ALL BEINGS ARE PROPORTIONAL TO THEIR
DESTINIES ;[*]

that is to say, the natural desires, inclinations, propensities,
instincts of all creatures are distributed to them in accordance,
in harmony with the work or function, the sphere of action, the
mode of existence, in a word the Destiny assigned to them by

---

[*] In speaking of Attractions, we mean the normal, natural, essential Attractions ;
in the case of Man, for example, we do not include perverted or depraved tastes
and inclinations, like those for drunkenness, theft, etc., nor subversive emotions,
like revenge, hatred, jealousy, envy — all of which are the effects of the perversion
of human nature in a Social Mechanism unsuited to it. These vicious and unnatural Attractions are in counter-march to Human Destiny ; it is only by studying them
according to the *Law of Inversion* that we can comprehend the true Destiny to which
they counterpoint.

We do not speak, either, of the artificial, accidental caprices, tastes, and whims
which we find in men whose Passions are misdirected or thwarted by false external
circumstances ; we do not hold that there is any Destiny corresponding to these factitious tastes. Take as an illustration the smoking and chewing of tobacco ; we do
not believe that these habits will exist in a true Social Order, but the taste which
gives rise to them, and which indicates that Man tends always to combine physical
with mental action, or that he has an abhorrence for non-action, point to customs
which, though dissimilar to those in question, have an analogy with them in principle. In like manner, gambling, a vice in Civilization, indicates in Man an Attraction for the unknown and hidden, for chance, surprise, intrigue, management, diplomacy ; the principle is good, while gambling is a perversion of it. In the same
way, the love of intoxication is an inverted effect of the love of excitement, exhila-
ration, enthusiasm ; it comes from the 12th Passion — Synthesism : there is no *direct*
Destiny corresponding to it ; that is, Man in a true Social Order will not seek in
intoxication for the means of that enthusiasm and exaltation which the Soul demands : he will find them in the poetic and ideal life of Association or the Combined
Order ; the love of intoxication, then, counterpoints, that is, points inversely, **to**
one branch of Human Destiny.

God—"The reindeer, for example," says FOURIER, "is destined
" to live among the snows and ices of the Arctic regions. God
" does not give it Attraction for the verdant fields and the
" products of our Temperate Zone ; this quadruped prefers the
" snows of the North and the mosses which they cover ; its At-
" traction, then, is proportional to its Destiny."   In like manner, the camel is destined to live in the desert ; it has no Attraction for the forests and shady groves of our climates ; it prefers the sandy wastes and the heat of the Torrid Zone : the Attractions of this animal, again, are proportional to its Destiny.

Taking the Law that "*Attractions are proportional to Destinies*" as our guide, we can, by a careful study of the Attractions
implanted in the human Soul, by a study of its essential wants
and requirements, solve all the intricate questions relating to human life and Destiny on earth, which now perplex the human
mind.

With the aid of this guide, we can :—

1. Determine the true and natural mode of life of Man on
Earth, the pleasures and enjoyments he should possess, the character of the custom, habits, institutions, etc., which he should establish, and the natural standard of Right and Wrong.

2. Demonstrate the goodness of the tastes, inclinations, propensities, and desires which we find universal among men — such
as the love of elegance, refinement, display, luxury, splendor and
wealth ; the taste for personal adornment and beauty, for sumptuous living, for change, travel, and adventure ; the love of power
and distinction ; the love of excitement and enthusiasm, and
other attractions and impulses which are found common among
men.

Moralists, and Ascetics, certain religious Sects like the Quakers, and a large class of persons with tame and feeble passions,
who believe in frugality, in abstemiousness, self-denial and other
negative virtues, make war upon all these tastes and inclinations, believing that they should be suppressed and kept down,
and that, if not positively vicious, they are at least immoral and
hurtful.   The Quakers, for example, would even proscribe Music as something sinful and contrary to the law of God.

The guide furnished us by Passional Attraction can alone settle differences of opinion and controversies upon all questions of

this kind; it is the only interpreter which we have in this respect of the Divine Will. If Attraction misleads us, then the Author of Attraction misleads us, and in that case there can be no principle of truth, justice, law, order, or wisdom, in the Universe, and, as a consequence, no standard of Right and Wrong, of Good and Evil for Man on earth.

Let us consult some of the Attractions implanted in the Human Soul, some of the interpreters to Man of the Divine Will, and deduce from them the Destiny to which they point.

The Sense of Sight or the Visual Attraction in Man, for example, finds its delight in beauty and harmony of form and color — that is, in the harmonies of painting, sculpture, and architecture, in beautiful scenery, and in external elegance and splendor of all kinds. Now if the Eye demands and can be satisfied only by these Harmonies, it is evident, according to the law of "Attractions proportional to Destinies," or inversely, of Destinies proportional to Attractions, that Man is destined to enjoy them, and that their enjoyment is perfectly legitimate. If this were not so, why would God have given to Man an Attraction for this branch of material beauty and harmony; why have given him a useless Attraction; why have tantalized him with a desire he could not gratify; why have violated a fundamental principle of Nature, that of adaptation of means to ends; why in short have gone counter to his three primary attributes — Economy of Means, Distributive Justice, Unity of System? The attraction in Man for artistic beauty and harmony in the external world, is a positive demonstration, then, that in the Natural or Divine Order of Society, Humanity is to enjoy everything that can please and charm the eye; that it is to inhabit palaces, to be surrounded with all the magnificence of art, and to live in the midst of material beauty, elegance, and splendor of every kind.

The same course of argument is applicable to the four other Senses or Material Attractions. The Attraction of the Ear for Harmonies of Sound is a proof that Music is destined to be a universal enjoyment of the Race; its elevating influence on the higher emotions of the Soul demonstrates its supreme utility, and the wisdom of God in imparting an Attraction for it to Man. The Attraction of the Sense of Taste for varied and agreeable flavors is a proof that Man is destined by God to enjoy a delicate and refined system of food — a fare as sumptuous as Nature can supply.

The Social Attractions implanted in the Soul, impelling Man to Social ties and accords, exciting in him a craving for sympathy, demonstrate that Man is a Social Being, that he is intended for Sociality and Association of all kinds, and that the great organic epoch of his Social Career will be one of UNIVERSAL ASSOCIATION, that all the diversified elements of Humanity — all the various races of men on earth — will be organized in one HARMONIOUS WHOLE, and that Social Unity and Harmony are destined to reign upon our Globe.

In like manner, the Intellectual Attractions in Man, with their craving to solve the mysteries of Nature, with their ceaseless curiosity to pry into the secret of things, to penetrate the Laws of Creation, to comprehend the plan of the great universal Whole which surrounds him, and of which he forms a part, are proofs that Man is to elevate himself to a knowledge of Universal Truth, to solve the problem of Universal Life, and to discover and comprehend the scheme of individual and collective Destinies.

Lastly, the sentiment in the Soul for the Infinite, its Attraction to commune with the Unseen and the Eternal, to grasp and identify itself with Universal Existence — which is the basis of the Religious Sentiment — is a proof that Man is in conscious, intelligent Unity with the Universe, and that through all ages, under the form of Worship — that is, of Unitary rites and symbols — he is destined to manifest his association with its phenomena and harmonies, to celebrate the Unity of individual with collective Destinies, and by connecting his labors and creations with and coördinating them to the plan of Divine or Universal Order, he is to elevate them in their various departments of Industry, Art, and Science to the dignity of religious acts, or acts based on Universal principles, and thus associate himself with the Supreme Harmonist in the realization of Unity and Harmony in the department of Creation over which he presides.

ATTRACTION in Man, then, prophesies, reveals, interprets to him his Destiny; it points as unvaryingly to that Destiny as the needle points to the pole. It is the Standard, the Criterion of truth in judging and deciding all questions of a moral or spiritual nature, as the Law of the Series is the Standard in deciding all questions relating to classification and organization.

Were the false systems of Society that now exist upon the Earth the permanent Destiny of the Human Race, Nature would have given men Attractions adapted to them; she would have given them Attractions for poverty and anxiety, for disorder and antagonism, and the other results which they engender. But as she has not given to men such Attractions, it is a positive demonstration that these Societies are not the permanent Destiny of the Race; that they are to pass away and give place to a Social Order, in which Attraction will find its natural employment and its full satisfaction.

The Universe is ONE—a great collective Whole, a vast Unitary Organism; co-relation, association, correspondence, mutual dependence, solidarity reign throughout this great, living ORGANIC UNITY. All the creations in it, from the lowest to the highest, from the plant and the animal to Man and the Planet, have each a function to perform, a mission to fulfil, a Destiny to realize. To impel and guide the living, self-acting creations to perform their infinitely diversified functions in this great Whole, Supreme Wisdom gives to them attractions adapted to this end; these Attractions are distributed in conformity with the general plan of Order which the Supreme Harmonist has established in Creation; their distribution is calculated with such exactness, and with such perfect conformity to that plan, that all animated beings are impelled to act and operate in their diversified spheres with perfect concert and harmony toward the accomplishment of a common end —the realization of UNIVERSAL UNITY.

During the period of the Social Infancy and Childhood of the Race, when Man is ignorant of the laws of Divine Harmony, and has not established a Social Order based upon those laws and adapted to Attraction, the Passions are in a state of general disorder and conflict, because they have to act in a Social Mechanism unsuited to them. To establish Order to some extent in the social world, and to bring the Passions to adapt themselves to existing laws and institutions, Man resorts to coercion and constraint, to moral precepts, punishments, etc. He enacts Penal Codes, builds prisons, erects scaffolds, organizes Armies and Police-forces, and as these means of Coercion do not reach every variety of evil, especially of moral evil, he holds up before the soul the terrors of a fearful retribution in another world.

If the repression of Attraction, if the system of constraint and coercion, and the government by fear and violence which now exist, were natural, were the design of God, and the permanent Destiny of Man, they would enter into the whole policy and plan of Divine Government; and if this were so, God, on the principle of Unity of System, would have given to Man *Counter-Attractions*, that is, Repulsions for the various functions he had to perform, and then have forced him to fulfil them from fear of punishment and other means of constraint; he would have given, for example, to the fruits, grains, vegetables, etc., on which Man subsists, insipid, bitter, or acrid flavors, and then have compelled him to eat them from the pains of hunger or the fear of starvation. Pursuing the same policy, he would have created the flowers without odor, or with odors repulsive to the Sense of Smell; he would have made the landscape repulsive to the Sense of Sight, have surrounded the earth with a murky atmosphere, have hung the heavens in black, and then, have forced Man, living in the midst of this repugnant scene, to execute all the works, labors, and functions on which his existence depended from fear of punishment, suffering, or death.

That this system of Coercion and Constraint does not enter into the plan of Divine Wisdom, is so evident, when considered abstractly or as a principle, that it requires no refutation ; and yet legislators, philosophers, and moralists, misled by the spectacle of the passions, misdirected or perverted by the influence of false Social Institutions, have made Coercion and Constraint the basis of their theories and systems ; they have proclaimed the viciousness of Attraction, and sought to repress or smother it by every means that human ingenuity could invent. For thirty centuries, since Reason began to theorize upon the Passions, this policy has been pursued ; we find it recommended by the Sages of Greece, by the Fathers of the Church, and the moralists and theologians of the present day. We think that Humanity has had enough of this doctrine, and that the time has at length come to discard and repudiate it, and to take as the basis of our faith, and as our guide in Social Politics, the doctrine of ATTRACTION, the inherent Goodness of Human Nature, and the possibility of realizing on Earth the reign of Universal Happiness and Harmony.

We will conclude this subject with a quotation from FOURIER in which he shows that Coercion and Constraint can not enter into the policy of Divine Wisdom:—

" It will suffice as a proof that coercion forms no part of the
" Divine Plan, to observe that God has not created upon the
" Earth any means of constraint invested with Divine authority
" and superior to any force which could be opposed to it by
" Man. We see on our Globe neither giants, nor centaurs, nor
" tritons, nor agents of any kind capable of vanquishing human
" armies, though it would have been so easy for God to have
" created on the land and in the seas beings of colossal size and
" strength, capable of at once subduing Man in case of rebellion
" against his will. The absence of such creations denotes that
" coercion does not enter into the plans of God, and that a So-
" cial Order emanating from Him would be exempt from it.

" If God did not possess the lever of Attraction he would be
" obliged to resort to Coercion—to create in the firmament co-
" lossal Planets which should urge on the smaller ones, restrain
" them, and compel them to move in their orbits. It would have
" been the same on the Earth, where God would have been
" obliged to create distinct species of men of monstrous size and
" power—to create Minotaurs, Giants, Titans, Centaurs, etc. to
" compel men to exercise Industry and to adopt any system which
" he might ordain. He would also have been compelled to cre-
" ate gigantic bees to force the smaller ones to gather honey, and
" gigantic beavers to force the smaller ones to construct their
" dams.

" Then again, these colossal species might themselves disobey
" God, if they were not impelled by Attraction to the service he
" had assigned to them. God would then be obliged to employ
" Attraction with some and Coercion with others, and to practise
" intentionally duplicity of system, when he could follow unity
" of system by imparting to all his creatures Attraction for their
" functions, which would lead them to prompt and cheerful obe-
" dience, and enthusiastic conformity to his will.

" How can we suppose that God, who is a being of supreme
" Goodness and supreme Wisdom, has taken pleasure in compli-

" cating the Social Mechanism, by coercive measures, which would
" render it necessary to double the number of agents for the
" maintenance of order and would cause the unhappiness of the
" great majority of mankind. How could God, whose pivotal at-
" tribute is Unity of System, deprive himself voluntarily of the
" marvellous lever — Attraction — which, already employed with
" entire success as the agent of sidereal harmonics, must accord-
" ing to the principle of Unity be equally adapted to produce
" harmony in the social relations of men ?

" It results from these indications, that God, in the social laws
" which he has destined for Man, can not have calculated on
" any other lever than that of Attraction, since he has not pro-
" vided any means of Constraint and Coercion. After this, how
" can we explain the inconsistency of men who wish, as they say,
" to conform to the designs of God, yet who, refusing to consult
" Attraction, his sole Interpreter in Social Mechanics, confide
" blindly in vague and arbitrary systems of Morality and Legis-
" lation notwithstanding that the tenacity of the seven subversive
" scourges has proved for three thousand years, the entire in-
" compatibility of these systems with the designs of God, and their
" incapacity to reveal the theory of Human Destinies and the
" Divine Social Code ?"

GENERAL VIEW OF ASSOCIATION.

We deem it proper, after the statement of general principles which has been made, to give some practical idea of the Social Mechanism which is to be deduced from them. This new social Regime we will call ASSOCIATION or the COMBINED ORDER, as it is based upon association and combination of all the elements which go to constitute the organization of Society.

To present the subject as clearly as possible, we will describe, in general outline, a single Association, containing about eighteen hundred persons, and comprising the complete scale of human characters. This social body would occupy a vast unitary edifice and would cultivate a domain about three miles square.

An Association of this extent, regularly organized in all its departments—industrial, artistic, scientific, educational, and domestic—is the primary element or germ of the Combined Order, as the town or village is the primary element or germ of the present Social Order. A state or nation in Civilization, however vast, is but a repetition of towns or townships; in like manner, a State in the Combined Order will be but a repetition of Associations. Now if we understand the organization of a single township in the present Order—its system of Industry, Property, Education, mode of Living, and Social Relations—we understand the whole organization of that Order; so if we understand the organization of a single Association, we shall understand the whole organization of the Combined Order, which, as we stated, is but a repetition of single Associations.

The four incoherent or subversive Societies—the Savage, Patriarchal, Barbaric and Civilized—are all based upon the system of isolated families living in separate households, with separate interests, aims, pursuits, and wants. This being the basis of the false or subversive Societies, it follows, according to the *Law of*

Inversion, that the basis of the true or harmonic Order of Society must be Association, and that an Order founded on such a basis, must produce results diametrically opposite to those produced by the isolated system—that is, must produce unity of interests, concert of action, and coöperation in all the pursuits and aims of life.

That Association is the true form and basis of human Society is evident from the following considerations:

It is only in a large Association, possessing ample capital, and vast industrial resources, that Agriculture, Manufactures, and the various branches of productive Industry can be united and prosecuted with unity of interest and concert of action, and with all the advantages of placing the producer and consumer side by side with each other.

It is only in such an Association, in which all varieties of human character are combined, in which a broad field is opened to social Relations, and in which general intelligence, politeness, and refinement reign, that Man's social nature can be fully developed and find full scope and satisfaction.

It is only in such an Association that every individual without exception can find a choice of congenial occupations, the enjoyment of the Arts and Sciences, agreeable and varied social relations, and the full and natural exercise of the physical, moral, and intellectual faculties with which he is endowed.

It is only in such an Association, with its system of Attractive Industry, its diversified pursuits, its congenial social relations, its independent mode of life, its institutions adapted to the Passions, together with the art, splendor, and refinement connected with all the details of existence, that PASSIONAL ATTRACTION can find an external world erfectly adapted to it.

It is only in such an Association, that the five Attributes of Divine Wisdom, or the five principles of Order and Harmony in Creation, can be practically realized on Earth.

Finally, it is only in such an Association that the complete Scale or Series of Human Characters, that is, all the varieties of tastes, inclinations, talents, and capacities, necessary to constitute what may be called the COLLECTIVE MAN—the INTEGRAL SOUL, —can be combined.

In connection with this last point, we will make an extract

from FOURIER, in which he explains the theory of what he terms
the PASSIONAL or COLLECTIVE MAN—the INTEGRAL SOUL ; we
shall find in it one of the strongest proofs that Association is the
Destiny of Man.

" Man, in the material sense, is composed of two individuals—
" one male, the other female. Analyze a hundred couples of both
" sexes, and on dissection they will be found (except in cases of
" malformation) to possess a uniform number of muscles, nerves,
" viscera, etc. ; no one among this hundred couples will be found
" with eleven or thirteen pairs of ribs, twenty-three or twenty-five
" vertebræ, fifteen or seventeen pairs of teeth ; variations infin-
" itely rare, like the absence of a pair of teeth, the addition of a
" sixth finger or sesamoidal bone, are deformities and not dif-
" ferences of species. The human Species, then, in the material
" sense, is composed of two bodies, a male and a female, and one
" such couple, taken at hazard, furnishes the complete type of the
" Material Man. It is not so with the Passional Man ; he is a
" compound Whole, composed of 810 individual souls or distinct
" characters, distributed in Series in about the proportion of 21
" males to 20 females.

" A hundred couples, compared in a material sense, will be
" found anatomically homogeneous ; but the same couples com-
" pared in a passional sense, or according to their characters,
" will be found radically different from each other ; among some,
" avarice would predominate, among others prodigality ; one
" would incline to frankness, another to deceit, and so on ;
" whence it is evident that the Passional Man is nowise complete
" in a single couple as is the case with the Material Man ; he
" is as far from complete in 100 couples, and would also be
" in 405 taken at hazard, since the assortment of characters
" might be defective and very discordant. To compose an In-
" tegral or Combined Soul, the characters of various degrees
" must be brought together in graduated proportion and arranged
" in classes, orders, genera, species, and varieties, as we arrange
" progressively the pipes of an organ. Let us add that among
" the 810 individuals forming the 810 characters, there must be
" 415 men and 395 women, so that there are not 405 of each
" sex.

" When the 810 characters are brought together and fully de-

" veloped, forming the complete Passional Man, we shall see
" them attracted naturally, without the least constraint, to all
" the functions of agriculture, manufactures, science, and art—
" the children spontaneously with their parents, and all with en-
" thusiastic ardor.   It will be seen that in this new Order the
" poorest individual may develop and satisfy many more of the
" Passions of the Soul than the richest Potentate can do at the
" present day, and the greater the inequalities in fortune, intel-
" ligence, etc., the easier will Association rise to a general Ac-
" cord, which will be as perfect as that of the muscles of the body,
" or the various instruments of a good orchestra—the latter be-
" ing an image of the Human Passions, which constitute an Or-
" chestra of 810 instruments.

    " In speaking of the integrality of the Soul, we have to rectify
" a fundamental error as respects the Passional Man.   Every
" individual believes that he possesses a complete integral Soul ;
" this is an error more gross than would be that of a soldier who
" should pretend that he formed by himself an entire regiment ;
" the reply would be (supposing the regiment to contain a thou-
" sand men) that he formed but a thousandth part of it.   The
" error of such a soldier would be far less absurd than that which
" has been committed in respect to the integrality of the Soul, for
" the soldier is of the same nature as the captain and the colonel ;
" he may replace them ; whereas in the great scale of Characters,
" a Soul with one dominant Passion, or Passion fully developed,
" is of a very different nature from a soul with two, three, or four
" dominant Passions, and can not take its place.   Let us make
" use of a familiar illustration.   If we wished to form a pack of
" cards, and a thousand aces of hearts were offered us, but one
" of the thousand would be of use ; a second would be superflu-
" ous.   It is the same in the Passional Mechanism, the 810 char-
" acters composing which may be compared to 810 different
" cards.   Now as a card of one particular kind, or a thousand
" such, would represent but a fifty-second part of a pack, so
" any one particular character, or a thousand such would rep-
" resent, not an integral Soul, but only the 810th part of it ;
" hence in Association but one of the thousand would be of use,
" and the 999 others would have to be rejected as superflu-
" ous.

" This truth, which will be distasteful to many, is but an ex-
" tension of the principle of corporal divisibility ; if a thousand
" men were presented to form a human body, we should have to
" reject 999, and to the one which remained add a woman. Now
" if, as is evident, the integrality of the human body requires
" two different bodies, should we be surprised that the integral-
" ity of the Soul may require two or even two thousand souls ?
" This is a truth of the most simple and palpable kind, the over-
" sight of which has led the philosophers into a labyrinth of er-
" rors in respect to human nature. Had they reflected upon the
" subject, they would long since have proposed the following prob-
" lem : Since a human body, taken isolatedly, is not an integral
" body, we must believe from analogy that a human Soul, taken
" isolatedly, is not an integral Soul ; and if two different bodies
" are necessary to form an integral body, how many different
" souls are necessary to form an integral Soul ? Are we to con-
" clude from analogy that the number is 2, 3, or 4, or indeed
" 200, 300, 400 ? and what rules should be observed in order to
" arrive at the solution ?

" The human body is not androgynous, like most plants — that
" is, it does not possess the faculty of reproducing itself without
" a distinct male and female body. A cabbage, if it could speak,
" might boast of constituting fully the cabbage species, for it re-
" produces itself, being provided with the male and female prin-
" ciples. It is not so with the human Species, which, sexually
" considered, is divided into a male and female body, and is
" unable to reproduce itself isolatedly. Other creations are
" composed of three sexes — the bee for instance. Now if Na-
" ture, which distributes everything by progression, has estab-
" lished the sexual progression of 1—2—3, respectively, for the
" bodies of the cabbage, the man, and the bee, it may well have
" established the progression of 1000—2000—3000, etc., for the
" integralities of souls — witness the bee, of which it takes as
" many as 20,000 to form a hive or the integral soul of the bee ;
" this soul, then, is composed of about 20,000 souls, distributed
" among three sexes.

" Can it be said that the three sexual bees — the queen, the
" working-bee, and the drone — form one integral bee ? No,
" since the three cannot form a hive ; they are only parts which

" associated with a large number of similar parts, form the in-
" tegral soul, capable of developing in full the faculties of the
" bee.

" A man would show that he knew nothing of bees, if, after
" passing his life in a country like Lapland, where there are
" no hives, he should judge this insect to be pernicious from
" the sight of a few isolated bees which had stung him. We should
" say to such a man : ' You are in error ; this little insect in its
" associated state is the most admirable of creatures.' Every
" one must admit that a being is spiritually incomplete so long as
" he is not associated with a sufficient number to enable him to
" fulfil his social functions, and we should say of two beavers, for
" example : Here, at any rate, is the entire species in the mate-
" rial sense, but it would take a hundred couples at least to form
" the species integrally in the spiritual sense — that is, to devel-
" op and exercise the natural social faculties of which the beaver
" is susceptible.

" It is thus with Man ; there has never been seen on our globe
" an integral human Soul in a natural and attractive social
" mechanism ; we see only parts of the integral Soul, existing
" without harmonic association : This would be the state of
" bees working isolatedly in a country where there were no
" flowers, which are the elements of their association ; they would
" be wild bees, social abortions, and not integral or associated
" bees. Such is Man in the Savage Horde ; he is not an Integ-
" ral Man ; he is not in his natural state, since he lacks two ele-
" ments — a knowledge of Industry, the Arts, and Sciences, and
" the theory of Passional Attraction — both of which are ne-
" cessary to enable him to elevate himself to his Destiny, to So-
" cial Harmony ; and in the Barbaric and Civilized Orders, he
" possesses but the first of these two means ; as a consequence
" he can not rise to his Destiny nor develop the Integral Soul.
" We shall not understand the nature of the Integral Soul till
" we have seen Man exercising without constraint the social and
" industrial faculties of which he is susceptible ; in the Civilized
" Order he acts only from constraint ; the proof of this is that if
" the prison and the scaffold should be abolished, this Order
" would be overthrown at once by the uprising of the masses."

By a variety of calculations — among others the above as

to the number of distinct Characters which constitute the complete Scale of Human Characters, or the integral Soul — FOURIER arrives at the conclusion that about 1800 persons (men, women, and children) are necessary to the formation of a complete or integral ASSOCIATION; this would be equal to say 300 families. The least number of persons with which an Association can be regularly organized is about 400. Below this number. the Serial Mechanism or the organization of Social and Industrial Relations in Series, would be impracticable; and without this Mechanism, the natural play and action of the Passions can not be secured, and Industry can not be rendered attractive — in other words, Passional and Material Harmony can not be realized.

Let us now proceed to give a sketch of an Association consisting of eighteen hundred persons, inhabiting a unitary Edifice, and cultivating a domain of say six thousand acres.

DOMAIN AND EDIFICE.

The Association or Collective Man, composed of its eighteen hundred individual Souls, would require for its field of operations a tract of land about three miles square. This domain would be laid out in fields, gardens, orchards, vineyards, parks, lawns, meadows, woodlands, etc., according to the nature of the soil and the industrial requirements of the Association. In the centre of the domain, a vast Unitary Edifice, a Palace complete in all its appointments, would be erected, serving as the residence of the Associates. This edifice should be planned throughout in conformity with the wants and requirements — material, social, and intellectual — of the Collective Man who is to inhabit it. In conformity with the principle in Nature which coördinates the Material and the Spiritual — as illustrated in the co-relation and unity of the body and the soul — the Palace of the Association should be an Architectural Organism perfectly adapted in its distribution and arrangements to the nature and requirements of the Collective Soul that is to inhabit it. We will point out some of the main features of the correspondence which should exist between the Collective Man and his abode.

The Palace of an Association will consist of three great divisions — a Centre and two Wings — forming a Series, and corresponding to the three-fold nature of Man, or to the three classes of Passions—the Material, the Social, and the Intellectual. The Centre of the Palace will correspond to the Social principle or element in Man; it will be devoted to uses, functions, pleasures, etc., of a social character—that is, to the service of the four cardinal Passions. In it will be located the banquet-halls, the halls of reception, the grand saloons, the ball-rooms, and the *Courts of the four Social Passions.* All social relations and pleasures of a collective character will be here concentrated; it will form so to say the Heart of the Edifice.

In one of the Wings will be located some of the workshops or Halls of Industry — those in which branches of manufactures and mechanics of a light and refined character are prosecuted: the heavier branches will be carried on in separate buildings adjoining the palace. In this Wing will be located also the industrial schools, so as not to disturb the other parts of the edifice. This Wing will represent the material or industrial element in Man. The other Wing will be devoted to the intellectual and scientific pursuits and functions of the Association; here will be located the reading-rooms, the library, the scientific collections, the museum, the university, and the studios of the artists : it will represent the intellectual element in human nature.

Thus the Palace of the Collective Man will correspond to the three great divisions of human life and activity, namely, the Industrial, the Social, and the Intellectual.

The private apartments of the members of the Association will be distributed through the upper stories of the entire palace : they will be of various sizes, with proportional rents, so as to suit all degrees of fortune, and all varieties of taste.

Architectural unity requires that all parts of the Edifice should be connected; in consequence, a spacious corridor or gallery, an enclosed piazza, will extend along the whole of one of the fronts of the Palace; by means of this covered communication, which will be spacious and elegant and decorated with works of art, persons will be able to go to all parts of the edifice with ease and facility, and without exposure to the inclemency of the weather or to sudden changes of temperature, which cause an incredible amount of disease under our present defective architectural arrangements. This spacious and elegant Corridor, of the entire height of the building and lighted by wide and lofty windows, will be one of the charms of the Palace of the Association; it will serve at times for exhibitions of works of Art, for horticultural displays, and other collective purposes.

A winter garden, planted with evergreens and exotic plants, and containing the green-houses, will be located in the rear of the central portion of the edifice.

At one end of the Palace will be erected the TEMPLE OF MATERIAL HARMONIES, in which the seven following branches of Material Art, in all the variety and magnificence of which they are susceptible, will be represented:—

1. SINGING, or measured vocal sounds.
2. INSTRUMENTAL MUSIC, or measured artificial sounds.
3. POETRY, or measured language.
4. PANTOMIME, or measured expression.
5. DANCING, or measured movement.
6. GYMNASTICS, or measured action.
7. PAINTING, or measured decoration.

PIVOT.—MEASURED MECHANICAL DISTRIBUTION, AND MEASURED COÖPERATION OF BOTH SEXES AND ALL AGES.

The nearest approach in the present Order to the Temple of Material Harmonies, is the Opera. The Opera, however, is merely a place of amusement, or considered in its best aspect, a means of developing one Sense, that of Hearing. The Temple of Material Harmony in the Combined Order will be a school of Universal Art; in it will be presented under the form of material emblems and harmonies the highest conceptions of the intellect; it will be a powerful auxiliary in educating the spiritual Passions through the medium of the Senses.

At the other extreme of the Palace will be located the TEMPLE OF UNITYISM in which Man will celebrate by appropriate rites and symbols, his Unity with the Universe, his association with universal life and harmony.

On the summit of the Edifice will be placed the observatory, telegraph, and signal-tower. From this point, communications with all parts of the domain and with neighboring associations, take place.

In the vicinity of the Palace will be located the granaries, stables, warehouses, manufactories, and other buildings which for various reasons require to be kept separate from the residence of the Association.

SYSTEM OF PROPERTY—INDIVIDUAL RESPONSIBILITY.

The lands, edifices, flocks, herds, machinery, and other property of the Association, will be represented by stock, divided into shares; the stock will be owned by the members according to their respective means. This system of joint-stock property, applied to the soil, while it secures individual rights in property, will secure at the same time unity of cultivation, and method and order in Industry generally.

No community of property will exist in Association; no confounding of interests will take place. On the contrary, the principle of private property and of individuality in all things will be strictly observed, and carried out to a much greater extent than in the present Order; for example, the Woman and the Child (the latter from the time that it begins to produce) will possess the right of property, and in fact all industrial rights, equally with Man.

An account will be opened in the books of the Association with every individual—man, woman, and child—debiting them respectively with what they consume, and crediting them with their share of the industrial profits of the establishment. The Association will deal with individuals, not with families; families can unite their interests if they wish, but the Association will keep them distinct, as it admits of no community of any kind. This principle of individual Liberty and Responsibility will be observed in all the details of life; each member of the Association, for example, will choose his own apartments, and live in a way to suit his individual tastes and means. The Association will balance its accounts once a year, when a settlement will take place with each member. At the end of every fiscal year, when the total annual profits are ascertained, a certain portion will go to the payment of dividends on Stock, and the balance will be awarded to Labor. The different kinds of Labor will not, however, be paid alike, but each according to the talent and skill exercised, and the repugnance overcome. The profits of the Association will thus be divided among the members according to their Capital, Labor, and Talent.

MODE OF LIVING.

The arrangements relating to the mode of living in Association will be sufficiently varied to suit all tastes and inclinations and all degrees of fortune, and allow the greatest liberty, with entire freedom of choice. In the eating department, for example, there will be both public and private tables ; there will be the Series of public banquet-halls fitted up with elegance and every convenience, and by the side of them there will be smaller rooms for the accommodation of private parties and groups of friends who may wish to dine by themselves. Individuals and families can also be served in their own rooms if they prefer. The price of living will not be uniform ; there will be a scale of prices, so that every individual may consult his tastes, means, or desire of economy. The same variety and freedom which exist in the eating department, will exist in all others. Association will in all things avoid uniformity, monotony, community, which are violations of the law of Harmony, and a certain source of discord.

UNITARY DOMESTIC ARRANGEMENTS — KITCHENS, NURSERIES, HEATING, LIGHTING, ETC.

The waste, incoherence, and complication of the present System will disappear in the Combined Order. An Association of eighteen hundred persons — equal to say three hundred families — would not have three hundred kitchens, three hundred kitchen-fires, three hundred sets of cooking utensils, and prepare three hundred separate meals as three hundred families now do. The Association would have one vast and well-organized kitchen, divided into four or five compartments for the different kinds of culinary preparations, with four or five fires, and the requisite number of skilful cooks, occupied alternately and devoted to a special function. The kitchen of an Association would be fitted up with elegance and with every convenience ; machinery and processes of every kind that can abridge or save labor will be introduced, so that culinary occupations will be simplified, and freed from the drudgery now connected with them. Those only who have an Attraction for the function will engage in it, and as their number will be comparatively small, the remuneration will be liberal. By these and other means, culinary labor will, in Association, be rendered honorable and attractive like other industrial occupations; it certainly should be, for the culinary art is one of the most useful and important to man.

The economies and collective arrangements introduced into the cooking department, will be introduced into all other departments of domestic labor, among others, into the Laundry, where a few large vats with proper machinery will take the place of the three hundred little wash-tubs of three hundred isolated households.

In connection with the subject of the Combined Kitchen of Association, we will remark that it is the primary practical condition of the *Emancipation of Woman*—her emancipation from pecuniary dependance on man, from domestic servitude, and from a low sphere of action. Efforts are being made to secure to Woman the rights which belong to her as an independent and rational being, and to elevate her to her true position. This subject may be discussed theoretically, but no important practical reform in this direction is possible so long as the isolated household and the isolated kitchen exist. Woman, or one half of the adult portion of the Human Race, must, under our present domestic arrangements, be absorbed in the petty details of the isolated household—in the kitchen, at the wash-tub, etc.—must spend her life in domestic drudgery and servitude, and be dependant upon Man for her support. If woman were taken out of the kitchen, man would have to take her place, for *the work must be done;* he would, then, sink into the condition in which woman is now placed.

If Woman would emancipate herself from domestic servitude, from dependence on Man, from inferiority of position, and from her present restricted and subordinate sphere of action, the isolated household and kitchen must be abolished, and the combined household and kitchen substituted in their place. In the vast kitchen of an Association, supplied with every variety of labor-saving machinery, thirty women would do the work which now absorbs three hundred; by this means two hundred and seventy would at once be set at liberty and be placed in a position to devote themselves to more useful, productive, elevating, and intellectual pursuits, while the thirty who remained, having an attraction for culinary functions, and working but a few hours a day at some special branch, in a spacious and elegant kitchen, and being well remunerated for their services, would find themselves in an independent and congenial position.

If Woman would free herself from the trammels which now bind her, if she would secure her pecuniary independence and would elevate herself to her true position, she must begin with abolishing the isolated household and the separate kitchen. She must set on foot a Reform which will descend to the pots, kettles, and wash-tubs of the domestic den, which are so many clogs from which she must first free herself as the preliminary condition of her emancipation and improvement.

The economy and unity which Association will introduce into the kitchen will be applied to the Nurseries and the care of children. In Association a collective sympathy for Childhood will exist, and will extend to it a fostering care and a Social Providence. The Association will consider itself the Collective Parent of all the children born upon its domain ; it will extend to them all the same advantages of education, and equal opportunities of development and cultivation. Animated by the spirit of collective philanthropy, it will, with the aid of its immense resources, organize for the care of its Infant World, the most perfect system that Art or Science can devise. The Nurseries of an Association will surpass in elegance and convenience, and in all their arrangements for preserving the health, and developing the incipient faculties of the child, anything which can now be secured by the wealthiest family. The nursery-rooms will be distributed in Series for children of different ages, and provided with the means of satisfying the tastes and instincts of each age. As perfect liberty in all respects will exist in Association, the mother can, if she prefers, keep her child in her own apartments ; the child however would not receive a tenth part of the care, nor enjoy a tenth part of the advantages for the development of its infantile faculties, that it would find in the Combined Nursery. The mother could visit her child as often as she pleased, or if she had a taste for the care of children, she could take part in the Group of Nurses (one of the most honorable in Association— the Nurses being considered as Collective Mothers) and be honored and remunerated for her services. In Association the maternal sentiment will be satisfied in a far higher degree than in the present Order, as all the charms connected with it will exist without the care and anxiety with which it is now allied.

As to the other arrangements, such as heating, lighting, and supplying the Palace with water, the Association will adopt the most perfect unitary system which Science can discover; the progress that has been made in our large cities where water-works and gas-works are established, give some idea of the immense facilities and economies which may be introduced in this respect; in fuel, for example, the saving will be nine tenths, and in domestic labors at least three fourths.

ORGANIZATION OF LABOR IN ASSOCIATION.

The Association will prosecute all branches of Agriculture adapted to the soil of its domain, will raise flocks and herds, carry on various branches of manufactures, cultivate the principal branches of the Fine Arts and Sciences, and organize a system of domestic service and general Education. The members of the Association will engage in these various pursuits and occupations as their tastes and capacities may dictate, and as they find in them attractive and lucrative fields of action.

All branches of Industry, Art, Science, Education, and of domestic or internal Service will be prosecuted by Groups of individuals, united voluntarily from a taste for the occupation and from sympathy of character. A Group may consist of any number of persons compatible with the nature of its operations, but not less than three, as a Group to be regularly constituted must have a Centre and two Wings. These Groups, the members of which are brought together from industrial and sympathetic attraction, will undertake the prosecution on their own responsibility of the branches of Industry, Art, Science, etc. in which they are engaged, will choose their own officers or directors, lay down laws for their own regulation, and be remunerated according to the nature and value of their labors or services. Liberty and Attraction, combined with Individual Responsibility, will thus be established in every department of human activity. Admission to the Groups will be open to all the members of the Association on condition of possessing the requisite capacity and attraction; means will exist for establishing equilibrium in the number of persons engaged in the various branches of labor.

Several Groups united together, distributed in regular order with a Centre and Wings, and prosecuting different parts or details of a branch of Industry, Art, Science, etc., will constitute a SERIES. Ten Groups, for example, cultivating ten varieties of the peach or pear, and distributed in an ascending and descending order, with a Centre, Wings, and Transitions, will form the *Series of Peach or Pear Growers;* twenty groups of ladies cultivating as many varieties of the Rose, will constitute the *Rose-Series;* a dozen groups of men working in iron—blacksmiths, locksmiths, cutlers, etc.—will form the *Series of Groups of Iron-workers;* and so with all other occupations and pursuits. Each Series will consist of as many Groups as there are varieties or branches of the particular work on which it is engaged. The Groups of a Series will form at least three Divisions—a Centre and two Wings—arranged in an ascending and descending order, with Transitional Groups at the extremes, when possible; the Quince Growers, for example, would form the Transitional Groups between the Pear and the Apple Series— the quince being a transitional fruit between the two. The Centre should contain more Groups than either of the Wings, and the Ascending Wing more than the Descending Wing. This distribution will be observed in every regularly organized Series. In a Series of twelve Groups, for example, there would be four Groups in the Ascending Wing, five in the Centre, and three in the Descending Wing; a Series of seven Groups would give rise to the following division: 2–3–2,—forming a less perfect Series than the foregoing, as the Wings are equal.

The Industrial Series in Association must be organized on the general plan of the Series in Nature, and conformably to the requirements of the Serial Passions which give rise to them, so that the latter may find free play and action, and an external mechanism suited to their nature and requirements. It is only on this condition that Industry can be adapted to the Passions and rendered attractive to Man.

There will be Dissonance and Rivalry between contiguous Groups cultivating varieties or prosecuting functions which are nearly alike. The rivalized Groups will call out individuality, emulation, and management, and thus satisfy the first of the three Serial Passions. There will be Accord, Concert, and League between Groups cultivating varieties too dissimilar to give rise to close comparisons, to competition and rivalry; this will create concord, fusion, corporate enthusiasm, and thus satisfy the third Serial Passion. By means of this alternate dissonance and accord, rivalry and concert between the Groups, two of the three Serial Passions — Analysism and Synthesism — will be satisfied. To satisfy the remaining one — Alternatism — there must be alternations of occupation, changes of scenes, incidents, and associates several times during the day (except, perhaps, in a few artistic and scientific pursuits which may require long application). This alternation will be possible in Association, as there will be a minute division of labor, and as individuals brought up in this Order will be prepared by a thorough practical and scientific education to exercise several branches of Industry, Art, and Science. Every member will belong to several Series, and will be engaged consequently in several different pursuits; the alternation from Series to Series will satisfy the second of the three Serial Passions; in addition, it will connect or interlace the various Groups and Series by ties of interest and sympathy.

Thus will be produced the three effects necessary to satisfy the three Serial Passions, and at the same time to secure the harmonious working of the Series — namely, accord, dissonance, and modulation; or concert, rivalry, and alternation.

FOURIER calls the Series, in which these effects are produced, the CONTRASTED, RIVALIZED, AND INTERLACED SERIES.

We have not the space to give even an outline of the Serial Organization of Industry; we will merely remark that in every department of Nature in which unity and harmony reign, they are the result of the application of the Serial system of distribution and arrangement. If, then, we would organize Industry in accordance with Nature and the demands of the Passions, and in unity with all harmonious organizations in the Universe, we must adopt the Serial Regime. The animal and vegetable kingdoms and the elements of the Arts and Sciences are distributed in Series, as also are the Passions, the forces that impel man to Industry, Art, and Science; as a consequence, the organization of Labor — physical and intellectual — must be in Series, in order to conform to the distribution of the elements of Art and Nature, and to the play of the Passions.

As this subject would require a regular Treatise for its elucidation, it is useless to undertake to explain it in a few paragraphs.

The various branches of human activity, with few exceptions, will be prosecuted in Association, as we have said, by contrasted, rivalized, and interlaced, that is, concordant, dissonant and alternating Groups and Series. Each Group will be entirely independent in its operations, managing its affairs in the manner it deems best, and be responsible for its works.

An Industrial Council, composed of experienced members, will preside over the Industrial affairs and interests of the Association, but without possessing the right of interfering in or of directing the operations of the Series; the Council will give advice when called upon and will be the general adviser of the Association in all its industrial operations. This combination, while it will insure liberty of action and individual responsibility, will secure the wisest prosecution of all branches of Industry.

The great practical aim of Association will be TO DIGNIFY INDUSTRY AND RENDER IT HONORABLE AND ATTRACTIVE. All the means and resources which Association can command, will be directed to this end, the attainment of which is the condition of ulterior progress and improvement of every kind.

Let us consider for a moment the supreme importance of Labor, or the activity of Man directed to production and creation.

It is Labor which cultivates and embellishes the earth and renders it a fit habitation for the Race; it is Labor which builds our edifices, manufactures our clothing, produces and prepares our food, works mines, constructs and navigates vessels, builds and runs railroads, digs canals, and in short executes all great works and improvements — thus creating the means of satisfying the material wants of Man.

Labor is the source of Man's material power and grandeur — the means by which he becomes the master of the material world, and makes all Nature tributary to him.

Labor is the source of the physical health and vigor of the Race; it is also to a great extent the source of its intellectual vigor — that is, of a sound and practical development of the mind, for it is only when it works upon matter and is obliged to study its inflexible facts and phenomena and the laws that govern them, that a check is put upon vague and arbitrary speculation, and that Reason is forced to become practical and positive, and to seek for laws and principles instead of devising fanciful theories and systems.

Lastly, Labor is the means by which Man is enabled to fulfil his Industrial function or Destiny of OVERSEER OF THE GLOBE.

Such being the noble mission assigned to Labor in the economy of Society, Association will feel the importance of organizing it on a true basis, so as to render it honorable and attractive and allure all mankind to its exercise.

We will point out three of the primary means by which Industry will be rendered attractive in the Combined Order.

1. Elegance, convenience, refinement, and splendor will be connected with everything relating to Industry and its prosecution; the gardens, orchards, parks, woodlands, fields, etc. will be laid out with the greatest taste and beauty, and Art and Science will be associated in every way with agriculture; the tools and implements of all kinds will be of the most convenient and elegant description; the workshops or Halls of Industry will be elegant, spacious, salubrious, and comfortable, will be decorated in unity with the functions prosecuted in them, and be supplied with every convenience for economizing and facilitating Labor; and, lastly, the Fine Arts, especially Music, will lend their charm to enhance the attractions which will be connected with every department of Industry.

2. The industrial organization, in all its details, will be adapted to the Social nature of Man. Individuals will be drawn together in their labors from affinity of tastes and character, thus rendering the Industrial Series delightful social gatherings, the charm of which will be heightened by the elegance and beauty of the surrounding scenes, and by the idea of being engaged in noble and useful pursuits. As persons of both sexes and all ages will coöperate together, the gatherings of the Series will be occasions for the meeting of friends, lovers, colleagues, parents, and children. In the useful field of Labor, the Social Affections will thus find scope and gratification.

3. In the Industrial Groups and Series there will be, first, choice of occupations and pursuits, which will enable each individual to exercise his particular talent or capacity and to distin-

guish himself in it, and thus satisfy the strong and legitimate demand in human nature for Individuality. Second, there will be alternation from occupation to occupation, with change of associates, scene of action, etc., which will prevent monotony and satiety, and will exercise alternately all parts of the body and all the faculties of the mind ; and, third, there will be accord of tastes and concert of action with intelligent coöperators, whose interest and zeal will insure perfection in all branches and departments of Industry. These three conditions will satisfy the primary demands of the three Serial Passions, as the other conditions enumerated will satisfy the demands of the five Senses and the four Social Passions.

We may add that in the Combined Order, Industry, Art, and Science will be the great avenues to fortune and distinction, as war, commerce, and political intrigue now are. As a consequence, men will engage with energy and enthusiasm in productive labors, as a means of satisfying these universal desires of the human heart.

We may lay it down as a principle that any pursuit, function, or occupation which satisfies one or more of the Passions will become attractive to Man, and will be engaged in voluntarily and with delight. Now in Association, Industry will be so organized as to minister to and satisfy all of the twelve Passions of the Soul ; it will consequently become attractive ; it will be invested with charms far exceeding any connected with the pleasures and pursuits of existing Society. Let us show briefly how each of the Passions will be satisfied in the prosecution of Industry in Association.

Sight. — This Sense will be gratified by the beauty of the gardens, orchards, parks, woodlands, etc. ; by the elegance of the workshops or halls of Industry, by fine tools, implements and working-dresses, by the presence of animated groups of laborers, and by the general splendor of the domain and its edifices.

Taste. — This Sense will be gratified by the perfection to which all products will be carried. The Groups, consuming the choicest qualities of their own products and testing with connoisseurs of their own and neighboring associations, the effects of various kinds of cultivation upon them, will be stimulated to make improvements in agriculture of every kind. In addition light repasts will be served in the fields and gardens, in the pavilions of the Series, after their work is over; and the pleasure of these repasts, when taken amidst the scenes of Nature, will strongly attract and charm the Sense of Taste.

SMELL.—This Sense will be gratified by the fragrance of the fields and gardens, and by the pure and balmy air of a highly-cultivated region; the industrial halls will be perfectly ventilated, and being contiguous to the gardens, will share in their fragrance. If this Sense were more developed and cultivated in Man, it alone would drive him from our foul cities and attract him to live and labor amid the freshness and fragrance of Nature.

HEARING.—This sense will be gratified by the subdued melody resulting from the thousand pleasing sounds of Nature commingling with the busy hum of Industry. In addition, Music which is now an accompaniment of War and Worship, and enlivens our parties and festivities, will in Association be connected in various ways with Industry, and its inspiriting and elevating influence will lend its aid in attracting Man to useful Labor.

TOUCH.—This Sense will be gratified by the perfect adaptation of tools and implements to the strength and the tactile perception of Man, by the comfort and convenience of the working-dresses, by the pleasant temperature of the halls of Industry, by various means of protection from the heat of the sun in agricultural labors, in short, by the adaptation of all the details of Industry to the tactile wants of Man.

Thus the five Senses will be gratified and delighted by the comfort and convenience, the elegance and refinement, the art and splendor, in a word, the *Industrial Luxury* that will be connected with every department of Labor. Let us now pass to the Social Affections.

FRIENDSHIP.—This Passion will be gratified in the industrial Groups and Series, as the members will be associated in their works from affinity of industrial tastes, and from sympathy of character. Individuals will join those groups only to which they are attracted by these two incentives. To this charm of pursuing a favorite occupation with friends, add the mutual confidence, the politeness, the freedom, the tone of equality which will reign amidst an enlightened and independent population, and we can easily conceive how Friendship will be gratified to its fullest extent, and how strongly it will attract man to the industrial gatherings in which it will find its gratification.

AMBITION.—This Passion will find full scope and every opportunity of gratification in the Combined Industry of Association; organized hierarchically, with posts of honor, ranks, grades, honorary distinctions, etc., it will offer the means of preferment, distinction, fame, to every individual in some branch of Labor. In the vast industrial enterprises of the Combined Order, Man will be able to distinguish himself far more than he has done on the murderous battle-fields of the Past; the genius of a Cæsar or a Napoleon will find a far nobler field of action in reclaiming and fertilizing a desert, or a Pontine marsh, than in slaying a hundred thousand men in battle. In Association, fame and fortune will be for great Producers and not for great Destroyers; for great Inventors, great Directors of Industry—not for great warriors, financiers, and other plunderers of Labor. By these means, the whole force of Ambition will be directed to Industry, and this Passion will find in it a true and natural field of action.

LOVE.—This Passion will be gratified in the Industrial Series by the meeting and coöperation of the Sexes in all the more delicate and artistic branches of Industry, and by the presence of Woman at the execution of works of great difficulty, which, in the Combined Order, will be transformed into industrial Tournaments. Some idea of the influence which she will exercise on Industry in the Future, may be conceived from the influence which she exercised in the days of Chivalry on the military spirit. Not only will LOVE be gratified in its ordinary degrees by the free and polite intercourse of the Sexes in the productive pursuits of Association, but its charm will be immensely enhanced by the reciprocal admiration which the display of taste, talent, devotion, energy, genius, etc., will call out.

Nature designed that the Social Affections should attract Man to useful Industry; that they should fulfil an important mission connected with it and with the general welfare of mankind. Our idle, sentimental parlor-loves are of no collective use, and serve no high or noble end; as a consequence they fade away and die like sickly flowers kept in a boudoir for the idle eye to gaze upon. It is only when Love shall be associated with Industry, Art, and

Science, and its potent influence shall be brought to bear to attract Man to fulfil his Social Destiny, that it will have a significance, a use, and that it will be gratified to its fullest extent.

PARENTALISM.—This Passion will be gratified in the Industrial Series by the meeting of parents and children, of adoptors and adoptives, and of the old and young generally. The pleasures of the parental and tutelary sentiment will be greatly enhanced by witnessing the useful functions of children in Industry, their alacrity, dexterity, ready obedience, devotion, and progress. If parents, particularly mothers, are now so strongly attracted to gatherings of children where sports or amusements alone are in question, how much more strongly will they be attracted to the Industrial Series where they will see their children engaged in noble and useful employments, developing their minds and bodies, and loved and caressed by all the older associates! Let Combined Industry once attract the women and children to its pursuits, and the men will soon follow.

Thus the four Social Passions, like the five Senses, will be satisfied by the Combined Industry of Association. We will now show that the three Serial Passions will be satisfied in like manner.

ANALYSISM.—This Passion, which when operating practically in social functions, manifests itself in the form of emulation, individuality, dissonance, etc., will be gratified by the opportunity which will be offered to every individual in the Industrial Series to exercise his or her special talent or capacity; by the generous competition and emulation between rival groups and worthy opponents; and by the constant exercise of minute analysis in perfecting the details of every branch of Industry.

ALTERNATISM.—This Passion—the love of change and variety, of new scenes, incidents, etc.—will be gratified by the opportunity which the Industrial Series will offer to every individual of changing occupations several times during the day—alternating from Series to Series, from physical to intellectual labor, etc. This alternation will be possible and easily practicable, because, first, every individual will execute in the Groups to which he belongs but one detail of a work; second, because a perfect industrial education will early have initiated him into a general knowledge of Industry; and, third, because all the main branches of

Industry, Art, and Science will be prosecuted in the same Association. If Industry in the Combined Order were not so organized as to admit of change and alternation, which are the source of balance and equilibrium, but were prosecuted monotonously, from twelve to sixteen hours a day as in the present Order, this fact alone would repel Man from it, even if all the other Passions were satisfied.

SYNTHESISM.—This Passion, the branches of which are love of accord, concert, harmonic contrasts, and combinations of all kinds—of the useful with the beautiful, the material with the intellectual, the social with the industrial—will be gratified by the concert and accord of Groups that are not in rivalry, but are contrasted harmoniously; by the union of industrial elegance and social enjoyment; and by the general concord and unity which will reign in the whole system of Associated Labor.

Let Industry be so organized as to satisfy in the manner we have described the twelve Passions of the Soul, and Man will be attracted to it by the whole passional force of his nature; it will become ATTRACTIVE to him because it will be the medium by which he will attain all the ends which the Passions desire; it will be a fairy-field in which they will find their expansion and full development—and he, his HAPPINESS.

INDIVIDUAL LIBERTY AND INDEPENDENCE IN ASSOCIATION.

A prejudice exists in most minds against Association from fear that Individuality and Personal Freedom will be sacrificed, that the individual will be subjected to arbitrary rules, to a strict discipline, and that moreover he will be forced into contact with uncongenial characters.

Let us dissipate this prejudice which is a source of alarm to so many persons. We will first examine the subject from a practical point of view, and point out the guarantees of individual liberty and independence which will exist in Association; we will then consider the subject in a higher light.

The principal practical guarantees are the following:—

1. *Individual Property.*—Every member of an Association will own stock, that is property in it, according to his means, and will thus possess individual liberty so far as property can secure it; he will receive a dividend on his stock, and this with his indus-

trial earnings, will constitute his income, which he can employ as he wishes. The right of individual property will be extended to Woman, and also to the Child from the time it begins to produce. Thus the independence growing out of the possession of property will be universal, so to say, in the Combined Order, whereas at present it is only exceptional.

2. *Free choice as to the mode of living.*—Every person in Association can follow his tastes and inclinations in his manner of living; he can choose his own apartments; he can live as retiredly or as publicly as he pleases; he can dine in the magnificent banquet-halls of the Association, amid animated groups, or in private with a party of friends in dining-rooms reserved for the purpose, or he may vary from one mode to the other, changing his company daily if it is agreeable to him.

3. *Free choice of occupations.*—Every member of an Association will be at full liberty to choose those pursuits which are adapted to his tastes and talents, and to vary them as the health of the body and mind may require. A large Association will prosecute numerous branches of Industry, Art, and Science, which will open to all ages and both sexes the greatest variety of attractive and lucrative pursuits. In this respect, how much greater will individual independence be in Association than in the present Order, in which the individual is confined monotonously to a single occupation. Nothing is more blighting to both mind and body than the monotony of Civilized Industry.

4. *Guarantee to every individual of the means of an ample support and of all social pleasures and privileges.*—The collective economics of Association, the system of Attractive Industry, and the employment of machinery on a vast scale, will insure the reign of universal abundance and wealth. Every individual, with the opportunities of attractive and lucrative employment which will be opened to him, will be sure of ample means of support for the present and the future, and thus be freed from harassing cares, and from the slavery which poverty, or the fear of it, now entails.

As to uncongenial social relations, to forced association with unsuitable or disagreeable characters, we will remark that in the Combined Order, after it is fully established, there will exist, by means of its system of education — unity of habits, of manners, customs, language, etc., together with general politeness, refinement and urbanity. Amidst a population universally educated, intimate and varied social relations will be one of the greatest charms of life. People judge of the Combined Order by comparing it with Civilization, and as they dread any association with the coarse, vulgar, and uneducated rabble of the latter, they imagine that extensive and intimate social relations will be repulsive in the former.

The means we have above indicated for securing individual liberty and independence, touch only the surface of the question ; we will now point out some of the higher resources which Association will possess for securing this end, and for developing Individuality in the highest degree.

At page 110 and following, we have explained that there exists a natural Institution with its laws for regulating the development and action of each Passion of the Soul. The Passion, developed and acting in the institution corresponding to it, will receive a true, full, and harmonious development, and operate in it according to its real nature, and with perfect liberty. As there is a natural system of hierarchical organization for the regulation of the passion of Ambition, a natural system of marriage for the regulation of the passion of Love, so there will be natural Institutions for the regulation of all the Passions of the Soul ; these institutions, perfectly suited to human nature, will develop integrally, all the passions and call out the talents and capacities of every individual. It is only by this means that Individuality can be fully developed, and personal Liberty fully secured.

Individuality consists in the integral development of all the faculties and passions implanted in the human Soul. The individuality of a Raphael or a Newton, for example, is called out only so far as their genius for art or science is cultivated, and a free field of action is opened to their labors. Had they been born serfs, slaves, or poor laborers — born in a position in which their natural powers had no chance of development — their *real* individuality would have been smothered. This is the lot of ninety-nine hundredths of men in Civilization ; not even the hundredth are placed in favorable circumstances for the development of their natures — that is their Individuality.

Liberty—that is true, integral Liberty—consists in being able to exercise freely and fully all the natural powers of the Soul. For a Raphael, Liberty consists in being able to exercise his genius for Art, that is, in being able to exercise the mental powers implanted in him in a manner suited to their nature. For a Newton, Liberty consists in being able to engage in the scientific labors for which his genius fits him, and to exercise his mind in the search for truth. To state the question strictly, we may say that *Integral Liberty consists in the integral development of the powers of the Soul, and their exercise in spheres of action perfectly adapted to them.* The possession of integral Liberty is the guarantee of the development of Individuality.

No real Liberty and Individuality are possessed by the immense majority of men at present; undeveloped or falsely developed, they are forced to spend their lives amidst poverty and anxiety, in repulsive pursuits or labors which outrage their natures, smother their natural capacities, violate their tastes, and thus practically degrade and enslave them. Individuality is lost in the social quagmire in which we live.

It is only in an Order of Society in which integral development and education will be secured to every individual without exception, and in which careers or fields of action as numerous and as varied as are human capacities, will be opened to all, that true Individuality and Liberty can exist. The highest idea now entertained of the latter is that of being able to cast a vote for some political intriguer, of not being dragged to prison without a writ of *habeas corpus*, and of exercising a kind of rude individualism, of selfish independence—and this is held up in opposition to the high ideal which the Combined Order presents to the Race collectively!

THE GLOBE UNDER THE COMBINED ORDER.

WE have given, in the preceding pages, a general idea of a single Association. It is, as we have explained, a union of *individual Souls* sufficient in number to constitute *the integral or collective Soul*—or the Social Man. It embraces the various social or humanitary elements—ages, characters, capacities, talents, tastes, inclinations, etc.—which are necessary to constitute the primary germ of the Combined Order of Society; it prosecutes the various branches of Industry, Art, and Science, and establishes the various social relations which are necessary to the life of man and to the fulfilment of human destiny.

The Association or Collective Man will inhabit a Palace, the plan and distribution of which will be perfectly adapted to the complex requirements of the integral *Soul*, of which the Unitary Edifice will be the great external body. The Palace will be located in the centre of a domain artistically and scientifically cultivated, which must be of sufficient size to furnish the Collective Man with a field of operations commensurate with his industrial activity, and with the elements of Nature—earth, air, and water—necessary to his support.

If the reader can picture to himself this scene—this social, architectural, and industrial Unity—he will have an idea of the primary element or germ of the Combined Order; by contrasting it with the incoherent village which is the primary civic organization of the present Social Order, he will have an idea of the radical difference between these two Societies. To form a conception of the Globe under the reign of universal Association, he has but to multiply in imagination these single Associations, and extend them over regions and continents till they cover the whole earth. A traveller on the Globe, in the future ages of Social Harmony, will see, at every few miles' distance, sumptuous palaces of various styles of architecture rising before him, surrounded by magnificent parks and gardens, by orchards, vineyards, fields, and woodlands, interspersed with fountains, works of art, and monuments of every kind, varying the landscape, and enhancing the effect of the natural scenery.

The Cities of the Combined Order will be composed of a greater or less number of these Palaces, brought in close proximity with each other, with vast warehouses or manufactories, with universities or other public edifices in the vicinity, according as these centres are devoted to commercial, manufacturing, scientific, or other pursuits of a general or collective character.

These cities will be the centres or pivots of districts, regions, and continents; the Globe itself will have its great capital—the Pivot of Administrative Unity on the Earth. The smallest city will be composed of a group of three or four palaces; the larger cities, of series of groups of these palaces. The capitals of the Combined Order will not be of such inordinate size as those of Civilization, the population of which is out of all proportion to the legitimate functions they perform; they are now immensely overgrown, because they are the centres into which flow the wealth, the vices, and the idleness of nations. The great capital of the Globe, which, most probably, will be located on the present site of Constantinople, will not contain, according to certain data, more than three hundred thousand inhabitants. The cities will be distributed systematically over the globe at points adapted to the prosecution of collective operations, and which are the natural centres of general relations; they will form the centres of districts or regions of Associations, whose general or external affairs they will administer. The Associations on the Globe will constitute a vast Series, of which the cities will be the Pivots. We will here remark, without entering into any explanations, that, from various calculations, it is estimated the globe, when fully populated, will contain about five thousand millions of inhabitants, and that the Associations spread over it will form a measured Series of the twelfth or highest degree, and will number about three millions.

Vast lines of communication, natural and artificial, will traverse all parts of the globe; as administrative Unity will reign on the earth, the artificial lines of communication—roads, railroads, canals, etc., constructed by man—will be laid out on a methodical and unitary plan; the streams and rivers, those "moving highways" prepared for man by Nature, will be regulated in their course, deepened and diked as may be necessary, and made universally serviceable. These communications are the veins and arteries of the great Social Body. A vast network of magnetic wires, radiating from the centre or capital of the globe, communicating with the sub-capitals, and through them with every Association upon its surface, will be the medium of transmission of the collective thought of humanity. This network of telegraphic communication will be the nerves of the great Social Body.

Industrial armies—or great collective industrial organizations, of which our destructive armies present an inverted image—will execute all works of a collective character. They will open brilliant spheres of action to true devotion and heroism, to the display of genius, and the acquisition of fame, far exceeding anything which the *inverted armies of our inverted Societies* can now possibly offer to man. If we had space to dwell upon the subject, we could show that the Industrial Armies of the Combined Order could undertake and execute stupendous works of which men have heretofore formed no conception, such as reclaiming and fertilizing the desert of Sahara; lesser works, like the draining of the Pontine marshes or the Dismal swamp, or the rewooding of a denuded mountain-range, would be easy tasks in an Order which could dispose of such gigantic industrial forces. The element of combative energy which exists in human nature, instead of being directed by man against his fellow-man, as is the case in the reign of Social Subversion, will be directed in Social Harmony against an unreclaimed and unsubdued Nature.

The globe, by means of the general labors of the industrial armies and the special labors of each Association, will be brought under a system of integral and scientific cultivation. The deserts of the Tropics will be fertilized, and their excessive heat tempered; while the regions of the North, being thoroughly cultivated, and the soil opened to the warmth of the sun, the snows, ices, and extreme frosts, will no longer invade the Temperate Zone. By the system of integral cultivation, the climate of the earth will be improved to an extent of which we can now form no conception, and will be brought into its natural state of equilibrium and harmony. The atmospheric and electric systems will be improved and refined in the same way, and the natural system of winds, or the Æolian Gamut, will be established; mild and genial breezes will then replace the deranged and irregular currents—the storms, hurricanes, and tornadoes, which now sweep over the earth.

An integral System of Unities will be established upon the globe, and first in importance, after some ages of social harmony, the unity of the Human Race itself. The various imperfect and mongrel breeds which now inhabit the earth—which are but the primitive and rude elements of a perfect race, as the crab-apple and the wild rose are the rude elements of the fine apples and roses which man now possesses—will give place to a magnificent and unitary Race, resulting from the highest development by proper minglings and crossings of the varieties of the human species. Political Unity will be inaugurated on the earth, and the administrative affairs of mankind will be managed with the unity of a single State or Nation. Industrial Unity, extending to all collateral branches — to weights and measures, to the currency, to exchanges or commercial affairs — will be established, as will Unity in the Arts and Sciences, in their processes, signs, nomenclature, etc. A universal language will be spoken, and on the basis of these lesser Unities will be reared that grand superstructure of Social Unity which is to govern mankind during the great central or organic phase of its career, or the long period of Social Harmony.

We could continue the subject indefinitely, but what we have said is sufficient to give the reader an idea of the material spectacle which the globe will present in future ages of social harmony, when Man, the Overseer and Harmonist placed upon it by Divine Wisdom to fulfil the useful and noble function of cultivating and embellishing it, and of realizing upon it UNIVERSAL MATERIAL UNITY, shall direct his industrial energy and genius to the accomplishment of this great work — his industrial Destiny.

We will not speak of the moral spectacle which Humanity will present in the future ages of Harmony, as it is a subject, the description of which would lead us into too abstruse a field. We will remark merely that on the basis of material Unity which we have described, Man, possessing all the resources necessary to his physical, intellectual, and spiritual development, living under a social order perfectly adapted to the natural or legitimate action of the passions, and on a harmonized earth, which will free the Soul from all subjection and slavery to matter, will be developed in his true or divine nature, and will appear in all that spiritual beauty, that moral splendor with which the benevolent Wisdom that rules in the universe, must delight in investing its spiritual creations, — the intelligent Beings whom it places on each planet as its delegate or vicegerent, with the mission to harmonize the material worlds over which they preside, and to realize upon them the spiritual or divine Life of the Universe.

THE MARRIAGE QUESTION,

OR

THEORY OF AMATORY RELATIONS.

In the whole domain of Social Science, there is no question which is surrounded with so many difficulties as this. Although it has been so much discussed, no writer, ancient or modern, with one exception, has thrown any light upon it, and the experience of the past, which is looked upon as the great teacher, offers little or no aid in its investigation; the reason is, that the passion of Love is so smothered or perverted, so falsely developed in present society, that it furnishes no indication of its true nature, or of the character of the Institution which should govern it. In addition, the preconceived notions and prejudices which prevail on the subject, render a full and impartial statement of it extremely difficult, in fact almost impossible.

The only person who has made a systematic investigation of this important problem is FOURIER; he has laid down the fundamental principles of the true Theory of Amatory Relations, and furnished the scientific basis upon which it rests.

Taking these principles as our guide, we shall endeavor to present in the following pages an impartial and scientific statement of the question. We shall treat the subject with special reference to the writings of FOURIER, and furnish the key to his Theory, which he has but partially explained. This is very important, for the part of his works which will give rise to the greatest prejudices, is that relating to the subject of LOVE and MARRIAGE.

The system of Amatory Relations which he predicts will exist in future ages of Social Harmony, has given rise to the accusation that he advocated a system of promiscuity, license, and sensuality; this accusation is wholly false. How could a great mind,

12

aiming at the elevation of the race, at the predominance of the moral over the material principle, at the reign of Order and Harmony on earth, propose a system which would lead to exactly the opposite results?

FOURIER has not given a complete statement of his Theory of Amatory Relations. He could not have given it without entering into a full analysis of the passion of Love and its functions, and without explaining the application to it of the Law of the Series—in fact, without giving the whole Theory of Passional Harmony. To explain this Theory, including the branch of Amatory Harmony, to a world having no idea that the Passions can be harmonized, would be as difficult as to explain to Savages, having no idea that Sounds can be harmonized, the Theory of Music.

FOURIER has presented only general sketches and descriptions, without entering into a regular exposition of his system, which would have been uninteresting and unintelligible to the mass of readers.*

In the brief exposition of the Theory of Amatory Relations which we propose to give, we shall consider:—

1. The fundamental principles upon which that Theory is based;

2. The fundamental nature of the passion of Love and the relations to which it gives rise;

3. The guide to be followed in seeking for a true System of Amatory Relations.

I. FUNDAMENTAL PRINCIPLES ON WHICH A TRUE THEORY OF AMATORY RELATIONS SHOULD BE BASED.

The principle from which we start is, that God in creating the Passion of LOVE and implanting it in man, must have precalculated its mode of action, and as a consequence must have de-

---

* We would particularly remark that FOURIER has not given what he held to be the true or natural system of Love Relations in the " *Theory of the Four Movements.*" It may be thought that the descriptions contained in page 120 and following of that work were intended as an exposition of his views. This is not the case; they relate only to the mode of union of the Sexes which he states will exist in the Order of Society that is immediately to succeed Civilization, and which he calls "Guarantism." The system of Amatory Relations he describes is deduced from the principles of that Order; it differs widely from the ultimate and harmonious system that will exist in ASSOCIATION.

termined upon a system of External Relations adapted to it, which would secure its true and harmonious development.

We take the ground, then, that there exists a Mode of Union of the Sexes founded in Nature, or, if we may use the expression, a *Natural or Divine System of Marriage.* The function of human reason is to discover that System, and not to invent and set up arbitrary laws and institutions of its own. This was the principle upon which FOURIER proceeded; he gave no Theory of his own devising, but sought to discover the Natural or Divine Theory.

In corroboration of the idea that God, in creating the passion of Love, must have determined upon the external conditions adapted to its action and development, let us ask:—if God has adapted the atmosphere to the lungs, the flavor of fruits and vegetables to the palate, colors to the eye, perfumes to the sense of smell, etc., is it not probable that he has followed the same course in respect to the Social Passions, and planned Institutions adapted to their nature and requirements ?

In seeking for the natural system of Amatory Relations, we should pursue the method which would be followed by a wise physiologist in seeking for a natural system of food; he would not, it may be presumed, propose an arbitrary system of his own, based on preconceived ideas of a proper combination of chemical substances, but would consult the attractions of the palate and the requirements of the stomach, and deduce a system from the indications they furnish; in like manner, we must consult the passion of Love, and deduce from it the system of external relations adapted to it.

In taking the passion of Love as our guide, we must consult:—

1. Its Attractions, or the tendencies and requirements of the Passion ;

2. The Law of the Series or Law of Universal Harmony, which regulates its action as it does all branches of life and movement.

We must study the Attractions of the Passion to determine the nature of the relations which should exist between the Sexes.

We must study the Law of the Series to ascertain the true

mode of action of the Passion, and the nature of the Institution which should govern it.

Attractions are proportional to Destinies. The Collective Attractions of the Race reveal, in their true and natural development, the Social Destiny of Man on earth and the Order of Society predestined for him.

Each special Attraction in turn reveals its own special function or destiny, and the external forms, conditions, and the Institution adapted to it. The saporous attraction or Sense of Taste, for example, reveals the nature of the food on which man is to live; the other senses—Hearing, Sight, Smell, and Touch—reveal the external conditions which should be established to secure their development and gratification.

In like manner, the passion of Love reveals the nature of the Institution which is destined for it, and which should regulate the Relations of the Sexes.

The first guide, then, which should be consulted in seeking for the true Mode of Union of the Sexes, is the Amatory Attraction in man—that is, the tendencies and requirements of the Passion of Love.

The second guide to be consulted is the Law of the Series or the Supreme Law of Harmony, which is applicable to the Passions as to all the other departments of creation.

The Series is Nature's universal mode of distribution and classification. The animal, vegetable, and mineral kingdoms are distributed in Series; the same order reigns in the moral or passional world; it is the plan of Divine Arrangement throughout the universe, and it is only by comprehending this arrangement, that human reason can see through the apparently confused and complicated facts and phenomena of Nature, and discover the general order that exists in her domain.

The Series lies also at the basis of all organization; the human body, for example, is a Series of organs and functions, and to understand its mechanism, we must understand the Serial Order that exists in it.

The Series again lies at the basis of all the material Harmonies which man has discovered or created; the existence of these Harmonies depends on the Serial distribution and arrangement of the elements or principles of which they are composed.

The stellar Harmonics are the result of a Serial distribution and arrangement of planets; musical Harmony is the result of a Serial combination and arrangement of sounds; Painting, Sculpture, and Architecture,—so far as these arts are perfected—result from a Serial arrangement of forms and colors; the human Skeleton, which is susceptible of so many harmonious movements, is, if we may use the expression, an osseous Harmony, formed by a Serial distribution of the bones which constitute it.

Harmony can exist in no branch or department of Creation, moral or material, except by a Serial arrangement of its constituent elements and principles. It follows, then, that man can create Harmony in the spheres over which he presides only by discovering and applying to them the Law of the Series.

Reasoning from analogy and unity of system, the law of Serial distribution and arrangement applies to the Social Affections,—Friendship, Love, Ambition, and Parentalism,—as it does to the departments above mentioned.

Each of these Affections or Passions is a Unity or Whole, composed of a certain number of elements; these elements are the different shades or varieties of the Passion; combined and arranged in Serial order, or according to the Law of the Series, they produce PASSIONAL HARMONY in their respective spheres.

The passion of Friendship, for example, is a Unity or Whole divided into shades or varieties of friendship; these regularly classified, extending from affection for a single individual up through various degrees to universal philanthropy or sympathy for the whole race, constitute the scale or gamut of Friendship, analogous to the scale of sounds, called the musical gamut.

Ambition, in like manner, is divisible into different kinds or varieties of aspiration, extending from the desire of personal elevation up through various degrees to the desire of the elevation of the whole human race; these varieties of the Passion, distributed in their natural order and succession, constitute the scale or gamut of Ambition.

The constituent elements of these Passions, combined and arranged according to the Serial Law, will produce two orders of Harmony in the social relations of mankind:— Ambition, Hierarchical and Corporative Harmony; Friendship, Amical Harmony, tending to the unity and solidarity of the race.

Let us remark that the distribution in scales or gamuts of the constituent parts or elements of any Unity or Whole, is the preliminary operation necessary to the creation of Harmony. It is only by such a distribution that we can perceive the relations of these elements,—the accords and dissonances or attractions and repulsions, etc.— to which they give rise. It is not until we have integrally analyzed any Unity or Whole, divided it into its constituent parts, and distributed them in regular order, that we possess the elements on which to operate to create harmony.

We now come to the point to which we wished to arrive, namely, that the passion of Love, like the sense of Sight and Hearing, like Friendship and Ambition, and in fact all the Passions, is not a *simple* but a *compound* Unity, and is divisible or distinguishable into a certain number of shades or varieties of Love; these shades or varieties, distributed in their regular order and succession, form the Scale or Gamut of the Passion, and give rise to a series of types of Amatory Character.

That there are different shades of Love, each giving rise to a distinct Character, is too evident to require demonstration. Do we not find the Prudish love and the Voluptuous, the Constant and the Coquettish, the Sentimental and the Ambitious, the Romantic and the Calculating, etc. ? We mention these varieties of Love, using terms in common use, merely to give a general idea of our meaning.

Let us suppose that the passion of Love were fully and harmoniously developed, so that we could distinguish all its shades or varieties — that is to say, all the different modes of Amatory Affection or Sympathy — and distribute them in a Scale or Gamut, we should then possess the means necessary to the realization of Harmony in the sphere of Love, as the musician with the scale of Sounds, has the means necessary to the creation of musical Harmony.

The view we take of the subject, then, is this:— The Passion of Love is a compound Unity or Whole, divisible into a certain number of shades or varieties of amatory sympathy. In this respect, it resembles all the other Unities in the universe. The human Soul, for example, is a Unity divisible into a certain number of passions, which are the constituent parts or elements of that Unity. The body is a Unity which, viewed internally, is divisible into a certain number of organs, and externally, into a certain number of members; color is a Unity divisible into a certain number of tints, and the sense of Sight, which perceives colors, is a Unity divisible into a certain number of chromatic perceptions; and so with sound and the sense of Hearing, and in fact with every other independent Unity or Whole in the universe.

Each variety of Love gives rise, as we have said, to a distinct Type of amatory Character; persons in whom that variety of love called the Coquettish is predominant, take the Coquettish character; those in whom Ambitious love rules, the Ambitious; and so on.

The different varieties or kinds of Love, distributed and classified in their natural order and succession, form the elements of a *Passional Series* which may be called the Amatory or Love Series. This Series is composed of groups; the groups, are composed of a certain number of persons possessing the same type of amatory character.*

---

* A few words of additional explanation in relation to the term SERIES. Considered in a restricted sense, a Series is a Chain, File, or Row of objects or attributes, classified and arranged in a certain regular, consecutive, and graduated order. A succession of sounds or of colors, a succession of the varieties of a species, of the species of a genus, provided they are distributed and classified in their natural order, is a Series. A jumble of different sounds does not form a Series, but the seven radical sounds, called in music the diatonic notes, distributed in a regular and graduated order, in their natural succession, do form a Series; that consecutive order as shown by the musical gamut, is Do, Re, Mi, Fa, Sol, La, Si, returning to and beginning anew with Do, an octave above. A jumble of colors does not form a Series, but the seven principal colors, distributed in the order shown by the prism, which divides the white ray of the sun — White being the Unity of color — into its constituent or component colors, do form a Series. The order of prismatic distribution of the colors is as follows:— *Violet, Indigo, Blue, Green, Yellow, Orange, Red.* In these two Series, the different sounds and colors follow each other in a specific order, in a regularly graduated succession; each has it place and bears a certain fixed relation to all the other elements in the Series. The distribution and arrangement of the elements may vary, and the Series still be perfect, provided the order of succession and classification be regular and based on a principle of unity; Sounds, for example, may be distributed in what is called Thirds, as *Do, Mi, Sol, Si, Re, Fa, La,* and the Series be perfect.

A regular classification of the elements of a Series shows the relation of each element to the others; in the Series of Sounds, it shows that *Do* is in dissonance with *Re,* and in semi-dissonance with *Si,* while it is in accord with *Mi, Fa, Sol, La,* though in slightly different degrees.

We will remark, here, that all the Passions, with the exception of Hearing, are at present so undeveloped or perverted, that it is impossible to distinguish the natural shades or varieties of which they are composed and to distribute them in Scales or Series; and even could this be done, it would be impossible in the existing Social Order to combine their elements so as to produce Harmony; the material arrangements of Civilization— that is, its incoherent system of Industry, its isolated households, etc. — are wholly unsuited to the play of the Passions and their harmonious action. It is only in a large Association, with a proper organization of its industrial, domestic, educational and other arrangements, that the Passional Series can be formed and Passional Harmony realized.

The division of the passion of Love into its shades or varieties of amatory sympathy, and their distribution in a Series, constitute the first work to be done in determining the theory of Amatory Harmony, and the true Order that is to exist in the relations of the Sexes.

These shades, or varieties as we said, give rise to a Series of

A Series then is a regular and systematic classification of the different elements or parts of any Whole, exhibiting the natural order and relations existing in and between those elements. Familiarly speaking, a Series is a Chain or Row of objects or attributes of the same nature, each occupying a given place and position in the Chain, and thus establishing the principle of Classification. Webster defines a Series, as "a continued succession of things in the same order, and bearing the same relation to "each other; in arithmetic and algebra, for example, a number of terms in succes- "sion, increasing or diminishing according to a certain law."

The first condition necessary to the discovery or creation of Order or Harmony in any department of Nature or in any branch of Art or Science, is the determination of the Serial Arrangement which reigns in it. The Naturalist, for example, can understand nothing of the order that reigns in the Kingdoms of Nature till he has regularly analyzed them and discovered the Serial distribution that exists in them; the musical Composer cannot create musical Harmony till he has analyzed sounds, and obtained a knowledge of the musical gamut or Series of Sounds. In like manner, it is impossible to establish harmony in the Passional Relations of human beings, until the Passions which give rise to them are analyzed or separated into their constituent shades or varieties, and these classified and distributed in Scales or Series. This is true of Love as it is of Friendship, of Ambition, and the other Passions of the Soul.

Considered in a more general and complex sense, the Series embraces all the effects, results, and relations, which grow out of the natural classification and distribution above described, and the Order and Harmony that reign in any department of the Universe in which the Serial arrangement exists. In this sense, the Serial Law is equivalent to the Law of universal Order and Harmony.

Characters; each distinct Character should be governed by laws and statutes corresponding and adapted to it; those suited to one type or variety of character would be found unsuited to another. The Coquettish or Ambitious love, for example, cannot be governed by the same rules and regulations as the Prudish or the Voluptuous love: if the same regulations be applied to all the different Characters, the inevitable result is that most of them are thwarted or perverted; this gives rise to deceit, hypocrisy, antipathy, disgust, hatred, etc.—effects which we everywhere behold in the conjugal relations of Civilization.

Individuals of the same type of Amatory Character would form a distinct Group or Corporation; hence there would be as many Groups or Corporations as there are distinct Characters; these Groups, regularly distributed and classified, would form the Scale or Series of Love Corporations; each Corporation would be governed in its relations and functions by a distinct Institution—that is, by a system of rules and regulations adapted to it. Thus there would be *a Series of Corporations, and a Series of Institutions regulating their relations.**

The Institution is the external form, the outward mechanism; the Passion, the internal force, the animating principle: the former should be adapted to the latter, as the body is adapted to the soul, as the musical instrument is adapted to the ear, as the steam-engine is adapted to the expansive power of steam. It is only on condition of the *perfect adaptation of the Institution to the Passion*, that the latter can act naturally and receive a harmonious development. If the Institution *is not adapted to the Passion*, the Passion is thwarted in its development, and forced into false and unnatural modes of action, giving rise to innumerable varieties of Passional Discord, examples of which we see everywhere in the relations of the Sexes.

The laws which are applicable to one variety of Love, or one kind of amatory Character, are not applicable, as we have stated, to the others. As a consequence, there must be as many Institutions—that is, as many sets of laws and regulations—as there are fundamental types of amatory Character. Let us suppose, for example, that the passion of Love, divided into its different

* Webster defines an Institution as embracing " the laws, rites, and ceremonies " which are enjoined by authority as permanent rules of conduct or government."

shades or varieties, gives rise to seven radically distinct types of Character; in this case, there should be seven Institutions or sets of rules and regulations for their government. Unity of system and certain general principles would exist in these Institutions, but they would vary in the details of their rules, regulations, rites, privileges, ceremonies, and obligations, according to the type of character, or the mode of action of the variety of the Passion they were to govern and regulate.

Thus, we repeat, there would be *a series of Amatory Groups or Corporations, each representing a type of amatory Character, and a series of Institutions corresponding to them, for their regulation and government.* These Institutions would lead to the full, free, natural, and harmonious development of Love in all its shades or varieties, and secure the reign of truthfulness, justice, frankness, courtesy, devotion, in a word, Order and Harmony in the love-relations of mankind.

The Series of Amatory Institutions, taken as a whole, would constitute ONE INSTITUTION — the integral Institution of Marriage- or the complete and natural System for the regulation of the relations of the Sexes.

In Civilization, there is but one Institution or one mode for the union of the Sexes, namely, Monogamic Marriage, or the exclusive and permanent union of a single couple for life; this union, enforced by law, is maintained irrespective of Love between the couple, or of their physical adaptation for the procreation of offspring.

The Monogamic Institution is adapted to that type of Amatory Character called the Constant or Faithful; it is not adapted to all the Characters, though more so to some than to others. The Ambitious Love, for example, which seeks for rank, fortune, and position in marriage, adapts itself better to the monogamic relation than a character less influenced by reflection and calculation, and which is further removed from the type of Constancy.

Monogamic Marriage supposes that the passion of Love is uniform or *mono-modal* in its action and development, that there are no shades or varieties in the Passion, and that the whole human race feel the amatory attraction in one mode and in the same manner; this is as great an error as to suppose that all persons have the same taste in the matter of food. The standard

of morality set up by the Monogamic Institution, leads to the condemnation, as immoral or vicious, of all the varieties of Love
except the Constant. Persons in whom the other types of amatory
attraction or affection predominate, are compelled to violate, secretly or openly, that standard. They are consequently denounced
as immoral or condemned as criminal; this gives rise, in the relations of the sexes, to deceit, hypocrisy, duplicity, and perfidy,
to wrong, outrage, and innumerable vices and crimes, resulting in
a vast chaos of passional Discord and Confusion.

In seeking to force all Characters to adapt themselves to one
standard, to one code of morality in the sphere of Love, this Passion is either:—

1st. Repressed and smothered in its development, in which case
it dies out in the soul, leaving it without the elevating and idealizing influence of this noble motor; or—

2d. Thwarted and violated in its action, in which case it rebels
against the Laws and Institutions set up for its regulation, and
engenders a series of subversive effects, to some of which we have
just alluded.

To determine whether the system of Monogamic Marriage is
the true and natural mode of union for the Sexes, we have but to
decide the following questions :—

Has God, in creating the passion of Love, assigned to it but
one form or mode of action—that is, created it mono-modal in
its development? In this case, Monogamic Marriage is the true
Institution.

Or, has he created the Passion with different modes of action
and development, that is, different modes of sympathy and affection? In this case, the Monogamic Institution is incomplete, and
adapted to only one variety of the Passion, or one type of Character.

We have now stated the problem, and furnished the data for
solving it. The passion of Love, created by God with specific
modes of action, necessarily reveals in its tendencies and requirements—that is to say, in its Attractions—the nature of the
Institution adapted to it.

It is the Passion, then, which should be studied and consulted;
it is in its demands, dictates, and behests that we are to seek for

the solution of the intricate question of the true **Theory of Amatory Relations.**

In closing this part of the subject, we will add the following extract from FOURIER'S manuscripts; though somewhat technical, it states the principles we have endeavored to explain, concisely and clearly.

" A PASSIONAL SERIES is an affiliated society or union of per-
" sons, composed of several Groups; these Groups represent the
" different shades of a Passion, and are to the Series what the spe-
" cies are to the genus; each Group exercises one of the shades
" or varieties of the generic Passion — or Passion which gives rise
" to the Series — but not all of them. Thus a Group of women
" of the constant type, and another of the inconstant, feel two
" kinds or varieties of Love of an opposite nature, but which be-
" long to or are branches of the same Passion.

" Each Group must be composed of individuals feeling an en-
" thusiasm for some one branch of the generic passion, and in-
" clined at the same time to disparage and look down upon the
" other branches. Suppose an Amatory Series to be composed
" of five groups: — the modest, the gallant, the voluptuous, the
" coquettish, and the prudish. (By the latter I mean women in
" whom age has produced a certain calm and reserve in the
" passion.) The varieties of the passion which give rise to
" these groups, are all branches of the same trunk, and, as incom-
" patible as they may appear, they concur equally in producing
" harmony, when the individuals who experience them are clas-
" sified and grouped according to the shades of their affection,
" and when the Series secures to the latter their regular action
" and development.

" The operation of a Passional Series is analogous to that of
" a geometrical series; the product of the extremes is equal to
" the square of the mean term. The two extreme groups agree
" together, and form a league against the central group; the lat-
" ter, from rivalry, seeks to surpass the others in devotion and
" generosity. In the Amatory Series of which I have just spoken,
" it is evident that the modest and the prudes, who form the two
" extreme ages and represent the initiatory and the declining
" phases of love, have sentiments which are similar and com·

" patible, though different, and that the voluptuous are the most
" opposed to these groups : but if some affair of interest should
" involve the honor of all the groups of the Series, the voluptu-
" ous would have the pride not to yield in disinterestedness
" and courtesy to the league of the modest and the prudish. It
" is understood that this generous rivalry takes place only in
" relation to matters out of the sphere of the generic passion, or
" the passion which gives rise to the Series. The varieties of
" Love tend to excite discord between the different Characters, and
" to form them into heterogeneous and incompatible groups ; and
" this very discord becomes the principle of their generous emu-
" lation in everything out of the sphere of the generic passion.
" The rivalry which exists between the groups stimulates each
" of them to signalize itself by noble acts, to enhance the *éclat*
" and palliate the eccentricities of its favorite shade of the
" passion.

" The power or influence of the central group is as it were
" redoubled, multiplied by itself, because it is the centre of op-
" position for the two extreme groups, which are in accord
" with each other. The result is an equilibrium which regulates
" the general opinion of the Series in any affair under consider-
" ation ; and all the intermediate groups between the central one
" and the extremes, present increasing and decreasing diversities
" of opinion.

" Thus we see, that in the Harmonic Order all men are not
" brothers and friends. To abolish differences of opinion, con-
" trasts of character, or antipathies even, would be to destroy
" the spice of life. But it must be observed that in the play of
" the Series, these passional dissonances operate between group
" and group, and not between individual and individual. It mat-
" ters little that the various groups are in discord, provided there
" exist ties of sympathy between the individuals composing them,
" out of the sphere of the generic passion.

" The more a Series is subject to internal dissonance, based
" on difference of tastes and opinions, the more prodigies it works
" for external concord. The concurrence of these two opposite
" influences is only a repetition of what takes place in material
" harmony, where we always find equilibrium established by the
" action of two forces, one of which is the inverse of the other.

" Thus in the planetary movements we find the centrifugal and
" the centripetal action.

" When the four Cardinal Passions, which lead to the forma-
" tion of social ties, can act freely in a social Order in which
" reign great abundance and entire unconcern for the morrow,
" and in which neither coercion nor prejudice exist, the human
" race tends to form Series of Groups in all the play of the Pas-
" sions, and to always separate and classify the different shades
" or varieties of a passion, each of which gives rise to a group
" of the series.

" We find the germ of the Series in the inclination which is
" common to every man to praise up his particular shade or vari-
" ety of taste and believe it preferable to similar tastes, while he
" pays no attention to those which are wholly different and there-
" fore admit of no comparison. Take for example several classes
" of men whose peculiar tastes are widely different, such as
" painters and poets, architects and musicians ; you will find the
" painter indifferent to the pursuit of the poet, and the architect
" to that of the musician, but it will not be the same with the
" painters or poets among themselves. Each will boast the su-
" periority of his favorite branch of art, and this will give rise
" to a classification of the parties into various groups, each group
" sustaining the superiority of its own favorite taste.

" A party of fifty painters may be formed into seven or eight
" groups of as many different tastes ; there would then exist
" among them the germ of a Series. This germ cannot exist
" among fifty individuals whose tastes are uniform. Fifty paint-
" ers of one taste, say for the Flemish school, would form a
" Group of painters, not a Series of painters ; but if among the
" fifty, eight were for the Flemish School, ten for the Roman
" school, fifteen for the Venitian school, they would then form a
" Series of painters.

" Now, supposing God designed to form the human race in
" Series in order to organize Harmony, we can then understand
" why he has given to human beings so great a diversity of tastes,
" and so much persistency in defending and extolling their favor-
" ite opinions ; for without divergent and rival tastes the Series
" could not be formed.

" We see, then, how absurd are the lamentations of the moral-

" ists who, not having discovered that man was destined for the
" Series, complain that we are not all in accord, all of one mind,
" all brothers and friends, eating black broth out of the same
" dish like the Spartans.

" An orchestra or choir furnishes an image or emblem of the
" Series. If all voices were of the same kind, if all musicians
" studied but one instrument, how could it be possible to form
" orchestras or choirs, which are nothing but assemblages or as-
" sociations of various affiliated groups, exercising the different
" branches of the same species of art? It is particularly in the
" Opera that God interprets to us his designs, by exhibiting to
" us Harmony produced by Series of Groups, and not by individ-
" uals acting incoherently, each according to his own fancy. The
" present Social Order may be compared to an Opera where the
" choristers and musicians should strive to see who could sing or
" play the most out of tune, thus producing a frightful discord,
" analogous to that of Civilization, in which every one acts indi-
" vidually, and without Serial Order in the play of the Passions.

" It will be said, with reason, that men are right in declaiming
" against diversities of taste and opinion, even admitting that they
" would produce emulation and concord in the Series, since in
" the present Social Order they produce frightful discord. This
" God himself could not prevent. He cannot have destined man
" to isolated and individual action; and if he has adapted har-
" mony to the collective action of the passions, it is in the order
" of things that individual action, out of the Groups and Se-
" ries, should cause universal discord."

The above extract from FOURIER gives a clew to the method
which he followed in studying abstract questions relating to the
passions. The standard or criterion he adopted in making researches in the new and unexplored field of Passional Harmony,
was the Serial Order which he found reigning throughout the
universe. Whether this standard is the true one or not, we leave
to reflecting minds to decide for themselves; we think it is.
There is at any rate great need of some standard, for on questions
of a moral or passional nature, men have no fixed principles, no
positive guide, no criterion of certainty to consult. They have
to refer to some imaginary authority, human or divine, or to

forge individual theories of their own. The Anglican Church with its synod of grave bishops, in undertaking to decide whether a man might marry his deceased wife's sister, had to refer to the eighteenth chapter of Leviticus, and then take an imperfect translation to get at its meaning. Other bodies of men, religious or secular, in order to settle similar questions in relation to the sexes, have to refer to St. Paul, or some one of the evangelists, and quote obscure sayings upon which scarcely any two of them agree. The men of positive science have not at all occupied themselves with questions of a passional or immaterial nature. Their achievements in the material sciences throw no light upon the moral sciences. In this sphere all is doubt, uncertainty and contradiction. If the Serial Order which reigns throughout the universe is not the standard or criterion of certainty in this domain, then we must wait with patience for future generations to discover and reveal it.

II. FUNDAMENTAL NATURE OF THE PASSION OF LOVE, AND OF THE RELATIONS TO WHICH IT GIVES RISE.

THE fundamental view which we take of the Human Passions, is that they are Forces or Motors, susceptible of being harmoniously developed, and of creating or evolving Harmony in the spheres in which they act, and that they were implanted in man to impel him to fulfil his Destiny, which is the realization of Universal Unity on earth :—

1. Unity with Nature or the Material World around him ;
2. Unity with his Race ;
3. Unity with the Universe and its principles of Order and Harmony.

If the Passions do not now create or realize Harmony, it is because the Theory of Passional Harmony, the law of their development, not having been discovered, nor true Social Institutions devised and established, they are obliged to act in a Social Mechanism which is not adapted to them, and which in every way thwarts and perverts their nature and prevents their harmonious play and action.

There is one Passion, however, which has been harmoniously

developed. It is the Sense of Hearing. The law which regulates its action, together with the theory of Sounds, having been discovered, and the instruments necessary to its exercise perfected, it has created or evolved the Harmony which corresponds to it, namely, the Musical.

It would seem as if Nature had designed that this Passion should receive a harmonious development during the period of Social Subversion, in order to furnish man with a guide by which to study the nature of the other Passions, and to lead him to conceive the possibility of their harmonious development, and of establishing Harmony in the various spheres which they govern.

Now, reasoning from analogy and unity of system, proceeding from the known to the unknown, let us ask :—

1. If one of the Senses has been harmoniously developed and has evolved or produced its corresponding Harmony, is it not probable that the other Senses also may be harmoniously developed and create Harmonies in their respective spheres; Sight, for example, in forms and colors; Taste, in flavors; Smell, in odors, etc. ?

2. If the five Sensuous Passions are susceptible of a harmonious development, and can harmonize the material elements — sounds, colors, odors, etc. — on which they operate, is it not probable that the four Social Passions, which are Motors of a superior order and so much more important in the Social Mechanism, are, in like manner, susceptible of a harmonious development, and of creating Harmonies in the spheres which they govern, namely, the Social Relations of Mankind ?

The problem thus stated appears to us to furnish its own solution. Following one of the fundamental laws of the Universe — Unity of System — it seems certain that if the Senses can produce Harmony in the material sphere, the Social Affections can produce Harmony in the moral sphere — that is, in the Social Relations of human beings. These relations are the elements of a vast system of Social Harmony, as sounds, forms, colors, odors, etc. are the elements of a vast system of Material Harmony.

Let us apply the general principles here laid down to the passion of Love; it is in this way that we can best demonstrate the important truth that this Passion can evolve Harmony in its

13

sphere and establish a perfect system of Order and Unity in the
Sexual or Amatory Relations of the race.

The action of the Passion of Love in evolving or creating
Amatory Harmony, is exactly analogous to the action of the
Sense of Hearing in creating Musical Harmony ; the two Passions operate in their respective spheres on the same unitary
principles and according to the same laws. The best means,
therefore, of arriving at a knowledge of the nature of the Passion
of Love, its true mode of action, and the conditions of its harmonious development, is to study the Sense of Hearing and take
it as our guide.

As Love is at present either imperfectly or falsely developed,
it is almost impossible to make a perfect analysis of it, and to
determine its true nature and the mode of development assigned
to it ; it is consequently indispensable to consult some Passion
or Faculty which has already been harmoniously developed, and
the true nature and mode of action of which are understood.
The only Faculty which fulfils these conditions, we repeat, is the
Sense of Hearing. Taking this Sense or Passion, then, as our
guide, and explaining the passion of Love by it, we may reason
as follows :—

The Sense of Hearing, considered as a Unity or Whole, is *one*
Perception or Sensation ; divided into its constituent elements,
it is composed of a series of Perceptions, and perceives the Scale
or Series of Sounds, comprising the radical vibrations of the atmosphere, and their effects or relations, such as accord, dissonance, measure, rhythm, etc. When the Sense is fully developed and properly cultivated, it distributes, combines, and classifies Sounds so as to produce Musical Harmony — that is to say,
a series of effects called intonation, accord, dissonance, time,
measure, modulation, rhythm, etc., which are the elements of
that Harmony.

In like manner, the Passion of Love, considered as a Unity or
Whole, is *one* Affection ; divided into its constituent elements,
it gives rise to a certain number of modes of sympathy between
the Sexes, from which spring all ties and relations of an amatory character. When the Passion is fully and harmoniously
developed, and can act freely and naturally, it distributes, combines, and coördinates those relations, operating on them as the

Sense of Hearing operates on Sounds, and produces a Harmony in its sphere analogous to the Musical; it calls out between the Sexes, politeness, devotion, reverence, courtesy, chivalry, ideality, and other effects that enter into the system of Amatory Harmony.

In the present Social Order, the Passion of Love is as undeveloped or as rudely developed as the Sense of Hearing among Barbarians and Savages, and engenders among us as much discord in the Relations of the Sexes as does that Sense among them in the Sphere of Sounds.

The discordant and subversive effects to which Love gives rise in present Society, may be classified under three general heads: 1st. *Moral Evils*, such as duplicity, hypocrisy, perfidy, suspicion, distrust, envy, jealousy, hatred, revenge, despair, insanity, etc.; 2d. *Vices*, such as prostitution and various sensual excesses which cannot well be mentioned; 3d. *Crimes*, such as seduction, rape, infanticide, suicide, murder, etc. To these subversive effects might be added a formidable catalogue of diseases which complete the circle of evils, and proclaim in a terrible manner the subversive development and action of the Passion in Civilization.

If, on the one hand, the Sense of Hearing when undeveloped or rudely developed, produces discordant combinations of Sounds, such as the horrible din of Savage tam-tams and war-songs, and, on the other hand, when harmoniously developed, the sublime Harmonies of a Mozart and a Beethoven, may we not infer from analogy and unity of system, that the Passion of Love is also subject to this dual action, and that if it produces in its present stage of development so much Discord and Disorder, it will, when truly and fully developed, produce an equal degree of Order and Harmony?

The position of FOURIER, in conceiving the possibility of harmonizing the Passion of Love and the relations to which it gives rise, may be compared to that of a great musical genius who, born among Savages and hearing their wild and discordant music, should conceive the possibility of a harmonious development of the Sense of Hearing, and by patient study and profound analysis, should discover the real nature and functions of that Sense, and evolve the Art and Science of Music.

In the preceding pages, we have spoken only of a true and harmonious development of the Passion of Love as the condition necessary to the realization of Harmony in the Relations of the Sexes; not wishing to complicate the subject, we have omitted mentioning certain conditions of a material or external character, which are also necessary to the attainment of this end.

The Sense of Hearing may be harmoniously developed and cultivated in the soul of the musician, and may be capable of directing him rightly in the creation of Musical Harmony, but unless he possesses certain external and material conditions — such as proper instruments, suitable halls, etc. — he cannot produce that Harmony. The same necessity exists in relation to the Passion of Love; certain external or material conditions must first be established before the reign of Harmony can be realized in the Amatory Relations of the Sexes.

The following are some of these conditions; they relate chiefly to the Industrial and Domestic independence of Woman, and her emancipation from pecuniary dependence on Man :—

1. A System of Refined and Attractive Industry, adapted to the nature of Woman.

2. Domestic Association or Combined Households, including
> Combined Kitchens,
> Combined Nurseries,
> Independent Suites of Apartments.

3. Institutions for the collective Care and Education of Children.

4. Reign of general Wealth, Intelligence, and Refinement in Society.

5. A Unitary standard of Morality.

A System of Refined and Attractive Industry, in which woman can engage without sacrificing the delicacy of her sex, is the only means of securing to her: 1st. Pecuniary Independence, which is the real basis of personal liberty; 2d. Health and Vigor, which are essential to a true and natural development of the Passions of the Soul.

The Combined Household, with its associated or collective domestic arrangements, will free woman from the petty domestic cares and drudgery to which she is now subjected, enable her to take part in the honorable and lucrative pursuits of Art, Science, and Industry, to achieve an independent position in society, and to follow the promptings of her nature.

The Institutions for the collective care and education of children, together with the Combined Nursery, will free woman from the enslaving care of children, and from the necessity of contracting or continuing the most incongruous unions, which often cause the misery of a whole life.

The reign of general wealth, intelligence, and refinement in society, is necessary to the existence of urbanity and confidence in social intercourse, and to freedom in social relations. True relations, especially between the Sexes, cannot be established except on condition that politeness, courtesy, self-respect, and sentiments of dignity and honor — which are impossible without general wealth, refinement, and intelligence — universally prevail.

A uniform or unitary Standard of Morality, based on a true knowledge of Human Nature and a true theory of the Passions, and accepted by all, must exist in society, in order to produce unity of opinion on all moral questions, and to lead persons of different types of Character to be tolerant to each other, and to accept the Passions as God created them.

The above conditions can be realized only in Association. It would be impossible, therefore, to establish a true system of Amatory Relations in the present Social Order, even if that system were generally known, and men desired to realize it.

Monogamic Marriage, or the exclusive and permanent union of a single couple for life, enforced by law, is the only system adapted to Civilization with its isolated households, kitchens, and nurseries, its separate interests, and the entire dependence of the woman and the child upon man. To organize true relations between the Sexes, we must first effect important changes in the material arrangements of society; we must reform our incoherent system of Industry and our Isolated Households, and establish a new industrial and domestic Order in their place.

The Social Mechanism is the external Organization in which the Passions have to act, and it is in vain to hope for their true, legitimate, and harmonious action in a Mechanism or Order which is unsuited to them, and which thwarts at every step and in every way their natural play and development.

III. GUIDE TO BE FOLLOWED IN SEEKING FOR THE TRUE SYSTEM OF AMATORY RELATIONS.

In seeking to discover true Social Institutions for the regulation of the action and development of the Passions, the primary object to be kept in view is not their individual gratification — nor the individual happiness of man which results from that gratification — but the *performance of the Functions and the attainment of the Ends assigned to them by Supreme Wisdom.* Individual happiness would follow as a result, for Supreme Wisdom always connects the individual with the collective good — makes the pleasure and the enjoyment of man dependent on the accomplishment of his Mission and Destiny on earth.

Let us glance briefly at the primary functions assigned by God to each of the three classes of Motors he has implanted in man, and point out the guide to be followed in determining the organization of the natural Institutions adapted to them.

The five Senses — the 1st class of Motors — were given to man to attract him to fulfil his Industrial Function or Destiny, that of Overseer of the Globe; they impel him to cultivate and embellish its surface, to develop its material resources, to supervise its animal and vegetable kingdoms, and to realize upon it the reign of material Unity and Harmony; they excite in him the love of Nature, associate him with her, and establish the tie between the moral and the material world. They were not given him merely to procure his sensuous or material enjoyment — Taste, for example, to procure him the pleasures of the table, and the other Senses material pleasures in their spheres — but to attract him to and guide him in the fulfilment of the above function of Terrestrial Overseer.

The four Social Passions — the 2d Class of Motors — were implanted in man to attract him to his Race, to induce him to form social ties and relations of all kinds with his fellow-creatures, and thus to lead to Association and the Social Unity of Mankind; they were not given to him merely to secure the individual enjoyment of social pleasures and social intercourse; their function is to unite and associate the individuals of the race, making Humanity ONE, so that through universal coöperation and concert of action, it may be able to fulfil the great and important work assigned to it on earth.

The three Intellectual Faculties—the 3d class of Motors—were given to man to attract him to discover the laws of Harmony by which the Universe is governed, and to apply them to the organization and regulation of the spheres which come under his control, so that he may realize on earth the Order and Harmony which reign in the universe. In fulfilling this function, they initiate him into a knowledge of the plan of creation, elevate him to communion with Divine Wisdom, and establish the association of the finite with the infinite Reason. They were not given him merely to gratify intellectual curiosity or an individual thirst for knowledge, but to effect a great work of organization on earth; intellectual happiness will follow as a result, but it is dependent on and subordinate to the fulfilment of the above function.

The Social Mechanism, with all its Institutions, should be so devised and planned as to enable Humanity to fulfil the three great primordial functions which we have above enumerated.

The four Cardinal or Social Passions are the highest order of Motors in man, as they are the agents which effect the Association and Social Unity of the race—the primary condition necessary to the fulfilment of all branches of Human Destiny. When they perform their true functions through the influence of Institutions which are adapted to them, they accomplish the high mission assigned to them, and lead to the reign of Social Harmony and Unity. When, on the other hand, they do not perform those functions, but are thwarted and perverted by false Institutions, they lead to disunion, antagonism, and discord, and establish on earth the reign of Social Incoherence and Anarchy.

Love being one of the four Cardinal Passions, and with Ambition exercising the greatest influence on the social relations of mankind, we see the supreme importance of its true and harmonious development, and of its fulfilling the functions assigned to it in the plan of Human Destiny.

From what precedes, we see that in seeking to discover an Institution which will secure the true and natural action and development of the passion of Love, and establish Harmony and Unity in the relations of the Sexes, we must first ascertain the functions which the passion has to perform and the work it has to accomplish, and take them as our guide.

In analyzing this Passion, we shall find that it has four radical and two pivotal functions to fulfil; we have mentioned the one which is most important in social mechanics—namely, the formation of social ties and relations of various kinds and degrees between the Sexes, constituting one of the Cardinal branches of the Association and Social Unity of the Race; we give the others in the following Table:

FUNCTIONS OF THE PASSION OF LOVE.

MATERIAL FUNCTIONS.

1. Procreation of the Species.............................Healthy Progeniture.
2. Interchange of the male and female influence.............Health of the Sexes.

SPIRITUAL FUNCTIONS.

1. Exaltation of the individual Soul............Refinement in Sexual Intercourse.
2. Union of the male and female elements of Humanity...Social Unity of the Race.

PIVOTAL FUNCTIONS. { Reciprocal Attraction of the Sexes to Industry, Art, and Science. Generation of the Religious Sentiment by Contact of the two Extremes of the series of the Passion.

It is the fulfilment by the Passion of Love of these functions which must be kept in view in studying and determining the nature of the Institution which is adapted to it, and which is to regulate the relations and intercourse of the sexes. An Institution which does not enable the Passion to fulfil its functions and attain the ends assigned to it by Divine Wisdom, is not the one predestined for it by that Wisdom. The truth or falseness, the morality or immorality of any system for the regulation of the relations of the Sexes, is to be judged and determined by this standard.

In connection with the question of the functions and uses of Love in Social Economy, we will make the following extract from FOURIER, which, in a few words, opens a wide horizon of thought :—

" A subject which appears frivolous at first sight, may, on ma-
" ture examination, be found to open a field of vast and profound
" calculations. This is the case with the Passion of Love, its

" accords and functions — a Passion which appears to be of slight
" importance in the Social Mechanism and scarcely worthy of
" analysis, but which, far from being a Motor without influence
" in the general economy of the Combined Order, will be one of
" the most powerful incentives to the formation of Industrial
" Combinations; for in Social Harmony, Love is an agent as
" powerful as Ambition in attracting the two Sexes to agricultu-
" ral and manufacturing labor.

" When I commenced the study of Passional Attraction in its
" application to Industry, I neglected for a long time to consider
" the resources which might be furnished by the Passion of Love.
" An explorer, in the commencement of his researches, is more
" or less influenced by the opinions of his age ; I participated
" therefore in the prejudices of Society which sees in Love an
" individual recreation only and not a lever in Social Mechanics.
" I judged it by the irregularities and excesses of which it is the
" source ; in short, I considered it unworthy of serious study,
" and this prejudice retarded the progress of my Theory. This
" was violating a wise precept of the philosophers, which en-
" joins an integral exploration of the whole domain of Nature.
" In studying the four Cardinal Passions, we should not stop
" at a partial investigation ; we should analyze all of them
" without prejudice for or against either of the four. If God
" has created them all, he has provided an employment for
" them all.

" The Passions should be studied in relation to the impulse
" they can give to agricultural and manufacturing Industry.
" The object of calculating the action of Passional Attraction is
" not to create amusements, but to create incentives to produc-
" tive labor. If fêtes and pleasures are brought into the account,
" it is only so far as they contribute to encourage labor, increase
" production, and augment the wealth of Society. The Com-
" bined Order does not admit of the employment of pleasures
" without assigning to them uses and functions ; but it possesses
" the art of utilizing all known pleasures and making them con-
" cur simultaneously in the work of enriching and harmonizing
" the Social World.

" Viewed in this light, Love, the subject of so much idle pleas-

" antry, becomes a matter of high importance, since in Social
" Harmony it leads to the formation of ties which tend to increase
" wealth and prevent discord ; the Creator could have had no
" other end than this in view. If any one of the Passions had
" appeared to him a source of discord and poverty, he would
" have excluded it from the Passional System. It is sufficient
" to know that he has given to a Passion like Love, great in-
" tensity, for us to conclude in advance that in Social Harmony,
" it will be a powerful incentive to attract man to Productive
" Industry."

*   *   *   *   *

" The Passion of Love appears to be a fit subject for pleas-
" antry, because it is superficially judged, and because men con-
" sider only its material element, and the material tie to which it
" gives rise. Certain writers, however, pretend to regard only
" the spiritual or sentimental tie, of which they have but the most
" superficial idea, since they are ignorant of the properties, the
" degrees, and the industrial uses of this branch of the Passion.
" Even when they profess to consider Love in its compound na-
" ture, as giving rise to two elementary ties—one Material, the
" other Spiritual—they are still far from comprehending the de-
" sign of Nature, which is that Love, as well as the three other
" Cardinal Passions, should be considered as a bi-compound Mo-
" tor, giving rise to four ties, namely :—

Two	Material Love.
Internal Ties.	Spiritual Love.

Two	Love applied to individual relations.
External Ties.	Love applied to Social Harmony.

PIVOTAL TIE.........Love applied to Universal Unity.

" If we should propose to those writers a series of calculations
" like the above in respect to a Passion which has been thought
" unworthy of serious consideration, they would find themselves
" greatly embarrassed. They would declare that they did not
" believe Love could have been designed for such important Func-
" tions. What opinion, then, must they form of that Being
" whom they call the Supreme Geometer, and who certainly is

" the Creator of Love as well as of the other Passions ?   When
" he created Love did he neglect his invariable Standard — the
" Laws of Geometry ?   Certainly not; for he has regulated the
" properties of Love on a uniform system with the three other
" Cardinal Passions and has calculated the action and relations
" of them all on strict geometrical principles."

THEORY OF THE ACCORDS OF LOVE.

CHARACTER OF MARRIAGES IN CIVILIZATION.

IN the preceding pages, we have treated the subject of Love and Marriage in a general and abstract sense. We have laid down the principles on which a true theory of Amatory Relations should be based, and have endeavored to furnish thinking and impartial minds with the data necessary for studying this important subject in all its bearings, and arriving at a clear and full comprehension of it. We have not entered into details and practical descriptions, which we should have been obliged to treat superficially, and which would have excited prejudice and led the majority of readers astray.

We will, however in closing, take up one detail of the subject, namely, the Accords to which the Passion of Love gives rise, and apply it to Marriages as they exist in the present Social Order.

Each of the four Cardinal Passions is composed of two branches or principles, or two kinds of Attraction—the one Spiritual, the other Material, as shown in the following Table:—

TABLE OF THE FOUR CARDINAL PASSIONS, WITH THEIR TWO PRINCIPLES OR BRANCHES.

AMICISM OR FRIENDSHIP.

Spiritual Principle. — Affinity from sympathy of character
Material Principle. — Affinity from coincidence of tastes and pursuits.

AMORISM OR LOVE.

Spiritual Principle. — Affinity from attraction of the heart.
Material Principle. — Affinity from attraction of the senses.

HONORISM OR AMBITION.

Spiritual Principle. — Affinity from coöperation for glory and honor.
Material Principle. — Affinity from coöperation for wealth and power.

FAMILYISM OR THE PARENTAL SENTIMENT.

Spiritual Principle. — Affinity from the tie of adoption.
Material Principle. — Affinity from the tie of consanguinity.

These Passions may be called into action by either of their two affinities. Friendship, for example, may be excited between individuals by sympathy of character, or by coincidence of pursuits in art, science, or industry. Love may be awakened by spiritual sympathy or the attraction of the heart, and by material sympathy or the attraction of the senses. The two affinities of which each passion is composed attract human beings to each other, give rise to the formation of ties between them, and lead to the Association and Social Unity of the Race.

Each branch of the Passions engenders when harmoniously developed a series of Accords, and when subversively developed a series of Discords. These Accords and Discords are of several degrees, as in Music, which is a symbol of the Passional System, and should be taken as a guide in its study.

We shall describe only the three primary Accords and Discords; they will be sufficient to furnish the reader with a standard by which to judge of the various amatory relations which, under the name of Marriage, exist in the present Social Order. We will not treat of the higher Accords, as the subject is a very intricate one, and is not necessary to our purpose.

ACCORDS OE THE 1ST, 2D, AND 3D DEGREES.

ACCORD OF THE 1ST. *Attraction in one branch of the Passion with indifference in the other.* — This Accord exists between a couple united by spiritual or material love alone; it is the exercise and satisfaction of but one branch of the passion, with indifference as to the other. If there were antipathy in either branch, the tie would degenerate and become a semi-accord or a semi-discord, according to the degree of the antipathy.

The Accord of the 1st gives rise to the simplest order of amatory relations admissible in Social Harmony. The present Social Order is so poor in passional sympathies, that very few marriages realize fully this Accord in either of its branches, that is to say, they neither realize a true spiritual nor a true material love. Unions which attain to the spiritual Accord of the 1st are considered as happy unions — model marriages. The fact is, that the great majority of marriages in Civilization are ties not of Love but of Friendship or of Ambition — that is, when any real affinity exists in them. The reader by studying carefully the elements of Friendship and Ambition, will see the truth of this remark.

ACCORD OF THE 2D. *Attraction in both branches of the Passion on one side, and in one branch on the other.*—This Accord exists between a couple one of the parties of which feels both spiritual and material love, while the other feels but one of these two loves. Such an Accord may exist between a man of genius who from age or some other cause is physically unattractive, and an accomplished and beautiful woman. He is attracted to her by both spiritual and material affinity, while she is attracted to him by spiritual affinity alone, by admiration of his noble character. His love, satisfied in both branches of the Passion, is *compound*, while hers, satisfied in but one of them, is *simple;* two affinities are felt on one side, and but one on the other.

ACCORD OF THE 3D. *Reciprocal Attraction in both branches of the Passion.*—This Accord exists between a couple united by both spiritual and material love—that is, by the tie of the heart and the tie of the senses. It is a *compound* Accord, since both of the affinities of the Passion are satisfied at the same time. It is found frequently in the early stages of marriage before domestic discord and monotony have destroyed it. It is also found in unions where the parties, not being legally united, can separate at will.

The Accord of the 3d is the elementary Accord in Passional Harmony, and the simplest that can be regularly employed. A love that is not *compound*, that does not satisfy both branches of the Passion, is unsuited to the nature of man, which is compound, and can perform no regular function in a world of Passional Harmony. This Accord corresponds to the Third in Music, which is one of the most pleasing of its Accords and recurs the most frequently in its Harmonies. The Accords of the higher degrees—the 4th, 5th, 6th, 7th, and the Pivotal—produce richer and more complex effects, but neither of them produces more simple charm and beauty. We will not describe these higher Accords in love, as there are no illustrations of them to be found in Civilization; they imply multiple loves in various degrees. The present Social Order, based on the exclusive and permanent union of a single couple for life, cannot admit any Accords beyond those of the 3d. But to condemn the higher Accords be cause they are unsuited to Civilization, would be like condemning the complicated harmonies of a Beethoven from a prepossession in favor of simple music.

As Love in its true or harmonious development gives rise to a series of Accords between the Sexes, so in its false or inverse development it gives rise to a series of Discords — that is, of antipathies and repulsions.

We will now describe briefly the first three Discords of the series, corresponding to the three Accords already given.

DISCORDS OF THE 1ST, 2D, AND 3D DEGREES.

DISCORD OF THE 1ST. *Antipathy or repulsion in one of the branches of the Passion, and indifference in the other.* — This Discord exists between a couple the parties of which feel either positive spiritual, or positive material aversion to each other — the aversion being confined to one branch of the Passion.

DISCORD OF THE 2D. *Antipathy in both branches of the Passion on one side, and in one branch on the other.* — This Discord exists when one of the parties of a couple feels both spiritual and material aversion, while the other feels but one kind of aversion, either spiritual or material. In this case there is *compound* antipathy on one side, and *simple* antipathy on the other.

DISCORD OF THE 3D. *Spiritual and material antipathy felt reciprocally by both parties.* — This Discord exists when the two parties of a couple are repulsive to each other, spiritually and materially. It is a *compound* antipathy on both sides.

This Discord is the lowest that can exist, and engenders the most repulsive relations possible between the Sexes. It is quite common in marriages in the present Social Order — much more so than appears, being masked from motives of policy. It is generated, spiritually, by the constant contact of antipathetic characters and by domestic monotony and conflicts; and materially by disease, poverty, etc. That human beings can live together in this state of compound antipathy and discord, hating each other spiritually and materially, and their union be considered perfectly right and proper, because legally ratified, shows the moral apathy, individual and collective, which reigns in our boasted Civilization.

The three Accords and the three Discords above described

give rise to *Six Modes of Relations between the Sexes;* of these, three are positively false, namely, the three Discords; two are incomplete, namely, the Accords of the 1st and 2d; while one only is a full and harmonious tie, namely, the Accord of the 3d.

Unions of the Sexes are true or false, noble or ignoble, harmonious or subversive, according to the amatory Accords or Discords that exist between them. Marriage as it now exists includes all these six modes of sexual relations. A couple legally married may be in passional Accord of the 1st, 2d, or 3d degree, or in passional Discord of the 1st, 2d, or 3d degree, and the marriage is considered in each case perfectly proper and moral. In the eyes of the law and of religion the relation is in all cases the same--namely, a legal union called Marriage.

With the knowledge of the theory of amatory Accords and Discords, the reader will be able to analyze Marriages as they now exist and determine their real nature. He must bear in mind, however, that the majority of marriages in Civilization are not based on the passion of Love; the relation is not of an amatory character, but grows out of some one of the other Passions.

Having thus given a criterion by which marriages in the present Social Order may be judged, we will now give a list of some of those which are contracted from motives wholly foreign to the Passion of Love.

CONVENTIONAL MARRIAGES IN CIVILIZATION.

1. MARRIAGE FOR A SUPPORT.—The number of young women who marry from this motive is very large. Living with poor parents or relatives who are unable to support them, they marry simply to be provided for. These marriages spring from the wants and requirements of the Senses; their incentive is physical necessity.

2. MARRIAGE FOR A HOME.—A young woman looks forward to the time when death or some other casualty will break up the paternal home, and marries with a view of securing a position for life. The motive here springs from prudential calculation, —one of the lower shades of Ambition.

3. MARRIAGE TO ESCAPE PARENTAL TYRANNY.—This motive often induces young women to marry in order to free themselves from domestic dependence and oppression. The incentive in such cases is love of independence, which is a want of all the Passions.

4. MARRIAGE FROM DREAD OF BECOMING AN OLD MAID.—As Society visits women with sneers and ridicule if they remain single beyond a certain age, they are often induced to marry from this reason alone. The incentive here is love of conformity, which springs from love of approbation—a branch of Ambition.

5. MARRIAGE FOR A HOUSEKEEPER.—These unions occur in the case of a widower left with a family of young children on his hands, or of an old man, retired from the world, who desires some one to take charge of his household or to keep him company ; in the latter instance, the motive springs from the gregarious sentiment in the human heart, which is the rudimental form of Friendship.

6. MARRIAGE TO OBTAIN AN HEIR.—These unions are very frequent among rich and aristocratic families, when it is desirable to transmit estates in a direct line. The motive in this case springs from Familyism combined with Ambition.

7. MARRIAGES TO UNITE ESTATES OR FORTUNES.—These unions are also common among the rich and the great, and are contracted for the purpose of consolidating the wealth of two families. The motive here springs from love of fortune and influence—the material branch of Ambition.

8. BUSINESS MARRIAGES, like that between an actor and an actress to unite their professional earnings, or between a widow and some one competent to conduct a business left on her hands, which she cannot manage. The union in these cases is a league to obtain a certain material end; it springs, therefore, from a branch of Ambition.

9. MARRIAGES TO OBTAIN PATRONAGE.—These are common among professional men who marry into families of standing in society in order to secure their influence. The motive here is desire of success, and belongs to one of the branches of Ambition.

14

10. MARRIAGES FOR MONEY.—These marriages are considered the most desirable and the most judicious in Civilization, and take place commonly in the higher classes who give the tone to society. The motive of such unions may be a desire of satisfying the love of luxury—the collective want of the five senses—or of acquiring power and influence, which is the aim of the material branch of Ambition.

11. MARRIAGES TO OBTAIN SOCIAL POSITION.—These are resorted to by the calculating and scheming to obtain admission to circles from which they would otherwise be excluded. The motive in this case is a desire of coöperation and league with superiors; branch of Ambition.

12. MARRIAGE OF A BELLE.—Unions of this kind, if they spring from admiration of personal charms, are based on Visual Attraction; if they spring from the desire of possessing a noted beauty, and there is competition among suitors, another motive is added—that of Ambition. On the part of the Belle there is generally calculation as to fortune or social position; these marriages present a curious mixture of heterogeneous motives.

13. MARRIAGES FROM SEXUAL ATTRACTION.—These unions are very common, particularly among young persons. They are based on the material branch of Love.

14. MARRIAGES FROM COMPULSION.—These are of several kinds. A suitor, for example, is threatened with a prosecution for breach of promise, and marries to escape the penalties of the law. A young woman is supposed to be compromised by the attentions of a lover; he is called on by some relative to repair the injustice he has done, and is induced by expostulations or driven by threats of violence to form a union against his will. The motives here are negative; in one case, the fear of losing money; in the other, the fear of disgrace or of personal injury.

15. SCHEMING MARRIAGES.—These unions belong to the category of ridiculous marriages. They are planned and executed by women who have been disappointed in previous engagements and have acquired experience in the wiles of the world. They fix upon some simple young man, inexperienced in such matters, and by various enticements, by plotting and managing, by arts

and blandishments, they draw him gradually into a union which he had no idea of contracting. The manœuvres which are resorted to in order to effect such alliances are often of the most amusing character. The motive on the part of the woman may spring from various sources ; on the part of the dupe, it is generally an impulse of benevolence.

16. MARRIAGES FROM COMPASSION.—These also belong to the ridiculous class. A man conceives a violent passion for a woman who so far from reciprocating it, has a positive aversion for him. As he can have no hope of winning her by direct appeals to her affections, he seeks to do so indirectly by working on her fears or on her compassion. He resorts to various means ; he threatens, for example, to commit suicide, and represents to her the responsibility she would incur by driving him to such an act. She is induced to tolerate his presence and attentions, and at last, from compassion or fear, she marries him to get rid of him. The motive on the part of the man may be love, or may be the desire of marrying a woman superior to him ; on the part of the woman, it is compassion or inverse-benevolence.

It will be observed that in the above list of Marriages, which might be greatly extended, there is but one (the 13th) contracted from Love, and that from the material or sensual branch of the Passion alone. All the others are formed from considerations wholly foreign to Love, and are not therefore in any sense amatory unions.

These false and artificial marriages are all sanctioned by Law and by Religion, and are considered perfectly right, moral, and sacred. This shows that in present Civilization, there is in reality no true and elevated moral standard. The ideas of right and wrong which prevail—at least in respect to the higher moral or passional relations—are based on usage, law, and conventional forms, irrespective of intrinsic truth and justice. A union in which sensuality, discord, and brutality exist, if it is consecrated by the civil or religious authorities, is held to be as true a marriage as one based on the highest and noblest sentiments.

In conclusion, we appeal to conscientious and reflecting minds to examine impartially the existing state of society in respect to the relations of the Sexes—to scrutinize carefully the antipathies, hatreds, and discords, the duplicity and perfidy, the sensuality and brutality, the excesses, vices, crimes, and other evils which exist in these relations—and decide whether some great change, some radical reform is not urgently needed and called for.

If they will not do this, but are willing to overlook the enormities engendered by the present system, let them at least be modest enough not to cry out against and denounce a Theory which proposes to remedy them, because it is at war with their prejudices, and would produce results opposed to their theoretical or abstract standard of morality, which is no where followed in Civilization.

In treating a question of an intricate character, and on which deeply-rooted prejudices exist, it is well to present it in different ways, and under different forms. For this reason, we add the following remarks of an old and distinguished disciple of FOURIER, which explain the subject in a popular and practical manner :—

FOURIER's views of the marriage relations, like those of all other relations, are always modified according to what he terms the laws of development, or the natural growth of society ; which growth resembles that of an individual from infancy to manhood.

The infant first develops its physical constitution, and then the moral and the intellectual faculties : first the body and then the soul. The human race, as a collective individuality, is subject to the same necessity of gradual development : first the material elements of social life are cultivated chiefly, and then the spiritual, combined with the material in higher and still higher powers and degrees.

The material principle of life in man, when severed from the spiritual, or placed above it, he deems animal and sensual, low and ignoble in character and bearing ; the spiritual principle is naturally human, noble and sublime in aspiration, but may become ridiculous when claiming independency of the material principle, and leading man astray in mystical ascetic mortifications of the flesh and supercilious contempt of physical relations and necessities.

True marriage is a perfect harmony of natural attraction and spiritual affection between man and woman : *false marriage*, a discordant union of the sexes from material interests and attractions, without mutual affection.

The growth and progress of society is gradually upward, from a predominance of the physical to a predominance of the spiritual, through an oscillating series of imperfections and approximations, until harmony between the natural and spiritual elements of human nature has been finally attained. FOURIER explains the various degrees of discords and necessities in every succeeding Period of social advancement, and in every phase of each particular Period. And hence it is, whence speaking of the marriage question, he is commonly misunderstood ; because he states that perfect Liberty and perfect Order will be one and the same thing in social harmony, when man and woman thoroughly developed in their spiritual nature, will become "a law unto themselves." He does not, however, state that they are one and the same thing in the Savage or the Patriarchal, the Barbaric or the civilized Periods of society. In these imperfect periods of social justice and development, he frankly states that individual liberty is partly incompatible with the necessities of an imperfect social order ; and that freedom can only be extended practically as the social order is advanced by the developments of science and useful inventions : these being the powers which emancipate the race from poverty and drudgery in all the physical relations and necessities of man and of society.

He describes the marriage tie as being generally more or less ignoble in Savage, Patriarchal, Barbaric and Civilized communities, because the sensual attractions and material interests usually predominate over the nobler spiritual attractions and higher interests of the soul. These low ignoble marriages, however, he admits, are sheer necessities of an imperfect social Order, and can only be improved and finally dispensed with, as Society advances in its growth toward higher manhood. Hence he describes the law of progress in each Social Period, and the modes in which the marriage ties will be first modified and then dissolved, and finally reorganized in what he terms the harmonial Order, where natural liberty and natural law combine the spiritual with the physical attractions in the free conjugial union of the sexes.

In what he terms the *civilized* or present period of progress, the marriage tie, though commonly ignoble from the vile predominance of Sensual attractions and material interests, should generally be indissoluble, because there is no other provision for the care of children, than that of their parents living in isolated households ; and the children must be cared for of necessity, whatever be the incompatibilities of temper and of feeling between man and wife. Another and a higher Period of social advancement, in which children will be duly educated and protected by society, that is, a state in which special institutions are established as a social Providence for childhood, is essential to the freedom of divorce, even between couples who become unhappy after marriage. This social period to which the world is gravitating in all civilized communities, FOURIER calls GUARANTISM, or a state of society in which mutual assurances are organized in almost every sphere of worldly interests, to protect the state and individuals against risks and casualties of all kinds, resulting from the accidents of nature and the fluctuations of industrial activity and individual enterprise. Before divorce can be admitted universally as a social liberty, Institutions to provide for the care and education of orphans and the children of divorced parents should be organized on the principle of mutual insurance against risks and casualties of this kind ; and such an institution would be one of the elements of progress on the principle of social order which FOURIER calls GUARANTISM.

This liberty of divorce in the period of "*Guarantism*," along with the development of other liberties of *self-possession* and enrichment by attractive industry, will gradually lead to a still further period of development in all the arts of life, in which women may and will become quite independent members of society, able to support themselves with ease by their own industry, without relying upon men for physical support and maintenance ; and therefore not being obliged to sell themselves to a husband for a legal claim to share his home, they will, according to FOURIER, claim independency, or what is now termed, "individual sovereignty," for themselves as well as for the other sex ; and generally refuse to be tied down for life, in physical and legal bondage, in opposition to the freedom of true marriage between soul and soul in spiritual unions and conjugal harmony.

The first reaction against what FOURIER terms the despotism of material interests in marriage, will be a contrary extreme of "*spiritual simplism*," or a wish to give undue predominance to spiritual freedom over matter and material interests in all the relations of life. This will constitute a transitional period, which he partially describes in the treatise on the "Four Movements," as the COMBINED HOUSEHOLD or the "Series of Nine Groups." These he describes as male and female societies living and working apart from each other in separate households. This liberty and independency being incomplete, and more or less unfavorble to the higher branches of economy and combination, will lead eventually, he affirms, to a still higher period of social development, in which the male and female independent corporations will coöperate in mutual associations, and institute conjugial relations on more perfect, though quite free, conditions of mutual interests and attractions; the physical and spiritual affinities being equally considered, without undue predominance of any one element of passion in the most important business of life, *i. e.*, the union of the sexes and the healthy reproduction and continuation of the human race.

This higher period of social development, FOURIER terms "SIMPLE ASSOCIATION," or "SOCIANTISM."

Liberty in this period, he still deems imperfect, as well as social order, both being enthralled by certain practical necessities, and hence he goes on to describe the next degree of social progress which he terms "COMBINED ASSOCIATION" or HARMONY; the eighth degree of progress toward perfection in social order and the destiny of man. This last degree is that which he has mainly dwelt upon in all his writings, and is therefore commonly described as "FOURIER's System of Society;" but that is a mistake, inasmuch as it is only one of a Series of Sixteen Periods of advancement in the social destiny of man, or of humanity upon this globe.

THE

SOCIAL DESTINY OF MAN,

OR

THEORY OF THE FOUR MOVEMENTS,

BY

CHARLES FOURIER.

PREFACE

TO

THE AMERICAN EDITION.

CHARLES FOURIER was born on the 7th of April, 1772, in Besançon, a city in the south-eastern part of France. His father was a merchant in easy circumstances, and gave him a liberal education. He was more or less engaged during his life in some department of business, so that he was not a mere theorist, secluded from society, but a practical man, familiar with the world and its interests. He was a witness and an involuntary participator in the great and terrible drama of the French Revolution. He came near losing his life on the scaffold, escaping as by a miracle. He lost his fortune at the Siege of Lyons by the confiscation of the merchandise in which it was invested. He was drafted in the army, and served for two years in the Cavalry.

The scenes of the great Revolutionary struggle produced, no doubt, a powerful impression upon his mind, and aroused it to a contemplation of the great problems of human Society.

The last years of his life were spent in Paris, where he died on the 10th of October, 1837, at the age of sixty-five.

It was in 1798, at the age of twenty-six, that FOURIER struck upon the first idea which led him on to the discovery of his THEORY OF UNIVERSAL UNITY. His first Manuscripts were written in 1803, 4, 5, 6; from these he made selections which compose the first work he published, entitled *Théorie des Quatre Mouvements et des Destinées Générales* (Theory of the Four Movements and of General Destinies). This work was brought out hurriedly in 1808, in order that it might appear before the law restricting the liberty of the press, then in contemplation by Napoleon, was promulgated. FOURIER's second and most important work was published in 1822, after he had devoted fourteen years more to his investigations in Social Science. He entitled it *Traité de l'Association Domestique-Agricole* (Treatise on Domestic and Agricultural Association). He chose this modest title to avoid all appearance of pretence, though in the Preface, he states that it ought to have been entitled *Théorie de l'Unité Universelle* (Theory of Universal Unity). His disciples in France, on publishing the second edition, after his death, gave to the work the last-named title. His third work was published in 1829, and was called *Le Nouveau Monde Industriel et Sociétaire* (The New Industrial and Social World). This work is a concise, practical statement of his doctrine, intended for popular circulation. His fourth work appeared in 1835, under the title of *La Fausse Industrie* (The False Industrial System). In addition to the above-mentioned works, FOURIER left numerous Manuscripts, most of which have since been printed in a monthly Review, published in Paris from 1845 to 1849, under the name of *La Phalange*. These manuscripts are of the deepest interest; they show the immense power and scope of FOURIER's genius, as he wrote them in entire freedom, and without being under the necessity of adapting them to the popular mind. It is our intention to publish the writings of FOURIER complete, or at least to publish all that are necessary to a full understanding of the magnificent Discovery he has given to the world.

We begin the Series of publications with his first work — *The Theory of the Four Movements* — although it presents the most incomplete statement of his system; in fact, FOURIER, after having more fully developed his principles, withdrew it from circulation. Our reasons for commencing with this work are, first, that it shows the course and order in which FOURIER'S discovery was developed in his own mind, and second, that, being the simplest and most spontaneous expression of his conception, the freest from analytical details and technicalities, it is the most fascinating and will be the most easily understood. Written in the ardor and enthusiasm of youth, when his intellectual vision first opened upon the sublime Destiny reserved to the Human Race on Earth, it will be found replete with poetry and charm, and may in fact be called the Romance of his Theory. It presents in bold outline the vast ideas the details of which he elaborated in his subsequent works. It is a survey, so to speak, of the new region which his genius had penetrated, and which he was destined to explore and describe.

In reading this work, it will be necessary to take into consideration the circumstances and influences by which the Author was surrounded — the country in which he lived, its social manners and customs, the spirit of the age, the immense political and intellectual agitation of the period, etc.; notwithstanding his universality, he could not avoid giving to his style and ideas a certain coloring borrowed from the period and the nation in which he wrote.

The reader, before taking up this work, must also divest himself as far as possible of two states of mind common to the generality of mankind, namely, Narrowness of View, and Prejudice.

1. NARROWNESS OF VIEW. Whoever would comprehend FOURIER, must be able to elevate his mind to a survey of the whole Universe, to contemplate its mighty phenomena with the same calmness that he contemplates the phenomena of every-day life; he must be able to view the career of a world or of a system of

worlds as he would view the career of an individual or of a
nation, bearing in mind that Life and Movement repeat themselves in all spheres, and that relatively there is nothing great
and nothing small in Creation. If he can not do this, he had
better close the book, for the statements of FOURIER, especially
those of a cosmical character, will appear so gigantic to him,
so far beyond the grasp of the human intellect, that he will be
lost in a boundless field of speculation, without landmark or star
to guide him.

2. PREJUDICE. The reader must divest himself of the prejudices of his age, social as well as moral, and contemplate dispas-
sionately the possibility of great changes in the Organization of
Society, and in all the relations of human beings. If he can not
look beyond the narrow horizon of the social world in which he
lives, and in which his opinions have been formed ; if his mind is
too timid or too inert to conceive the possibility of fundamental
changes in the politics, morals, and religions of Humanity ; if he
believes that the present Order of Society is permanent, is to last
forever, he will enter upon the study of this work wholly unprepared. The criticisms of FOURIER will appear severe and unfounded, while the social changes which he points out and predicts will seem impracticable and visionary, and the reader will
lay down the book, declaring with the multitude of common
minds, petrified by social prejudices, that FOURIER was a wild
Theorist, a mad Innovator.

Parts of the work — those treating of the Relations of the Sexes
— will be looked upon by persons who accept the prevailing morality as the absolute standard of right and wrong, as false and
immoral. To consider this subject from a purely scientific point
of view will require great independence of thought and impar-
tiality of judgment. What adds to the difficulty is that FOU-
RIER expresses himself without the least reserve, leveling the
most severe criticisms against existing morals and customs, and
using common colloquial terms which in many cases but imperfectly express his ideas : moreover, he was led to make partial

and incomplete statements from the impossibility of treating the subject fully in a few chapters.

FOURIER, in an article upon this work written in 1818, remarks as follows :—

" Care should be taken in reading this work, not to fall into an error very common with the French, namely, that of expecting in a Prospectus the details which belong to a Treatise. They complain that they can not understand how the proposed changes are to be effected. If I had wished to explain this, I should have given a Treatise and not a Prospectus. It was not advisable to present my whole Theory at once, and as I published only an Announcement of it, I did not feel bound to give anything but sketches adapted to excite curiosity, and to create a desire for the Treatise which will satisfy it. In publishing this Volume, I had two objects in view—to sound public opinion, and to protect myself against plagiarism.

" I have given to the Essay different tones, and forms sometimes startling, in order to mask various experiments I was making on popular prejudices, which in France are stronger than in any other nation. To sound these prejudices one after another, it seemed best to distribute the work after the fashion of Harlequin's coat, composed wholly of fragments and variegated with many colors ; it may be accused of want of method, but it has enough for a Travesty.

" The first part of the work, the Cosmogony, is not positive, though containing many details very exact, which the positive theory has since confirmed. In 1814, I had not made the discovery of the general scale or gamut of Creation, which serves as a guide in this kind of calculation. In the Treatise, the Cosmogony will be exact, like the other parts of the work.

" An error of method very serious was that of dividing Movement into four branches instead of five, namely, one Pivotal and four Cardinal. In 1808, I was ignorant of the theory of Pivots, and frequently omitted them. This irregularity does not affect the substance of the work. The Satirists who have expended their wit on the *Theory of the Four Movements* would have certainly done better to rectify these errors. The journals of Paris, while admitting that its reasonings are well put, well followed out, have replied to them by railleries according to French usage, but raillery is not refutation. Moreover, to pay the French in their own coin, since they deal only in raillery, I felicitate them on the striking benefits they have reaped from Civilization since the epoch when I indicated to them the issue from it, by paying for its prolongation with so much bloodshed and expenditure.

" A new science does not arrive at perfection at the first start, especially when the Author is alone at the work. Now in 1807, I was only in the eighth year of my discovery ; there remained an infinity of problems for me to solve before I could complete the whole Theory. I should not have hurried in coming before the public, had I not been pressed by the requests of inquisitive friends who demanded of me at least a Synopsis, and who induced me to give it by the fear of a law against the Press which was then threatened, and by which France was gagged the following year. To avoid this, I prepared the Essay precipitately.

" I had already solved some of the principal problems, and among others that of the formation of the *Passional Series*, and of the distribution of a Phalanx of Domestic Harmony with 810 characters, rivalized and contrasted. I also possessed the secret of the equilibrated distribution of profits, in direct ratio of masses and inverse of the square of distances.

" It was possible then from that epoch to make an exit from Civilization. The French, however, have preferred to remain in it, and it has cost them since a loss of a million and a half of young men killed in battle. This is the best reply which can be made to their pleasantries, for which they have been well punished."

We add the following extracts from the Preface to the edition of the *Theory of the Four Movements*, published in Paris by the disciples of FOURIER, after his death :—

" When FOURIER, who made the Discovery which Destiny had reserved to his genius, in 1799, had elaborated his Conception during eight years, he contemplated giving it to his contemporaries. His first project was to publish, successively, under the title of *Theory of the Four Movements*, eight Memoirs, of which the first two were to have been simple Prospectuses or Announcements of his Discovery. The six others were to have been devoted to the Regular Exposition of his System. Now it will easily be understood that these eight Memoirs would have been very far from containing a complete statement of FOURIER's Theory. The volume which appeared in 1808, under the title of *Theory of the Four Movements*, was only the first of the proposed eight Memoirs; that is to say, half of the Prologue which was to precede the descriptive exposition of the System. It was simply an experiment to awaken the attention and sound the state of feeling of a Public to which FOURIER, Master of the World which his thought had conquered, and embarrassed with the immensity of the riches he held in his possession, did not yet know how to communicate so many treasures.

*　　*　　*　　*　　*　　*　　*　　*　　*

" The reader must be on his guard against looking in this volume for FOURIER's Science, for the knowledge of his Theory, the exposition and demonstration of the theorems of his doctrine, and, especially, against considering it as an elementary Work. Far from this, the *Theory of the Four Movements*, though the first of the productions of FOURIER in chronological order, is, in methodical order, the last to be read. The book is a first explosion of Genius; it is a startling and marvellous eruption, throwing out on every side floods of poetry, of beauty, and of science, the sudden flashes of which open to the mind myriads of horizons, new and immense, but shut out instantly from the view, and which produce upon the intellect the effect of a dazzling fairy scene, of a gigantic Phantasmagoria.

*　　*　　*　　*　　*　　*　　*　　*　　*

" The reading of the work gave rise to so many erroneous opinions in respect
to FOURIER's system, that he resolved to suppress it entirely. He rarely
alluded to it in his subsequent writings even when he borrowed passages from
it. He abstained for a long time from speaking of the work, and it was only
by yielding to great importunity on our part that he informed us, in 1830, that
a large part of the edition was probably to be found among the old stock of a
bookseller in Paris, where in fact we found it. ' The Theory was not complete,' said FOURIER, ' when I published this work ; it contains many errors :
and then it is not a book finished, digested ; its style is not that of science,
there is too much of hyperbole in it,' etc. And when we spoke to him of a
second edition, he never ceased to repeat that the work ought to be rewritten
almost entirely."

*   *   *   *   *   *   *   *   *

In another part of the Preface, speaking of the charge that
FOURIER wished arbitrarily to change institutions and customs
now regarded as sacred, and substitute for them others of an immoral tendency, the writer says very aptly :—

"FOURIER WISHES nothing. He brings to Humanity neither laws, nor
prescriptions, nor new precepts, nor a new morality. FOURIER makes no
pretension to impose *anything* upon Humanity ; legislation is not his task ;
he presents neither Leviticus, nor Deuteronomy, nor a Table of Command-
ments ; he does not present even a Constitution. FOURIER brings a NEW
SCIENCE, and he asks that it be verified ; that is all. Has FOURIER discovered the Law of UNIVERSAL HARMONY ? Or, in a more circumscribed
sphere, has he discovered the Natural Law of SOCIAL HARMONY ? Here is
all we have to decide upon. We have not to discuss whether what FOURIER
proposes is moral or immoral ; the only question is, if what he proposes is true
or false. If FOURIER's THEORY is true, if in the domain of Social Science it
is conformable to the nature of things, to the Law of Universal Order, and
if, at the same time, it is contrary to Morality, so much the worse for Morality, which must govern itself accordingly."

Notwithstanding any imperfections in style and mode of pre-
sentation which may be discovered in the present work, the intelligent and impartial student will look beyond these defects,
and occupy himself only with the substance of the Theory ; he
will then see the grandeur, the vast sweep of FOURIER's conceptions ; he will see a deep underlying truth in all his statements,
and will recognise in the Theory of the Four Movements one of
the most extraordinary productions of the human mind.

For our own part, we unhesitatingly assign to it this high
rank ; in the domain of original thought and conception, it has

no equal; it treats boldly of problems the most profound and the most universal, the most practical and the most imaginative; it is, in truth, a magnificent Epic, sung by a mighty Genius who had penetrated the secret of the plans of God, and revealed the glorious Destiny reserved to Man on Earth. It is not measured cadences nor flowery images which constitute its poetic grandeur, but vast conceptions, profound intuitions, and immense scope of thought. It is an Epic of which God and Humanity are the Heroes, and in which the wisdom and the goodness of the one, and the high Destiny of the other are for the first time revealed in the light of absolute Law and Principle. Unlike the Epics of a Dante or a Milton, which sing of Hell and its demon inhabitants, of a God of Wrath and Vengeance, of a fallen and accursed Race, outcast from Heaven, of a Future over which appalling doubt and uncertainty hang, of a Universe shrouded in the dark pall of a gloomy theology, FOURIER's Epic sings of a glorious Destiny for Humanity on Earth, of the approaching reign of Social Harmony, of a World redeemed and regenerated by the discovery and application of the Laws of Divine Order, of a Globe resplendent with the creations of human Art and Industry, of a God who governs by Attraction, and of a Universe of grandeur, of harmony, and of happiness, the Divine Order of which Man is destined to realize on this Planet.

CONTENTS.

PART II.

DESCRIPTIONS OF VARIOUS BRANCHES OF PRIVATE AND DOMESTIC DESTINIES.

FIRST SECTION.

On the Combined Household of the Seventh and Twenty-Sixth Periods, and the Ennuis experienced by both Sexes in the Isolated Household.

CORRECTIVES WHICH WOULD HAVE LED TO THE SIXTH PERIOD.

SECOND SECTION.

On the Splendors of the Combined Order.

PART III.

CONFIRMATION DRAWN FROM THE INCOMPETENCY OF THE SPECULATIVE SCIENCES IN ALL PROBLEMS RELATING TO THE CIVILIZED MECHANISM.

THEORY OF THE FOUR MOVEMENTS.

PRELIMINARY DISCOURSE.

On the heedlessness of Civilized Nations in overlooking or disdaining the two
branches of study which would have led to the discovery of the Theory of General
Destinies,* — namely, the study of Agricultural Association † and of Passional Attraction : —
And on the pernicious results of this heedlessness, which for over two thousand years
has uselessly prolonged the duration of Social Chaos — that is to say, of the Civilized, Barbaric, and Savage Orders of Society, which are not the Destiny of the
Human Race.

When we consider the number of great geniuses which Civilization has produced, especially during the eighteenth century, we
are tempted to believe that they have exhausted every scientific
career ; far from hoping for great discoveries, we do not expect
even those of minor importance.

This idea is now to be dissipated. Men are about to learn
that the sciences already acquired amount to hardly a fourth of
those which remain to be acquired, and that all will be revealed
at once by the Theory of General Destinies. This theory is the

---

* By General Destinies is meant the past, present, and future career of Man and the
Globe in their relation to the Universe. — *Note by the Translator.*

† It should be borne in mind that when Fourier speaks here, and in other parts of
the work, of the importance of Agricultural Association, and the results which are to
follow its establishment, he includes among these results the extension of the principle
of Association to all departments of industry, and to every branch of human relations.
Hence in the present translation it has been deemed advisable in some cases, for the
sake of clearness, to substitute the word Industrial for Agricultural, and in others to
use simply the term Association — the idea always being *Association, or Harmonic Combination, in all the branches of industry, and of all the passions and faculties of the human soul.* — *Note by the Translator.*

key to all discoveries accessible to the human mind; it is to initiate us immediately into sciences which, according to our present slow methods, might have cost thousands of years more of study. Its announcement will excite distrust, in the beginning, from the mere fact that it promises to elevate man to a knowledge of his Destiny. I think it proper, therefore, to make known the indications which put me on the track. This explanation will prove that the discovery required no scientific effort, and that the humblest man of science might have attained to it before myself, if he had possessed the requisite qualification—freedom from prejudice. It was in this respect that I had an aptitude for the calculation of Destinies, which the philosophers, who always support and extol dominant prejudices even while pretending to combat them, have always lacked.

Under the name of philosophers, I include here only those engaged in the uncertain sciences—the politicians, moralists, political economists and others—whose theories are incompatible with experience, and have for their only rule the caprice of their authors. It will be borne in mind, then, that whenever in the course of the present work I speak of the philosophers, I allude to those of the uncertain school, and not at all to those engaged in the positive sciences.

I.

INDICATIONS AND METHODS
WHICH LED TO THE ANNOUNCED DISCOVERY.

NOTHING was further from my thoughts than researches on the subject of Destinies. I partook of the general opinion which regards them as impenetrable, and which ranks all calculations upon them with the visions of astrologers and magicians. The study which led me to their investigation related only to certain industrial and political problems of which I will here give some idea.

After the incompetency of which the philosophers gave proof in their first practical experiment—the French Revolution—all agreed in regarding their science as an aberration of the human intellect. The floods of light which they pretended to have shed upon moral and political questions, seemed no longer anything but floods of darkness; what else, indeed, can be found in the writings of these savants, who, after having spent five-and-twenty centuries in perfecting their theories, after having brought together all the lights of ancient and modern times, make their début by engendering as many calamities as they promised benefits, and causing Civilization to retrograde toward Barbarism?

Such was the result of the first five years during which France was subjected to the experiment of philosophic theories.

After the catastrophe of 1793, all illusions were dissipated, and the moral and political sciences were repudiated and condemned, past retrieve. From that time, it should have been seen that humanity had nothing to hope from any existing theories, that social happiness must be sought for in some new science, that political genius must be directed in some new path; for it was evident that neither the philosophers nor their rivals knew how to remedy social miseries, and that, under the doctrines of either, the most shameful calamities—among others general indigence—would be sure to prevail.

Such was the first consideration which led me to suspect the existence of a social science hitherto unknown, and which stimulated me to seek for its discovery. Far from being daunted by my limited knowledge, I thought only of the honor of grasping what twenty-five learned centuries had failed to discover.

I was encouraged in my researches by the numerous indications of the aberration of human reason in the past, and above all by the aspect of the calamities which everywhere afflicted the world of industry; calamities such as pauperism, fraud, maritime spoliation, commercial monopoly, the slave-trade, and innumerable other evils, which lead one to doubt whether civilized industry* be not a scourge invented by God for the chastisement of the human race. I argued from this, that there must be in our industry some subversion of natural law; that perhaps it was exercised in a manner opposed to the designs of God; that the tenaciousness of so many scourges must be attributed to the absence of some plan intended by Providence but unknown to our men of

* As the word Industry will recur very often in the following pages, it is important to observe that it is never used in the restricted sense, as signifying application or diligence, but always in the enlarged or generic sense, as comprising all branches of agriculture, manufactures, and the mechanic arts. — *Note by the Translator.*

science. Finally I thought that if human society were affected, according to the opinion of Montesquieu, "with a chronic debility, with an organic disease, with some secret and latent poison," the remedy must be found by leaving the beaten paths of the uncertain sciences, which for thousands of years had sought for this remedy in vain. I adopted, then, for a rule in my researches, the principle of ABSOLUTE DOUBT of all existing theories, and ABSOLUTE DEVIATION from all existing methods.

Since no one before myself has made use of these two methods, it will be well to define them.

1. ABSOLUTE DOUBT OF ALL EXISTING THEORIES.—Descartes had an idea of this method, but while boasting and recommending Doubt, he made only a partial and improper application of it. He raised doubts that were ridiculous; he doubted his own existence; and he devoted himself more to refining upon the sophisms of the ancients than to seeking after useful truths.

The successors of Descartes made still less use of the principle of Doubt than he; they applied it only to what displeased them. For example, they called in question the necessity of religion, because they were opposed to the priests; but they were very careful not to call in question the necessity of the moral and political sciences, which were their means of livelihood, and which are now found to be very useless under governments which are strong, and very dangerous under governments which are weak.

As I had no connection with any scientific parties, I resolved to apply the principle of Doubt to them all, without distinction, and to suspect even what was universally approved. I applied it, then, to Civilization, which is the idol of all the philosophical schools, and is regarded as the limit of perfection; though what can be more imperfect than this same Civilization, which drags all possible calamities in its train? What can be more doubtful than its necessity, or its future permanence? Is it not probable that it is but one link in the chain of social existence? If it has been preceded by three other forms of society — the Savage, the Patriarchal, and the Barbaric—does it follow that it will be the last because it is the fourth? On the contrary, may not still others be established; and may we not see a fifth, a sixth, a seventh Social Order, which shall prove less disastrous than Civilization, and which have remained unknown only because no one has sought to discover them ? We must, then, apply the principle of Doubt to Civilization; we must doubt its necessity, its excellence, and its permanence. But these are doubts which the philosophers dare not raise; for by suspecting Civilization they would bring the suspicion of nullity upon their own theories, which are all identified with Civilization, and will fall with it the moment a better Social Order shall be found to take its place.

The philosophers, then, are restricted to PARTIAL DOUBT, since they have to sustain their systems and the interests of their class ; for fear of compromising these, they have in all time evaded every important social problem. For myself, who had no party to support, I was able to adopt the principle of ABSOLUTE DOUBT, and to apply it, from the outset, to Civilization and its most cherished institutions.

2. ABSOLUTE DEVIATION FROM ALL EXISTING METHODS.—I assumed that the most certain means of arriving at useful discoveries, was to avoid entirely the paths followed by the philosophers, who have never made the least discovery of use to society, and who, notwithstanding the immense progress of industry, have never succeeded even in eradicating general indigence. I adopted the resolution, therefore, to place myself in constant opposition to the uncertain sciences ; for considering the multitude of authors who had written upon them, I presumed that every subject they had treated must be completely exhausted, and I resolved to interest myself only in those problems which no one of them had ventured upon.

I therefore avoided all questions relating to the Throne or the Altar, to which the philosophers have devoted themselves, without intermission, ever since the origin of their science. They have always sought for the means of social welfare in administrative and religious innovations ; I applied myself, on the contrary, to seeking for it in operations which had no connection with either the government or the priesthood—operations which depended entirely upon measures of industrial and domestic reform, and which were compatible with all governments, without requiring the aid of any.

In following these two guides, ABSOLUTE DOUBT of all existing theories, and ABSOLUTE DEVIATION from all existing methods, I could not fail to open for myself a new career, if any there

were; but I certainly had no expectation of discovering the
Theory of General Destinies. Far from aspiring so high, I con-
fined myself at first to the investigation of certain comparatively
simple problems, the two principal of which were AGRICULTURAL
ASSOCIATION, and the INDIRECT SUPPRESSION OF THE COMMERCIAL
MONOPOLY OF ENGLAND. I cite these two problems because they
are inseparably connected, and are solvable one by the other.
The monopoly of Insular Powers can be destroyed, indirectly, only
by the establishment of Agricultural Association, and as soon as
Agricultural Association is effected, it will put an end at once,
and without striking a blow, to insular monopoly, maritime spoliation, stock-jobbing, bankruptcy, and all the other scourges
with which civilized industry is afflicted.

I hasten to explain these results in order to interest the reader
in the question of Agricultural Association, which has seemed of
so slight importance that the savants have never deigned to notice it.

The reader is here reminded that I have thought it necessary
to make known the calculations which led me to my discovery.
It is for this reason that I am about to treat of a subject which
will appear almost devoid of connection with that of General
Destinies; I mean the subject of Agricultural Association. For
myself, when I commenced to reason upon it, I did not for a
moment presume that so modest a calculation could lead to the
Theory of General Destinies; but since it has become the key to
this theory, it is indispensable that I speak of it at some length.

II.

AGRICULTURAL ASSOCIATION.

THE solution of this problem, so long neglected, led to the solution of all political problems. It is well known that the smallest means sometimes produce the greatest results; it is with a
metallic needle that we master the lightning, and guide our ships
through darkness and storms. It is with a means equally simple
that an end may be put to all social calamities; and while civilized nations are bathing themselves in blood in wars for commercial supremacy, the world will doubtless learn with great
interest that an industrial operation is about to terminate these

wars for ever, without the least violence, and that the maritime monopoly of England, so oppressive to the continental nations, is to fall before the power of Agricultural Association.

Association was not practicable in antiquity, owing to the slavery of the laboring classes. The Greeks and Romans sold the laborer like a beast of burden, and that with the consent of the philosophers who never protested against this odious custom. These sages are in the habit of considering everything that they have not seen in practice, to be impossible. They imagined that their slaves could not be emancipated without overthrowing society; nevertheless they have been emancipated, and society is better organized than before. The philosophers have the same prejudices in respect to Industrial Association which they had in respect to the abolition of slavery; they believe it to be impossible because it has never been tried. Seeing families working separately, they think there is no means of associating them. Or at least they pretend to think so; for upon this subject, as upon every other, they are interested in representing all problems which they are unable to solve as insolvable.

Nevertheless it has more than once been perceived, that if the inhabitants of a township could be united together in an Industrial Association, if two or three hundred families of different degrees of fortune, and engaged in agriculture, could be associated so as to secure equitable remuneration in proportion to their labor and capital, the economies and improvements which would result would be incalculable.

The idea appears at first to be gigantic and impracticable, on account of the obstacles which would be opposed to such an Association by the passions;* an obstacle the more discouraging because it can not be overcome in Associations on a small scale.

---

* By the passions Fourier means those forces, motive-powers, springs of action, impulses in man, which are variously described by the philosophers as sentiments, feelings, affections, sympathies, instincts, desires, loves, faculties, etc.

They are the *motors*, or motive-powers which prompt or impel men to action. In their unity they constitute the soul or active principle in man. Like all the forces of creation they are subject to two modes of development; one, *direct* or harmonious, producing good results; the other, *inverse* or discordant, producing evil results, such as hatred, jealousy, envy, malignity, misanthropy, etc. According to Fourier the five senses — taste, sight, smell, hearing, touch — as well as the four social affections, friendship, love, ambition, and parentalism, must be considered as passions, since they all prompt men to action.—*Note by the Translator.*

It would be impossible to form an Association of twenty, thirty, forty, or even a hundred individuals; at least eight hundred would be necessary to form a complete or Attractive Association. By this I mean one the members of which would be attracted to labor by emulation, self-respect, ambition, and other influences compatible with those of interest. Such an Association would inspire men with a passion for agricultural pursuits, which at present are so repulsive that no one adopts them as an occupation except from necessity or fear of want.

I will not detail the researches which the problem of Association cost me; it is an Order so entirely opposed to existing ideas, that if I did not prepare the reader for it by a sketch of the immense advantages which will result from its establishment, any description would appear ridiculous.

An Association, supposing it to number a thousand persons, offers such enormous advantages to industry, that the indifference which prevails on the subject is almost inexplicable; and yet there exists among us a class of men, the political economists, who are professedly devoted to questions of industrial improvement. The negligence of these economists in not seeking to discover some system of Association, is the more inconceivable from the fact that they themselves have indicated several of the advantages which would result from it. For instance, they have perceived, as any one might have perceived with them, that three hundred families associated together would have one granary kept in good order, instead of three hundred granaries kept in bad order; one dairy carefully attended to instead of three hundred dairies managed generally with extreme ignorance; that instead of sending a hundred milkmen to market, they would send but one; that in various cases, especially in Summer, they would have three or four large fires instead of three hundred small ones, etc., etc. These are some of the economies which have been recognized by different observers, who have not, however, indicated a twentieth part of the advantages which would result from Agricultural Association.

Association has been thought impossible because no means had been discovered for organizing it; but was this a reason for concluding that they could not be discovered — that they ought not to be sought? When it is considered that Association would triple and often decuple the profits of every branch of industry, it will not be doubted that God has provided the means for its realization; for he must first of all have fixed upon a plan of Industrial Association, since it is the pivot or basis of human society.

Persons fond of dispute will here raise a host of objections. "How," they will ask, " are you to unite in an Association a number of families, one of which, for instance, possesses a hundred thousand francs or more, and the other not a stiver ? How will you reconcile so many different and conflicting interests, or harmonize so many opposite characters ? How, in a word, absorb the jealousies of individuals in a plan of general and combined operations ?" To this I reply — by the allurements of wealth and of pleasure.

The strongest passion of the great majority of men, in the country as well as the city, is love of gain; and when they see an associated township, the chances being equal, yield three, five, seven times as much as a township of isolated families, and at the same time secure to all the associates the most varied enjoyments, they will forget all their rivalries and hasten to organize Association, which will extend itself at once, and without the least intervention of law, throughout all regions; for the passion for fortune and pleasure is universal in every part of the globe.

In a word, the theory of Association, which is about to change the condition of the human race, satisfies the passions common to all men, and wins them by the allurements of fortune and luxury. It is this which will guarantee its success among Savage and Barbaric as well as Civilized nations; for the passions of men are the same the world over.

The details of this New Order, to which I shall give the names PROGRESSIVE SERIES, or SERIES OF GROUPS, and PASSIONAL SERIES, it is not important to give.

I mean by these terms an assemblage of several associated groups devoting themselves to the various departments of a given branch of industry, or to the development of a particular passion.

In another part of the work I shall give some idea of the organization of these Series, the description of which, though far from sufficient, will serve to correct any erroneous notions which may be formed in advance as to their mechanism.

The Theory of the Passional Series is not arbitrarily imagined like our Social Theories. On the contrary, the order of these Series is in all points analogous to that of the geometrical series, of which they possess all the properties.

The passions, which have been supposed to be the enemies of concord, and against which so many volumes have been written which are now about to sink into oblivion—the passions, I repeat, tend only toward that harmony, that social unity to which they have been thought to be so much opposed; but they can never be harmonized except so far as they are regularly developed in the Series of Groups. Out of this mechanism they are incomprehensible enigmas—unchained tigers. It is this which leads the philosophers to say they must be repressed—an opinion doubly absurd, first, because the passions can not be repressed, and, second, because if they should be repressed, Civilization would rapidly decline and revert to the Nomadic State, in which the passions would still be as pernicious as among ourselves; for I believe as little in the virtue of shepherds and shepherdesses, as in that of their eulogists.

The Combined Order, which is to succeed to Civilized Incoherence, admits neither of moderation, equality, nor any of the philosophic virtues; it requires that the passions be ardent and refined; and from the moment Association is established they will be harmonized in exact proportion as they are active and numerous.

Not that the New Order is to effect any change in our passions. That would be impossible either for God or for Man; but their direction may be changed without changing their nature. For example, if a man without fortune, and having an aversion to marriage, has the chance to marry a woman with a hundred thousand francs income, he will consent with pleasure to form this tie, though the day before it was repugnant to him. But would he, for that, have changed the nature of his passions? Not at all; but his dominant passion, love of money, would have changed its mode of development; it would have adopted a means of gratification which the day before was displeasing; but it would not, for that, have changed its nature, but only its direction.

If, then, I assert that in the Combined Order men will adopt different tastes from those which they have at present, that they will prefer living in the country to living in the city, it must not be supposed that in changing their tastes they will also change their passions; for they will never be guided by any other motive than love of riches and pleasure.

I insist on this remark in order to meet a silly objection which will be raised by certain obtuse persons, who, when they hear of the changes in tastes or customs which are to result from the Combined Order, cry out at once:—"You are going to change our passions then!" Certainly not; but they will have opened to them new spheres of action which will assure to them a three-fold, four-fold greater development than they find in the Incoherent Order in which we now live. It is for this reason that we shall see the Civilizees acquire a strong aversion to habits which they now find agreeable—such, for instance, as the life of the family. They will observe that in the family, children do nothing but cry, quarrel, destroy, and refuse all kinds of labor, while these same children, in the Series of Groups, will engage voluntarily in industry; will emulate each other in usefulness; will instruct themselves, of their own accord, in agriculture, manufactures, the sciences and the arts; and that while thinking only of amusing themselves, they will all the while be engaged in profitable employments. When parents see this New Order, they will find their children adorable in the Series, and detestable in the isolated household.

When they observe, also, that in the palace of a Phalanx (this is the name I shall give to an Association which cultivates a township) the living is so wonderfully managed that for a third of the expense of the family-table they will find in the Series a fare three times as delicious and abundant, so that one can live three times as well as in the family for a third of the cost, and avoid, at the same time, most of the trouble of marketing and cooking; when they see, finally, that in the business relations of the Order no one is ever subjected to the least fraud, and that the masses, so clownish and dishonest in Civilization, become conspicuous for their integrity and politeness in the Series, they will conceive for this family-life, for these cities, for this Civilization, now the objects of their affection, nothing but repugnance; they will wish to organize themselves at once into a Phalanx, and to dwell in its palace. But will they have changed their passions, in thus disdaining the customs and the tastes which please them at present? No, but their passions will have changed their direction, without having changed either their object or their nature.

We must carefully guard ourselves, then, against believing that the Order of the Series, so unlike Civilization, will operate the least change in the nature of our passions; they have been and always will be unchangeable in producing discord and poverty out of the Series, and harmony and wealth in the Combined Order, which is the Destiny of Man, and the organization of which in a single township will be imitated spontaneously in all countries owing to the simple allurement of the immense advantages which this Order assures to every individual, whatever his fortune or condition.

I pass now to the results of this discovery in relation to science.

III.

PASSIONAL ATTRACTION,
AND ITS RELATION TO THE POSITIVE SCIENCES.

Is it from contempt, from inadvertence, or from fear of failure, that learned men have neglected to apply themselves to the problem of Association? It matters little what their motive has been, but they have certainly neglected it; I am the first and the only person who has considered it. Hence it follows that if the Theory of Association, unknown up to the present time, should lead to other discoveries, if it is the key to any new sciences, they should fall to me alone, since I only have sought and grasped this theory.

As for the new sciences to which it opened the way, I shall restrict myself to indicating the two principal; and as this detail will not interest a large number of persons, I shall be as brief as possible.

The first science I discovered was the THEORY OF PASSIONAL ATTRACTION.

When I perceived that the Combined Order assured a full development to the passions of both sexes, of all ages, and of all classes; that in this New Order men would acquire increase of vigor and of fortune in proportion to the activity of their passions, I conjectured from this that if God had given so much influence to Passional Attraction, and so little to reason, its enemy, it was with a view to lead us to this New Order which would, in every sense, satisfy our attractions. I believed from that time that Passional Attraction, so much decried by the philosophers, was the interpreter of the will of God in respect to the organization of society, and I proceeded at once to the *Analytic and Synthetic Calculation of Passional Attractions and Repulsions*. This calculation pointed, in all respects, toward Agricultural Association. If, therefore, men had thought of making this analytic and synthetic study of Passional Attraction, they would have discovered the laws of Association without even seeking for them. This thought, however, never occurred to any one, not even in the boasted eighteenth century, which, though pretending to apply the most searching analysis to everything, never attempted to apply it to Passional Attraction.

The Theory of Passional Attractions and Repulsions is a positive theory, and applicable throughout to the theorems of geometry; it is, moreover, susceptible of great developments, and will furnish new material to the philosophers, who, I imagine, must be greatly embarrassed to find some luminous and useful subject upon which to exercise their metaphysics.

To continue on the connection between the new sciences.

I soon perceived that the laws of Passional Attraction were in all respects conformable to those of Material Attraction as explained by Newton and Leibnitz, and that there was UNITY OF SYSTEM BETWEEN THE MOVEMENT OF THE MATERIAL WORLD AND THAT OF THE SPIRITUAL WORLD.

I suspected that this analogy must extend *from general laws to particular laws;* that the attractions and properties of animals, vegetables, and minerals, were perhaps distributed according to the same plan as those of Man and the planets; of this, after making the necessary researches, I was convinced. Thus was discovered a new positive science, namely : — *The Analogy of the Four Movements — the Material, the Organic, the Animal, and the Social; in other words, the Analogy between the Modifications of Matter and the Developments of the Passions of Men and of Animals.*

The discovery of these two positive sciences revealed to me others of which it is unnecessary to give here the nomenclature;

16

they extend even to literature and the arts, and will establish positive methods in all the branches of human knowledge.

From the moment that I possessed the theory of Passional Attraction, and of the Unity of the Four Movements, I began to read in the occult book of Nature; her mysteries were gradually revealed, and I had removed the so-called impenetrable veil. I had entered a new scientific world. It was thus that I arrived gradually to the calculation of Universal Destinies, or, in other words, to the discovery of the fundamental system on which is based the laws of all Movements, present, past, and future.

After such a success, which should most astonish us, the stroke of fortune that unveiled to me so many new sciences, by the aid of a little calculation on Association which was the key to my discovery, or the heedlessness of twenty-five learned centuries, which, though they have exhausted so many other branches of study, have never given to this calculation so much as a thought? I believe that the question will be decided in my favor, and that the extent of my discoveries will seem less astonishing than the heedlessness of the ages which have overlooked them.

I have already consoled the learned in their misfortune, by apprising them that a harvest of glory and fortune is prepared for them all. I bring more new sciences than were found mines of gold at the discovery of America; but not having the necessary acquirements for developing all these sciences, I take for myself but one—that of Social Movement. I abandon all the others to the erudite scholars of every class, who will create from them a new and magnificent domain.

How much they stood in need of this re-enforcement! The whole learned class were reduced to the last extremity, and restricted to the most pitiful gleanings. All the known sciences had been sifted and pressed out to the last grain, until there remained no other resource than to create new sophisms for the purpose of combating them, and to create a double number of volumes by advocating and refuting each error.

But from this time the scene changes. The learned are about to pass from absolute destitution to abundant riches. The harvest will be so great that they all may hope to share in it, and to establish for themselves colossal reputations; for they will have the first working of this scientific mine, of which they will seize upon the richest veins. After the appearance of the second Memoir, in which I shall treat of the Animal and Organic Movements, each of them will be able to find subjects within his competency, from which he may compose treatises on Positive Science. I insist upon this name Positive Science, because it is lavished, without the least reason, upon vague and capricious sciences, like botany for instance, the various systems of which are only arbitrarily classified tables, having no connection with the method of Nature, which coördinates the forms and properties of all created things according to a common type—the mathematical system of the human passions.

I have shown that the sciences are about, at last, to be systematically developed, and to be based, without exception, upon an invariable method. In the second Memoir I shall give some idea of this method, which will be found applicable to all our passions. It shows in every thing that exists the symbol of some passional action or development; and this analogy will give even to the most repulsive studies, such as anatomy for instance, a greater charm than is afforded at present by the study of the flowers.

Among the happy results which will flow from this method, must be mentioned, first of all, the discovery of special remedies for all diseases. There is no malady which has not one or several antidotes drawn from the three kingdoms of nature; but the science of medicine having no regular theory for proceeding in its researches after unknown remedies, is obliged to feel its way for centuries, and even for thousands of years, until chance throws one in its path; hence it has not yet found the natural absorbents for the plague, for hydrophobia, or for the gout; they will be discovered through the Theory of the Four Movements. The science of medicine, like every other, will pass from its long infancy, and, by the calculations of the theory of *counter-movements*, will attain to all the branches of knowledge which have hitherto eluded its research.

IV.

ABERRATION OF HUMAN REASON THROUGH THE INFLUENCE OF THE UNCERTAIN SCIENCES.

SCIENCE and renown are very desirable, without doubt, but they are far from sufficient unless accompanied by fortune. The possession of knowledge, of academic honors, etc., do not of themselves lead to happiness, which consists, first of all, in the possession of wealth; hence in Civilization learned men, as a general rule, are unhappy because they are for the most part poor; they will enjoy the favors of fortune only in the Combined Order which is to succeed Civilization. In this new Social Order every man of science and every artist, if he possess real merit, will be sure to amass a colossal fortune.

But while I proclaim the brilliant career which is to be opened to the positive sciences and to the arts, in what terms shall I announce the storm which is about to burst upon the old idols of Civilization — the uncertain sciences? Must I put on the sable garb of mourning to announce to the politicians and moralists that their final knell is tolling; that their immense world of volumes is about to crumble into dust; that the Platos, the Rousseaus, the Voltaires, and all the champions of ancient and modern philosophy are about to be swept into oblivion?*

As for their present disciples, they should think only of the fortune which is in store for them; of the pleasure of penetrating, at last, into the sanctuary of Nature, the portals of which their predecessors were unable to open.

And have not the philosophers, in all time, foreseen the blow which awaited them?

I see the prognostications of it even in their most celebrated writers, from Socrates, who hoped that one day the light would descend, to Voltaire, who, impatient to see it descend, exclaimed : —

"How dense a night still veils all Nature's face!"

They all confess the inanity of their sciences and the aberration of this human reason which they pretended to perfect; they all join in saying with their compiler Barthelemy: "These libra-

---

* I speak not of their literary productions, but only of those which relate to political and moral science.

ries, pretended treasuries of sublime knowledge, are but humiliating depositories of contradictions and errors."

Alas! it is too true.. During the twenty-five centuries that the moral and political sciences have existed, they have accomplished nothing for the good of humanity; they have served but to increase human perversity, and that in proportion to the improvement of their reformatory theories; they have succeeded only in perpetuating poverty and crime, and in constantly reproducing the same scourges under different forms. After so many fruitless trials for the amelioration of society, there remains to the philosophers nothing but mortification and despair. The problem of human happiness is an insuperable obstacle to them; and is not the mere spectacle of the poor who crowd our cities enough to prove to them that their floods of philosophic light are only floods of darkness?

Meanwhile a universal disquietude attests that mankind has not yet attained to the destiny to which Nature would lead it, and this disquietude seems to presage some great event which is to change the condition of the race. The nations of the earth, harassed by misfortune, grasp eagerly at every political or religious reverie which offers them a glimmering of happiness; they are like the poor invalid who counts upon a miraculous cure. It seems as if Nature whispered into the ear of the human race that it is destined to a happiness the paths to which have hitherto been unknown, and that some wonderful discovery is about to dispel at once the darkness of Civilization.

Human reason, whatever boast it may make of its achievements, will have accomplished nothing for the happiness of man till it have procured for him that *social fortune* which is the object of all our aspirations; and I mean by social fortune a graduated wealth which places the least opulent beyond the reach of want, and insures to them in any event, as a minimum, that condition which we call *a moderate competence.* If it is undeniable that riches are the principal source of happiness to Man, after health, then human reason, which has been unable to procure for us comparative riches or graduated wealth, has produced nothing by its pompous theories but useless verbiage utterly without result; and if the discovery which I announce should give us nothing but science, always the same science, without giving us riches, which are necessary before science, it would be, like our moral and political theories, only a new reproach to human reason.

The Theory of Universal Destinies is about to fulfil the aspirations of the whole human race, by insuring to every individual that graduated wealth which is the object of all our desires, and which can be found only in the Order of the Series. As to the Civilized Order from which we are about to emerge, I shall demonstrate that far from being the Industrial Destiny of Man, it is only a passing scourge with which most globes are afflicted during the first ages of their existence; that it is for the human race only a temporary malady like teething in infancy; that it has lasted *two thousand three hundred years too long*, through the inadvertence and the pride of philosophers, who have neglected all study of Association and of Passional Attraction; in a word, that the Savage, Patriarchal, and Civilized Orders are only rugged paths, progressive stages, by which the race advances gradually to a better Social Order—to the Order of the Series, which is the Industrial Destiny of Man, and out of which the efforts of the wisest potentates can not in any way remedy the misfortunes of nations.

It is in vain then, philosophers, that you pile up volumes upon volumes in your researches after human happiness, so long as you fail to extirpate the root of all social evils, namely, INDUSTRIAL INCOHERENCE, which is the antipode of the designs of God. You complain that Nature refuses to you the knowledge of her laws; but if you have been unable to discover them up to the present time, why do you hesitate to recognize the insufficiency of your methods, and seek new ones? Either Nature has not destined Man for happiness, or your methods are condemned by Nature, since they have not been able to wrest from her this secret which you pursue. Do you find her as rebellious against the positive sciences as against yours? No; because the students of those sciences really study her laws instead of dictating laws to her, and you study only the art of stifling the voice of Nature—of stifling Passional Attraction, which is the interpreter of Nature, since it leads in every way toward the organization of the Series. And what a contrast between your blunders and the prodigies wrought by the positive sciences! Every day you add new errors to the old, while every day we see the positive sciences making new achievements, and spreading a lustre over the present century equal to the disgrace which your visionary schemes have imprinted indelibly on the eighteenth.

We are about to behold a spectacle which is witnessed but once in the career of any globe—the rapid transition from a state of Social Incoherence to a state of Social Harmony; this is the most brilliant effect of Movement which can take place in the universe; the hope of it should console the present generation for all its sufferings. Every year during this grand metamorphosis will be worth whole ages of previous existence, and will be marked by a host of events so surprising that it would be ill-advised to describe them without previous preparation. It is this which has determined me to postpone the account of the Theory of the Combined Order to the third Memoir, and to announce, for the moment, only general results. Of this character will be the voluntary acceptance of industry by the Savage tribes; the consent of the Barbaric nations to the emancipation of women and slaves, whose freedom is necessary to the organization of the Combined Order; and the establishment of Unities all over the globe, such as unity of language, unity of weights and measures, unity of typographic characters, etc.

As for the details of the Combined Order—the pleasures it will secure to us—it is necessary, I repeat, to use great precaution in announcing them to the Civilizees. Disheartened by continual misfortune, and by the doctrines which the philosophers have diffused, they believe that God has destined them to a life of suffering, or, at least, to but a moderate degree of enjoyment. They cannot suddenly conform themselves to the idea of the happiness which awaits them. If, without due precaution, we should depict to them the delights they are about to enter upon in so short a time, they would become indignant; for supposing the longest delay possible, two years would suffice to organize an Association, and a few more to extend the organization over the entire globe.

The Combined Order, from its commencement, will be all the more brilliant from the fact that it has been so long delayed. It might have been attempted in Greece, in the time of Solon, for that age had attained to a sufficient development of industry and art to warrant its proceeding at once to its inauguration; but, at the present day, the means of wealth and refinement are at least double what they were among the Athenians. They knew nothing of cotton and silk fabrics, nor of sugar and other productions of America and the East, nor of the compass, the telescope, nor hardly any other modern inventions. I do not exaggerate, then, in saying that our means of wealth and refinement have at least doubled. We shall accordingly enter so much the more brilliantly upon the Combined Order; and it is now that we are about to reap the advantages of the progress made by the eighteenth century in the positive sciences, which up to this time have been signally unsuccessful in advancing human happiness.

As long as Civilization lasts, our scientific discoveries will be more detrimental than useful to human happiness, for while increasing the means of enjoyment they increase the privations of the multitude, who are destitute of the necessaries of life; they add but little, moreover, to the pleasures of the rich, whose life is irksome for want of variety in their enjoyments; and they engender more and more corruption by multiplying temptations to cupidity.

Up to the present time the sciences, in augmenting the means of wealth and luxury, have promoted only the interest of the dishonest and scheming, who in the Civilized and Barbaric Orders attain to fortune sooner than any others. This anomaly leads us to one of two conclusions, either to a belief in the malevolence of God, or in the malevolence of Civilization. Rationally, we can admit only the latter, for we can not suppose that God is malevolent, though he really would be so if he had condemned us to vegetate for ever in our disastrous Civilization.

The philosophers, instead of looking at the question from this point of view, have sought to evade the problem which is thus presented by human perversity; problem which leads us either to suspect Civilization or to suspect God. They have adopted a spurious doctrine, that of Atheism, which, assuming that there is no God, dispenses the savants from the trouble of studying his designs, and authorizes them to advance their capricious and irreconcilable theories as the standard of right and wrong. Atheism is a very convenient opinion for moral and political ignorance; and those who have been called strong-minded for having professed Atheism, have shown themselves thereby to be very weak in genius. Fearing to fail in their investigation of the designs of God in respect to the organization of Society, they have preferred to deny the existence of God, and to extol Civilization as the height of perfection, though in secret they abhor it, and the sight of its calamities makes them doubt even Providence itself.

On this point it is not the philosophers alone who are at fault. If it is absurd not to believe in God, it is not less absurd to believe in him but partially — to believe that his Providence is limited, and that he has neglected to provide for the most urgent of our wants, namely, a Social Order calculated to promote the happiness of the human race. When we behold the prodigies accomplished by modern industry — a first class ship, for instance, and so many other wonderful inventions, all of which are premature, considering our social and political infancy — can it be believed that God, who has lavished upon us so many sublime discoveries, would refuse to us that of Social Science, without which the others are as nothing? Would he not be blamable, and inconsistent with himself, to initiate us into so many noble sciences if they were calculated only to produce a state of society reeking with vices and crimes, like Civilization?

V.

GENERAL PREJUDICES OF THE CIVILIZEES.

WHEN I bring forward a discovery which is to deliver the human race from the chaos of the Civilized, the Barbaric, and the Savage Orders — which is to insure to Man more happiness than he has dared to hope for — which is to open to him the whole domain of the mysteries of Nature, from which he believed himself for ever excluded, — the masses will not fail to accuse me of charlatanism, while the sages will think they are using moderation in treating me simply as a visionary.

Without stopping to notice such petty attacks, for which every discoverer should be prepared, I will endeavor to dispose the reader to be impartial.

Why have the most celebrated discoverers — Galileo, Columbus, and so many others — been persecuted, or at least ridiculed, before being heard? There are two prominent reasons, namely:—

1. GENERAL MISFORTUNE. — If a discovery promises happiness

to the human race, men are afraid to indulge in the hope of a good which appears so uncertain; any theory which awakens their ill-reppressed desires, and sharpens their present sense of privation by too brilliant a prospect, they at once reject;—just as we see the poor man who comes unexpectedly into a fortune, into an inheritance, refuse at first to believe it; he repulses the bearer of the good tidings, and accuses him of insulting his misfortune.

This is the first obstacle I shall encounter in announcing to the world that it is about to pass to a state of happiness of which, during five thousand years of what has been considered irremediable misery, it has lost all hope. I should be much better received if I announced a more moderate condition; it is this which has decided me to present the picture of the approaching happiness of the race in the most subdued colors. But when it shall come to be known in its full extent, the world will be astonished that I had the patience to temporise, or to defer the publication; and will wonder that I could use such reserve, and adopt so icy a tone, in announcing an event which should excite so much enthusiasm.

2. SCIENTIFIC PRIDE.—This will be the second obstacle I shall have to struggle against. Every brilliant discovery excites the jealousy of those who have failed to make it. Men become indignant that some one they had never before heard of should, by a lucky stroke of fortune, suddenly become famous. They do not pardon a contemporary who has succeeded in penetrating mysteries which any one of them might have penetrated before him. They do not forgive him for eclipsing the light of known sciences, and leaving the most illustrious savants in the rear. Such a success becomes an affront to the existing generation. People forget the benefits which a discovery is to confer upon them in reflecting upon the mortification with which it covers the the age that has overlooked it; and every man of science, before reasoning about it, wishes to avenge his wounded pride. Such are the reasons why the author of a brilliant discovery is ridiculed and persecuted before he is either judged or examined. Such jealousy is not indeed exhibited toward a Newton, because his calculations are so magnificent that ordinary men of science can make no pretensions to them; but men attack, men vilify a Columbus, because his idea of discovering a New Continent was

so simple that any one might have conceived it as well as himself. In such a case, people unite to perplex and embarrass the discoverer, and seek to prevent the trial of his plans.

I make use of this illustration to render the general malignity of the Civilizees toward discoverers more palpable.

When an ignorant Pope launched the thunders of the Church and of public opinion against Columbus, was he not more interested than any one else in having the plans of Columbus succeed? Without doubt; for hardly had America been discovered, before the Sovereign Pontiff distributed empires over this New World, and found it very convenient to profit by a discovery the very idea of which had excited all his wrath. The Head of the Church in this inconsistency was like all other men; his prejudices and his pride blinded him as to his interest. If he had reasoned about the matter, he would have perceived that the Holy See, having the power at that epoch to extend its temporal sovereignty over unknown lands, and to subject them also to its spiritual empire, was interested in every sense in encouraging the search for a new continent. But such was the pride of the Pope and his counsellors, that they refused to reason. This is a littleness of mind common to all ages and to all persons. Every one must expect to be persecuted in proportion to the magnificence of his discovery, especially if he be a man wholly unknown, and not recommended by some previous discovery to that of which chance has furnished him the key; witness the man whom I have cited, Christopher Columbus. He was ridiculed, disgraced, excommunicated for seven years, for having announced a New Continental World. Ought I not, then, to expect the same treatment in announcing a New Social World?*

---

* If I had to do with an equitable age, one which was seeking sincerely to penetrate the mysteries of Nature, it would be easy to prove to it that the Newtonians have only half-explained the laws of the Movement which they have treated, namely, the Planetary Movement. As a proof of this, if we should interrogate them as to the system by which the stars and planets are distributed, they would remain silent. Their most learned writer, Laplace, could not give the shadow of a solution to either of the following problems: —

What are the laws by which the heavenly bodies are distributed — by which they are assigned particular ranks and positions?

Why is Mercury the first in order?

Why is Herschel, smaller than Saturn, so far from the Sun; and why should not Jupiter, then, be nearer to the sun?

No one can go against public opinion with impunity; and philosophy, which reigns over the nineteenth century, will raise more prejudices against me than superstition raised in the fifteenth against Columbus. Still, if he found in Ferdinand and Isabella sovereigns less prejudiced and more enlightened than all the brilliant geniuses of the age, may not I, like him, count on the support of some sovereign more far-seeing than his contemporaries? And although the sophists of the nineteenth century will repeat with those of the fourteenth that *there is nothing new to discover*, may it not happen that some potentate will be willing to try the experiment which was made by the sovereigns of Castile? They certainly hazarded very little in risking a vessel with the chance of discovering a New World, and of acquiring empire over it; and a sovereign of the nineteenth century might say: " Let us risk a square league of land for trying the experiment of Association; it is certainly hazarding very little to have the chance of extricating the human race from Social Chaos, of ascending the throne of Universal Unity, and transmitting the sceptre of the world through all time to our descendants."

What is the cause of the greater or less eccentricity of orbits?

What are the laws of the grouping and the revolutions of the heavenly bodies?

Why do certain stars revolve, as moons, round a centre, like the satellites of Jupiter, Saturn, and Herschel?

Why do others, like Venus, Mars, etc., move in an independent orbit?

Why has Herschel, sixteen times smaller than Jupiter, eight moons, while the latter has only four? Is not the colossal Jupiter entitled to the greater number of moons? He should, according to his dimensions, attract sixteen times as many as Herschel. This distribution is singularly opposed to the theorem that attraction is exercised in direct ratio to masses. Why, by virtue of this theorem, does not the enormous planet Jupiter attract, and cause to revolve about him, the four little stars Juno, Ceres, Pallas, and Vesta, which are so near to him? In attracting these he would only have eight moons, like Herschel, which is sixteen times smaller than Jupiter, and would still have but a very light charge.

Why has Saturn luminous rings, and Jupiter not, when Saturn receives from his seven moons more light than Jupiter from his four?

Why has the Earth a moon and Jupiter not?

Why has not our moon, like Venus and the Earth, an atmosphere?

What is the difference of functions between satellites, revolving like the moon round a centre, central planets like the Earth and Jupiter, and isolated planets like Venus, Mars, Mercury, Vesta?

What are the changes to which the distributive system of the heavenly bodies has been and is to be subjected?

What are the unknown planets? Where are they stationed? Where must we look for them? What are their dimensions and functions?

In pointing out the prejudices which will be raised against me, I have wished to forewarn the reader against the sarcasms of the host of critics who decide abruptly upon matters of which they are ignorant, and who reply to arguments by pleasantries, the mania for which has extended even to the common people, and has thus diffused the habit of raillery among all classes.

When the evidences of my discovery shall be produced, and the time approaches for gathering its fruits; when Universal Unity is seen rising up from the ruins of Barbarism and Civilization, the critics will suddenly change their tone from disdain to admiration; they will seek to raise the discoverer to the rank of a demi-god, and debase themselves as much by excess of adulation, as they are now about to by excess of raillery.

As to impartial men, who constitute but a small portion of the public, I like their distrust, and I invoke it; but I invite them to suspend their final judgment till I have explained the Mechanism of the Series.

On twenty pages of questions like these our scientific men remain dumb. Of the laws of *distribution* they have no idea; they are, in fact, ignorant of most of the laws of the Sidereal Mechanism, which, nevertheless, they flatter themselves to have fully explained. And I, who since my discoveries of 1814 have been able to reply pertinently to all these questions, have I not finished the task which the Newtonians have only sketched out without completing?

The knowledge of the Sidereal System would include after all but one branch of the laws of Universal Movement; there would still remain to be explained, among others, the Passional or Social Movement, on which depends the unitary organization of the human race — the advent of man to his Social Destiny — and this could be discovered only by studying the laws of Movement as a whole, of which the Newtonians have explained but one branch, and that very unimportant to human happiness.

In bringing forward this theory of Universal Movement, it would be necessary, in order to insure its examination and trial, to support it by the authority of some great name. If it had been Newton, or one of his rivals or successors — like Leibnitz or Laplace — who had announced the THEORY OF PASSIONAL ATTRACTION, the whole world would have smiled on him; under such auspices every one would have seen in it a very natural extension of the THEORY OF MATERIAL ATTRACTION — a logical result of the Unity of the Universe, by virtue of which every principle of Material Harmony must be applicable to the Theory of Passional or Social Harmony; and on such an announcement, made by a Newton or some other eminent person, the whole race of critics would have applauded his discovery even before examining it; his victory would have been chanted before he had even entered the lists. But if the discovery is the work of some man hitherto unknown, of a provincial, of a scientific pariah, of some intruder, who, like Piron, has the misfortune not to be even an academician, he incurs the anathemas of the whole cabal. — *Note added by Fourier in* 1818.

The first two Memoirs* do not touch this matter; they have no other object than to prepare the way, and to familiarize the human mind with the high destiny which is in reserve for it.

VI.

PLAN.

In these two Memoirs I shall consider the following questions:—

What are Destinies?

Of what branches is the Theory of General Destinies composed?

What indications and what means had the human mind for arriving at the discovery of the Theory of General Destinies?

As it would be difficult for me to treat these questions isolatedly, I shall not separate them.

There will be many repetitions found in these pages, and perhaps in order to fix the attention of the reader upon a subject so new, and so opposed to the philosophic prejudices with which the world is imbued, there should have been still more.

I shall divide this Prospectus into three parts, namely, the EXPOSITION, the DESCRIPTION, and the CONFIRMATION.

1. THE EXPOSITION.—This will explain certain branches of General Destinies. A subject so elevated and so vast will not interest a large number of readers, but it will be accompanied with details sufficiently curious to compensate for any dryness. This first part, then, is addressed to the *Inquisitive*, to studious men who are not afraid to encounter a few obstacles for the sake of penetrating profound mysteries. They will be agreeably surprised at various developments here presented on the origin of the different forms of society, on the method of their future succession, and on the material and social revolutions of our own and other globes.

2. THE DESCRIPTION.—This will make known certain details of private or domestic destinies in the Combined Order. It will also contain some sketch of its enjoyments, and in this respect will

---

* The work we are translating was considered by Fourier, at the time he published it, only as a first "*Mémoire-Prospectus.*" His intention was to publish a second volume of the same kind, and to follow these two Memoirs with a regular and scientific exposition of his discovery, developed in six little Memoirs of about a hundred and fifty pages each, which he announced at the end of the volume.—*Translator.*

be addressed to the *Lovers of Pleasure.* In getting a foretaste of the delights of the Combined Order they will perceive to what degree the human race has been misled by the philosophers who have blinded us for so long a period as to the means of attaining to such a happiness, by their obstinate criticisms of Passional Attraction, and by their attempts to repress and to stifle it, instead of making it a profound and systematic study.

3. The Confirmation.—This will consist of illustrations drawn from the falsity of prevailing ideas. I shall argue from the systematic blunders of the Civilizees, and among others the most recent, or that which reigns exclusively over their politics, namely, the Commercial System. I shall point out, in the progress of this system, the increasing degeneracy of the uncertain sciences, and the revolutions to which we are more and more exposed under their auspices. This third part will be addressed to the *Critics;* they will perceive that discredited as the philosophers appear to be, society is more and more influenced and mystified by them; that our Commercial Theories, last resource of the sophists, are the most foolish inventions which have ever appeared, and worthily fill the measure of civilized absurdities.

By means of this arrangement I trust to have adapted the Prospectus to the tastes of all classes of readers, each of whom may perhaps be ranged in one of the three categories—the Inquisitive, the Lovers of Pleasure, or the Critics.

I invite them all to bear in mind that in a Prospectus I cannot stop to give proofs, and that in announcing so many wonderful events, so many marvelous results, I have no desire to impose upon their credulity. My aim is to excite an interest in the subsequent Memoirs, which will contain the demonstrative theory of many new sciences. These sciences will be found all the more marvelous from the fact that every person can be easily initiated in them, since they result logically from a very simple calculation on *Agricultural Association.* Such was the modest germ of the most brilliant of discoveries; thus the greatest river is often at its source but an humble spring, and the avalanche which crushes villages in its fall is at its birth but a few flakes of snow.*

---

* As for this Prospectus, now that I can judge of it after an interval of ten years, I feel that there should be added to it, seeing the progress the Science has since made, a commentary larger than the book itself.—*Note added by Fourier in* 1818.

PART I.

EXPOSITION OF GENERAL DESTINIES.

PREFATORY REMARKS.

ANTICIPATING the charge of dryness which might be brought against this first part, I have already stated that it is intended in nowise for the frivolous, but only for the serious. Persons who have had from me some account of the delights of the Combined Order will naturally expect to find here some description of them; to see the Series in full operation; to read nothing but fascinating details of their interior life, of their delicious banquets, of the variety in their loves, festivals, dramatic performances, adventures, voyages, etc.,—and of the elegance and refinement which they introduce even into the most insipid employments.

Some who have trembled with impatience on hearing of these pleasures, so unknown in Civilization, will be eager to have a complete tableau of them; but regularity requires that before descending to these minor details I make known, first of all, the General Destinies of the planet.

I shall therefore treat, here, of a period of *eighty thousand years*, which will comprise the vegetable career of the globe. I shall speak of the various creations which will succeed those we now see, the first of which will commence in about four centuries. I shall make known the physical modifications which the globe is to undergo during these eighty thousand years, seventy thousand of which will see the boreal pole under full cultivation by the effect of a luminous ring, or boreal crown, which will appear after ten centuries of the Combined Order.

This will be to commence, as I have already said, by presenting difficulties; but if I proceeded without method, for the sake of satisfying the curious, I should lay myself open to criticism; for although I am giving only synopses here, and not theories, it is proper at least that before touching upon what concerns the destiny of individuals, they should bear upon the general affairs of the globe.

In course of the work there will be found various tables the nomenclature of which may seem to be improper and badly chosen, for I do not pretend to be a master of the French language. It is important, then, to consider ideas rather than words, in the choice of which I confess my incompetency. In this respect, I shall adopt more correct nomenclatures when they are communicated to me.

THE PRINCIPLE OF EXCEPTION.

I MUST commence with a short dissertation upon this subject, in order to spare the reader the trouble of making an infinity of objections which otherwise he will be sure to raise.

The calculations on Attraction and on Social Movement are all subject to an eighth or a ninth of exception; this must always be understood even when I fail to mention it. For example, if I say, speaking in general terms, that the Civilizees are very unhappy, I mean that seven eighths or eight ninths of them are reduced to a state of privation and misfortune; that an eighth only escape from the general unhappiness and enjoy a lot worthy of envy.*

If I add that the happiness enjoyed by the small minority of Civilizees is all the more aggravating for the majority from the fact that the favorites of Fortune are the least worthy of her benefits, it will be found again, that this assertion allows of an eighth or a ninth of exception, and that one in eight of those who are favored by Fortune deserve to be so. This shadow of equity serves only to confirm the systematic injustice which reigns in the Civilized Order.

I conclude, then, that the exception of an eighth or ninth which

---

* Was it not necessary that God should raise some men to a state of happiness which is refused to the great majority? Without this precaution the Civilizees would not be conscious of their misfortune. The sight of the prosperity of the few is a stimulus well calculated to operate upon the ravants, who are generally poor, and excite them to seek for a new Social Order capable of procuring for Civilizees the happiness of which they are now destitute.

may be applied to all my assertions will serve only to confirm them ; it will be useless for me to mention the exceptions in each instance, and useless, also, for the reader to raise any such objections, which will only serve to support what I may have advanced. I shall take care to repeat this observation more than once in order that it may not be forgotten.

The exception is not fixed invariably at an eighth or a ninth, since it varies more or less ; but the eighth or ninth is the more frequently applicable, and may be admitted in most general calculations.

I.

DEFINITION AND DIVISION.

DESTINIES are the present, past, and future results of the mathematical laws of God in respect to Universal Movement.

UNIVERSAL MOVEMENT is divided into four principal branches, the *Social*, the *Animal*, the *Organic*, and the *Material*.

1. THE SOCIAL MOVEMENT.—The theory of this explains the laws by which God regulates the order and succession of the various social mechanisms, or forms of society, on all inhabited globes.

2. THE ANIMAL MOVEMENT.—The theory of this explains the laws by which God distributes passions and instincts to all beings of past or future creation on the various globes.

3. THE ORGANIC MOVEMENT.—The theory of this explains the laws by which God distributes properties, forms, colors, savors, etc., to all substances created or to be created on the various globes.

4. THE MATERIAL MOVEMENT.—The theory of this, already explained by modern astronomers, has made known the laws by which God regulates the gravitation of matter for all globes.*

---

* A copy of the original work, annoted by Fourier, in 1818, rectifies this division of the branches of Movement, giving five instead of four, as follows : —

PIVOTAL MOVEMENT : The *Social* or *Passional*.

CARDINAL MOVEMENTS :
- The *Aromal*.*
- The *Instinctual*.
- The *Organic*.
- The *Material*.

* The *Aromal Movement*, or system of distribution of aromas, known or unknown, — directing Man and the animals, forming the germs of winds and of epidemics, controlling the material relations of the planets, and furnishing the germs of the creations upon them.

There is no effect of Movement which is not comprised in one of these four divisions. The four united constitute the Universal Movement; of these four we know only the laws of the last, namely, the *Material Movement*. This, again, has been only partially explained, for the astronomers, while indicating the laws of the existing order in the planetary worlds, are ignorant what changes these worlds may have undergone a hundred thousand years since, and also what changes they may undergo a hundred thousand years hence. In a word they are ignorant how to determine the past and future revolutions of the universe. This calculation, which will be brought within the comprehension of all, forms a part of the Theory of the Material Movement; hence it will be seen that it had not been fully discovered.

II.

HIERARCHY OF THE FOUR MOVEMENTS.

I SHOULD have devoted an entire chapter to this subject, but as it would not be understood by most readers, I restrict myself to saying a few words upon it in a note.* The reader may pass

---

* The Four Movements are dependent upon two things: —

FIRST DEPENDENCE. — The laws of the Four Movements are coördinated to mathematics. Without this dependence there would be no harmony in Nature, and God would be unjust.

In effect, Nature is composed of three eternal, uncreated, and indestructible principles.

1. *God, or Spirit;* the active and moving principle.
2. *Matter;* the passive principle, which is acted upon.
3. *Justice, or Mathematics;* the regulative principle of Movement.

To establish harmony between these three principles, it is necessary that God, in acting upon and modifying matter, should be in accord with the law of mathematics; otherwise he would be arbitrary, both in his own eyes and in ours, from the fact that he would not be in accord with a justice positive and independent of himself. But though God submits himself to mathematical laws which he can not change, he finds in this both his glory and his interest: his *glory*, in that he can demonstrate to Man that he governs the universe equitably and not arbitrarily, — that he acts upon matter according to laws which are not subject to change; his *interest*, in that his accord with mathematical laws furnishes him the means of obtaining, in all Movement, the greatest number of effects with the smallest number of means.

We know, already, that two of the Movements — the Material and the Organic — are in accord with geometry; that all bodies, animate and inanimate, are constructed, moved, and modified, according to its laws. Here, then, are two of the Four Movements, coördinated to natural justice, and independent of God.

It remains to be shown that the two other Movements — the Animal and the Social — *follow the same rule*, and that all the passions, even the most ignoble, produce, alike

this note over, for it is not necessary to an understanding of what follows, and can be interesting to but a few persons.

In Man and in the animals, only such effects as are geometrically regulated by God. For example: —

The properties of Friendship are calculated according to the properties of the Circle; —

The properties of Love are calculated according to the properties of the Ellipse; —

The properties of Paternity are calculated according to the properties of the Parabola; —

The properties of Ambition are calculated according to the properties of the Hyperbola; —

And the collective properties of these four passions — Friendship, Love, Paternity, Ambition — are calculated according to the properties of the Cycloid. So that every theorem of geometry has served as the type for some passion either of Man or the animals; and this passion invariably preserves its relations to the theorem which regulated its creation. It will be seen, in another part of the work, that the Passional Series, or Series of Groups have also for their type, the order and the properties of the geometrical series.

SECOND DEPENDENCE. — The Social Movement is the type of the three others; the Animal, Organic, and Material Movements are coördinated to the Social, which is the first in order. In other words, the properties of every animal, vegetable, and mineral — and even of every group of stars — represent some effect of the human passions in society; and *every created thing*, from the atom to the star, presents a tableau of the properties of some passion in Man. For example: —

The groups of Stars comprising the Milky Way represent the properties of Ambition; —

The groups of Planets revolving round Suns represent the properties of Love; —

The groups of Satellites revolving round Planets represent the properties of Paternity; —

The groups of Suns, or Fixed Stars, represent the properties of Friendship.[*]

So that our passions, so much decried by the philosophers, perform, according to the law of God, the first part in the Movement of the Universe; they are all that is most noble, after himself, since he has willed that the whole universe should be so arranged as to symbolize the effects which they produce in Social Movement.

It follows from the above that when a globe comes to know the laws of Social Movement, it will discover, at the same time, the laws of the other Movements, since the latter are, in all points, hieroglyphs of the former; hence if we did not yet know the laws of the Material Movement, determined by modern astronomers, they would be discovered now by their analogy with those of the Social Movement which I have penetrated, and which furnishes the key to the whole system of the three others. It is unfortunate for the human race that the savants commenced their studies just where they should have been completed, that is with the laws of the Material Movement which were the most difficult to determine, and which opened no way for arriving at a knowledge of the laws of the three others.

This note will be found very inadequate, being a mere sketch which did not admit of my entering into more minute details.

* Defective Illustrations; there are many other sidereal groups, but in 1807 I did not know the potential calculations of groups either in sidereal relations or in passional relations.—*Note added by Fourier in* 1818.

III.

THE SOCIAL MOVEMENT.

It has been seen by what precedes that the order and succession of the various social mechanisms possible on the different globes must be determined by the Theory of the Social Movement, which embraces the present, the past, and the future.

A fine subject this for satirists!

"You are going to inform us, then," they will say, "what is going on in other worlds—in the Sun, the Moon, Jupiter, Sirius, the Milky Way, and in the whole planetary universe."

Certainly I am; and you will be informed, also, what has taken place there in the past, and what is to take place there for ages to come; for the chart of General Destinies can not be read partially; we can not determine the Destiny of one world without possessing the calculations which will unveil the Destinies of all worlds.

This knowledge of the condition of other globes is not so indifferent to you as you may imagine; for it will be demonstrated to you that your souls will traverse them during future ages, and that the eternal happiness which your religions teach you to hope for will depend upon the condition of these other globes, in which your souls will be again conjoined to matter after having passed eighty thousand years on the globe we now inhabit.

You will then understand the social mechanisms existing on the different planets, and the fortunate or unfortunate revolutions to which their inhabitants are subject. You will learn that our little globe has been for five or six thousand years in the most unfortunate condition in which a globe can be placed. But the calculation which will reveal to you the happiness enjoyed on other planets, will reveal to you at the same time the means of introducing on your own a happiness nearly equal to that of the most fortunate worlds.

I pass to the account of the social revolutions which our own globe is to undergo.

IV.

PHASES AND PERIODS OF SOCIAL DEVELOPMENT ON THE THIRD PLANET, CALLED THE EARTH.

THE reader will here learn a truth of the highest importance; it is this, that the ages of happiness will be of seven times longer duration than the ages of misfortune, such as that in which Man has lived for thousands of years.

This may seem a matter of indifference to us when it is considered that we have lived in an unhappy period; but the Theory of the Social Movement will demonstrate to you that your souls, in future ages, will participate in some manner in the lot of souls still living upon the earth; you will participate, then, during seventy thousand years, in the happiness which is in preparation for this globe, and it is with this view that you should take an interest in the account of the future revolutions which the Social Movement is to undergo upon your own planet. The existence of the human race on the Earth will comprise a period of say eighty thousand years. This number, like every other relating to the Social Movement, is calculated within about an eighth.

The social career of Man on the globe, the duration of which is thus estimated at eighty thousand years, is divided into four phases, and subdivided into thirty-two periods, according to the following Table: —

PHASES.

Two phases of Ascending Vibration, or Ascension.
Two phases of Descending Vibration, or Declension.

ASCENDING VIBRATION.

First Phase.
Infancy, or Ascending Social Incoherence, $\frac{1}{16}$ 5,000 years.

Second Phase.
Growth, or Ascending Social Combination, $\frac{7}{16}$ 35,000 "

DESCENDING VIBRATION.

Third Phase.
Decline, or Descending Social Combination, $\frac{7}{16}$ 35,000 "

Fourth Phase.
Caducity, or Descending Social Incoherence, $\frac{1}{16}$ 5,000 "

Total.... 80,000 years.

The two phases of Social Incoherence or Discord comprise the periods of misfortune.

The two phases of Social Combination or Unity comprise the periods of happiness, the duration of which will be seven times longer than the periods of misfortune.

It will be seen by the preceding table that in the career of the human race, as in that of individuals, the periods of suffering are at the two extremities.

We are now in the first phase, in the age of Ascending Social Incoherence, which precedes our advent to the Social Destiny of the race; hence during the five or six thousand years of which our chronicles have preserved the history, mankind has been extremely unhappy. Nearly seven thousand years have elapsed since the creation of Man, and during that period he has passed only from torment to torment.

The immense amount of suffering to which the race has been subjected cannot be appreciated till we come to know the superlative happiness reserved for us, the possession of which we are about to obtain through the discovery of the Laws of Movement. We are about to enter upon the second phase in our social career, that of Ascending Social Combination.

The two phases of Incoherence, though very short, contain each seven social periods; in all   **14 Periods of Incoherence.**

The two phases of Combination, though very long, contain each but nine social periods; in all   **18 Periods of Combination.**

Total   **32 Periods or Societies.**

Total, thirty-two periods, or possible forms of society, without counting the mixed. The Table of these thirty-two periods will be found annexed.

On the inspection of this Table, the first thing which strikes us is the narrowness of the views of the philosophers, who would persuade us that Civilization is the ultimate limit of Human Destiny, whereas it is only the fifth of the thirty-two possible forms of society, and is one of the most unhappy of the ten periods of misfortune, which are : —

The 2d, 3d, 4th, 5th, 6th, in the Phase of Infancy ;

The 31st, 30th, 29th, 28th, 27th, in the Phase of Caducity.

I call these periods of misfortune, because there is no real happiness for Man except in these periods, the mechanism of which is based upon Series of Groups, and not on Isolated Households.

The periods 1 and 32, 7 and 26, are organized in Series, but of an imperfect description; the 7th and 26th are embryos of the regular Series of Groups, and would be organized in case the human race should fail of the scientific calculation of Association, and discover only its germs. These imperfect Series are still very happy; I shall give some account of them in the second part, which will treat of the Collective Household.

The human race is about to advance to the eighth social period (Simple Combined Series), which will be established all over the globe, and will last at least four hundred years before we can pass to the ninth. The latter can be organized only by the aid of new creations, and of the Boreal Crown, of which I shall speak hereafter.

During the course of its first phase, the Social Movement presents the image of a man recoiling from a chasm in order to obtain the necessary impetus for springing over it. This is designated in the preceding Table by the words *recoil, spring,* and *leap.* It is a recoil to fall back from the first period which is happy, to the fourth which is the most unhappy. But a new force is thus acquired — namely, that of agricultural and manufacturing industry — which augmenting during the fifth, sixth, and seventh periods, gives to the human race, at last, the means of overleaping the chasm which separates Chaos from Harmony.

The thirty-two forms of Society must not be counted as sixteen; for the sixteen of the last two phases although reproductions, in an inverse order, of the sixteen of the first two phases, undergo great changes in their reappearance. For example, Civilization will be as calm when it shall reappear at the decline of the Social World as, now while the race has all the ardor and impetuosity of youth, it is turbulent. The period of latter-Civilization will be subdued by the consciousness of a lost happiness, and by grief at not being able to reorganize the Series, the mechanism of which will be obstructed, disorganized, and broken up by the eighteenth and last creation which will be deleterious, like that which we now see.

The first phase or Infancy is the only one of which the duration is not fixed and whose course is irregular. It should have been limited to five thousand years; but God, in endowing Man with free will, could not prevent certain globes from being led astray by the uncertain sciences, and by the prejudices they diffuse against Nature and Attraction. These globes, stultified by philosophic doctrines, may remain for a long time in a state of blindness, and believe themselves skilled in social science while ignorant how to produce anything but revolutions, indigence, fraud, and carnage. So long as men persist in this belief, and until reason rises up against false science, we must not be surprised if social disorder continue to prevail. And is it possible to conceive a more frightful state of disorder than that which now reigns on our globe? One half of the earth is overrun by wild beasts, or, which is the same thing, by Savages; while on the other half, which is under cultivation, we see three quarters inhabited by Barbarians or cut-throats, who enslave their laborers and their women, and are in all respects a disgrace to humanity. There remains, then, one eighth of the globe, which has fallen to the Civilizees or rogues, who boast of their social improvements while extending indigence and corruption to the last degree. Where on any globe can be found more frightful disorder? And when we see nations accepting a philosophy which has led to such political chaos, is it at all astonishing that the human race is thousands of years behind-hand in its social career; that it has passed seven thousand years in an infancy which should have lasted hardly five thousand; and that it has arrived only to the fifth of the seven infantile periods—not attaining even to the sixth, where it might have found at least some degree of happiness?

In the two ages of Ascending and Descending Social Combination, which are about to commence, and which will comprise seventy thousand years, the progress of the Social Movement will be regular. In the course of this long period of happiness, the sixteen social metamorphoses, or changes of period, will be determined by new creations which will succeed each other regularly, and which, yielding new products in each of the three kingdoms, will cause corresponding modifications in the state of society. But these changes will consist chiefly in varieties of enjoyment, and will in no case produce disastrous revolutions, except during the transition from the twenty-fourth to the twenty-fifth period which will cause a rapid decline, and will announce the caducity of the globe.

For the rest, if a child six or seven years of age ought not to trouble himself about the infirmities which will come upon him in his eightieth year, so we, like him, should think only of the happiness which is near at hand, and of which the Earth never before had such pressing need.

V.

REMARKS ON THE ANTERIOR SUBVERSIVE CREATION, ASSIGNED TO THE FIRST PHASE AND TO THE EIGHTH PERIOD WHICH OPENS THE SECOND PHASE.

THE creation whose products we now see upon the Earth is the first of twenty-six creations which will appear successively during the social career of the human race.

I speak here only of the *substances* of the three kingdoms, and not of the creation of the globe itself.*

In order to engender the various productions which have appeared on the old continent, Nature employed a period of about four hundred and fifty years. The creations in America took place subsequently, and were conducted on a different plan; but on both continents they occasioned great convulsions. Those in the Harmonic Order will be effected without commotion.

Since it is a delight to God to create, it is for his interest to prolong that delight; and if the time for the conception, gestation and birth of a child embraces a period of nine months, he must have employed a proportional space of time for creating the three kingdoms. This period is estimated in the present theory at $\frac{1}{132}$ part of the social career, which gives say four hundred and fifty years for the period of the first creation.

Every creation is effected by the conjunction of a boreal fluid which is male, with an austral fluid which is female. A planet is

---

* A copy of the original work annoted by Fourier has in the margin the following remark : —

"In 1807 I knew the Theory of Creations but very imperfectly; two will take place at the commencement of Social Harmony, and will yield immense riches in the three kingdoms."

a being which has two souls and two sexes, and which procreates like the animal and the vegetable by the union of two generating fluids. The process is the same, with perhaps a few exceptions, in every department of Nature, for the planets, like the vegetables, combine the two sexes in one and the same individual.

To believe that the Earth will bring forth no more new creations, but will limit itself to those which we now see, would be like believing that a woman who has been able to bear one child can not bear a second, a third, a tenth. The Earth also will bear successive creations; but the sixteen harmonic will be effected with as much facility as the two subversive ones—the first and the eighteenth—have cost and will cost commotions.

On every globe the first and the last creations are regulated on an opposite plan to that of the intermediate creations, and yield as result an abundance of injurious productions with but a diminutive number which are useful. In the intermediate or harmonic creations, the contrary takes place; they yield as result an affluence of beautiful and useful productions with a diminutive number, an eighth, of useless, and none which are pernicious.

Thus the first creation, that which we now see, has borne an immense number of noxious beasts on land, and still more in the seas. Persons who believe in demons might fancy that Hell itself had presided over this creation, and that in the form of the tiger and the monkey they beheld the spirit of Moloch and Belial. And I ask, what could Hell itself, in all its fury, have invented worse than the rattlesnake, the bedbug, the legions of insects and reptiles, the monsters of the sea, the plague, hydrophobia, leprosy, syphilis, the gout, and so many malignant poisons devised for the torment of man, and for making this globe a social pandemonium?

I have indicated the causes of the baneful system which determined the first creation, in a preceding note, in which it is stated that the effects of the three Movements, the Animal, the Organic, and the Material, represent the play of human passions in society. Now as the first creation was to form a tableau of the seven periods of Social Infancy, to the use of which it is devoted, God in this creation must have depicted the frightful results which our passions were to produce during these seven periods, by corresponding creations; and as certain virtues were to exist in the course of the first and seventh periods, he must have represented these by certain useful and beneficent productions, which in the three kingdoms of this truly demoniac creation are found in very small number. It will be seen hereafter what kind of productions will result from future creations, both on land and in the seas. At present we are ignorant how to use even the few good productions furnished by the first creation; and I shall cite as a proof of this, four quadrupeds, the vicuna, the reindeer, the zebra, and the beaver. We are deprived of the two former by our unskilfulness, our cruelty, and our general dishonesty; but for these obstacles herds of reindeer and vicunas might be raised in all the chains of high mountains where these animals could be acclimated. Other social vices deprive us of the beaver, which is not less precious for its fur than the vicuna for its fleece, and of the zebra which is equally valuable with the horse for its speed, its vigor, and its beauty. There prevails in the arrangement of our stables and in our treatment of the brute creation, a coarseness, an ignorance, which renders the domestication and training of these animals impossible. We shall see from the commencement of the eighth period, and we should see even in the seventh, the zebra and the quagga domesticated among us like the horse and the ass, beavers constructing their edifices and forming their republics in the midst of our most populous districts, and herds of vicunas as common in our mountains as flocks of sheep; while many other animals, like the ostrich, the deer, the jerboa, etc., will also come and associate themselves with Man as soon as they find attractions strong enough to retain them. But these attractions the Civilized Order is utterly unable to supply. Thus the present creation, at best so scanty in useful productions, is rendered doubly so by our social ignorance which deprives us of most of the good offered to Man by the three kingdoms.

The new creations can not commence till the human race shall have órganized the eighth social period; till then, and during the existence of the first seven Orders of Society, this second creation can never be witnessed.

Meanwhile the Earth is violently agitated by the need of creating; we see this by the frequency of the aurora-borealis, which is a symptom of the rut of the planet—a useless effusion of prolific fluid which can not combine with the fluid of the other planets till the human race shall have accomplished the preparatory works. These works can be executed only in the eighth period which is about to be organized. The population of the globe must first be increased to its minimum complement of two thousand millions, which will require at least another century; for women are much less prolific in the Combined Order than in Civilization, where the life of the isolated household makes them generate children by the legion—children of whom misery destroys a third, while another third is swept off by the numerous diseases which the Incoherent Order causes to prevail among the young. It would be better to propagate fewer children, and preserve them,—a thing impossible for the Civilizees, who for this reason can not bring the globe under general cultivation; and despite their frightful pullulation they suffice only to cultivate the land which they occupy.

When the two thousand millions of inhabitants shall have cultivated the globe up to the 60th degree North, we shall see the Boreal Crown appear, which will furnish heat and light to the icy regions of the Arctic Zone. These new regions opened to industry will permit the population of the globe to be increased to its full complement of three thousand millions. Then the two continents will be brought under full cultivation, and there will no longer be any obstacles to the Harmonic Creations, the first* of which will commence in about four centuries after the establishment of the Combined Order.

VI.

THE BOREAL CROWN.

When the human race shall have cultivated the globe up to and beyond the 60th degree North, its temperature will become comparatively mild and regular, the rut of the planet will acquire more activity, and the aurora-borealis, becoming more frequent, will be found stationary round the North Pole, opening out in the

---

* I have since discovered that this first creation will appear four years after the foundation of Universal Harmony; it is the Austral Crown which will appear at a later period, say in about four hundred and thirty-two years after this foundation. I said nothing in 1808 of this Austral Crown, concerning the birth of which I had no certainty The theory of Cosmogony was then but little advanced, and I preferred saying too little to hazarding what was still conjectural. — *Note added by Fourier in* 1818.

form of a ring or Crown. Its fluid, which at present is only luminous, will then acquire a new property, that of distributing heat as well as light.

The Crown will be of such dimensions as always to be at some point in contact with the Sun, the rays of which should embrace its outer circle ; it should present an arc to the Sun even at the greatest inclination of the Earth's axis.

The influence of the Boreal Crown will make itself strongly felt over a third of the northern hemisphere ; it will be visible at St. Petersburg, Ochotsk, and in all the regions of the 60th degree North.

From the 60th degree to the Pole the heat will go on increasing, so that the polar centre will enjoy about the same temperature as Andalusia and Sicily.

At this epoch the entire globe will be brought under cultivation, which, in regions hitherto uncultivated, like Siberia and Upper Canada, will cause a softening of the temperature of from ten to twenty and even twenty-two degrees.

The climates in the vicinity of the 60th degree will become modified by two causes, by the influence of general cultivation and by the influence of the Boreal Crown, owing to which only moderate winds will come from the Pole, like those which come from Barbary to Genoa and Marseilles. These causes combined will establish in the 60th degree the temperature now enjoyed in the regions of the 45th degree under full culture, such as Bordeaux, Lyons, Turin, Venice. The cities of Stockholm, St. Petersburg, Tobolsk, and Yakutsk, which will be on the coldest line of latitude, will enjoy a temperature, save certain modifications caused by the vicinity of mountains and seas, like that of the South of France, and of Lombardy. The maritime coasts of Siberia, now impracticable, will possess the mild temperature of Nice and Naples.

A more important amelioration which we shall owe to the Boreal Crown will be the prevention of all atmospheric excesses ; excess of cold·and heat, excess of humidity and dryness, excess of storms and calms. The influence of the Crown, combined with the influence of universal cultivation, will produce all over the globe a graduated temperature which at the present day can exist on no part of it. The climates which will be the coldest on the Earth, such as the line between St. Petersburg and Ochotsk, will enjoy at that epoch a more agreeable temperature than is found at present at the most celebrated resorts, such as Florence, Nice, Montpelier, and Lisbon, which are favored by the softest and serenest skies. I estimate that these places have about four months of fine temperate weather, but after the appearance of the Boreal Crown, the 60th degree — that is to say the line of St. Petersburg and Ochotsk — will have at least eight months of fine season, and the certainty of a double harvest. (See the note below, in which I point out the causes of long winters and of other climatic disorders to which the globe is subjected during the first phases of the Social Movement.*)

* Besides the natural cause of winters, which is the inclination of the Earth's axis, there are three incidental causes which concur to render them four times more severe than they should be, and which will not be found in the Combined Order; these causes are : —

1. The uncultivated state of the globe and especially of the regions about the North Pole;

2. The vast fields of Polar ice, which increase the intensity of the cold during the absence of the Sun;

3. The icy winds which blow from the Pole and counteract the influence of the Sun at the return of Spring.

On the birth of the Boreal Crown, these three causes of intense cold will be neutralized. The regions in the latitude of St. Petersburg will be more certain of a double harvest than those in the latitude of Tuscany are at present, and the 60th degree will enjoy a longer season of fine weather than can be found at the present day on any part of the Earth; this I will now explain.

As soon as the regions about the Pole shall receive light and heat from the Boreal Crown, and be brought under cultivation, nothing will be able to counteract the influence of the Sun on the approach of Spring, at which epoch, we have now a second winter by the effect of the cold winds which extend from the Pole over the whole hemisphere; it is owing to this cause that the winters in France extend into May and consume the pleasantest portion of the Spring.

After the advent of the Crown, the Polar winds will be tempered, even in Winter, and the climate of the 60th degree over which they blow will thus become softened; there will be no other cold winds than those which originate in the vicinity of the 60th degree, which latitude, even in winter, will receive heat from two points, from the North as well as from the South. Foliation will commence, then, at St. Petersburg early in March, and in the 70th degree earlier still; while it will be well advanced in Paris and Spitzbergen during the month of February. Such would be the course of Nature if she were not thwarted by Polar winds and emanations which impede germination at the return of Spring, and give us a second and factitious winter worse than the first.

What constitutes a fine season is a well-regulated variety of temperature. A light frost in the month of January, provided it be of short duration, and come on gradually, at a suitable time, without being accompanied by chilly fogs or bleak winds, seems as agreeable to us as a fine day in Spring. Such will be the winters in the New Order. The grape will be grown in the 60th degree, while the orange will be cultivated in the

Before demonstrating this future event—the birth of the Boreal Crown—let me point out various indications which seem

53d and the 70th. Warsaw will have groves of orange-trees as Lisbon has now, and the vine will be less exposed at St. Petersburg than it is at present at Mayence; for the metamorphosis of the polar winds into soft zephyrs will protect it from violent changes in temperature, which now constitute one of the principal causes of impoverishment all over the globe.

The chilling influence of the Pole renders our winters much too rigorous during the month of January which is their natural season, and causes them to recommence at the exit of January when they should cease. These two circumstances suffice to make our hemisphere, up to the 40th degree in Europe and up to the 30th in Asia and America, where the cold is much more severe, an abode truly detestable; Philadelphia and Pekin, which are on the line of Naples and Lisbon, have winters more disagreeable, more bleak than those of Frankfort and Dresden which are higher North by eleven or twelve degrees.

It will be objected that if there is to be so little cold in the Temperate Zone, the heat on nearing the Equator will be insupportable. It will be nothing of the kind. Other causes will contribute to temper the Equator, and will render the summers of Senegal less oppressive than those of France. A graduated and benignant temperature will succeed to the hurricanes and tempests which extend from the Equator over the Temperate Zones, and the climates will be regenerated at the centres as at the extremities of the globe. I shall not speak here of the causes which will correct the equatorial climate, since they have no relation to the Boreal Crown.

To conclude; when these various influences for the softening of the temperature shall be brought to bear upon the atmosphere of the Earth, the worst climates, like Ochotsk and Yakutsk, will be able to count upon from eight to nine months of fine season, and on a sky exempt from storms and fogs, which will be rare even in the vicinity of the sea, while in the inland parts of the continent they will be nearly unknown.

It is understood that these ameliorations will be modified by high mountains and the proximity of seas, especially at the three continental extremities near the South Pole, which is to have no Crown, but will remain for ever shrouded in frost. This, however, will not prevent the regions in the vicinity of this Pole from participating in various ways in the influence of the Crown, which among other things will change the savor of the sea, and decompose or precipitate its bituminous particles by the diffusion of a boreal fluid. This fluid combined with the salt will give to the water a slightly acidulated and pungent taste. It will be easy then to free it from its saline and citrine particles which will render it soft and thus enable our ships to dispense with loading themselves down with casks of water. This decomposition of sea-water by the boreal fluid is one of the necessary preliminaries to the new marine creations. These creations will consist of a host of amphibious servants for drawing vessels, and for the service of the fisheries, in place of the legion of monsters now infesting the sea, which will all be exterminated by the effect of the boreal fluid and its purification of the seas. An instant extermination will purge the ocean of these horrible creatures which in their implacable wars serve only to symbolize the fury of our passions. We shall see them all stricken with sudden death, as we shall see the odious customs of the Civilizees, the Barbarians, and the Savages suddenly extinguished to make place for the virtues, which will be honored and triumphant in the Combined Order, since they will become the avenues to fortune and pleasure.

N. B.—The Caspian Sea and other salt basins in the interior, like the Sea of Aral, and even the Black Sea which is almost isolated from the ocean, will be but slightly to announce it; and, first, the contrast in form between the lands toward the South Pole and those about the North Pole. The three Southern continents narrow to a point on approaching the Pole, so as to keep human relations away from these latitudes. The Northern continents, on the contrary, have a form exactly opposite; they spread out on nearing the Pole and surround it so as to receive the rays from the luminous ring which is one day to crown it; and they pour their great rivers in this direction as if to attract human relations toward the Arctic Seas. Now if God had not intended to crown the Northern Pole with a fructifying ring, it would follow that the distribution of the continents which surround it, would present a phenomenon of incongruity; and God would seem all the more unwise in such a distribution from the fact that he has acted with extreme wisdom at the opposite points, for he has given to the Southern continents a form perfectly adapted to a Pole which will never have a fructifying crown.*

The objection might be raised that God has extended the Southern point of America too far, thus causing a temporary hindrance to navigation; but his intention was that this route should be abandoned, and that canals navigable for large vessels should be cut through the isthmuses of Panama and Suez. These works, and so many others, the idea of which dismays the Civilizees, will be only child's play for the industrial armies of the Spheric Hierarchy.

Another prognostication of the Boreal Crown is the defective position of the Earth's axis. If we suppose that the Crown is never to appear, the axis to be of service to the two continents, should be inclined $\frac{1}{24}$ or $7\frac{1}{2}$ degrees toward the meridian of Constantinople, so that this capital would be in latitude 33° N. It would result from this that Karskoe Straits and the two North-

and slowly affected by the boreal fluid. They will receive none of the sub-marine currents which, proceeding from the North Pole, will be diffused through the oceans and gulfs, but will inhale the more subtle aromas which, emanating from the Crown, will permeate the whole atmosphere. Hence the fish contained in these bituminous reservoirs will not be destroyed by the boreal fluid; its small quantity and its slow and imperceptible introduction will enable them to accustom themselves to it in two or three generations, and to become more vigorous than they are in the bituminous waves, just as fruits become finer and more savory by being grafted.— *Note by Fourier.*

* It will have one, but at a later period than the other pole.—*Note added subsequently by Fourier.*

ern extremities of Asia and America would be advanced 7½°
further among the ices of the North Pole. This would be sacrificing the most useless part of the globe for the benefit of all the
others. We may judge of this by some details relative to the
Polar and Temperate regions.

As for the Polar regions, let us observe that Karskoe Straits
being completely useless, owing to the projection of the N. E.
Cape, it is of little importance that these Straits be extended
somewhat further into the ice, since they are already useless for
navigation. But their approach seven or eight degrees nearer the
pole would lower by the same distance the most valuable region
of the Frozen Zone ; this region is the Gulf of Archangel, or the
White Sea, which would become perfectly navigable, since the
North Cape in Lapland would be only in 64° N. on a line with
Jacobstat, the last town in Finland. Maritime relations would
be extended easily to the mouths of the Obi and of the Yenessei,
which would gain fourteen degrees of heat by this readjustment
of the axis, and fourteen more by the effect of cultivation of which
Eastern Siberia would become susceptible. Then would be established water-communication between the extremities of the great
continent, and the productions of China, shipped from the bend
of the Hoang-Ho to Lake Baikal, would be transhipped at small
expense to Europe by way of the Angara and the Yenessei.

In our Temperate Zone the important outlets, such as the Sound
and the Channel, would be ameliorated in the same manner by
being brought five or six degrees nearer to the Equator. The
Gulfs of St. Lawrence and of Corea would not be subjected to any
material change in latitude, but the whole Baltic would gain full
seven degrees, and St. Petersburg would be in the present latitude of Berlin. I do not speak of the equatorial regions, since
a change of 7½° would be of no importance in those latitudes.

Toward the 45th degree, the Southern point of America would
be brought a little nearer to the Equator, which would be an advantage to it. The Southern points of Australia would gain still
more in the same sense. As for the Southern extremity of Africa
it would descend from 35° to 42°, and would remain equally practicable for navigators, who in any case will abandon it sooner or
later for the Canal of Suez.

Let any one trace on a map of the globe the latitudes coördinated to this hypothesis of a change of axis, and he will see that it would be for the advantage of the whole Earth, save only certain regions, like Kamschatka, which are unworthy of attention. Now God would have placed the Earth's axis in the manner I have indicated if we were not destined to have the Boreal Crown, by means of which this axis, now so absurdly placed, will be found in the position the most conducive to the general good— a peremptory indication of the necessity of the Crown and of its future appearance.

This fact of the absurd position of the Earth's axis has not been observed hitherto, because the philosophical modes of reasoning prevent our making any critical analysis of the works of God, and drive us to the extreme position, either of disbelief in Providence, or of a blind and stupid admiration, like that of certain savants who admire everything, even to the spider, the toad and other vermin, in which, until we know the reason of their creation, it is impossible to see anything but a cause of reproach to the Creator. The defective position of the Earth's axis necessarily leads us either to question the wisdom of God or to divine the future advent of the Boreal Crown, which will justify the Creator's apparent mistake. But our false modes of reasoning, and our tendency on the one hand to atheism, or on the other to blind admiration, having prevented our forming any impartial judgment of the works of God, we have not known how to determine their necessary correctives, nor to foresee the material and political revolutions by which he himself will effect them.

I have entered into these details in order to prove that the material distribution of continents, and of lands generally, has not been made by chance. I shall give a second proof of this when treating of the Archipelagoes, in the chapter on Insular Monopoly. Chance is about to lose the high potency which is attributed to it by Philosophy at the expense of Providence. It will be seen that God has restricted it within the narrowest limits. As to the forms of continents, which are here in question, far from their being the result of chance, God has calculated the fitness of things even to the extent of preparing a special site for the capital of Universal Unity. Even now we are struck with the unique and wonderful provisions he has made for combining usefulness with beauty in the location of Constantinople; and every one, divining from this the design of God, exclaims : " Here should be the Capital of the Globe !" it will necessarily be so ; and at its antipode will be placed the first meridian of Universal Unity.

I should add, on this subject of the Boreal Crown, that the prediction of this electric phenomenon will not seem at all extraordinary when we consider the rings of Saturn. Why should not God accord to the Earth what he accords to other globes ? Is the existence of the Polar Crown more incomprehensible than that of the equatorial belts of Saturn ?

The aspect of these two luminous rings should before now have dissipated our prejudices in respect to the Sun, which has been ridiculously regarded as a world inflamed. Herschel is the only one who has well described it :—" A grand and magnificent world, bathing in an ocean of light." The thing was evident from the moment the two rings of Saturn were discovered. If God can give circular belts to a globe, he can give those which are spherical ; he can also give polar rings and even polar caps. We have now to learn the theory which regulates this distribution, and which will admit our globe to participate in a favor that up to the present time has been enjoyed only by Saturn. There are groups of stars each of which has some luminous ornament for supplying heat to one or both of its poles, and if our group is generally destitute of them, it is because it is one of the poorest in the firmament ; for I shall show that our thirty-two planets (not counting the Sun and the Moon) are only the remains of a constellation, only a small cohort of stars, badly organized, like the remnant of an army destroyed in battle. Other constellations have four or five hundred planets arranged in series of groups ; that is to say, with satellites revolving round satellites, and all provided with rings, crowns, polar caps, or other ornaments. If this favor be reserved for our globe it is an attribute inherent to its rank of sub-cardinal in the major gamut of planets.

VII.

FIRST PERIOD OF ASCENDING SOCIAL SUBVERSION (THE CONFUSED
SERIES).—TRADITION IT HAS LEFT OF A TERRESTRIAL PARADISE.

GOD created sixteen species of men; nine on the old continent,
and seven in America.   The details as to their diversity are of
little importance.*

The three races having respectively straight, convex, and con-

---

* Among the sixteen primitive races we must first distinguish four heterogeneous
races, namely:—

1. The Northern Dwarfs, such as the Laplanders and the Samojedes;
2. The Southern Giants, such as the Patagonians;
3. The native Albinoes, such as the Bedas of Ceylon, and the Darienese of America.
4. The native Negroes, with flat faces, of Guinea. There existed Albinoes and
Negroes of original creation, though the human race has itself the faculty of reproducing them. Among the four heterogeneous races, the Albinoes were the only one
common to the two continents.

These four heterogeneous races are very different from the twelve others. The latter approach more nearly to a common type, and may be called the homogeneous races.
The regular determination of their original differences is a calculation of Organic
Movement. which I shall not here treat of. I wish merely to expose the timidity which
has hitherto been exhibited in discussing the origin of races. We find learned men
still debating how America could have been peopled. It would seem as if God had
not the power to create on the new continent as well as on the old; and because certain
disparities are found, such as the Esquimaux having beards, while other aboriginal
races have none, it has been concluded that the Esquimaux came from the old continent of which they are neighbors. This is an error. The Esquimaux are of primitive
origin, like many other races, and the differences which exist are in no way the result
of chance.

The twelve homogeneous races were divided into two lots, seven on the old continent, and five in America. If among the latter we find some destitute of beard, while
their neighbors are covered with it, there is nothing in this at all astonishing. The
sixteen races must necessarily have presented certain differences, which the Theory
of Movement will explain, and which are still found very distinct all over the globe.

Despite invasions, despite the carrying-off of women and slaves, and the amalgamations which have resulted, the form of the face has been in each instance preserved,
and nothing has been able to destroy the original types. Customs even have produced
little or no changes, so that our physiognomies are still similar to those of the ances-
tral races whose portraits have been transmitted to us for three thousand years. Differences in race should not then be attributed to chance or to amalgamations; we
should see in them, as in all the varieties of creation, the effect of a distributive theory
which we have not yet learned, but which will be revealed in the laws of the Organic
Movement.

I ask pardon of the fabulists who make the whole human race to spring from the
same stock. One must indeed be opposed to all evidence to believe that the convex
faces of Senegal, and the concave of China, that the Kalmucks, the Europeans, the

cave faces, were placed in the Temperate Zone, between latitudes 30° and 35° N. (I speak only of the old continent.) It was in these latitudes that Man could organize the Primitive Society, or the *Confused Serial Order*. This society could not have lasted more than about three centuries. I have already notified the reader that I should not explain this Order till I came to speak of the eighth social period, at which epoch a Serial Order will be organized much more complete than the primitive which is here in question.

The first men came from the hands of God happy, since they were enabled to form an order of society organized in Series; and all Societies of this kind are more or less happy because they permit the free development or action of the passions.

Most beasts of prey and reptiles were created near the Equator, though some, such as the wolf, were created in the higher latitudes; it was not till they had spread toward the 30th and 35th degree N. that the men there placed were annoyed by such creations. They were surrounded, on the contrary, with an abundance of the best animals and vegetables then existing; there were some animals even which are now unknown, such as the mammoth, which, not being provided with the means of defence, must necessarily have perished with the primitive Society, to which it rendered great services.

The various races of men, in the beginning, had no social organization. It was not instinct alone that impelled them to form the Series; they were led to do so by four favoring circumstances which do not at present exist, namely :—

1. ABSENCE OF PREJUDICES.—From this resulted, as a natural consequence, freedom in Love, which in the incoherent Order, or Society organized in isolated families, is inadmissible.

2. THE SMALL NUMBER OF INHABITANTS. —From this resulted a superabundance of herds, fruits, fish, game, etc. The first groups of men were placed by God at long distances from each other; hence considerable time had to elapse before they became sufficiently numerous to encroach upon each other's territories.

Patagonians, and the Laplanders, are all shoots from the same tree. Throughout the four kingdoms, God establishes shades or varieties distributed in ascending and descending series; why then in creating the human race should he depart from an order which he has followed in all other created things, from the insect to the star?

3. THE ABSENCE OF REPRESENTATIVE SIGNS OF WEALTH.—
The first races of men had no skill in the mechanic arts, and were
deficient in all articles of a fixed value, such as the arms and
ornaments of the Savage tribes; on the other hand, they had per-
ishable productions in great abundance, and the difficulty of accumulating these, suggested the idea of *advance-payments in
kind*, which favored the relations of the Series.

4. THE ABSENCE OF BEASTS OF PREY.—This contributed toward maintaining the greatest gentleness in manners, checking the
invention of murderous weapons, preventing the spirit of war,
and preserving animals like the mammoth, which have since become extinct.

5. THE PRIMITIVE BEAUTY OF CREATED THINGS.—It is a great
error to suppose that the animals and plants, at the epoch of their
creation, were such as we now see them in their wild state. The
urus and the mufflon are not original creations, but degenerations
from the ox and the sheep. The herds created by God were superior to the finest breeds of Switzerland and Spain; the same
perfection prevailed among the fruits and flowers. "Everything
as it came from the hand of God," says Rousseau, "was good."
This is a truth which he hazarded without proof, and which he
weakened in the next line by adding: "but in the hands of
Man everything has degenerated." It was not Man who reduced
the animals and vegetables to the condition in which we now see
them, both in their wild and domestic state; it was Social Incoherence, which, by disorganizing the Order of the Series, caused
the deterioration of all productions, even of Man himself, whose
original height, for the race with straight faces, was 6 ft. 8 in.
This race attained easily to the age of 128 years (8 times 16).
All other productions possessed corresponding vigor, and the
roses of creation were superior to those of our finest gardens.
This general perfection was maintained during the whole of the
first social period, which was organized in Series by the concurrent aid of the five circumstances just cited.*

---

* A copy of the original work, annoted by Fourier, adds three other circumstances,
namely:—

6. ABSENCE OF ANTERIOR NATIONAL RIVALRIES.
7. IGNORANCE OF THE FAMILY INSTITUTION.
8. UNITY IN LOVE.
   (No. 8. is referred back, by a sign, to No. 1.)

Peace reigned during that period, not because of the general prosperity, but by virtue of a faculty inherent to the Series, namely, that of systematically developing and coördinating the passions, which out of the Series clash with each other and produce wars and dissensions of every kind.

It must not for an instant be supposed that there was anything like equality, anything like community of goods in this Primitive Order. I have already said that all such philosophic chimeras are incompatible with the Combined Order, which requires, on the contrary, graduated inequalities both in character and wealth. This system of graduated fortunes was established in the beginning, though the art of writing was unknown by which to regulate and adjust the interests of each associate.

The passions were more violent at that epoch than they are now; for the pastoral simplicity of which we read never existed except in the writings of the poets. The men were proud, sensual, and capricious; it was the same with the women and children. These pretended faults were the means of social concord, and when the Series shall be reëstablished, they will become the means of social concord again.

VIII.

DISORGANIZATION OF THE SERIES.

The primitive Serial Order was broken up by the concurrence of circumstances opposed to those mentioned in the last chapter. The excessive increase of population soon engendered poverty. At the same time the multiplication of beasts of prey coming from the equatorial regions, or from the North, led to the invention of murderous weapons, while the love of depredation became the more general from the fact that the infancy of the race, and the obstacles in the way of agriculture, did not permit that superabundance of accumulation necessary for the mechanism of the Series. From this state of things sprung the institution of marriage, the division of society into isolated and incoherent families, and, as a consequence, the transition to the Savage, Patriarchal, and Barbaric Orders.

During the existence of the primitive Serial Order, the human race enjoyed a lot so happy in comparison with that of the Savage and Patriarchal Orders, that the people, when they saw the Series disorganizing, naturally fell into a state of despair.

The last supports of the Serial Order were the children. They covered the social retreat, and continued in a state of harmony a long time after their parents had fallen into a state of discord. Men were then ready to adopt the isolated household, and the system of exclusive marriage, the idea of which was suggested by the general increase of poverty. The more this poverty increased, the more the chiefs of the different tribes were interested in establishing this system, which was destined finally to prevail.

Before resorting to this extreme, various measures, more or less inadequate, were tried in order to sustain the primitive Society, and when the impossibility of continuing this fine social Order was at last recognised, the chiefs, perceiving that regret for past happiness was plunging their people into apathy, and disgust for labor, sought to weaken the recollection of a happiness which could not again be restored, and the accounts of which served only to disturb the harmony of the Social Order which had succeeded to the primitive.

Hence the leaders agreed to falsify the traditions of former prosperity, the recollection of which could not be banished so long as there remained any ocular witnesses of it; but succeeding generations, which had not seen the order of the Industrial Series, were easily deceived as to its ever having existed. Contradictory accounts were intentionally circulated for the purpose of exciting doubt; and from these accounts sprung the fables, more or less absurd, which we find accredited throughout the East, of a Terrestrial Paradise from which Man had been expelled.

From the same source, also, sprung numerous other fables, invented for the purpose of falsifying the authentic traditions, which the chiefs of the different nations were interested in disguising. These fables, which form the basis of the old religions, contain the germ of a great truth, namely, that previous to the existing forms of society, there existed a happier order of things, confused traditions of which have been preserved among the oriental nations by whom it was enjoyed.

Among the means resorted to for the purpose of disguising this truth, may be mentioned the mysterious revelations and initiations instituted among the ancient priests of the East. It is almost certain that these mysteries, in their origin, were only traditions of the Primitive Order. But as the increasing sufferings of the people called for redoubled exertions to conceal from them the knowledge of any such society, it had to be restricted to a very small number of the initiated. By suppressing the tradition more and more, it became limited at last to so small a number of adepts, that the real possessors of the secret might have all been destroyed by a war or any other great disaster; still the priesthood doubtless continued their mysterious initiations, which no longer had any foundation in truth, but were only a species of jugglery used to sustain the importance of their order. It is to be presumed that the priests of Isis and of Brahma were already reduced to this degree of ignorance, and had no idea of the existence of the Primitive Order; at all events in those rude ages, when the art of writing had not been invented, and when every narrator added his own fancies to the traditions which had been handed down to him, all notions of this order must have been greatly distorted. The Orientals are as much given to romancing as the Gascons of France, and I calculate that, at the end of three hundred years, the tradition in question was so much disfigured by accessory fables as to have become incredible even to the initiated.

There remained, then, only the fundamental truth of a former state of happiness, lost without hope of recovery. From this fact the priests inferred the anger of God, the banishment of Man from a terrestrial Paradise, and other fables, calculated to intimidate the people and lead them according to the views of the sacerdotal body.

I have thus sufficiently explained why the world has remained in such entire ignorance as to the usages of the Primitive Order. This ignorance is about to be dissipated; the theory of Social Movement will remove all obscurity from the subject, by pointing out, with the greatest minuteness, what was the mechanism of this first Society, to which succeeded the Savage, the Patriarchal, and the Barbaric.

IX.

THE FIVE SOCIAL PERIODS, ORGANIZED IN INCOHERENT FAMILIES; OR THE SECOND, THIRD, FOURTH, FIFTH, AND SIXTH.

I SHALL treat of these five social Periods in the same chapter. To give a chapter to the details of each would require too much space; it would be departing from the plan of this outline, which is not even a regular abridgment.

Omitting the second or Savage Order, which has but little interest for us, I pass to the third or Patriarchal Order. This is a form of society almost unknown. Though believed to be a Primitive Order, it did not prevail among any people during the first ages. Men of all races, at the epoch of the Creation, were exempt from prejudices, and never thought of considering freedom in love a crime. Their vigor and longevity led them to the opposite extreme—to orgies, incests, and other voluptuous excesses. When men lived, as a rule, to the age of 128 years, and consequently had a hundred full years to give to the passion of love, how could they have been persuaded, like our moral Civilizees, that they should pass a hundred years with the same woman, without venturing to love another? It was a long time before circumstances made it necessary to restrain the freedom of love; the race had to lose much of its primitive vigor before it consented to regulations so contrary to the tastes of robust men. But as the vigor of the race visibly decreased when the Serial Order was broken up, this decline led to coërcive regulations in respect to love, and opened the way to the Savage, Patriarchal, and other Societies.

There prevails as much ignorance in relation to the Patriarchal state as to the Primitive. Abraham and Jacob, as they are represented to us, were far from being virtuous men; they were petty tyrants, given to wickedness and injustice, and possessing harems and slaves according to Barbaric usage. They were little despots, or pachas, ruling over a small region, and indulging in every species of excess. What could be more cruel and unjust than Abraham sending Hagar and her son Ishmael into the wilderness to die of hunger, without the least reason, if not that he had possessed this woman long enough, and had no more desire for her? It was this motive which induced him to condemn the mother and her young child to death. Such were the patriarchal virtues in all their glory, and you will find nothing in the whole conduct of the Patriarchs but acts equally odious.

Nevertheless, philosophy would take us back to patriarchal customs. The philosopher Raynal, in his history of the two Indias, commences with a pompous eulogy of the Chinese, whom he represents as the most perfect of nations, because they have preserved their patriarchal usages. Let us examine their pretended superiority.

China, the fine agriculture of which is so much vaunted, is so poor that the people are seen eating by the handful the vermin with which their garments are filled. It is the only country in the world where roguery is legalized and honored. Every tradesman in the land possesses the right to sell by false weights and measures, and to practise other frauds which are punished even among Barbarians. The Chinese prides himself on this corruption, and when he has cheated any one, he calls in his neighbors to receive their congratulations and to laugh with him at the expense of the dupe, to whom the law allows no redress.

China is the most litigious nation in the world. Nowhere else are pleadings conducted with such vehemence. The baseness of the people is so great, ideas of honor are so unknown among them, that the public executioner is one of the intimate friends, one of the grand officers of the Emperor, who causes the lash to be administered to his courtiers in his own presence. The Chinese are the only people who publicly despise their gods — who drag their idols through the mud when they fail to grant what is asked of them. It is the nation which has carried infanticide to the greatest extent. It is well known that the poorer classes among the Chinese expose their infants on the dunghill to be devoured alive by swine, or send them floating down the river, attached to hollow gourds. The Chinese are the nation the most jealous and the most cruel toward women, whose feet they incase in iron from their infancy, so that they may be unable to walk. As for children, the father has the right to gamble them away, and to sell them as slaves. Finally, the Chinese are the most cowardly people on the face of the earth, and in order not to frighten them, it is the custom to have the guns of their fortifications pointed upward, even when they are not loaded.

With such manners and customs, of which I have given but an imperfect outline, the Chinese laughs at the Civilizees because they are less knavish. He accuses all Europeans of being blind in business matters, and says that the Dutch have but one eye, while the Chinese have two. (The distinction is flattering for the Dutch, and also for Civilized commerce.)

Such are the patriarchs lauded by the philosophers, and who are offered to us by Raynal as models. Raynal certainly knew, better than anybody, that China was a sink of social vices, and the moral and political sewer of the globe; and yet he lauded its customs, because they were in conformity with the doctrines of philosophy—with its sophisms respecting the life of the isolated household, and the system of fragmentary industry on which it is based. This is the true reason why, despite its odious results, the philosophers extol the patriarchal life. The Chinese and the Jews, who are the nations most faithful to patriarchal ideas, are also the most knavish and the most vicious on the globe.

To set aside this testimony of experience, the philosophers depict China only in bright colors, without regard to its corruption, or to the horrible misery of its people. As for the Jews, their social vices are attributed to the persecutions they have undergone; but persecution, on the contrary, tends to ennoble the proscribed. The Christians were never more honorable than when they were the objects of general persecution, without being sustained by any prince, or having any rallying-point. How is it that religious persecution has produced such different results upon the two races? This is explained by the fact that the Christians in their misfortune, adopted the associative spirit, which in a proscribed race becomes the source of noble passions. The Jews preserved the patriarchal spirit, which is the source of vile passions, and which degraded them even in the day of their power. And where was there ever a nation more contemptible as a body than the Hebrews, who never made the least progress in the arts or sciences, and were remarkable only for the habitual practice of crimes and brutalities, the recital of which provokes indignation on every page of their disgusting annals.

This digression would naturally lead to an analysis of the

patriarchal spirit, and of the vices and dissimulations to which it gave rise in the human heart. But this brief Memoir not admitting of such discussions, I return to my subject, and restrict myself to pointing out the ignorance of the Civilizees on the subject of Federal Patriarchism, which was the third period of Ascending Social Incoherence.

Federal or Compound Patriarchism is constituted by the union of neighboring hordes, free, and united under a common rule, according to the custom of the Tartars. The patriarchal families, in this state of things, are interested in ameliorating the condition of legitimate wives, and in gradually augmenting their civil rights and privileges until they possess the partial liberty enjoyed by women in Civilization. This policy becomes for the Patriarchal Order a means of transition from the third Period, and an entrance to the fifth Period or Civilization.

The Civilized Order can not grow out of either the Savage or the Barbaric Order; neither Savages nor Barbarians ever voluntarily adopt our social customs. The Americans, notwithstanding all the allurements they have held out and all the stratagems they have employed, have not yet induced any tribe of Aborigines to adopt Civilization. This Order, according to the natural bent of the Social Movement, must spring from Federal Patriarchalism, or at least from some greatly modified form of Barbarism, like that of the ancient Orientals which in several respects resembled Federal Patriarchism.

As to Simple Patriarchism, like that under Abraham and Jacob, it is an Order which leads only to Barbarism—a state in which every father becomes a satrap who sets up his caprices for virtues, and in the family exercises the most revolting tyranny, as in the case of the patriarchs just mentioned, who were men as vicious and as unjust as were ever seen on the throne of Algiers or Tunis.

The Savage, the Barbaric, and the Civilized Orders are but little better understood than the Patriarchal Order. When I shall have occasion to treat of the phases and characteristics of each Period, I shall show that all our philosophic theories are as deceptive in their views of Civilization as of the means of escaping from it, and passing to the sixth Period.

This sixth Period, Guarantism, is one the discovery of which might have been made by the philosophers, since it is but a little removed from Civilization, and still preserves the isolated household, the institution of marriage, and the principal attributes of the philosophic system, though it greatly diminishes the number of revolutions and the amount of indigence. But however easy it might have been to discover this sixth Period, how could the philosophers have succeeded in advancing the human race beyond Civilization, when they were ignorant even of the means of elevating it to that point — in other words of raising the Savages and Barbarians to the Civilized State? They have not even known how to aid the progressive movement of Civilization; and when I come to analyse the Civilized mechanism, and to point out its four phases, I shall show that it has arrived at the third only by chance, without the philosophers ever having had the least influence on the progress of their cherished Order. Instead of accelerating it, they have retarded it, like those foolish mothers who in their infatuated devotion spoil their children by administering to all their caprices, and thus sowing the seeds of disease, and causing the child to sicken and die, even while they believe themselves to be serving it. It is thus that the philosophers have acted in their enthusiasm for Civilization. They have always made it worse even while seeking to perfect it. They have ministered to its dominant prejudices, and have thus, instead of seeking the road to truth, propagated error. We see them again at the present day giving in blindly to the commercial spirit which they ought rather to combat, if it were only for the sake of consistency, since they ridiculed trade for two thousand years.

Finally, if it had depended on the Philosophers, Civilization would still have been in its first phase and have preserved Barbaric Institutions, such as Slavery, so much lauded by the philosophers of Greece and Rome.

A proof of the general ignorance which prevails in respect to the Civilized mechanism, is found in the unforeseen calamities which are visited successively upon every generation. The most recent was that of the affiliated Revolutionary or Jacobin Clubs, no idea of which had been conceived in 1789, notwithstanding the learned analyses which had been made of Civilization. There are other calamities which will spring up successively, but which the philosophers do not at all foresee; among these is the impending Commercial Feudalism, which will be found no less odious than the reign of the Clubs. This will grow out of the influence which the commercial policy gains from day to day over society. Its encroachments will produce an innovation truly terrible, and which the Civilizees are far from suspecting. But let no one be alarmed at this prognostication ; far from exciting terror, it should excite only joy, since, through the Theory of Social Movement, we are about to acquire the means of providing against and preventing all political calamities.

X.

REGULAR CONTRAST BETWEEN SOCIETIES BASED ON THE SERIES, AND THOSE BASED ON ISOLATED FAMILIES.

THE first and seventh societies, which are formed in Series, present in every respect a regular contrast to the second, third, fourth, and fifth societies which are organized in families. (The sixth forms an exception.)

In the four last, the interest of the masses is in opposition to those of the individual, so that governments, in operating for the good of the majority, are obliged to use coërcion. This does not occur in societies formed in series, for in these the general good coïncides so perfectly with individual interests and desires, that the administration has only to notify the people of any public measure agreed upon, and it is at once conformed to. Everything is settled and executed by the Series on a given day, and upon receiving a simple notice. But in the four incoherent societies, coërcion is necessary even in the case of measures evidently salutary, and the adoption of which would cause no personal inconvenience or damage, as, for instance, uniformity in weights and measures. If we were in the seventh period (or even in the sixth), the government would restrict itself to notifying the people of such acts, and in each province and township they would be carried out immediately, and without further orders.

Resistance in the second, third, fourth, and fifth societies, to measures of general utility manifests itself in corporations as well as among individuals ; for example, in Turkey the constituted authorities are opposed, like the people, to the introduction of military discipline, though they feel its necessity.

The second, third, fourth and fifth societies, which are characterized by general poverty, revolutions, the marriage institution, fraud, etc., have the property of *mutual repulsion;* that is, of constant intercommunication without either society having the desire to imitate the other. We see the Barbaric Order, without having any desire to adopt its usages; it, on the other hand, sees ours, without any wish to adopt the usages of that. It is the same with all the four societies organized in isolated families. They have the property, like the wild beasts, of being incompatible with each other; and if they were all in presence—that is, if their frontiers were contiguous—no one of them would show any desire to assimilate with either of the three others. It should be observed, however, that the sixth society has some affinity with the fifth.

The first and seventh societies, as well as all the others based on the Serial Order, have the property of *mutual attraction.* The only exception is in the case of the first society, which would offer but little attraction to the richer classes of the fourth, fifth, and sixth societies.

The seventh would possess a strong attraction for all classes, although it is only a preliminary step to the state of true happiness, which man will commence to enjoy in the eighth. Still, the seventh is so happy in comparison with the Civilized Order, that if it should be organized at once, many feeble and sensitive persons would be overcome with excitement and regret, at suddenly seeing so much happiness which they themselves have never enjoyed, though they might have done so.

As for the eighth period, which is about to commence, in order to give an idea of the attraction it will exercise, I shall borrow the words of an author who says: "If men could behold God in all his glory, the excess of their admiration would, perhaps, cause their instant death." Tell me what is this "glory of God"? It is nothing else than the reign of the Combined Order which is about to be established, and which is the most magnificent conception of Divine wisdom. If we could suddenly see this Order, this sublime work of God, such as it will appear when it is in full operation, there is no doubt that many Civilizees would succumb to the violence of their emotions. A simple description of it would excite, in many of them, especially among women, an enthusiasm bordering on insanity; or would render them indifferent to present amusements, and incapable of performing the labors required in Civilization.

The societies organized in isolated households—the second, third, fourth, fifth and sixth—have the property of exciting repugnance for agricultural and manufacturing industry, and for the arts and sciences; the children in these societies rebel against labor and study, and the moment they are free to act as they please, become ungovernable and destructive. This inclination on the part of children to destroy as soon as they are left at liberty, is a remarkable peculiarity in the human race. In the societies organized in Series, the child will acquire opposite tastes; he will constantly be employed in some kind of labor, and by engaging at once in numerous minor occupations, now performed by full-grown men, will become of incalculable service. Finally, he will receive in the Series what we shall call *natural education;* in other words, he will instruct himself without the instigation or supervision of any one. As soon as he can walk, he will be left to his own will, without any other advice than to amuse himself as much as he pleases with groups of other children; emulation, and the impulse given by the Series, will be sufficient to initiate the child, by the time he is sixteen years of age, in all branches of art and science, and in the practical knowledge of agriculture and the mechanic arts. This education will cost him nothing; on the contrary, he will have acquired a small fund, the fruit of the labors performed during his infancy, and performed, not from compulsion but from emulation and attraction, and while amusing himself, as he supposes, with the Series of children, who of all classes will be the most devoted to labor. (See note below on the hierarchy of Harmonic Attraction.*)

* The development of Passional Attraction will be accomplished by means of three concurrent, competitive, and independent elements; namely, *children, women, and men.* I place the men in the third rank, because attraction is established by commencing with the weak and then communicating itself to the strong; that is to say, the state of things which will produce industrial attraction, will draw children more powerfully than their parents, and women more powerfully than men; so that in this Order, it will be the children who will give the strongest impulse to labor; and, after them, the women, who, in turn, will excite the men to industry.

I do not enter into any details as to this incomprehensible statement; but when given, they will make every one see that the mechanism of Attraction will be in every respect the opposite of that of Civilization. How, in fact, could it be otherwise, since nothing can be more opposed to Nature than Civilization?

Out of the Passional Series there can be no natural education. The instruction which children receive in Civilization, varies according to the caprice of teachers and parents. It has nothing in common with Nature which would attract the child to all kinds of labor, alternated regularly from hour to hour. It is thus that children will be trained in the Combined Order, where they will acquire great vigor and activity, because they will be engaged in continuous and varied exercises, none of which will be carried to excess. Out of this Order, children become dull, rude, feeble, and ungainly. This explains why, after the dissolution of the Primitive Series, the human race began to degenerate in size: as soon as the Serial Order shall be reëstablished, it will improve in this respect. I do not mean the adults, but the children brought up in this Order. The human race will gain two or three inches in height each generation, until it has attained to the average stature, for the men, of seven feet. They will arrive at this point at the end of about nine generations. The vigor and longevity of the race will increase, but not at the same rate, up to the sixteenth generation. At that period the full term of life will be a hundred and forty-four years, while physical strength will be developed in the same proportion.

The intellectual faculties will be developed more rapidly. I estimate that a single generation will suffice to change those living automata we call peasants, and who, in their extreme rudeness, are more like brutes than human beings, into men.

In the Combined Order, men in the humblest circumstances, born in an agricultural Phalanx, will be initiated into all branches of knowledge; and this general proficiency will not be at all surprising, since Association will lead every one to engage eagerly in the study of the arts and sciences, which (as will be seen in the Second Part) will open the way to immense fortunes.

The first, second, and third societies do not admit of agricultural and manufacturing industry on a large scale; this begins to appear, first, in the fourth or Barbaric Society. If it had been possible for an extensive system of Industry to grow up in the first Society, the human race would have been exempted from the misfortune of traversing the five unhappy Periods—the second, third, fourth, fifth, and sixth—and would have advanced immediately from the first to the seventh, that is to say, from the Confused Series to the Simple Initiatory Series. This is an advantage enjoyed by the inhabitants of suns, and of planets with belts, like Saturn; these are not subjected to the disgrace of becoming Savages, Barbarians, and Civilizees. They preserve the organization of the Series during the whole course of their social career, and are indebted for this happiness to the abundance and superiority of the productions furnished them by the first creation.

This first creation, which exercises a great influence on the condition of the different globes, was so poor and scanty on our own, that it could not long furnish the Primitive Series with the elements necessary for their operations. The Series require numerous and varied occupations; hence they could not be formed near the Equator, where God had placed certain races of men who were hindered from the beginning in their operations by the number of wild beasts, reptiles, and insects, which paralyzed all attempts at industry. It was equally impossible to form the Primitive Series in the two Americas, which were deficient in the principle aids to labor; for they possessed neither horses, cattle, sheep, swine, nor fowl.

In later times it was found impossible to establish the Series in Otaheite, where, nevertheless, there existed the germ of the Associative Order since there was some degree of freedom in the passion of love. Had this island possessed the useful animals, vegetables, and minerals found on the old continent, the Passional Series would have been found there, all formed, when the island was discovered.

In the fourth Society, the Barbaric, man commences to develop a system of Industry. In the fifth, Civilization, the arts and sciences appear; and thereafter Man is provided with all that is necessary for organizing the Passional Series, and of developing them on a scale of great magnificence. The sixth Period is only an avenue to the Industrial Series, which is partially formed in the seventh.

The second Society, the Savage, and the fourth, the Barbaric, are stagnant, and have no tendency toward a superior order. Savages have no desire to adopt Barbarism, which is superior to their Order in respect to Industry; and the Barbaric races refuse obstinately to embrace Civilization. These two

Societies, the Savage and the Barbaric, remain unchangeably attached to their old habits and customs, whether good or bad.

The third, fifth, and sixth societies tend more or less toward progress. Witness Civilization, which is violently agitated with the desire of improvement. Its sovereigns are constantly trying new experiments in government; and its philosophers propose some new moral or political system, daily. Thus Civilization labors theoretically and practically to attain to the sixth society, but without being able to reach it, the reason being, I repeat, that this change depends upon industrial and domestic operations, and not upon administrative measures, with which philosophy is exclusively occupied, without ever contemplating the least innovation in social and domestic relations.

I add an illustration drawn from the respective prevalence of honesty and fraud, the former prevailing in societies organized in Series, and the latter in societies organized in isolated families.

In the first case, the practice of truth and honesty assures to every one much greater advantages than can be derived from the practice of fraud. Hence every individual, vicious or virtuous, loves and practises honesty as being the road to fortune. Thus during the term of the twenty-four harmonic societies, (including Guarantism,) we find that in all industrial relations there prevails the utmost integrity.

In the eight Societies organized in isolated families, the contrary is the case. Fortunes are made only by means of craft and fraud. During these eight periods, therefore, dishonesty must be triumphant; hence we see that in Civilization, which is one of the Societies organized in isolated families, there is hardly any success except through the practice of dishonesty and injustice— the exceptions being so rare as only to confirm the rule.

The Second Society, the Savage, and the Sixth, Guarantism, are less favorable to fraud than the Civilized Order; but nevertheless when compared with the twenty-four societies organized in Series, they are sinks of perfidy and injustice.

All the arrangements of the Combined Order will be in regular and striking contrast to existing usages, and will even sanction what we consider to be faults and vices, as for instance gallantry and epicurism. The Associations in which these pretended faults are the most rife, will be those in which industrial art will be carried to the greatest perfection, and whose wealth and splendor will be the most conspicuous.

Strange as such assertions may seem, it gives me pleasure to repeat them in order to call attention to this great truth, that God must have formed our characters to suit the Combined Order, which will last 70,000 years, and not the Incoherent Order, the duration of which will be but about 10,000 years. Now, reasoning from the requirements of the Combined Order, it will be seen that there is nothing either vicious or faulty in our passions.

Take, for example, some given character—say the Housekeeper. In the Civilized Order, it is desirable that all the women should have a taste for the cares of housekeeping, since they are all destined to be married, and to take charge of isolated families; yet if you study the tastes of young women, you will perceive that hardly one in four of them would make a good housekeeper, and that the other three have little or no inclination for the duties of such a position, but have a decided taste for dress, for coquetry, for amusements, etc. It is inferred from this, that the characters of three fourths of the young women are defective, when in truth the defect is in our social mechanism. In fact, if all young women had a passion for housekeeping, as is desired, the result would be that three fourths of the sex would be unsuited for the Combined Order, which is to last 70,000 years; for in this Order, the labors of the household are so much simplified by association that they will not employ a fourth part as many women as they now require, so that it will amply suffice if a fourth or a sixth of the women make good housekeepers. God, therefore, must have observed this proportion by distributing the taste for housekeeping in a ratio adapted to the seventy thousand years of happiness, and not to the five thousand years of unhappiness, in the midst of which we now live. How would women be adapted to the Combined Order, if there were four hundred of them to do what would only require one hundred? The result of such a state of things would be the abandonment of the other functions devolving upon them, and we should feel that God had exhibited but little wisdom in giving to all women a taste which he should have restricted to a fourth of them.

The truth is that women are very well as they are, that three fourths of them are right in disdaining the cares of housekeeping, and that all the fault lies in our Civilization, which is incompatible with the nature of the passions, and with the designs of God.

The argument is the same in respect to all the other passions. It will be shown in the Theory of the Combined Order that all the various characters of men are good, and are wisely distributed, and that what is necessary is not to correct nature, but to develop it. A child seems to us made up of faults, because he is gluttonous, capricious, rebellious, quarrelsome, insolent, inquisitive, and indomitable; but such a child is the most perfect of all: he is the one who in the Combined Order will be more ardent and indefatigable in useful labors than any other. At the age of ten, he will hold the highest rank in the Series of children; and the honor of presiding over them in their labors and at their industrial parades, will cause him to make light of the most arduous toil.

In the existing order of society, I must admit that such a child is insupportable; and I say as much of all children; but I can not admit that any of them are vicious. Their pretended faults are the work of Nature. This tendency to gluttony, to mischief, which we seek to repress in all children, was given to them by God, who knows very well how to calculate his plan for the distribution of human characters: and I repeat that what is false is Civilization, which is adapted neither to the development nor to the proper employment of the characters created by God,— that what is false is philosophy, which refuses to confess that the Civilized Order is opposed to the designs of Nature, though it obliges us to stifle in children their most general tastes, such as the tendency to gluttony and wilfulness among boys, and to dress and display among girls; and so with all other ages, the tendencies or attractions of which are such as God has judged necessary for the Combined Order, which is the synthesis or full development of Attraction.

It is time now to speak of the Analysis of Attraction, to which the philosophers have never paid the least attention.

XI.

THE STUDY OF NATURE, INTERPRETED BY PASSIONAL ATTRACTION.

WHEN we compare the immensity of our desires with the limited means we have for satisfying them, it would seem as if God had acted inconsiderately in giving us such ardent and uncontrollable passions,—passions created, as it were, only to torment us by exciting a thousand cravings, not a tenth of which can be gratified in the Civilized Order.

It is in reasoning from this point of view, that the moralists pretend to correct the work of God by moderating and repressing the passions, which they are ignorant how to gratify, and which they have not even analyzed; for of the twelve passions comprising the principal springs of action of the soul, they recognise only nine, while of the four most important of these, they have but very imperfect ideas.

The nine passions already recognised are the five material or sensuous appetites, which exercise more or less influence over every individual, and the four spiritual or psychical appetites, namely:—

6. Friendship.
7. Love.
8. Parentalism, or the Family sentiment.
9. Ambition, or the Corporative sentiment.

The moralists would give to these nine passions a tendency or development wholly opposed to the designs of Nature. What have they not said for two thousand years past in order to moderate and change the five material or sensuous appetites; to persuade us that the diamond is a vile stone, that gold is a vile metal, that sugar and spices are vile products, all worthy only of contempt; in fine that the thatched cottage with simple nature is preferable to the palaces of kings? It is thus that they have sought to extinguish the sensuous passions, and they have been equally unsparing with the spiritual passions. What, for instance, have they not vociferated against ambition? To hear their declamations, one would suppose that man should desire only the humblest and least lucrative positions; that if a place were offered him with 100,000 francs salary, he should, out of respect to morality, prefer one with but 10,000. In their ideas of love, they are still more absurd. They preach nothing but exclusiveness and constancy, which are incompatible with the desires of Nature, and to which no one submits, when he possesses full liberty. None of these philosophic caprices, called "duties," have the least foundation in Nature. Duty comes from Man; Attraction comes from God. If we wish to know the designs of God, we must study Attraction—study Nature only—without accepting the idea of Duty, which varies in every age and in every country, whereas the nature of the passions has always been and will always remain unchangeably the same among all races and in all lands.

Let us give an illustration of this taken from the relations between the parent and child. The moralists would establish equality of affection between them. On this subject they preach certain sacred duties which Nature in no way inculcates. To discover her dictates, let us forget what *ought to be*—in other words what is *duty*—and analyze what *is*. We shall find that the natural affection of the parent for the child is three-fold that of the child for the parent. This appears disproportionate and unjust on the part of the child; but whether it is unjust or not is of no consequence; what we want to know in such a study is, I repeat, not what *ought to be*, but what *is*.

If instead of seeking to correct the passions, we should seek to ascertain what was the design of Nature in giving them a direction so much opposed to our ideas of duty, we should perceive very soon that this pretended duty has no relation to justice, as is shown in the case in question—namely, in the disproportion between parental and filial love. This inequality is based on sound reasons. If children return but a third of the love bestowed upon them by their parents, there are three causes for it:—

1. Up to the age of puberty the child is ignorant in what consists the quality of father or genitor. He can not appreciate this relation nor take any account of it. At the early age when filial affection is formed, the nature of the act which constitutes paternity is carefully concealed from him; he is not susceptible, then, at this period of *filial* love, but only of *sympathetic* love. Attachment out of gratitude for the care given to his education ought not to be required of him. This feeling is above the moral

faculties of a child. If we required a love resulting from reflection from a being incapable of reflection, we should be more childish than the child itself. Besides, its gratitude is *friendship* and not *filial love*, which children at a very early age can neither know nor feel.

2. The child more advanced in age, from seven to fourteen, is beset by the remonstrances of his parents, which are often accompanied by bad treatment; and as he has not reason enough to appreciate the necessity of the restraints imposed upon him, his attachment is graduated in proportion to the favors he receives. Hence we frequently see that a grandfather, a neighbor, a domestic, is dearer to the child than his own father, and fathers have no right to complain of this; if they have any sagacity, they ought to know that the child (for reasons above given) is susceptible only of *sympathetic love*, and that such a love is established in proportion to the kindness and discernment they exhibit in the exercise of their paternal functions.

3. When the child, arrived at the age of puberty, comes to know in what consists the quality of father and mother, he perceives the interested motives of their love for him; these are based on the souvenirs of conjugal love, on the hope that the child will minister to their ambition or their caprices, and on the pleasure he afforded them as an infant when he was the delight of their leisure hours. Having attained to the knowledge of such facts, the child can not feel himself much indebted to his parents for having procured them so many pleasures in which he has had no part. This knowledge, instead of increasing his affection, diminishes it. He finds that he was begotten from love of pleasure, and not from love of himself; that his parents have, perhaps, begotten him against their will, having already more children than they wanted, or possibly wishing for a child of the opposite sex; in brief, at the epoch of adolescence, when filial love commences to be born in the child, a thousand considerations come up to dissipate the prestige of paternity, and to make the importance which is attached to it seem to him ridiculous. And, then, if the parents have not been able to conciliate his esteem and friendship, they will discover in him no sentiment of filial love, not even the third which Nature has fixed upon as the debt of affection which the child owes to the parent, and which, when we reflect

that education in the Combined Order will give the parents no trouble, will seem sufficient.

As for the present, if the difficulties and responsibilities incident to education seem to give to parents an unlimited claim to the love of their children, it is because attention has not been paid to the three circumstances already mentioned, namely:—

1. The ignorance of children in their early years as to what constitutes paternity.

2. The disgust they experience, as they grow older, from the abuse or improper exercise of paternal authority.

3. The contrast they observe, on attaining to the age of reason, between the high pretensions of parents, and the imaginary claims upon which such pretensions are founded.

When other circumstances are considered, such as the partiality of parents, at which the neglected child is so justly offended, it will be understood why he feels only a third as much affection toward his parents as he receives from them. If he feels any more than this, it is the effect of sympathy, and not of consanguinity. Thus it is often seen that a child has much more attachment for one of his parents than for the other, whose claims are the same in his eyes, but whose character does not suit him.

These are truths which the Civilizees will not confess, nor accept as a basis for their social calculations. Poor in enjoyments, they would fain be rich in illusions. They arrogate to themselves a right of property in the affection of the weaker party. Are they husbands of sixty years, they pretend that a wife of twenty should love them to the exclusion of all others; and we all know how little ground there is for such pretensions. Are they fathers, they wish to be considered as models, as gods, in the eyes of their children, and if they obtain only the degree of love which they merit, they cry out "Ingratitude!" In the absence of real attachment, they console themselves with fanciful delusions; they like to have exhibited to them in novels and plays extremes of filial love and conjugal fidelity, of which not even a shadow is found in their households. The Civilizees, in feeding upon these moral chimeras, become incapable of studying the general laws of Nature, or study them only in their own caprices and their despotic pretensions, accusing Nature of injustice without seeking to fathom her decrees.

To discover these decrees, we should not stop at ideas of *duty*, but proceed to the analysis of PASSIONAL ATTRACTION, which appears vicious to us only because we are ignorant of its object and functions, but which, vicious or not, has never been the subject of systematic study.

XII.

THE PASSIONAL TREE AND ITS BRANCHES, OR GRADUATED DIVISIONS OF THE FIRST, SECOND, THIRD, AND FIFTH DEGREES.

LET us commence with the first division which furnishes three branches. We shall treat hereafter of the trunk or UNITYISM, considered as the source of all the passions, which are three in the first division, twelve in the second, etc.

The first division furnishes three passions, which are sub-focal attractions, impelling and guiding all ranks and all ages. These three passions are

1. Love of Luxury, or attraction for material splendor;
2. Love of Groups, or attraction for society;
3. Love of Series, or attraction for order.

Let us examine these sub-focal attractions in their minor divisions, according to the number of passions furnished by each in the next succeeding scale, which gives twelve branches, forming the Passional Gamut, analogous to the musical gamut.

FIRST SUB-FOCAL ATTRACTION, LOVE OF LUXURY. — This branches into five secondary passions, which we will call the material or sensuous Passions.

LUXURY is internal and external. It is internal when it relates to Health and guarantees to us the full and direct exercise of all the senses; these can not be satisfied without the aid of Wealth. It is in vain that one has a good stomach, or a fine appetite, if he lack the means of buying a dinner. He who is without money is condemned to starvation — to the martyrdom of the senses, which can not be satisfied without the aid of wealth, to which, in Civilization, everything is subordinate. It is with the four other senses as it is with Taste; each, without the aid of wealth, is reduced to the minimum of gratification. It is in vain that one has a good ear for music unless he has money; the doors of the opera will be closed against him, and he will see vulgar persons entering, with no ear, but having well-filled purses.

The possession of internal luxury, or Health, is not sufficient, then, for our happiness; we require, in addition, external luxury, or Wealth, which guarantees the full development and gratification of the senses, of which internal luxury guarantees only the conditional development. The exception only confirms the rule. A poor girl marries a rich old dotard who insures to her a life of enjoyment, and the full possession of certain sensual pleasures (good living, rich dresses, etc.), which, before, she lacked. In this case one of the five senses, the fifth—that of Touch, in its amative action—intervenes to insure to her, by means of wealth, the gratification of the four other senses which otherwise would have had, at most, only internal exercise, or health—in other words only capacity of development without positive development—but which without the aid of the wealth furnished by the rich husband would have been thwarted in every way, the privation extending perhaps even to the sense of touch, for the poor have few means of gratifying their amatory desires.

Let it be understood, then, that Luxury is not simple but compound, in other words is internal and external. This is an important principle to establish in order to show the vagueness of existing theories on all questions of Unity of Movement; witness the discussion as to the simple or compound nature of light. If Light were a simple substance, it would follow by virtue of the Unity of Nature, that Luxury must be simple, Luxury being the first object or focus of Passional Attraction, as the Sun, the pivot of Light, is the first object or focus of Material Attraction. Now Luxury being compound, as we have just seen, Light must also be compound, that is unless there is duplicity of system in Nature — duplicity between the Material and the Passional Movement.

SECOND SUB-FOCAL ATTRACTION, LOVE OF GROUPS. — This branch furnishes four secondary passions which we will call the Affectional.

Major
{ 1. Group of Honor, or the corporative sentiment ;
{ 2. Group of Friendship ;

Minor
{ 3. Group of Love ;
{ 4. Group of the Family, or Parentalism.

Legislators would subordinate the whole social system to the last of these four groups, that of the family, to which God has assigned very little influence in social harmony, because it is a group based on a material or forced bond, and not a free, passional union dissoluble at will.

It was worthy of men who in all their calculations are in contradiction with Nature, to take as Pivot of the social mechanism the one of the four groups which should have the least influence, since it is not voluntary or free. In the Harmonic Order, this group will have no active employment except when absorbed by the three others, and operating in their sense.

As all constraint engenders falsity, the latter must necessarily prevail in proportion to the influence of the Family Group, which is neither free nor dissoluble ; hence there is nothing more false than the two Orders of Society, the Civilized and the Patriarchal, in which this group predominates. The Barbaric Order, though more oppressive than ours, is however less false, being less influenced by the family group which is one of the most fruitful sources of duplicity of action which can be found in Movement. As a fixed and indissoluble bond, it is foreign to the spirit of God who would govern only by attraction—that is by liberty in all social ties and impulses.

THIRD SUB-FOCAL ATTRACTION, LOVE OF SERIES ; — or affiliation of groups, leagued together in Series, and possessing the same properties as the geometrical series. This third branch furnishes three of the twelve secondary passions, which we have called Distributive Passions, and which tend to a social and domestic mechanism wholly unknown in Civilization ; it was known, however, in the Primitive Order, and is the secret of the lost happiness which is to be regained. It is therefore on the art of forming and organizing the Series of Groups that the calculations of passional harmony must principally depend.

If men of science believed in the Unity of the Universe, of which they are continually writing, they would have inferred that since the whole Universe and all its creations are distributed in Series, it is necessary, in order to bring Man into unity with it, to establish a similar order in the play of the social and domestic passions.

It has not pleased them to admit this analogy, nor the necessity of making researches as to the formation of the Passional Series, the secret of which I reveal.

As I do not explain the Series in this volume, but give only a superficial sketch of them, it has appeared to me useful to define the passions which tend to their formation. Of what use would it be to describe three new motor-powers of the soul without describing the uses which should be made of them in the social and domestic mechanism?

We shall often have occasion to remark the division of the twelve secondary passions into five corporal or sensuous passions, and seven spiritual or psychical (four affectional and three distributive), with their collective focus or passional trunk, Unityism, a passion which comprises the three primary branches, and is the result of their combined action.

Unityism is the tendency of the individual to associate or identify his own happiness with that of all who surround him, and with the whole human race, now so antagonistic. It is an unlimited philanthropy, a universal benevolence, which can not be developed till the whole human race shall be rich, free, and just, conformably to the requirements of the three sub-focal passions —Love of Luxury, Love of Groups, and Love of Series—which require,

In their first development, *Graduated Wealth* for the five senses ;
In their second development, *Absolute Liberty* for the four groups ;
In their third development, *Distributive Justice* for the passions bearing this name.

As Unityism comprises the three primary passions, it includes also the twelve secondary, which branch from the three primary. To compare Unityism to the white ray which contains the seven solar colors would be incorrect. It should be understood that this ray contains five other rays which are not perceptible to the eye, namely, rose, buff, chestnut, dragon-green, lilac. (I am certain only of the rose and the fawn.) The white ray then contains, in fact, twelve rays, of which it shows only seven, as the musical octave contains twelve sounds, seven of which only are pronounced. It would not be at all exact, therefore, to represent Unityism as being the union of the seven spiritual or psychical passions, which we call the affectional and distributive, since this union supposes the play of the material or sensuous passions as a consequence of the twelve secondary combined.

In this Prospectus there is wanting a complete definition of Unityism, or the synthesis of the passions ; but as this has no development in the Civilized Order, it will suffice to fix attention on the counter-passion, or SELFISM, which reigns so universally in this Order that our ideologists have made of Self or the Me the basis of all their calculations. It was natural in studying the Civilizees to observe in them only the subversive passions, which have their regular scale like the harmonic passions.

Unityism, or universal philanthropy, is unknown to our philosophers; instead of this passion, they have conceived only of its subversive or counter-development, the mania for subordinating everything to individual interests. This odious tendency has various names in the learned world; among the moralists it is called selfishness, while among the ideologists it is named the Me, a new term which says nothing new, and is only a useless paraphrase of selfishness, of which the Civilizees have always been accused, and with reason, because their social order, in establishing the reign of poverty and oppression, tends to subordinate the twelve passions to Selfism, which thus becomes a subversive focus, taking the place of Unityism which is the harmonic focus.

Happiness, the common pursuit of mankind, being the development of Unityism, which comprises the development or play of all the passions, we may, in order to simplify our studies, explain the action of the three primary passions, Love of Luxury, Love of Groups, and Love of Series, or at most the twelve secondary which are the sub-divisions of the three primary.

It is useless to extend details prematurely to the 32 tertiary passions, still less to the 134 quartiary, and so on, since the complete development of the 3 primary assures that of the 32 tertiary, the 134 quartiary, the 404 quintiary, etc.

In this Prospeqtus, therefore, it will amply suffice to reason from the development of the three primary or sub-focal passions, and from that of the twelve secondary, which are the radical passions of the octave, or Passional Gamut.

The five material or sensuous passions tending to luxury, and the four affectional tending to groups, are well known; it remains for us to explain the three distributive passions whose combined development produces the Series, which is the true law or method of social organization.

Our task, reduced to its simplest form, is then to determine the play of the third primary passion, namely, the Serial. It is this passion which keeps in balance the two others—the sensuous and the affectional—or Love of Luxury and Love of Groups, the discord between which, without the intervention of the Serial passion or Love of Series, would be permanent.

The accord of the three produces happiness by insuring the development of the great focal passion, Unityism, which is the source of all the passions, the common trunk from which spring the branches of each division.

The classification of these branches I have already given ; let us repeat that the passional tree, the trunk of which, Unityism, (a passion unknown to us, and which is the counterpart to Selfism), gives in the first division 3 passions, in the second 12, in the third 32, in the fourth 134, in the fifth 404,—plus the pivot, which is never counted in Movement.

The characters and temperaments are classed, with slight variations, in the same order. The temperaments are four in number in the second degree, plus the focus or pivot. The fourth degree may vary from thirty to thirty-two, and so with the others.

We might extend the analysis of the passions, characters, and temperaments to powers of the 6th, 7th, and 8th degrees ; but the 5th, in the beginning, will suffice to satisfy curiosity, since it forms the basis of the Phalanx of Passional Harmony, which is the Social Destiny of Man. In the Treatise I shall be more full.

As there is Unity between the material and passional worlds, the system of attraction is very faithfully depicted and followed in sidereal mechanics. We see there thirty-two keys in the planetary gamut, gravitating collectively about Unityism, or the Sun, by the equilibrium of our solar system with the general system of the stellar universe.

Passing to subdivisions, and beginning with those of the first degree, the planets in our system gravitate around three sub-foci.

1. Around Luxury, symbolized by the solar pivot.

2. Around Groups, symbolized by the planets.

3. Around Series, symbolized by the accolade of the four groups, and of the transitional or ambiguous planets.*

Let us now pass to a sketch of the twelve radical passions, or those of the second power.

---

* Fourier calls those planets transitional, ambiguous, or mixed, which have no moons but revolve around the sun in independent orbits.—*Translator.*

XIII.

THE TWELVE RADICAL PASSIONS FORMING THE PASSIONAL OCTAVE OR GAMUT.

I HAVE already given the classification of these passions as follows : 5 Sensuous, 4 Affectional, 3 Distributive. The latter are hardly known in Civilization. We see only germs of them, and even this excites the choler of the moralists, who are the inveterate enemies of all pleasure. The influence of these three passions is at present so slight, and their manifestation so rare, that they have not even been distinctly classified. I might have named them the Connecting, the Alternating, and the Graduating passions, but have preferred to designate them by the numbers 10, 11, 12. I postpone giving any definition of them because it would not be believed that God, notwithstanding his omnipotence, could invent a Social Order capable of satisfying three passions so insatiable in their demands for luxury and enjoyment.

The seven affectional and distributive passions relate to the soul rather than to the body, and rank as primitive passions. Their combined action engenders a collective passion—or one formed of the union of the seven others, as white is formed by the union of the seven primitive colors. I shall name this thirteenth passion, Harmonism, or Unityism. It is still less known than the 10th, 11th, and 12th, which I have not yet explained, but the general influence of which we may reason upon without fully understanding them. This is what I shall now do.

Although these three passions, the 10th, 11th, and 12th, with the 13th, Unityism, are completely repressed by our civilized habits, their germs nevertheless exist in our souls, besetting and tormenting us according as they are more or less active in each individual. Hence it is that many Civilizees pass their whole lives in ennui, even when they possess all the objects they desire. Witness Cæsar who, seated on the throne of the world, was astonished to find in so exalted a position nothing but lassitude and void. This dissatisfaction and uneasiness in the mind of Cæsar had no other cause than the influence of the four stifled passions, and especially the 13th, which exercised a very powerful influence over him. Hence he enjoyed his elevation and good fortune all the less from the fact that it left him nothing to covet which might absorb his attention or divert his mind from the action of this 13th passion which was dominant in him. This is the general experience of the great in Civilization. Their souls being violently agitated by the four undeveloped passions, it is not strange that we find the mass of men more satisfied with mediocre enjoyments, than the great are with all their luxury and splendor. These boasted splendors — thrones, palaces, sovereignties, wealth — doubtless constitute a a real good whatever the philosophers may say to the contrary; but they have the property of arousing the four suppressed passions without satisfying them. Hence the middle classes can enjoy themselves more with their moderate resources, because their commonplace routine of life excites only the nine sensuous and affectional passions, to which the Civilized Order allows a certain degree of development, whereas to the three distributive passions, and to the 13th, Harmonism, it allows little or no scope.

In general the influence of the three distributive passions produces characters which are accused of being corrupt and are called false, dissipated, debauched, etc. The thirteenth, or Harmonism, produces those which are called eccentric — persons who seemed little at their ease in this world, and who can not accommodate themselves to the usages of Civilization.

The Barbarians are nearly destitute of these four passions, which their social condition has no tendency to awaken. Hence they are more contented than we, notwithstanding their brutal customs that affect but the nine sensuous and affectional passions which are the only ones active in them.

To sum up: if perfect happiness for the human race is to be found only in the Order of the Groups and Series, or Association, it is because this Order will insure full development and scope to the twelve radical passions, and, consequently to the thirteenth which is a combination of the seven principal passions. Hence it follows that the humblest individual, man or woman, in this new Order, will be much happier than at present is the most powerful monarch; for the true happiness of man consists in the development and gratification of all his passions.

The twelve radical passions are subdivided into numerous shades which dominate more or less in each individual, and lead to the formation of an infinite variety of characters, the number of which may be estimated at 810. Nature distributes these characters among the children of the two sexes at hazard, so that among eight hundred and ten children, taken promiscuously, may be found the germs of every kind of talent of which man is capable. That is to say, each one of them is endowed naturally with a capacity competent to make him equal to some one of the most gifted geniuses who have ever lived—such as a Homer, a Cæsar, a Newton, etc. Hence, if we divide the thirty-six millions of inhabitants constituting the population of France by 810, it will be found that there exist in this empire forty-five thousand persons capable of equalling Homer, forty-five thousand capable of equalling Demosthenes, and so on ; that is provided they are properly instructed from the age of three years, and have received that *natural education* which develops all the germs distributed by Nature ; but this education can take place only in the Progressive Series or the Combined Order. It may be conceived, then, how great will be the number of celebrated men in this new Order, since the population of France alone would furnish the above-mentioned number of each kind. When, therefore, the globe shall be duly organized, and have a population of three thousand millions, it will contain, commonly, thirty-seven millions of poets equal to Homer, thirty-seven millions of astronomers equal to Newton, thirty-seven millions of dramatists equal to Molière, and so on with all imaginable talents. (These, of course, are only proximate calculations.)

It is then a great error to suppose that Nature is parsimonious in the distribution of talents. On the contrary she is prodigal of them far beyond our desires or wants ; but it is for us to discover and develop their germs, and on this subject we are as ignorant as is the Savage in respect to the discovery and working of mines. We have no art, no touch-stone for discerning the destiny marked out by Nature for each individual, in other words for discovering the germs she has implanted in each human soul. These germs are stifled and trampled under foot by civilized education, so that scarcely one in a million of them is ever developed. The art of discovering them is one of the thousand marvels which will be revealed by the theory of the Progressive Series, in which Order all the different germs of talent which

Nature has implanted will be developed in every individual to the highest degree.

Since the eight hundred and ten different characters are distributed at hazard among children, we ought not to be astonished at the habitual contrast which is remarked between parents and children, a contrast which has led to the proverb, " miserly father, prodigal son." From this results the constant ruin of family interests. We see a father build up an establishment at great cost and with great labor which is afterward neglected, broken up, and sold by the son, because he happens to have opposite tastes. This is for parents an inexhaustible source of complaint against Nature. The new Order will explain this apparent injustice, even in cases the most revolting, as for instance the abandonment of the poor who, the more they stand in need of assistance the more they are denied it, whereas the rich, who are above material wants, find, themselves for that reason overwhelmed with the favors of fortune. The influence of this malevolent spirit seems to pervade every department of Civilization. It exhibits Nature to us in every way as the most inveterate enemy of the poor, the honest, and the weak. Everywhere we recognise the absence of a divine Providence and witness the permanent reign of the demoniac spirit, which at times, however, is accompanied by some glimmerings of truth, though only to teach us that justice is banished from the Civilized or Barbaric societies.

> " Je ne suis, de tout temps, quelle injuste puissance
> Laisse la paix au crime et poursuit l'innocence.
> . . . . . Autour de moi, si je jette les yeux,
> Je ne vois que malheurs qui condamnent les dieux."[*]—*Racine.*

When we come to recognise in the Theory of Attraction that Civilization has the property of developing the twelve radical passions in an *inverted order,* and of making them produce as many vices as their natural and combined development would have produced virtues, all these temporary disorders will seem to us ordinances of the highest wisdom. The regular order and succession of the calamities with which God overwhelms us, and which he will continue to inflict upon us as long as we persist in

---

[*] Tell me what Power it is which in all time
Virtue pursues and sanction gives to crime ;
For round me everywhere, in fearful odds,
I see but miseries which condemn the gods.

living in a state of industrial incoherence, will then excite our admiration ; and we shall recognise that the apparent incongruity in the action of the passions results from the profound calculations by which God prepares for us the immense happiness of the Combined Order; we shall learn, in fine, that Passional Attraction, which the philosophers so much revile, is the wisest and most admirable of all the works of God; for it alone, without the least coërcion, and without other support than the allurements of pleasure, will lead to the establishment of universal Unity on the globe, and, during the career of 70,000 years of Social Harmony upon which the world is about to enter, will banish from our midst not only wars and revolutions, but all poverty and injustice.

XIV.

CHARACTERISTICS, TRANSITIONS, AND PHASES, OF THE DIFFERENT SOCIAL PERIODS.

EVERY Social Period has a fixed number of characteristics or constituent properties. For example, *Religious Tolerance* is a characteristic of the sixth Period and not of the fifth ; the principle of *Hereditary Government* is a characteristic of the fifth and not of the fourth ; and so on.

To say that the characteristics of the different Periods result from the play of the seven primitive or radical passions, that their development varies, changing from Period to Period, would excite a desire for a definition of those passions, which I do not wish to consider in this Memoir.

Speaking only of Civilization, or the fifth Social Period, I will state that it has sixteen characteristics, fourteen of which result from the play, direct and inverse, of the seven primitive passions, and the other two from the inverse development of the passion of *Unityism*, or Harmonism.

Every Society has certain characteristics borrowed from superior or inferior social Periods. For example, French Civilization has partially adopted *Unity in Industrial and Administrative Relations.* This method, which is one of the characteristics of the sixth Period, was established by the adoption of a uniform Metrical System, and the Code Napoleon — two institutions not properly belonging to the Civilized Order, which has among its characteristics *Incoherence in Industrial and Administrative Relations.* In this respect, then, we have departed from Civilization, and grafted from the sixth Period or Guarantism, which is to succeed Civilization. We have done this also in other respects, especially in the matter of religious toleration. The English, who practise an intolerance worthy of the Twelfth Century, are in this respect more in keeping with Civilization than the French. The Germans, again, are better Civilizees than either, owing to the incoherence which exists in their laws, customs, and industrial relations. In Germany we find at every step different weights and measures, different coins, different laws and usages, by which a stranger is much more easily duped and plundered than would be the case if there were unity of system in these departments. This chaos of relations is favorable to the Civilized mechanism, the object of which is to carry deception and fraud to the greatest perfection ; and this end is accomplished by the full development of the sixteen special characteristics of Civilization.

Nevertheless, the philosophers pretend that by the adoption of the principle of religious tolerance, and industrial and administrative unity, Civilization has greatly improved. This is a very false way of stating the case ; they should rather have said that the *Social Order has been improved while Civilization has declined.* In fact, if the sixteen characteristics of the sixth Period should be successively adopted, the result would be an end of Civilization, which would be destroyed by the attempts made to perfect it. The Social Order would be better organized, but Society would be found in the sixth Period, and not in the fifth. These distinctions as to characteristics lead to an amusing conclusion, namely, that *the little of good we find in Civilization is due only to the adoption of principles and institutions which are opposed to it.*

If we wish to render Civilization worse than it now is, we should adopt certain characteristics of the Patriarchal Order, which are perfectly compatible with it; for example, *Commercial license,* or liberty to sell by false weights and measures and to deal in adulterated goods. All these frauds are legally permitted in China, where every tradesman uses false weights and sells adulterated goods with impunity. In Canton you purchase a fine-looking ham, and, on opening it, find only a mass of clay ingeniously covered with slices of meat. Every shopkeeper has three kinds of weights: one too light, to deceive purchasers, another too heavy, to deceive sellers, a third exact, for his private use. If you allow yourself to be caught by any of these rogueries, the magistrate and the public will laugh at you; they will inform you that *commercial liberty* exists in China, and that notwithstanding this alleged vice, the vast Chinese empire has sustained itself for 4000 years better than any empire in Europe. From this we may conclude that the Patriarchal State and Civilization have no connection with truth or justice, and can very well sustain themselves without admitting either of these virtues, the exercise of which is incompatible with the characteristics of both of these societies.

Without designating the characteristics of the various Periods, I have shown how each borrows frequently those of both superior and inferior Periods. It is without doubt an evil to introduce those of inferior Periods, as, for instance, the *legal toleration of false weights and measures*, which is a characteristic of the third Period, or the *affiliated Jacobin Clubs*, which are a civil jannissariat borrowed from the fourth Period or Barbarism.

It is not always an advantage to introduce characteristics of a superior Period; in certain cases they may degenerate by this political transplanting, and produce bad effects; witness the *right of divorce*, which is a characteristic of the sixth Period, and which has produced so much disorder in Civilization that it has been found necessary to restrict it to the narrowest limits. Nevertheless, freedom of divorce will be of great use in the sixth Period, and will contribute eminently toward domestic harmony. It is only in this Period that it can combine with other characteristics which do not exist in Civilization.

It will be seen from what precedes, that there are precautions to be observed in engrafting a characteristic of one Period on another, as in transferring a plant from one climate to another. It is a mistake, for instance, to suppose that *Religious Tolerance* can be introduced among Civilizees without restrictions; in the long run, unless religions suited to the morals of the fourth, the third, and the second Periods (like Mohammedanism, Judaism, and Idolatry) were excluded, it would produce, in agricultural states, more harm than good. At the present time, however, the admission of such religions is a matter of indifference, as Civilization is drawing to its close.

Each of the incoherent Societies experiences more or less the want of institutions borrowed from the next higher social Period. No one of them feels this need more than Civilization, which sees the falseness of its own characteristics, as for example, the duplicity that prevails in the relations of love. In our novels, romances, and plays, and in our social intercourse, taunts on this subject are universal; and though satire has become insipid from frequent repetition, it is re-echoed from day to day as if it were new. It is aimed principally at the women, and very unjustly, for in love-matters the two sexes vie with each other in deception. If the men seem less false, it is because the law gives them more latitude, and declares allowable in the stronger sex what in the weaker it declares to be criminal. It will be replied, that the consequences of infidelity are very different in the two cases; but when the woman is sterile, or when she takes care of her illegitimate child without charging it upon a man not acknowledging it, the consequences are the same. Had there been a law insuring to woman the free exercise of the passion of love in these two cases, infidelity in love affairs, which is the object of our just sarcasms, would have greatly diminished, and we might without the least inconvenience have adopted the principle of free divorce. But as it is, the Civilizees, in consequence of their tyranny over woman, have failed to pass to the sixth Period to which such a law as that just mentioned would have conducted them. There was a means, however, much better adapted to bringing men as well as women to frankness and sincerity in affairs of love, and which would have enabled the social body to pass to Amorous Liberty by means of an indirect and purely economical operation; this was the Combined Household, or the Domestic Order of the seventh social Period of which I shall speak in the Second Part.

In each Period there is a characteristic which constitutes the *Pivot of the Social Mechanism*, and the absence or presence of which determines the change of Period. This pivotal characteristic always relates to the passion of Love. In the fourth Period it is the *Absolute Servitude of Woman*. In the fifth, it is *Exclusive Marriage and the Civil Liberty of the Wife*. In the sixth, it is *Love-Corporations*, which will assure to women the privilege above mentioned. If the Barbarians should accept *Exclusive Marriage*, they, by this simple innovation, would in a short time become Civilizees. If we should adopt the harem and the buying and selling of women, we should soon become Barbarians; and if we should adopt amatory guarantees as they will be established in the sixth Period, we should find in this measure an issue from Civilization and an entrance into that Period. In general the pivotal characteristic, that is, the institution which forms the basis or constitutes the pivot of the Period, and which always relates to the passion of love, gives rise to all the others; but the collateral or branch-characteristics do not give rise to the pivotal, and tend but slowly toward a change of Period. The Barbaric Order may adopt as many as twelve of the sixteen characteristics of Civilization, and still remain Barbaric, unless it adopts the pivotal characteristic, namely, exclusive marriage and the civil liberty of the wife.

If God has given to usages and customs growing out of the passion of love so much influence over the social mechanism and the changes to which it may be subjected, it is owing to his horror of oppression and violence. It is his wish that the happiness or unhappiness of human societies be proportioned to the amount of liberty or constraint which they permit. Now God recognises no liberty which is not extended to both sexes; hence he has decreed that all the abominable societies—such as the Savage, Barbaric, and Civilized—should have for their pivot the servitude or slavery of Woman, and that all the Harmonic Societies —like the sixth, seventh, and eighth Periods—should have for their pivot, the *progressive emancipation of Woman.*

These truths are not relished by the Civilizees. They judge woman by her character in Civilization, by the dissimulation which our customs impose upon her, in refusing her any liberty. They believe this duplicity to be the natural and invariable attribute of the female sex. Nevertheless, when we consider the difference between the cultivated women of our large cities, and the concubines of a harem, who believe themselves to be mere automata created for the amusement of man, we may infer how much greater would be the difference between the former, and the women of a truly enlightened nation in which the sex should

be advanced to a state of entire liberty. And what would be the
character which entire liberty would develop in such women?
This is a question which the philosophers take good care not to
raise. Animated by the spirit of oppression, by a secret disdain
of woman, they seek to beguile her by stale compliments and
senseless flattery into blind indifference to her lot; they even
stifle in her the idea of inquiring what would be the character
of her sex in a social Order which should loosen her chains.

In each of the thirty-two Periods of the Social Movement, there
are uniformly four Phases. Thus each Period—like Barbarism,
Civilization, etc.—may be divided into four ages, namely, Infancy, Growth, Decline, Caducity. In the Third Part I shall
give a table of the four Phases of Civilization, which is now in
its third Phase or Decline. Let me explain the sense of this
word.

A society may fall into decline by the effect of its social improvements. The Savages of the Sandwich Islands and the
Aborigines of America, who adopt certain branches of agricultural and manufacturing industry, without doubt improve their
social condition, but they depart, for this reason, from the Savage
Order, one of the characteristics of which is repugnance to Agriculture. These tribes, therefore, present to us the Savage Period
in decline through the influence of social improvement. It may
be said, in the same sense, that the Turks are Barbarians in decline; for they are adopting various characteristics of Civilization, such as hereditary government and other institutions which,
being similar to those of Civilization, tend to the decline of Barbarism. Before the abdication of Selim, they had adopted military tactics, which are a characteristic of Civilization; they have
since perfected their Barbaric Order by suppressing regular
troops, the adoption of which was an anti-Barbaric measure borrowed from Civilization.

These examples will suffice to explain what I have said above,
namely, that a "*Society may fall into a state of decline by the
effect of its social improvements.*

The first, second, and third societies lose by declining, since
their declension approximates them to the fourth—Barbarism
—which is the worst of all. But the fourth, fifth, sixth, and
seventh, gain by declining, since their declension brings them

nearer to the eighth, which is the entrance to the Combined Order.

The four Phases—Infancy, Growth, Decline, and Caducity—have each their special attributes. For example, the attributes of the first Phase of Civilization are exclusive marriage and the slavery of the agricultural laborers. Such was the Order existing among the Greeks and Romans, who were only in the first Phase of Civilization. The second and third Phases have also their peculiar attributes: and when I come to indicate the four Phases of Civilization, it will be seen that the philosophers have always sought to retard it, to maintain it in the state of Infancy; that it was chance which conducted the race from the first to the second Phase, from the second to the third, and that when this progress was accomplished, the philosophers had the tact to arrogate to themselves the honor of ameliorations which in fact they never dreamed of.

I have already given a proof of this in the fact that among the Greeks and Romans no philosopher ever proposed any plan for the emancipation of the slaves; not for an instant did they concern themselves with the lot of those unfortunate victims whom Vedius Pollion caused to be devoured by lampreys for the smallest fault, and whom, when they became too numerous, the Spartans slaughtered by the thousand. Never did the philanthropists of Athens or Rome deign to interest themselves in their lot, nor even to protest against these atrocities. They believed, at that period, that Civilization could not exist without slaves. The philosophers always believe that social science has arrived at its ultimatum, and that the best which exists is the best which is possible. Thus, seeing that the Civilized Order is not quite so bad as the Barbaric and Savage Orders, they have concluded from this fact that Civilization is the best Society possible, and that no other would ever be discovered.

Between the various social Periods there are mixed or mongrel Societies which are compounded of the characteristics of several Periods. The social system in Russia is a compound made up from the fourth and fifth Periods—Barbarism and Civilization. Society in China is the most curious in respect to the mingling of elements, which has ever existed on the globe. It presents, in about equal proportions, the characteristics of Patriarchism,

Barbarism, and Civilization. Hence the Chinese are neither Patriarchs, Barbarians, nor Civilizees.

Mixed Societies, such as the Russian and the Chinese, have the properties of mixed or mongrel animals, like the mule; that is, they have more vices and at the same time more vigor than the original stock.

It is next to impossible to find a pure society, that is to say, one exempt from mixture, and having no characteristic borrowed from superior or inferior Periods. I have already remarked that the Barbarians of Asia have nearly all adopted the principle of hereditary government, which is a characteristic of Civilization, and therefore a departure from the Barbaric Order. This Order is the purest in Algiers, where the throne belongs legally to the strongest pretender. I have also remarked that there exist among us several institutions belonging to a higher Order than Civilization.

I must now finish this thesis which would require a regular exposition of the characteristics of each social Period, and, above all, of the sixteen characteristics of Civilization, and of the special attributes of each of its four Phases.

XV.

COROLLARIES ON THE MISFORTUNES OF GLOBES DURING THE PHASES OF SOCIAL INFANCY AND INCOHERENCE.

HAPPINESS, about which men have reasoned so much and so absurdly, consists in having many passions and abundant means of satisfying them. At present we have but few passions and hardly means sufficient for satisfying a fourth of them. It is for this reason that our globe is, for the moment, among the most unfortunate in the universe. If other planets experience as much misfortune, it is impossible for them to experience more, and the theory of Movement will show that more refined social torments than those we endure on this miserable globe could not be invented even by God himself.

Without entering into any details on this subject, I restrict myself to the remark that the most unfortunate planet in the system is not always the one which is the poorest. Venus is poorer than we, while Mars and the three new planets are poorer still;

their lot, however, is less unhappy than ours, and for the following reason :—

The globe the most unhappy is that the inhabitants of which
have passions disproportioned to the means of satisfying them.
Such is the case, at present, with our own globe. This renders the condition of the human race so oppressive that we see
the general dissatisfaction extending even to sovereigns, who,
while enjoying a lot universally envied, complain nevertheless
that they are not happy, though they are free at all times to
exchange conditions with any of their subjects.

The cause of this temporary misfortune of our globe I have
explained in the preceding pages; it is that God has given to
our passions an intensity suited only to the two great phases of
the Combined Order—phases which will comprise about seventy
thousand years, in the course of which every day will afford us
enjoyments so intense, so varied, that our souls will hardly suffice
for them, and we shall be obliged to develop all the passions systematically in order that we may be competent to appreciate
and enjoy the innumerable delights thus presented by this New
Order. Had our miserable Civilization been the ultimate destiny
of man, God would have given us passions tame and apathetic, as
recommended by Philosophy—passions suited to the wretched
existence the human race has supported for five thousand years.
The passional activity and vehemence of which we complain constitute the guarantee of our future welfare and happiness. God
has formed our souls for the ages of happiness, which will last
seven times longer than the ages of misery. The certainty of our
having to suffer from five to six thousand years of preparatory
torments, was not a sufficient reason for determining him to give us
feeble, philosophical passions, since, though these would have well
accorded with the miseries of Civilization and Barbarism, they
would not have at all accorded with the seventy thousand years of
the Combined Order upon which we are about to enter. We should
therefore render thanks to God, even now, for the activity and
vehemence of our passions, which have been the subject of absurd
attacks simply because men have been ignorant of the social Order which is to develop and satisfy them. The question arises,
should God have given to us the faculty of foreseeing the brilliant Destiny reserved us, in order to obviate this ignorance?

Doubtless not. Such knowledge would have been for our first parents the cause of continual grief, for the imperfect development of Industry made it a necessity for them to remain in the incoherent Order. Even had they foreseen the future happiness of the race, they would still have fallen into the Savage State, since the Combined Order could not have been organized until Industry and the Arts were developed to a high degree, which was very far from being the case during the first Period. Many ages were necessary for the creation and development of the resources necessary to the establishment of the Combined Order, and our first parents would have refused to perfect Industry merely for the good of generations not to be born till the lapse of thousands of years. The people would thus have been seized with universal apathy ; no man would have been willing to labor for a happiness so distant that neither the living nor their descendants for many generations could hope to enjoy it. Even at present, when we boast of our intelligence and philanthropy, men refuse to engage in certain works because the enjoyment of them must be deferred for a generation. How then could our first parents, who were less cultivated than we are, have taken an interest in labors the fruit of which would not be gathered for two thousand years ? For at least twenty centuries were necessary in order to carry Industry and the Arts to that degree of perfection required by the Combined Order.

What then would have happened if the first races of men had foreseen a social harmony which could not be born till after so many years of industrial progress ? It is probable that far from laboring for the benefit of the twentieth century to come, they would have taken pleasure in laboring against it ; that they would have said with one accord : "Why should we be the servants of men to be born thousands of years hence ? Let us abandon, let us stifle in its birth, this Industry whose fruit will be only for them ! Since we are denied the happiness reserved for the Combined Order, let our successors be denied it like ourselves, for two thousand, for twenty thousand years ! Let them live as we have lived !"

Is not such the character of man ? Witness parents, who constantly reproach their children for possessing luxuries which they did not enjoy in their young days. Even if it required but twenty years to organize an Association, where is the old man who would take any interest in such an enterprise? Fearing not to live for that period, such a man would decline to engage in labors for the benefit of his successors, since he would have no certainty of himself enjoying the fruits.

If I announce with so much confidence the near approach of Universal Harmony, it is because the organization of the Combined Order might be effected within two years after a given Association had prepared the necessary edifices and lands. If these preparations were already made, if the edifices and lands suitable for a Phalanx could be procured now, this fine social Order might be inaugurated at once. Now as the organization of the first Association would require hardly two years, and as the oldest man hopes for at least two years more of existence, he would be pleased with the idea of seeing it in operation before his death, that on beholding it he might exclaim after the manner of Simeon: "Lord! lettest now thy servant depart in peace, for mine eyes have seen the happiness that thou hast prepared for all thy people."

It is at present that man may quit this life without regret, since he may be certain of the immortality of the soul, which could have been demonstrated to him only by the laws of social Movement. Up to this time we have had such vague notions of the future life, such frightful pictures of it, that the doctrine of immortality has been not so much a consolation as a terror. Hence the belief in it has been very feeble, and it was not desirable that it should become stronger. During the existence of the incoherent Order, God does not permit us to acquire any definite ideas of the future life; for if the doctrine of immortality were demonstrated beyond doubt, the poorer classes in Civilization, the moment they felt sure of another existence which could not possibly be worse for them than the present, would be led, in their wretchedness, to put an end to their lives. There would then remain on the earth only the rich, who have neither the ability nor the inclination to engage in the arduous and repulsive labors now performed by the poor. Civilized Industry would thus fall into decline by the death of those who support its burdens, and a globe would continue permanently in the Savage State owing to the one fact of its belief in the immortality of the soul.

But God, having occasion to maintain the Civilized and Barbaric Societies for a certain period, in order that they might serve in leading the way to other and better societies, has left us in profound ignorance on the subject of immortality, till Civilization and Barbarism shall have passed away. He has identified the calculations which establish the certainty of a future life with those which reveal the means of advancing the world to a higher social Order than the Civilized or Barbaric, during the existence of which two societies the mass of laborers and slaves, were they certain of another existence offering them a chance of escape from their terrible sufferings, would hasten to put an end to their lives by self-destruction.

This question of the happiness reserved to the soul in another life, gives an opportunity to expose the absolute ignorance of the Civilizees in respect to the laws and designs of Nature. How little you understand her laws when you make future happiness to consist in the separation of the material and the spiritual elements, and when you pretend that after the dissolution of the body the soul will isolate itself from matter, without which there would be no enjoyment even for God himself.

All that is necessary here, on the subject of the future life, is to undeceive you as to the conflict you suppose to exist between the lot of the departed and that of the living. Cease to believe that the souls of the former have no connection with this world. Between the present and the future life there are intimate ties. It will be demonstrated to you that the souls of the departed vegetate in a state of languor and anxiety, in which, until the present condition of the globe shall be ameliorated, our own will participate after this life. So long as the earth continues in a state of social chaos so contrary to the designs of God, the souls of its inhabitants will suffer from it in the other life as well as in this, and the happiness of the departed will commence only with that of the living—with the disappearance of the Civilized, Barbaric, and Savage Orders.

If it were difficult to organize the Combined Order, the establishment of which will become the signal for the happiness of the departed as well as of the living, this revelation would become a source of pain and even of despair; but the extreme facility of establishing it will render precious to us a Theory which comes to dissipate our illusions as to the future life, upon which we shall enter only to partake of the unhappiness and the anxiety to which the souls of all are subjected while waiting in the other world for the harmonious organization of the Globe.

The theory of the social Movement, by making known to us the condition reserved for the soul in the various worlds which it is to traverse during eternity, will show that after this life it will be again united to matter, without ever isolating itself from material enjoyments. This is not the place to enter either upon this discussion, or upon the causes which will temporarily deprive our souls of the faculty of remembering their former existence. Where were they before inhabiting our present bodies? God, creating nothing from nothing, could not have formed our souls from nothing; and if you believe they had no existence before the body, you are near to believing that they will return to that nothingness from which your prejudices would make them spring. In pretending that the soul may be immortal after this life without having been so previous to this life, the Civilizees have shown themselves to be very inconsistent. The Barbarians and Savages, in their rude ideas of metempsychosis, are much nearer the truth: this dogma approaches it in two respects;—first, in that it does not suppose our souls to have sprung from nothing; second, in that it does not isolate them from matter after this life. Here are at least glimpses of the truth; and it is not the first time that rude nations have shown themselves more sensible than the conceited Civilizees, who, with all their jargon about progress and perfectibility, plunge deeper and deeper into the abyss of moral and political subtleties, and thus incur the risk of stagnating a thousand years longer in Civilization.

EPILOGUE.

ON THE PROXIMITY OF THE IMPENDING SOCIAL METAMORPHOSIS.

In reflecting upon the sketches I have given of past and future social revolutions, what doubts and suspicions will spring up in every
mind! At first men will float between curiosity and distrust.
Seduced by the idea of penetrating the mysteries of Nature, they
will fear being deceived by some ingenious fiction. Reason will
whisper them to doubt; passion will urge them to believe.
Amazed to see a mortal unroll before their eyes the chart of the
divine decrees and survey past and future eternities, they will
yield to the power of curiosity, and be overcome with joy to know
that at last man has been able

"The august decrees of Destiny to unveil,"

so that before experience has pronounced upon my theory, I shall
perhaps have more proselytes to moderate than skeptics to con-
vince.

The views I have just given of General Destinies are too
superficial not to excite numerous objections. I foresee them
all. They have been made to me many times in private confer-
ences when I have given various explanations which this first
Memoir does not admit of. It will be useless for me to attempt
to remove any doubts till I have explained the mechanism of the
Series, a knowledge of which will dissipate all obscurities and
resolve all possible objections.

Meanwhile I restrict myself to saying that the two first Memoirs will not treat of the theory of the Social movement, but
will have no other object than to satisfy the impatient, to give
a few sketches which have been solicited, to describe some
of the results of the Combined Order, and to gratify the enthusiastic, who wish to anticipate the publication of the Treatise and
satisfy themselves, by various indications, that the Theory of
Human Destiny is at last discovered. What we desire we can
easily be made to believe; and there are readers who will not
wait for more ample developments before giving to the discovery
their entire confidence. Wishing to sustain these in their hopes,

and at the same time to confirm those who hesitate, I insist, especially, on the facility of entering without delay upon the Combined Order. This facility is so great that from the present year (1808) we may see the commencement of the organization of Universal Harmony. If, in order to form an experimental Association, a prince would employ one of the armies which the continental peace has left in activity; if he would draft twenty thousand men to make the preparatory works, it would be possible, by transplanting trees with a portion of their native soil (as is done in Paris), and by making the first constructions of brick, to so accelerate the enterprise that at the close of the spring of 1808 the first Association might be in operation. Then the chaotic Civilized, Barbaric, and Savage Orders would soon disappear from the face of the globe, carrying with them the unanimous malediction of the whole human race.

It will be seen by this what reasons we have for throwing off our lethargy, for laying aside our apathetic resignation to the misfortunes and despair engendered by the dogmas of philosophy, which teach the inefficacy of Providence in social affairs, and the incompetency of the human race to discover its future destiny.

If the calculation of future events were not within the competency of man, whence comes this mania, common to the entire· race, of wishing to fathom Human Destiny, at the very mention of which the most impassive being experiences a tremor of impatience?—so impossible is it to root out of the human heart this passion for knowing the future! And why has God, who does nothing without a purpose, given to us this intense desire, if he has not provided the means of some day satisfying it? At last that day has arrived, and mortals are about to participate with God in the knowledge of future events. I have already given a slight sketch of them in order to lead the reader to the conclusion that if this knowledge, so marvellous and so long desired, depends upon the theory of Agricultural Association and Passional Attraction, nothing can be more worthy to excite our curiosity than this theory, which will be communicated hereafter, and which will open to the world the Book of Eternal Decrees.

"Nature," say the Philosophers, "is concealed by a brazen veil which the efforts of ages will never be able to penetrate."

A very convenient sophism, this, for ignorance and self-conceit! What we are unable to do ourselves we like to feel that no one else can do.

If Nature is veiled, it is not with brass, but at most with gauze. Since Newton has discovered the fourth branch of her mysteries, it is an indication that she would not refuse us a knowledge of the other branches. When she has accorded one favor, it would be silly to suppose that she will accord no more. Why then have the philosophers been so timid in her presence, when she has tempted them by allowing a corner of her veil to be raised?

They boast of having diffused floods of light; but whence have they obtained it? Surely not from Nature, since according to their confession she is concealed by a brazen veil which no one can penetrate. It is by such brilliant paradoxes that the philosophers communicate their own want of faith, and persuade the human race that nothing will be discovered because their science has never discovered anything.

Meanwhile, despite the incompetency of such guides, society continues to make some progress, as we see in the case of the suppression of slavery; but how slow is our advance in the career of social good! Twenty scientific centuries elapsed before the least amelioration was proposed in the condition of the slaves, from which it would seem that thousands of years are necessary to open our eyes to a truth, or to suggest to us an act of justice. Our men of science, who boast their love for the people, are utterly ignorant of any means for improving their condition. The attempt of the moderns for the emancipation of the negroes resulted only in shedding seas of blood and aggravating the sufferings of those whom it was proposed to serve; and ignorance still prevails as to the means of emancipation, though the operation was demonstrated to be possible by the abolition of ancient slavery and serfdom, from which fact, however, we have thus far been unable to deduce a theory of gradual emancipation.

It is to chance, then, and not to the moral and political sciences, that we owe the little of progress made in the social world; but for every new discovery thus made we have to pay centuries of social and political commotion. The onward movement of society may be compared to that of the sloth, whose every step

is counted by a groan. Like it, Civilization advances with inconceivable slowness. In each succeeding age it tries new theories which serve only, like thorns, to lacerate those who grasp at
them.

Unfortunate Nations! You are on the verge of a great social
metamorphosis which seems to be heralded by a universal commotion. It is now, indeed, that the times are big with hopes for
the future, and that the excess of suffering must lead to the crisis which precedes recovery. To behold the repetition and the
violence of political convulsions, it would seem as if Nature were
making a supreme effort to shake off a burden which oppresses
her. Wars and revolutions devastate successively every part of
the globe. Political storms, for a moment lulled, break forth
anew, multiplying like the heads of the hydra beneath the blows
of Hercules. Peace is but a delusion, a momentary dream,
and Industry, since an island of commercial monopolists and
spoliators has embarrassed the intercourse of nations, discour-
aged the agriculture and manufactures of two continents, and
transferred their workshops into nurseries of pauperism, Industry, I say, has become the scourge of the toiling millions. The
ambition of colonial possession has opened a new volcano. The
implacable fury of the negro race threatens to transform America
into a vast charnel-house, and to avenge the exterminated aborigines by the destruction of their conquerors.

The commercial spirit has opened new fields to fraud and rap-
ine, spreading war and devastation over the two hemispheres and
carrying the corruptions of Civilized cupidity even into Savage
regions. Our ships circumnavigate the globe only to initiate
Barbarians and Savages into our vices, our excesses, and our
crimes. Thus Civilization is becoming more and more odious as
it approaches its end. The earth presents only a frightful political chaos, and invokes the arm of another Hercules to purge it
from the social abominations which disgrace it.

Nations! your presentiments are about to be realized. Breathe,
and forget your former miseries, for a fortunate discovery
brings to you at last the Social Compass which, but for your
impious distrust of Providence, you might have discovered a
thousand times. Learn (and I can not repeat it to you too often)
that, before all things else, Providence must have determined the

laws of the social mechanism, since they constitute the noblest branch of Universal Movement, the direction of which belongs to God alone. Instead of recognising this truth, instead of devoting yourselves to studying what were the designs of God in respect to the organization of society, and what means he might have chosen to reveal them to us, you have discarded every idea which admitted of the intervention of Providence in human relations; you have reviled, defamed Passional Attraction —the eternal interpreter of his decrees; you have confided yourselves to the guidance of the philosophers, who would place Divinity below themselves by arrogating its highest functions— by assuming to regulate the Social Movement. To cover them with shame, God has suffered Humanity, under their auspices, to bathe itself in blood for twenty-three scientific centuries, and to exhaust the career of misery, ignorance, and crime. Finally, to complete the opprobrium which rests upon these modern Titans, God has willed that they should be vanquished by a discoverer who is a stranger to the sciences, that the theory of Universal Movement should fall to the lot of a man almost illiterate.

Your political and moral theories, the shameful result of ancient and modern sophistry, are about to be confounded by a mere merchant's clerk, and this is not the first time that God has made use of the humble to abase the exalted, and that he has made choice of the obscurest of men to bring to the world the most important of messages.

END OF THE FIRST PART.

PART II.

DESCRIPTIONS OF VARIOUS BRANCHES OF PRIVATE OR DOMESTIC DESTINY.

ARGUMENT.

THE horizon is about to light up; we pass to dissertations which have nothing scientific in them, but will be within the comprehension of all.

In the First Part, I have presented to the inquisitive a sketch of great future phenomena. In this Part I shall present the lovers of pleasure with a sketch of various delights which the Combined Order may enable them to taste even in the present generation. I insist on the proximity of the social transformation, because in respect to pleasures no one likes delay, especially in an age like the present, when the excess of misfortunes makes every one so impatient for a change.

In giving these pictures of approaching happiness, my intention, as already expressed, is to engage the reader in the theory of Association and Attraction which promises so many joys, and to make him desire that it may be found practicable. In proportion as we become interested in the accuracy, the justness of the theory on which are founded such great hopes, we shall become interested imperceptibly in its study.

In accordance with these considerations, I wish to present my theory of Association and Attraction, little by little, unfolding it gradually in each Memoir, and finally collecting the details together and giving the whole doctrine in a body. In a word, I would present the theory in proportions graduated according to the curiosity excited in the reader. I believe these precautions necessary in order to secure the acceptance of a Treatise which, if I should present it abruptly and without preparing the way for it, would be disdained like any metaphysical science. In giving certain descriptions of the Combined Order, my difficulty will not be to embellish the picture sufficiently, but to soften it down—in other words, to raise but a corner of the veil. I have already said that if the picture were presented without due precautions, it would create too much enthusiasm, especially among women. Now my desire is not to produce infatuation, which might be the case if I presented the Combined Order in all its brilliancy, but to appeal to reason. Hence, in the pictures which are to follow, I shall glide over all the pleasures of the new Order, which will be made known only as far as may be necessary in order to expose the ennuis and absurdities of Civiliza-. tion.

The perspective I shall present will be contained in two Sections.

The first Section, relating to the seventh Period, will treat of the pleasures of the Combined Household in that Order, and of the ennuis of the isolated Household in Civilization.

The second Section, which relates to the eighth Period, will treat of the splendors of the Combined Order.

To moderate the surprise which will be excited, and to proceed by degrees, I shall commence with a description taken from the seventh Period, the pleasures of which, though immense compared with those of Civilization, are yet moderate compared with those of the Combined Order, which latter I shall not treat of till we come to the second Section.

This first Section will contain nothing startling, and will not therefore be open, like the second, to the reproach of being either absurd, gigantic, or impossible.

SECTION I.

ON

THE COMBINED HOUSEHOLD OF THE SEVENTH AND TWENTY-SIXTH PERIODS,

AND

THE ENNUIS EXPERIENCED BY BOTH SEXES IN THE ISOLATED HOUSEHOLD.

PRELIMINARY.

THE Combined Household of which I am about to speak is a domestic institution belonging to the seventh and twenty-sixth Periods. It holds a middle rank between the isolated household of the Civilizees and Barbarians and the Associated Household, which will reign in the eighteen periods of Universal Harmony.

In the Combined Household, men and women will enjoy an existence so agreeable and so free from vexations, that it will become impossible to decide any one of them to adopt the permanent marriage relation required by our isolated households.

Before speaking of the manners and customs which will grow out of the Combined Household, I shall examine whence proceeds the blind prejudice of the Civilizees in favor of permanent marriage.

The reader must bear in mind that I confess the necessity of this bond in Civilization, and that I criticise it only in comparison with the new Social Order, in which a different form of union between the sexes will require a freedom in love-relations which in the present order is inadmissible.

It will also be borne in mind, that on the subject of marriage and the life of the household, as on all other subjects, my assertions are subject to an eighth of exception.

I.

ENNUIS OF MEN IN THE ISOLATED HOUSEHOLD.

IF we reflect on the innumerable inconveniences connected with permanent marriage and the life of the isolated household, we shall be astonished at the folly of the male sex in never having devised the means of escaping from this kind of life. Leaving aside the rich, it seems to me that our domestic life is anything but amusing. Among other evils attendant upon it, I shall mention eight which afflict more or less all husbands, and which in the Combined Household will disappear.

1. THE RISK OF UNHAPPINESS. — What game of chance can be more frightful than that of an indissoluble bond in which a man stakes the happiness of his whole life by incurring the risk of incompatibility of character?

2. THE EXPENSE. — In the present Order this is enormous, as we shall presently see by comparing it with the immense economies which will result from the Combined Household.

3. THE VIGILANCE REQUIRED; — the obligation to watch over the economical details of a household, the management of which can not be prudently left to others, but requires the constant personal supervision of the husband.

4. MONOTONY. — This must be very great in our isolated households, since husbands, notwithstanding the diversion afforded by their business, resort in crowds to public places of entertainment — clubs, coffee-houses, theatres, etc. — to relieve themselves from the satiety and ennui of family life. For the women, the monotony is still greater.

5. STERILITY. — This threatens to defeat all projects of happiness. It disconcerts plans in respect to family succession, causes estates to pass into the hands of collateral heirs whose avidity and ingratitude are disgusting, and inspires the husband with

aversion for a sterile companion, and hatred of a conjugal bond which has deceived all his hopes.

6. WIDOWER-HOOD.*—This reduces a man to the condition of a galley-slave by throwing upon him all the cares of the children and the household ; on the other hand, if the husband dies before the wife, anxiety lest the children shall fall into mercenary hands, and the prospect of the disasters which may happen to his young family, embitter his last moments with gall.

7. FALSE ALLIANCES.—The disappointment resulting from alliances with other families, which in their subsequent conduct rarely realize the hopes of interest or pleasure founded on the connection.

8. CONJUGAL INFIDELITY.—This vice is common in all countries, notwithstanding the many useless precautions taken in order that the husband may not experience the retributive justice due for his own conduct previous to marriage.

In seeing these and other evils connected with permanent marriage and the isolated household, how is it that men have neglected to seek some means of escape from so many kinds of servitude, and to effect some domestic innovation which might result in something less intolerable than the present household life ?

In political affairs, it is said that the laws are made by the strongest party. In domestic affairs, the case appears to be different. In establishing permanent marriage and its natural result, the isolated household, the male sex, though the stronger, has not made the law to its own advantage. One would say that such an Order must be the work of a third sex which had sought to condemn the two others to ennui ; for what could be better calculated than permanent marriage and the isolated household to produce lassitude, venality, and perfidy in the relations of love and pleasure ?

Marriage would seem to have been invented as a reward for the perverse ; the more false and intriguing a man is the more easy is it for him to attain through marriage to opulence and public esteem. It is the same with women. Employ the vilest stratagems in order to make a rich match, and the moment you succeed you become a little saint—a person of family and of position.

---

* We coin this term—which, for the rest, is as legitimate as widow-hood—because there is no word in the English language expressive of the condition of the widower.
—*Translator.*

Suddenly to acquire great wealth for the trouble of winning a young bride is so lucky a stroke of fortune, that a depraved public opinion is ready to pardon anything to the successful intriguer who accomplishes it. He is unanimously voted to be a good husband, a good son, a good father, a good brother, a good son-in-law, a good neighbor, a good citizen, a good republican. For such is the style of the eulogists of the present day; they can not praise any one without pronouncing him perfect from head to foot. And it is thus they praise every adventurer who succeeds in marrying a fortune. A rich marriage may be compared to baptism, by the promptness with which it effaces all previous stains upon the character. Parents can not do better, then, in Civilization, than to stimulate their children by every possible means, good or bad, to make rich matches; for marriage, a true civil baptism, atones in the eyes of public opinion for all previous faults. The public has not the same indulgence for other *parvenus;* on the contrary, it taunts them for a long time with the means by which they obtained their wealth.

But for one person who attains to riches and happiness by marriage, how many others find in this bond the torment of their whole lives? These will certainly admit that the subjection of woman is not an advantage to man. What dupes are men to forge for themselves chains which subject them to continual restraint, and how justly are they punished, by the ennuis of such a bond, for having reduced woman to a state of dependency and subjection! Admitting that the life of the household guarantees a man against some of the disadvantages attached to celibacy, it fails to secure positive happiness, even in case of perfect agreement between the parties; and if they possess characters eminently adapted to each other, there is nothing to prevent them from living together in an Order where love is free and the social arrangements differently organized.

It will be shown by the descriptions of the new Domestic Order, that marriage does not offer a single chance of happiness which would not be found in case of entire liberty. In order to blind men to the evident incompatibility of marriage with the passions of man, philosophy preaches the doctrine of fatalism; it contends that we are destined in this life to tribulation, that we ought to know how to resign ourselves, etc., etc. Not at all.

All that is necessary is to discover a new Order of Society adapted to the demands of Nature, to the requirements of the passions. and this is what has neither been sought for nor proposed.

I wish presently to put the reader on the track of this new Order and to give an idea of its domestic life, the organization of which would have been so easy.

Let us further examine the evils connected with permanent marriage and the isolated household. These institutions have the property of depriving us in every sense of *positive happiness*— that is, of real pleasures, such as freedom in the passion of love, good living, absence of care, and other sources of enjoyment, which the Civilizees do not think of coveting, because philosophy accustoms them to look upon the desire of positive pleasure as a crime. Despite all the arguments used to wheedle men into marriage, as a child is wheedled into taking medicine, despite all the honeyed eulogies of domestic bliss, we still see men frightened at the idea of a permanent union, especially after they have arrived at the age of reflection. It must be that the bond is a very formidable one since men hesitate so long before contracting it. I make an exception of the rich, for in a household which commences with affluence, everything is charming, though even in this case, men are in no haste to give up their former pleasures for the sake of rendering themselves slaves to a wife, to whom they must always be paying the most assiduous attentions under the penalty of conjugal infidelity, and of having to support children not their own, but which the law forces them to accept. *Is pater est quem justæ nuptæ demonstrant.* (The father is the man designated as such by the fact of marriage.) And this is only one of the dangers to which men are exposed by marriage ; hence they consider it as a trap laid for them, as a perilous leap. Before taking this leap they exhaust all the calculations of chances. The conclusion of all these calculations is that the one thing to be looked after is money, so that if one is to be deceived by a woman, the dowry at least may be made sure, and also that a compensation may be found in fortune for the inconveniences and ennuis of marriage. Such are the arguments used by men on this subject; such the calculations they make before entering upon this sacred tie — upon the philosophic delights of family life.

It is certain that there is as great a distance between these calculations and love, as there is between the isolated household and an agreeable life. Doubtless, comforts may be had in the houses of the rich, who compose the very small minority, say an eighth in society, but as for the seven eighths, they merely vegetate, and are filled with jealousy at seeing the comforts enjoyed by the other eighth. All however, rich and poor, are so weary of the domestic monotony of the isolated household that we see them seeking pleasure away from their homes, plunging into anti-domestic dissipations, haunting public places — theatres, balls, concerts, etc. — keeping open house when they are rich, and when they lack the means of doing this, giving each other alternate entertainments.

In the seventh Period, of which I am about to give certain details, these recreations which are purchased so dearly in the present Order, will be enjoyed at little or no expense by all. This Order will assure to every one a constant variety of festivals and other social entertainments, and a freedom of which not a shadow is found in our family repasts, where there reigns a constant and unnatural restraint, a conventional tyranny, so different from the freedom even now enjoyed at some of our private parties, and especially at what are called picnics.

As for these family repasts which are so insipid from the incongruous mixture of ages and characters among the guests, and so burdensome owing to the trouble of preparation, it should be remarked that even this commonplace enjoyment is only possible for the rich. But how miserable the lot of the numerous families which, for want of fortune, are wholly deprived of what are called pleasures, and are reduced to that state of intestine war which the proverb well defines in saying: "Asses fight when there is no fodder in the rack!" And how many families there are that, despite their opulence, fall into this domestic discord which, among the great majority who are soured by poverty, is all but universal.

True, there are exceptions to be admitted. We find not only individuals but whole nations who easily submit to the yoke of marriage. Such are the Germans, whose patient and phlegmatic temperament is much better adapted to conjugal servitude than the volatile and restless character of the French. These exceptions are relied on as a defence of marriage, in favor of which only such instances are cited as are exceptions to the general rule. Doubtless such a tie is suited to a man who has passed the meridian of life, and who wishes to isolate himself from the corruptions of the world. I am willing to believe that a woman may find a charm in the society of such a man, and may disdain for him the whirl of fashionable life; but how is it that the masculine sex postpones these virtuous ideas till after having passed fifteen or twenty years in gallantry and dissipation? Why, in withdrawing from the world, do not such men take wives like themselves, who are matured by experience, instead of hoping to find in a mere girl virtues more precocious than their own which have been so tardy of development? It is amusing to see the men in Civilization, who pretend to be superior in reason to woman, require of her at the age of sixteen an amount of judgment which they themselves do not acquire till thirty, and after having spent their youth in every kind of dissipation. If they attained to reason only by pursuing the paths of pleasure, why should they be surprised that women prefer to take the same road? Their domestic policy, which depends on the fidelity of a young tendril, in no way accords with the designs of God. If he has given to young women a taste for exciting pleasures, it is a proof that he has not destined them either for permanent marriage or for the life of the family, which requires a taste for retirement and quiet. Hence husbands are necessarily unhappy in the isolated household, since they generally marry persons to whom Nature has not given a character adapted to this kind of life.

And here the philosophers intervene and propose to *change the passions of man, and to repress Nature.* Absurd pretension! We know too well with what success it is crowned. Despite all the systems of the moralists, happiness is not found in our households; a universal cry is raised against the monotony and ennui of such an existence, and it is the men especially who make this complaint,—they who made the law, and fancied they were making it to their own advantage! And what would the women say if they had the right to complain? And what must be thought of an institution which is oppressive to the stronger sex who established it, and more oppressive still to the weaker sex who are not permitted to complain of it?

We hear praised the apparent harmony of those households in

22

which a young woman endures with heroic devotion the persecutions of a jealous husband retired from the world. But is not this a state of warfare worse even than that which prevails in certain German villages, where the husband suspends over the chimney a rod called the "family peace-maker" and which, in the last resort, puts an end to conjugal quarrels?

The tyranny of marriage, though less apparent among the refined classes, is none the less real. Why, then, do not the two sexes rise up against a Social Order which subjects them both to so many vexations? When we see these domestic wars among all classes of people, why not admit that the conjugal state is not the final destiny of man? Instead of seeking some palliative for the evil, means should have been devised for emancipating both sexes from the tyranny of household-life, which breeds and develops all the elements of discord and ennui *without producing any good that may not be found in a state of entire liberty.*

II.

THE COMBINED HOUSEHOLD.

I SHALL now speak of the method which may be substituted for our present Domestic Order. It is a measure borrowed from the seventh Social Period. I shall call it the *Combined Household, or Series of Nine Groups.* It may be organized in eight or ten groups, but the number nine is better adapted for a regular balance in the play of the passions.

To organize this Household, an edifice should be constructed suitable for the accommodation of a hundred persons of different degrees of wealth; eighty persons of one sex, and twenty domestics of the two sexes. There should be suites of apartments of different prices, so that every person can choose according to his means; there should also be halls and saloons for various public purposes.

The Series in its internal relations should be formed, so far as is possible, of nine Groups, each containing nine persons. (It should be borne in mind that these numbers are not imperative, and that I indicate everything approximatively.) For example, for the repasts, there should be nine tables distributed three and three in the respective halls of the first, second and third class of prices; and in each hall the three tables should be served at consecutive hours—say at one, two, and three o'clock in order in every respect to avoid uniformity; for uniformity, tameness, and mediocrity are the three natural enemies of the passions and of Harmony, since the equilibrium of the passions can not be established except by a regular contrast of opposites.

The Series should have three compatible occupations. For instance, one Series of artisans could carry on the three trades of carpentry, joinery, and cabinet-making. This Society should have a name and an escutcheon—say the Oak. Further on should be the Series of the Lilac, composed of women, carrying on the business of mantua-making, millinery, and shirt-making.

Each associate should furnish an amount of capital regulated by a progressive scale, for instance, 4,000, 8,000, 12,000 francs; or 0, 1000, 2000; or if the founders are rich and wish to establish a magnificent Series, their subscriptions might extend to 100,000, 200,000, 300,000 francs, taking care always that the first class furnish triple that furnished by the third. This capital will serve as a guarantee for all the advances made by the Series in the way of rent, provisions, etc., to each member.

These Societies admit no coercive statutes, no monastic constraints. For example, the groups or individuals of the third class may sometimes order the fare of the second or of the first class, the directors giving credit to all who do not abuse it. The palaces or mansions of neighboring Series should intercommunicate by means of covered galleries protected from the air, so that in the relations of pleasure and business there may be a guarantee against the inclemency of the weather, from which so much inconvenience is experienced in Civilization. The members should be able to go day and night from one palace to the other by means of passages well heated or ventilated according to the season and without any risk, as in the present Order, of being constantly wet, bespattered, and exposed to colds and inflammations by passing suddenly from hot rooms to the open streets. On leaving a ball or banquet, persons wishing to sleep away from their apartments should be able to pass from one edifice to another under cover, and without overshoes or furs, or even the bother of taking a carriage. Instead of having to traverse three or four streets, as in Civilization, they would merely have to go through the public galleries of three or four contiguous edifices, without being exposed to either the cold or the heat, the wind or the rain. This system of sheltered communications is one of the thousand conveniences reserved for the Combined Order, of which the Unitary Palace of the Series gives a partial idea.

To organize the Series in balanced rivalry with each other, there should be formed eighteen in regular gradation; namely, nine masculine and nine feminine; but this organization would be more costly than a Phalanx of the Combined Order. The trial might be made with six Series, three of men, and three of women. By means of this rivalry, though it would be on a small scale, the Series would put an end to the three philosophic virtues — uniformity, tameness, and mediocrity — at once. For example, the Series of the Willow, being the poorest of the six, would pique itself on carrying neatness, dexterity, politeness, and the other qualities compatible with its small fortune, to the highest degree, while in matters in which it could attain only to mediocrity, it would make no pretension.

Societies of this kind will not, like the Combined Order, admit of extreme contrasts, such as that which exists between the poor man and the millionaire; these disparities which will be harmonized in the eighth Period, are not adapted to the seventh which is here in question.

In the eighth Period, Association is *contrasted*, and in the seventh *shaded;* thus the Combined Household, or Series of nine Groups, though composed of members unequal in fortune and in other respects, should not have too great a dissimilarity between them, whereas a Phalanx of the eighth Period would bring together the most extreme contrasts.

We see in our large cities a germ of the Combined Household, as in the case of the Clubs and Casinos, which already cause the insipid family group to be deserted. They afford relaxations and amusements of various kinds at less than a tenth of what they would cost in the private household. Every kind of pleasure becomes economical both in respect to money and trouble, all the preparations being carefully made by persons specially appointed for the purpose, as will be the case in the Combined Household. But Clubs and Casinos are based on a principle of equality which interferes with the development of ambition, whereas the Combined Household, being subdivided into nine rivalized and unequal groups, will open a vast field to it in the three characters of patron, patronized, and independent. I do not speak of the arrangements relative to children, nor of their education in such a household, because to explain such details, it would be necessary to give a synopsis of the whole Period. Let us confine ourselves to reasoning on the hypothesis that six Combined households are established; two composed of the opulent class, two of the middle class, and two of the poorer class. And let us suppose these six Series placed at once in the midst of Civilization—in a city like Paris or London. What would be the result of a domestic innovation so foreign to our old customs of social incoherence and isolation?

Observe, first, that in order to found these Series, it will not be necessary to overthrow and devastate empires as happens whenever an attempt is made to carry out the visionary schemes of the philosophers. On the contrary, the work will be entirely a pacific one; and instead of ravaging the earth to establish the rights of man, we shall peaceably establish the rights of woman by allotting to her three of the proposed Associations which will admit of nine classes of fortunes for each sex.

As for the results which this social inoculation would produce, these are enigmas which I leave to the inquisitive, but I will endeavor to furnish the key to them.

In administrative economy, what advantage would not a government find in dealing with a Series which paid its taxes on a fixed day and on simple notice, instead of treating with twenty isolated families, half of which would defraud the government, and the other half refuse to pay till forced to by the law. In case of contravention of the laws, no penalties would be inflicted except those which are simply humiliating, such as removing the escutcheon from over the entrance of the edifice. What increase of revenue and what facility of administration would be secured in case a whole nation should be organized in Associations or Series of this kind! Might not governments, while diminishing the taxes by a third, find themselves one half richer owing to the economy in collecting, and in the increase of taxable products which would result from combined Industry?

In domestic economy, how great would be the diminution of individual expenses! Might not a person in the Combined Household live on a thousand francs income much better than on three thousand in the Isolated Household, and avoid, in addition, the trouble of marketing, supervision, and other details which would be attended to by the group of major-domos of each tribe?

Persons who have no inclination for the functions of major-domo or other domestic employments, would not be in any way occupied with the details of the household, and on quitting work would think of nothing but enjoying themselves at the various tables and parties of the Series, and of the neighboring Series of both sexes which would reciprocate invitations and visits. In this way, parties so expensive among us would in the end cost but little or nothing to the respective hosts. In fact an Association would not levy a profit either upon its members, whom it would indemnify every time they were absent from a meal, nor on its guests whom it would treat on the same terms as its own members, so that, balancing the account, every one could pass his time at social parties without expending a stiver more than if he had remained alone in his own room. As for the fare, I have stated that by means of combined labor, it would cost only a third of the trouble and expense which it costs in our isolated household.

To judge of the variety and charms afforded by the meetings of guests from various Series, it is necessary to understand the relations of Industry and of Love in the Seventh Period, to explain which here would require too much space.

In respect to manners and customs, it will be seen that in each Series, however poor, there will reign an *esprit de corps* — a jealousy of the honor of the Series; and that the first of the three classes will become the standard for the two others who will aim to imitate it. This *esprit de corps* will suffice to do away with the most offensive habits of the civilized populace, such as rudeness, vulgarity, untidiness, meanness, etc., by which a Series would consider itself disgraced. It would instantly dismiss any member who should be guilty of them.

These results would be due to the rivalry between the two sexes. The feminine Series would always be eager to distinguish themselves by courtesy, and to make up for deficiency of fortune, by excess of urbanity. Such a spirit would be incompatible with the popular institutions of the Civilizees, who do not possess either of the three following means for polishing the manners of men.

1. Competition between feminine and masculine corporations.

2. Emulation between the three classes of the same Series and the groups of each class.

3. The pecuniary independence which will be enjoyed in the seventh Period, in which the subordinate functions will be three times as lucrative as they are in the incoherent Order.

Our present Societies being destitute of these three means of social refinement and elevation, we should not be astonished that they tend to rudeness and vulgarity in all the trades and professions of the middle and lower classes. Nevertheless we find some among them, the soldiers for instance, who already have very noble tendencies, and are ready to sacrifice their lives for the honor of a corps in which they have little or no enjoyment. This enthusiasm common among soldiers, shows what advantage might be derived from *esprit de corps*, if it existed between the two sexes, as will be the case in the seventh Period, when all the domestic and social evils of Civilization will disappear. Among those evils must be mentioned domestic servitude, or *personal service*, which will not be admitted in the seventh Period. In this Order, as a rule, domestics will not be in the service of individuals but of the Institution ; each of them will devote himself to the associates whose characters are most in sympathy with his own ; this privilege of choice will render domestic service agreeable to inferiors as well as superiors. It is friendship rather than interest which will bring the parties together, and this is another charm unknown in Societies organized in families, in which domestics are generally the secret enemies of their employers. The three principal causes of this are : —

1. *The low rate of wages,* which are so reduced in the incoherent Order. Domestic service in this Order being very complicated, requires three times as many agents as in the Combined Household, and their pay must in consequence be reduced to a third what it would be in the latter.

2. *Incompatibility of character between the employer and the employed,* which renders the former tyrannical and establishes

in domestic relations an extreme coldness which is augmented by fear of theft and other frauds, which can not occur in the Series.

3. *Multiplicity and Complication of Domestic Functions.* This will cease to exist in the Combined Household, in which every domestic will choose a function suited to his taste, and will devote only a portion of his time to domestic service. In the present Order, servants being compelled to perform twenty different functions, half of which are disagreeable to them, conceive a disgust for their calling and often hate their employers, even before knowing them. On the other hand, domestic service in the Series will offer numerous advantages to both servant and master; so that in all respects this Order will have the faculty of converting occupations which are a constant source of vexation in the Civilized Order, into positive pleasures.

The old especially will be delighted with this new Order. There is nothing more sad than the condition of the old and of children in Civilization; this Society does not admit of functions adapted to either of the two extremes of life, so that infancy and old age become a burden to the community. Children, however, receive a certain degree of attention in anticipation of their future services; but the old, from whom nothing is expected but their property, are neglected, importuned, secretly railed at, and often hurried to the grave. Some respect is paid to them among the rich, but among the peasantry, nothing is more afflicting than the treatment they receive. They are slighted, thrust aside without ceremony, and reproached every hour with their useless existence.

These scandalous abuses will cease in the Combined Household in which the old will have functions not less useful than those of men in the prime of life; and, when in good health, they will enjoy an existence as delightful as during the best periods of their lives. To judge how marvellously the Combined Order will be found suited to the human passions, it should be observed that Nature has distributed to us our various tastes in a proportion and variety adapted to this new Order and in constant disproportion to the requirements of the Civilized Order.

I will give a proof of this which has already been presented, but which it is well to repeat. I have said that the majority of women have no taste nor aptitude for the cares of the household. Most of them are annoyed and harassed even by the cares of a small family. Others of them, on the contrary, make mere sport of domestic labors, and excel in them to such a degree that we should judge them competent to conduct a household of a hundred persons. Nevertheless Civilization requires of all women that they have a uniform taste for domestic labors which they all may be called on to perform. How happens it, then, that Nature refuses this taste and aptitude to three fourths of them? It is to preserve the proportion suitable for the Combined Order which will employ but one fourth of them in such functions.

If we continue our analysis of the inconveniences connected with our present domestic life, with the isolated household, it will be seen that all its vexations spring from one cause, namely, from *social incoherence*, which requires of every man and woman capacities and tastes which Nature has given to but a very small number, in order not to exceed the wants of the Combined Order which is our Destiny, and which ordinarily will employ but ten persons where we employ a hundred. It would have been useless, therefore, for Nature to have distributed in profusion such and such tastes which we consider so praiseworthy, such as that for housekeeping, which tastes, if they were as common as is required by Civilization, would become superfluous and inconvenient in the Combined Order.

I dwell on these facts in order to reproduce and enforce a conclusion which I have several times announced, namely, that there is nothing vicious or defective in our natural tastes and characters; that they are distributed in a variety and proportion adapted to our future Destiny; and that there is nothing vicious or defective on the earth but our incoherent Order that can not in any way accommodate itself to the nature of the passions, all of which are adapted to the wants of the Combined Order, the germs of which will be found in the Combined Household.

III.

DEBASEMENT OF WOMAN IN CIVILIZATION.

Is there a shadow of justice to be found in the position forced upon woman in Civilization. Is not the young girl an article of merchandise offered for sale to any one who wishes to negotiate for her possession and exclusive ownership? Is not the consent she gives to the conjugal tie a mere mockery ? Is it not forced upon her by the prejudices which beset her from infancy ? Society would persuade her that the chain she is about to wear is woven of flowers. In respect to the rights of woman, is public opinion any more advanced at the present day than in that rude age when a certain Council of Macon discussed the question whether women have souls ? — a question which was decided in the affirmative by a majority of only three votes !

The laws of England, so much vaunted by the moralists, accord to men various rights equally dishonoring to the female sex ; such is the right of pecuniary indemnity given to the husband as a compensation for the infidelity of the wife. The forms are less gross in France, but the system is essentially the same. Here, as everywhere, young women languish, fall sick, and die for want of a union imperatively commanded by Nature, but which prejudice forbids them under penalty of ignominy and ruin, until they have been legally sold. Such events, though rare, are still sufficiently frequent to attest the slavery of the weaker sex, a contempt for the demands of Nature, and the absence of all justice in respect to woman.

The happy results which would have followed the extension of the rights of woman may be judged of by the experience of all countries. We find that the noblest nations have always been those which have accorded to woman the most liberty. We see this among the Barbarians and Savages as well as among the Civilizees. The Japanese, who are the most industrious, the most brave, and the most honorable among Barbaric nations, are also the least jealous of and the most indulgent toward woman. So true is this, that the wealthy Chinese make the voyage to Japan to indulge in amatory pleasures forbidden them by the hypocritical customs of their own nation.

The Otaheitans, for the same reason, were the best of all Savage tribes. Considering their limited resources, no tribe ever carried industry to such an extent. The French, who are the most liberal in many respects toward woman, are also among the best of the Civilizees, from the fact that they are the nation the most flexible — the one which can be the most easily excited by enthusiasm to do great things. And despite certain faults, such as frivolity, individual vanity, and uncleanliness, they are nevertheless the first Civilized nation, from this simple fact of their flexibility of character, which is the quality most opposed to the character of Barbarians.

We may observe, in the same sense, that the most vicious nations have always been those which have reduced woman to the greatest subjection. Witness the Chinese, who are the refuse of the globe—the most knavish, the most cowardly, the most wretched of all industrial nations; accordingly they are the most jealous and the most intolerant in respect to woman.

Among modern Civilizees, the least indulgent to the female sex are the Spaniards; hence they have remained behind all the other European nations, and have acquired no lustre in the arts or sciences.

As for Savage tribes, examination will prove that the most vicious are those which have the least respect for woman, and among whom her condition is the most miserable.

We may lay it down as a general rule, then, that *social progress and changes of Period are accomplished in proportion to the progress of Woman toward Liberty, and that the decline of society takes place in proportion to the diminution of her liberty.*

Other events influence these political vicissitudes and changes, but there is nothing which leads so rapidly to social progress or decline as modifications in the condition of woman. I have already said that the simple adoption of the harem or the seclusion of women, would change the Civilizees in a short time into Barbarians, while the simple abolition of the harem would cause the Barbarians to become Civilizees. In a word, *the extension of the rights of Woman is the fundamental principle of all social progress.*

CORRECTIVES

WHICH WOULD HAVE LED TO THE SIXTH PERIOD.

AMATORY MAJORITY; AMATORY CORPORATIONS; THEIR RESULTS.

IV.

AMATORY MAJORITY.

A GREAT evil for our globe is that among Civilized sovereigns there has never been found one who was friendly to woman, that is to say, just to woman. Some of them have been gallant, but between gallantry and equity, the measures for securing which I am about to point out, there is a great distance. At first sight, and until their influence is understood, these measures may appear to be germs of disorder.

The first measure of equity in respect to woman would have been to accord to her an *Amatory Majority;* to affranchise her at a certain age from the humiliation of being exposed to sale, and of being obliged to deny herself the pleasures of love till the arrival of some stranger to negotiate for and marry her. I consider that woman should have been declared mistress of her own destiny in amatory relations—suitable rules being adopted for their regulation—at the age, say, of eighteen.*

---

* The remarks of Fourier in this and some of the following chapters will be found harsh and severe, and to many will appear coarse and vulgar; but as applied to society in France and in many other parts of Europe, they are perfectly true — in fact below the truth. As Civilization grows older and more corrupt, they will become equally applicable to society in this country, as in fact they are to some extent in our large cities, even now.

Persons to whom the innovations proposed by Fourier appear immoral, must remember that they are not farther from our more liberal systems of divorce than the latter are from the indissoluble marriage of the Catholic Church. Besides, when people reason upon the moral bearings of the question, they ought, if they have any candor and common sense, to take into consideration the wide-spread system of prostitution which exists throughout Civilization, and which is *one of its permanent institutions*—as perma-

At eighteen, a woman has passed four years in pubescence ; this, I think, is a sufficient delay for the young men of her neighborhood to have had time to reflect, and to choose whether to take her or to leave her.

Since men wish, according to the law of the strongest, that amatory enjoyment be interdicted to every young girl, in order that she may be reserved for the first adventurer who shall come to bargain for her, ought not some provision to be made for those who have finally no chance of obtaining a possessor ? Ought they not, after having been kept in waiting for several years, to be put in possession of their liberty — to be allowed to provide for themselves as it best pleases them, and to take lovers legally, *which at present they take without this permission?* She who has not found a husband after frequenting balls and watering

nent as marriage itself. There reigns then in existing society an extensive system of licentiousness in love affairs, which in a wiser social Order would wholly disappear, and this fact ought to be taken into account as a counterbalancing consideration — and certainly a very important one. We say nothing of illicit intercourse so prevalent in society, nor of solitary vice. In fact the passion of love, with the excesses, diseases, and vices, to which in its subversive development, or when smothered, it gives rise, is the rock upon which thousands wreck their health or happiness. Certainly, then, some corrective is deeply to be desired.

With regard to innovations in love-relations, various plans have been proposed by thoughtful minds. Goethe in one of his novels (ELECTIVE AFFINITIES) proposes that men and women should form a preliminary marriage to be binding for three years, at the expiration of which time, if the parties find the union congenial, they should then form a permanent tie. Others propose that marriage should be a contract like any other, which being formed by the will of the parties can be dissolved at the will of the parties ; in this case, provision would have to be made by one or both of them for the support of the children. To us it seems that the most practicable and the most commendable innovation would be to establish a system of honorable divorce by which parties who are antipathetic and repulsive to each other could separate without dishonor, and without losing public esteem.

Society should rise to the conception that it is the sympathetic union of souls that constitutes true marriage, and not the legal union of bodies — that *the spiritual and not the material should govern.* However, the more closely we examine the subject of Divorce, the more evident it appears that certain material or external arrangements must be made in society before any important modification can be made in respect to marriage. Industry must first be so organized as to open spheres of congenial activity to woman, so that she can honorably earn her own livelihood, and thus secure her pecuniary independence. The Combined Household must take the place of the Isolated Household, which is a domestic prison whence a couple once having entered and installed themselves find it almost impossible to escape. Besides, the complication of domestic labor in the isolated household entirely absorbs the woman and leaves her no opportunity to take part in productive industry, art, or science, and thus achieve a position and a destiny for herself. — *A. B.*

places, theatres and churches for four years, has but little chance of ever finding one ; the reasons which have kept husbands away will operate as well after the four years of candidacy as before. Besides, if marriage is so useful in Civilization, it is proper to stimulate men to it by the fear of not obtaining the first love of women whom they have left in waiting beyond the age of eighteen.

There is nothing more revolting than to see so many young girls, often of fine personal attractions, neglected because they lack the charm of gold in their favor. And how is it that parents who *have them on their hands* have never thought of proposing a reform in customs so prejudicial to families of limited means, which are the most numerous and the most worthy of protection ?

In view of the above considerations, and to bring about an amatory reform, women should be divided into two classes — the vestals, under eighteen, and the emancipated, over eighteen. After this age they should acquire the right of contracting amatory relations, suitable laws being made for providing for the children resulting therefrom. (*It is to be borne in mind that this is a measure for the sixth Period, and not for Civilization.*)

Public opinion should unite with justice in demanding this measure. It is well known that young girls who attain to twenty years of age without being married are ridiculed by men, and stigmatized as old maids. Their abandonment is made the subject of derision ; they are covered with sarcasm, assailed by ribald jokes, and often driven to contravene the law by taking lovers in secret. Men are so slanderous, so unjust in respect to women, that they pursue them with ridicule in any case, whether they have preserved or lost their chastity, after the age when this burden becomes too painful to be borne.

Where would have been the risk in according to women amatory liberty after the age of eighteen, and what advantages have been obtained from the repressive policy of the philosophers ? With their systems of canting education, which give to young ladies an affected indifference for love, they have succeeded only in making conjugal infidelity all but universal. Another system, then, more conformable to the demands of Nature, could hardly produce more of this vice than we have at present. And would it not be worth while, offsetting vice against vice, to try an Order less oppressive, less degrading for woman? Without doubt, for amatory freedom develops among the classes who possess it in the largest degree, some of the finest traits of character: I allude to Ladies of Court, and Courtesans of high life.

It is among these classes of women that we find some of the happiest developments of character; their good qualities combined would constitute perfection.

Ladies of Court, where gallantry reigns, are characterized by a frank and open character, easy and polished manners, and an expansive tone which inspires friendship. They seduce at once the man who sees them for the first time; he fancies he has found women superior to human nature—so much do they differ from our prim prudish housewives, who are mere conventional machines, contracted souls in whom love when it exists leaves no room for any other passion, and who are dead to friendship, to all taste for the fine arts, and to every noble affection.

Doubtless these Ladies of Court have their vicious side, but they give to their gallantry varied charms, and a touch of nature and of magnanimity. And how can they be blamed for having the art to embellish vice, since it alone is destined to reign in Civilization?

The Courtesans of high life, apart from certain vices incident to their position, possess many noble qualities: obliging, charitable, cordial, if they only had good incomes, their characters would be really noble; witness that of Ninon. By being accustomed to a life of pleasure, they lose that suspicious, crafty spirit, those ill-repressed desires, wholly sensual, which we observe in commonplace souls, full of moral pretense, in those conventional beings who, amid all their parade of sentiment, betray at every instant a sensuality which they persist in denying —a sensuality which does not disparage a woman when it is in balance with the affections of the soul, as is the case with women openly gallant.

The character of woman, if it combined the good qualities of the classes above-mentioned, would soon attain to perfection; and such would be the effect of a social Order in which the female sex were placed in possession of amatory liberty. In wishing to attain but one end, that of making good housekeepers, we fail in all, for having desired too little. Our young girls, inflated with prejudices and philosophy, and in whom all the passions are smothered, are no longer natural beings; gnawed continually by unsatisfied desires, their minds are in a state of continual distraction; they work with disgust, skim over the studies taught them, forget after marriage all that they have learned, and unless the husband has the tact for controlling and guiding them, become bad housekeepers. The world dazzles them and leads them astray all the more easily from their having had no experience, whereas an experienced woman is less infatuated by pleasures, and, knowing the arts of gallants, becomes the more easily attached to the household, and to her husband whom she considers as a protector against masculine persecution. Such a wife makes the happiness of a weak man: he obtains from her true conjugal love, which is nothing else than a league of interests between the married couple—a coalition against social perfidies.

How many other men there are who are unable to accommodate themselves to these women all honeyed over with sentiment, these philosophic automata whose character is an impenetrable enigma, and who, with their affected ingenuousness, excite the distrust of the philosophers themselves, who know better than anybody that we can count little on this air of candor which education gives to young girls. Every woman of licentious conduct appeared as virtuous before marriage as any one; this veneer of chastity is a mask which deceives nobody, in no way promotes marriages, and ends only in practising women in dissimulation. We know that a breath of love arouses their passions and develops in them a character before unknown, the goodness or malice of which is an impenetrable riddle even to experienced men. In a word, this balderdash of philosophic education is but a circle of errors, like all civilized customs, and ends only in plunging husbands into the disgrace they were most anxious to avoid. What perplexes the philosophers, is to see that everything tends to that infidelity which is the object of their constant alarm ; hence these savants vary their systems of education every day, without any other result than masking instead of changing the inclinations of young girls.

Naturam expellas furca, tamen usque recurret.

They take alarm if they see women cultivating the arts and sciences, and would have no other talent developed among them but that of housekeeping; these are their own words which we hear even on the stage. They think only of thwarting the love of pleasure, see nothing in the future but cuckolds, are crabbed and fault-finding as regards the tastes of women, and as suspicious as the eunuchs about a harem.

And when we come to disembroil their systems of education, which vary every day (for every day there appear new treatises on morality which are never in accordance with previous ones) what fruit do we reap from them for the advantage of young girls? Do we see those who are imbued with prejudices, but without fortune, getting married? No; with all their virtues, they are left aside.

How is it that an age so inclined to experiments of all kinds, an age which has had the audacity to overthrow thrones and altars, has truckled so servilely before amatory prejudices — the only ones an attack npon which might have produced some good; and why is it that no one has thought of applying to this subject the theories of liberty which have been so much abused? Everything concurred to invite a trial of their effect on the passion of love, since the happiness of man is proportioned to the liberty enjoyed by woman. Suppose that there could be invented a means for restricting all women, without exception, to that chastity required of them, so that no woman could form any amatory relation before marriage, nor possess, after marriage, any other man than her husband; it would result from this that no man could have in the whole course of his life any other woman than the one he had espoused. Now, how would men look upon the prospect of being restricted all their lives to the possession of one woman who might prove disagreeable to them the day after marriage? Certainly the majority of men would be in favor of strangling the author of an invention like this, which would put an end to all gallantry; and the most ardent enemies of such an Order would be the philosophers themselves; whence we see that men are personally opposed to their own maxims of chastity, and that the happiness of the male sex is established in proportion to the resistance of woman to the principles of Civilized morality; their strict observance would cause the despair of

23

nearly all men, *individually*, without excepting the philosophers, who, being more given to intrigue than others, would be as much confounded by the triumph of their amatory maxims as they were in 1789 by the triumph of their political maxims.

Another conclusion which may be drawn from the present discussion, is that the Civilizees are in complete ignorance as to the destiny and functions of the passions in the social system; for, by adopting the modification proposed in favor of woman—the distinction of an Amatory Minority and Majority—several results would be attained exceedingly advantageous to the cause of good morals, in Civilization. Among other abuses which would be extirpated, I shall mention *Amorous Confusion*, which is one of the sixteen characteristics of Civilization. I shall presently compare it with the system of Amatory Corporations; these are a characteristic of the sixth Period, of which every one will be pleased with the descriptions, because it is the Period most akin to our own, and the most intelligible to the Civilizees, of whom it preserves various domestic usages, such as the isolated household.

V.

AMATORY CORPORATIONS.

UNDER the name of *amorous confusion*, I designate the custom we have of admitting no degrees of vice and virtue in the relations of love. For example, if it is a question of adultery, all conjugal infidelity is equally culpable in the eyes of the moralists, who call down upon a woman the wrath of heaven and earth for the smallest fault. Nevertheless there are degrees of guilt in adultery as in everything else. Is not connection with a woman who is barren, or with a woman already pregnant, in fine, any connection which does not result in pregnancy, much less grave than one that leads to false paternity? A distinction should be made, then, between such connections and adultery truly culpable, like that which causes the breaking up of families, or which introduces into them heterogeneous offspring. By refusing to admit these distinctions, and wishing to confound and condemn in a mass all kinds of adultery, they have all been rendered excusable; the indulgence due to some has been extended to all. Public opinion has attacked the persecutors of woman with ridicule, and under the name of

cuckoldry we have come to excuse and make light of odious perfidies which the law confounds with very trifling offences.

We have failed of our end, then, by excess of injustice and oppression, and succeeded only, in love affairs, in causing the triumph
of falseness and depravity. If, according to the philosophers,
all amatory pleasures, out of marriage, are criminal, it becomes
necessary to play the hypocrite, deny everything, and deceive continually; hence it is that every woman and young girl pretend
to be models of fidelity and continence; but if degrees of virtue
and vice were admitted in gallant affairs, we should see the introduction of loyal customs which would promote the cause of
truth as well as of pleasure.

Admitting the distinction of amatory minority and majority,
women emancipated after the age of eighteen would take part,
according to their inclinations, in one of the three following corporations:—

1. *The Constant,* united in permanent marriage according to
the Civilized Method.

2. *The Capricious,* enjoying the liberty of divorce.

3. *The Gallant,* having statutes less rigorous still.

This order of things, the details of which it would require too
much time to enumerate, would realize most of the reforms at
present vainly attempted in amatory relations. For example, it
would prevent seduction and the consigning of young girls to
celibacy. If we see so many of them vegetating all their lives,
waiting for a husband, or yielding to illicit loves, it is because,
in the first case, the men have the privilege of trifling with them
by constant delays, and in the second case, because they see no
end to their disheartening celibacy; but the period being fixed
at eighteen years, men would have no chance to dally with or
seduce a young girl; if she yielded she would be rejected or
ignominiously suspected by her corporation.

In such an Order, adultery would be restricted to very narrow
limits; a seducer would have little success among married women,
for they would run the risk of being suspected even without material proofs, and classed in the list of doubtful, or, if the charge
were proved, of inconstant. Wives would find themselves under
the supervision of the other two corporations; and hence a woman would not dare to contract the conjugal bond without she

had a decided taste for constancy. As a consequence, people would not marry till late in life, at the age when the passions are calm, and marriage would be restored to its true function, which is to be the support and solace of old age; it is a retreat from the world, a bond of reason, designed not for the young, but for persons of mature age.

Then would be dissipated the prejudice which attaches ridicule to the idea of marrying a woman who has had a previous amour. A young girl would be in no way degraded for having had such an amour, since she would have waited till the age of eighteen, the time required by the laws. A man would marry her without any more scruples than are felt in espousing a widow who has children. If it is a disgrace to be the second possessor in marriage, why are men so eager to espouse a rich widow and charge themselves with the education of the children of others? Men overlook all these considerations, and yet feel themselves compromised by marrying a young girl who has had a previous liaison, though she has had no children. It will be seen by this that our ideas of honor and virtue are only prejudices which vary according to changes in the laws. A law would suffice to cause public opinion to conform to the demands of Nature, and to place in the rank of decent pleasures those amours which it is ridiculous to call vices, since among men they are declared to be gallantries; from which it would appear that men can be gallant only in proportion as women give themselves up to vice — an absurd contradiction, though not more so than prevails in all our civilized customs and opinions.

Then would disappear the selfishness and the servile spirit engendered by the conjugal bond, which corrupts especially the character of women. They adopt all the vices of a husband without adopting his good qualities, and this is the natural result of the servility inspired in them. Marry a young Agnes to a Robespierre, and in a month she will be as ferocious as he, and will flatter him in all his crimes. This servile tendency of wives would be corrected by the rivalry of the women of the other corporations, whose leading trait would be a determination to sustain a noble and independent character, and to preserve themselves free in every respect from the defects inherent to the conjugal state — among others from selfishness, which marriage carries to the highest degree, and which accounts for married persons having an extreme distrust of their fellow-men. Nothing is more difficult than for two married couples to live together in the same household. The incompatibility extends from master to servant, and in every household there is the strongest objection to receiving a married couple into the family. This is because men are well aware that the conjugal spirit creates a league between the married couple against all who surround them, and that it stifles all noble passions and expansive ideas; hence the married class is the most sordid, the most indifferent to public or private misfortunes, and their anti-social spirit is so well understood, that it is considered to be greatly in praise of a man to say: " Marriage has not changed him; he has preserved the amiable character of a bachelor."

Then shall we see degrees recognized in virtue and vice, a reputation for these qualities reduced to its just value, and an end put to all perfidy, duplicity, and dissimulation in the affairs of love.

Such an Order is the least of the regular developments which may be given to amatory relations; any system which should restrain the passions more, would fall necessarily into the errors of philosophic equality and confusion, of which we see at present the odious results.

VI.

FALSENESS OF THE OPPRESSIVE SYSTEM IN THE RELATIONS OF LOVE.

It is to be remarked that in the disorder which prevails at the present day in matters of love, women have obtained the only privilege which should have been refused to them, namely, that of making a husband accept a child which is not his, and on the face of which Nature has written the name of the veritable father. Thus, in the only case in which the woman is culpable, she enjoys the protection of the law, and in the only case in which the man is truly outraged, public opinion and the law agree in aggravating his disgrace. How is it that the Civilizees, who are so intolerant in respect to the pleasures of women, consent to bow their heads so submissively to the yoke, — to adopt a child evidently the fruit of adultery, and to confer upon it their name and property when they should send it to the Hospital for Foundlings. It is thus the designs of philosophy are carried out.

These shameful inconsistencies are found throughout the Civilized mechanism, and when we observe them calmly, how can we think otherwise than that Civilization is a society of maniacs ? — all the more so because they admit the principle of social progress and amelioration, but refuse to apply it. They know that the advance from Barbarism to Civilization was accomplished only by improving the condition of woman. This fact should have induced them to give a still greater extension to her rights. Such a course would have led to the establishment of the sixth Period, while the complete emancipation of woman would have led to the seventh. From this it will be seen that the means of social progress were well known and easy of application, and that we should have entered upon the true path from the moment we were willing to set aside the oppressive system of the philosophers in respect to woman. Do they not themselves know that perpetual fidelity in love is contrary to human nature ; that though we may induce a few simple characters of both sexes to adopt such a morality, we shall never bring the mass of men and women to it, and therefore that any legislation which requires tastes and characters so incompatible with the passions, can produce only theoretical absurdities and practical disorders ? Has not such been the result of the policy pursued in respect to love for twenty-five hundred years ? The system of the present day is only a continuation of the oppressive customs which reigned in the dark ages, customs which it is absurd to require in an age when men boast their respect for the laws of Nature.

To judge of woman by the defective character which she exhibits in Civilization, is as if we should judge of the nature of man by the character of the Russian peasant, who has no idea of honor or liberty ; or as if we should judge of the beaver by the stupidity which he exhibits in the domestic state, whereas in a state of liberty and combined labor, he becomes the most intelligent of all quadrupeds. The same contrast will be found to exist between the oppressed women of Civilization and the free women of the Combined Order. In the latter they will surpass the men in devotion, in loyalty, and in true nobility ; but out of the free and Combined Order woman becomes, like the domesticated beaver or the Russian peasant, a being so inferior to her destiny and to her natural capacity, that, judging her superficially and from appearances, we are inclined to look upon her with disdain. It is not surprising therefore that Mahomet, the Council of Macon, and the philosophers generally, have raised the question whether women have souls, and instead of breaking their chains have sought only to rivet them.

It is an instructive fact that whenever women have had a chance to develop their natural powers on a throne assuring to them free scope and development, they have shown themselves superior to men. Is it not notorious, that out of eight female sovereigns who have been free and without husbands, seven have reigned with glory, whereas out of eight kings we count, as a rule, seven whose reigns were feeble? And if certain women have not shone upon the throne, it is because, like Mary Stuart, they faltered and shuffled before amatory prejudices, which they should have boldly trampled under foot. When they have adopted this course, what men have swayed the sceptre better than they? The Elizabeths and Catharines did not fight in their own persons, but they knew how to choose their generals, and that was enough to secure them good ones. In every other branch of administration, have they not been able to give lessons to man? What prince ever exhibited more firmness than Maria Theresa, who at a disastrous moment, when the fidelity of her subjects wavered, when her ministers were seized with stupor, undertook, by herself alone, to restore courage to the whole people? She knew how to intimidate the Diet of Hungary by her bold policy; she harangued the Magnates in the Latin tongue, and brought her very enemies to swear on their swords to die for her.

Here, then, is an indication of the prodigies which feminine emulation will accomplish among women in a Social Order which shall give free scope to their faculties.

And you, sex of oppressors, would you not surpass woman in the defects with which you reproach her, if a servile education had formed you, like her, to believe yourselves nothing but automata, created to be slaves to prejudices, and to cringe before a master whom chance had allotted to you? Have we not seen your pretensions to superiority confounded by Catherine, who trampled you beneath her feet? By appointing special favorites, she humbled man to the dust, and proved that even when entirely free he can be debased lower than woman, whose servitude is compulsory and therefore excusable. To confound the tyranny of men, we ought to have for a century or so a third or hemaphrodite sex stronger than either of the others. This new sex should make men feel, by application of the lash if need be, that they were made for its pleasures as well as women ; then should we hear the men protesting against the tyranny to which they were subjected, and confessing that strength is not always the test of right. Now why do they refuse to accord the privileges, the freedom and independence which they would demand of this third sex, to woman ?

I do not pretend here to criticise Civilized education, nor to insinuate that we should inspire the women of the present day with the spirit of liberty. Doubtless every social Period should train up its youth, of both sexes, to reverence dominant absurdities ; and if in the Barbaric Order it is necessary to imbrute woman and persuade her that she has no soul, in order that she may allow herself to be sold in the market and imprisoned in the harem, it is also necessary in the Civilized Order to break the spirit of woman from infancy, so as to adapt her to its philosophic dogmas—to the servitude of marriage, and to the degradation of falling into the hands of a husband whose character is the exact opposite of her own. Now as I would blame a Barbarian who should educate his daughter for the usages of a Civilization in which she will never live, so would I blame a Civilizee who should educate his daughter in the spirit of freedom and intelligence adapted to the sixth and seventh Social Periods, to which we have not yet arrived.

If I bring accusations against the present system of education and the servile spirit it engenders in woman, I speak with a view to other forms of society, in which it would be useless to distort their natural characters by filling their minds with absurd prejudices. I point out to woman the distinguished position to which she may attain, as shown by the example of those of her sex who have surmounted the influence of education and resisted the oppressive system necessitated by the conjugal bond. In calling attention to those who have known how to exercise their own wills, from viragos like Maria Theresa to women of a more subdued cast like the Ninons and the Sévignés, I am justified in saying that woman in a state of liberty will surpass man in all the faculties of mind and body which do not depend upon physical strength.

Men have an idea of this already, and when woman gives the lie to the charge of inferiority brought against her, they become indignant and take alarm. Masculine jealousy breaks out especially against female authors. Philosophy has denied them the privilege of academic honors and sent them ignominiously to the kitchen.

And do not our learned women deserve this affront? The slave who apes his master merits from him nothing but disdain. What have women to do with the stale glory of composing books, of adding a few more volumes to the useless millions already written? What they had to do was, to have become not writers but liberators, social Spartacuses—geniuses to concert the means of delivering their sex from its present abasement.

Civilization weighs especially upon woman; it was for woman, therefore, to attack it. What is her existence at the present day? Her life is a life of privations, even in the world of Industry, in which man has usurped everything even to the minute occupations of the needle, while we see women devoting themselves to the arduous labors of the field. Is it not scandalous to see stalwart men of thirty years dancing behind a counter, and running about with their brawny arms serving coffee at table, as if there lacked women and children to perform the light duties of the shop and the household?

What then are the means of subsistence left for women without fortune? The loom, the needle, or, if they happen to possess charms, their persons. Yes, prostitution more or less disguised, is almost their only resource, and this again brings upon them the condemnation of the philosophers.

Such is the abject condition to which women are reduced by Civilization, which, with its system of conjugal slavery, they have never even dreamed of attacking. This inadvertence has been the less excusable since the discovery of Otaheite, the manners and customs of which were a hint from Nature, and should have suggested the idea of a social Order combining the exercise of a highly developed system of industry, with freedom in the passion of love. This was the only problem worthy to engage the attention of female writers, and their neglect of it is one of the causes which have increased the disdain felt for them by men. The slave is never more despicable than when he blindly submits to his chains and thus satisfies the oppressor that his victim was born for slavery.

Our learned authoresses, far from devising means for the deliverance of their sex, have espoused the cause of civilized morality ; they have shut their eyes to the subjection of their companions, whose fate they themselves have known how to avoid, but for which they have sought no remedy. The female sovereigns who might have served their sex in this way, and who, like Catherine, had the good sense to despise all prejudices, have still done nothing for the emancipation of woman. No one has suggested the idea of her enfranchisement, no one indicated any method for establishing freedom in the relations of love. Had such a method been suggested, it would have been accepted and put to the test the moment an equitable prince or princess had appeared on any throne.

The study of these means of emancipation was a task peculiarly obligatory upon learned women. In neglecting it, they have tarnished, eclipsed their literary glory, and posterity will bear witness to their selfishness and sycophancy ; for if these women have generally known how to free themselves from dominant prejudices, and to choose their own pleasures, they are none the less pointed at and inveighed against for their exercise of such freedom.

This tyranny of public opinion should have sufficed, it seems to me, to provoke the indignation of honorable women, and to stimulate them to attack popular prejudices, not indeed by useless declamations, but by seeking for some innovation which should extricate both sexes from the frightful and degrading condition of permanent marriage. Far from there being any tendency to lighten the chains of woman, the prejudice against her enfranchisement is constantly on the increase.

Three circumstances have contributed in modern times to increase the disposition to oppress the weaker sex, namely :—

1. The introduction of syphilitic diseases, the dangers of which

transform voluptuous pleasures into debauchery, and tend to restrain the freedom of relations between the two sexes. (These diseases will be extirpated by the Combined Household.)

2. The influence of Catholicism, the dogmas of which, being hostile to amatory pleasures, deprive them of their legitimate influence in the social system, and add the force of religious prejudices to the old tyranny of the conjugal bond.

3. The birth of Mohammedanism, which, by aggravating the misfortune and the degradation of women in the Barbaric Order, misleads us as to the condition of women in Civilization, because it is less deplorable.

These three circumstances formed a tissue of fatalities which rendered any amelioration founded on the extension of the rights of woman more impossible than ever—unless, indeed, chance had raised up some prince opposed to existing prejudices, and having sufficient good sense to make a trial of the system I have suggested, in some small province. This act of justice was the only one which Nature demanded of human reason, and it is a just punishment for our rebellion against her will, that we have failed of finding a transition to the sixth and seventh Periods, and have remained twenty-five centuries too long in the abyss of philosophic darkness and civilized abominations.

SECTION II.

ON THE SPLENDORS OF THE COMBINED ORDER.

PRELIMINARY.

In order to understand the Splendors I am about to describe, we must first understand the organization of the Passional Series, by which the reader will be convinced that an Order so contrary to our present usages must produce diametrically opposite results; in other words, must produce as much magnificence, as our incoherent system produces misery and ennui.

ORDER OF SUBJECTS TREATED IN THIS SECTION.

Lustre of the Arts and Sciences.
Operatic Representations and Knight Errantry.
Gallant Policy for the levying of Industrial Armies.

The reader must bear in mind that to accomplish the prodigies I am about to describe, the Combined Order will have the aid of four new passions which we are hardly conscious of in Civilization, where everything is opposed to their development.

These four passions, which I have named,

10*th. The Dissident or Cabalistic,*
11*th. The Alternant or Modulative,*
12*th. The Composite or Connecting,*
13*th. Harmonism or Unityism,*

can not be brought out except in the Progressive Series, and as we are not accustomed to such exciting and delicious passions, they will seem to us as new as love appears, to young persons who experience it for the first time.

This perspective will not be at all flattering for those who have already passed the heyday of youth in our dull Civilization. But let them take courage ; these pleasures will be for all ages, and their postponement will cause despair only during the interval which is to elapse before the foundation of the Combined Order.

VII.

LUSTRE OF THE ARTS AND SCIENCES.

To judge to what degree of splendor the arts and sciences will be carried in the Combined Order, we must first understand what honors and rewards it will bestow upon scientific men and artists.

Every Association will prepare, annually, according to the decision of the majority, a table of the inventions and compositions which have appeared and been accepted during the year. Each of these productions will be judged by the competent Series ; as, for instance, a tragedy by the Series of Literature and Poetry.

If a work is esteemed worthy of recompense, a sum will be fixed upon to be adjudged to the author ; for example, twenty cents to Racine for his tragedy of *Phèdre.*

Each Phalanx having made up the list of prizes or recompenses to be adjudged, will forward it to the Central Administration, which counts the votes of the different Associations and makes up the list for the whole Province. This is sent to a higher administration by which the provincial returns are verified and made up in the same way. Thus the returns arrive by degrees to the Supreme Administration at Constantinople — the future capital of the Globe — where the final verification takes place, and where are proclaimed the names of the authors crowned by the suffrages of the majority of the Associations of the globe. The author or inventor has adjudged to him the average of the sums voted by this majority. If a million Phalanxes vote ten cents, a million twenty cents, and a million thirty cents, the recompense will be fixed at twenty cents. Suppose twenty cents are awarded to Racine for his tragedy of *Phèdre,* and sixty cents to Franklin for the invention of the lightning-rod, the Administration would send to Racine drafts for the sum of

$600,000, and to Franklin the sum of $1,800,000 drawn on the Congress of their respective nations. This sum would be paid by the three million Phalanxes of the globe.

In addition, Franklin and Racine would receive the triumphal decoration and be declared Citizens of the Globe, and wherever they travelled they would enjoy in every Phalanx the same privileges and prerogatives which are accorded to its highest authorities.

These awards, the payments of which would be trifling for each Association, would be immense for the authors and inventors, especially as they may be frequently repeated. It might happen that Racine and Franklin would earn a similar sum the following year for having distinguished themselves by some other production obtaining the suffrages of the Globe.

The smallest works, provided they were received with general favor, would bring immense sums to their authors; for if the globe should adjudge to Haydn one cent for a given symphony, to Lebrun two cents for a given ode, Haydn would receive $30,000 and Lebrun $60,000 for a work which might not have cost them a month's labor. They might earn this sum several times in a single year.

For works like those of the sculptor, which can not be exhibited to the whole globe, other means of recompense will be devised.

It follows from what has been said, that in the Combined Order superior talent, of whatever kind, will assure to its possessor an immense fortune, and artists and men of science will have no occasion for soliciting protection or patronage; far from this, anything of the kind would serve only to humiliate both the patron and the patronized.

Suppose that Pradon, after much solicitation, succeeds in interesting in his tragedy of *Phèdre* twenty neighboring Associations in which he has friends, and where he has secured the performance of his piece; suppose even that these Associations have had the weakness to award a recompense to Pradon, of what account would be the vote of twenty Phalanxes out of three millions? And what mortification would be experienced by these twenty Phalanxes when the returns should come to be published at the capital of the globe! It would be seen, from the whole number of votes, that an unknown play called *Phèdre*, and composed by one Pradon, had found acceptance in twenty Associations, all compeers and neighbors of the said Pradon. It will easily be conceived that such an announcement would cause alike the author and the twenty Associations which had patronized him to be covered with disgrace all over the globe. But what would happen despite all the intrigues of Pradon? Simply that the twenty Associations whose support he had solicited would not care to expose themselves to mortification and disgrace, by giving their suffrage to a play of such little merit; that far from being able to count on half the suffrages of the globe, such a play would not be accepted at twenty leagues distance in any Association where Pradon had no particular friends.

It is thus that in the Combined Order all patronage and favoritism will serve only to mortify an author, without being of any advantage to him, while the man of real talent will rise at once, without the aid of either intrigue or solicitation, to immense reputation and fortune. There will be but one means of success, namely, that of delighting a majority of the Phalanxes of the globe.

After this digression on the unitary recompenses which will be awarded to men of science and art in the Combined Order, let us examine what will be the effect of such a system on some particular branch of art—say the *Opera*.

VIII.

OPERATIC REPRESENTATIONS.—KNIGHT-ERRANTRY.

I HAVE said that means will be found in the Combined Order for causing every artist or man of science whose talent is local, and can be appreciated only by his own Association, to be compensated by the whole globe. A famous surgeon, or a celebrated cantatrice, can not display his or her skill before the whole world like a poet or engraver, whose works circulate everywhere; but they will nevertheless receive the recompenses of which I have spoken, and which, in the case of transcendent talent, will soon amount to hundreds of thousands. Hence every man in humble circumstances will study only how to develop in his child some decided talent. The moment a marked capacity for some branch of science or art is manifested, the father will be intoxicated with joy, and his neighbors will overwhelm him with felicitations. Everybody about him will exclaim: "Your child will become a famous author, a famous artist; he will receive the Triumphal Decoration, and accumulate an immense fortune:"—and we all know how such a prognostication flatters the ears of parents, even when they are rich.

Who, then, will be the persons the most ardent and indefatigable in their studies? They will be the poor, and the children of the poor. Now as the Opera requires the study of all the arts and sciences, even of mechanics, which are indispensable to it, the poor will be anxious for no one thing more than to see their children taught and trained upon the stage of their Phalanx, under the direction of the rich, who in all countries have a partiality for the dramatic art. Hence the children in Association will all be accustomed, from a very early age, to figure in dramatic or lyric performances, in which they will take part with some Series formed for practising declamation, singing, dancing, instrumental music, etc. All classes, rich and poor, will engage in these exercises, since the Phalanx, performing only for its own amusement and that of its neighbors, becomes a company of Amateurs. Hence an Association of a thousand persons would have at least eight hundred performers or musicians competent to figure on the stage; for every child will have been dramatically and artistically educated, and will be eager to take some theatrical part.

In the Combined Order, a child of four years will not dare to present himself for admission to the corps of Neophytes, or to the General Parade, unless he knows how to figure in the dances and manœuvres of the Opera.

It has been seen in the chapter treating of Passional Attraction, that among every 810 persons Nature distributes all the talents necessary for excelling in the different branches of human activity. Hence an Association of 1,000 persons would necessarily have in its ranks eminent performers of all kinds; that is, if the capacities of each were cultivated and developed from infancy, as will be the case in the Combined Order. In this Order the child will be emancipated from the tyranny of institutions and prejudices, and will always devote himself to the employments for which nature destined him. His progress will be due solely to emulation. The only artifice which will be employed to make excellent performers of children, will be to take them in a body to the neighboring Associations, where they will see the representations given by their rivals, with whom they will enter the lists.

There is no occasion for asking who will pay the cost of the Opera. It will only be necessary to establish *one*, for the example to be imitated by all the Associations on the globe. If the Associations are in regular rivalry no one of them will have any peace till it has equalled its neighbors ; and in order to build an opera-house, has not each its Series of masons, carpenters, mechanicians, painters, etc., and productions of every kind to exchange for the requisite materials ?

If each Association having a population of a thousand persons, has at least seven or eight hundred competent to figure as performers, musicians, and dancers, it can give, itself alone, as varied performances as a large capital like London or Paris. The result would be that in the poorest Associations of the Alps or the Pyrenees, an opera would be found equal to that of Paris ; I might even say superior, for Civilized education, neither in the study of the arts, nor in refining the taste, can accomplish the prodigies which will result from the system of natural education.

If to the performers of a given Association we add those of neighboring Associations, how brilliant will be the theatrical representations at festivals and celebrations, where the amateurs of several Phalanxes will be brought together, and where will be seen a combination of talent greater than could be furnished by a dozen capitals like Paris ! And as the poorest man can be present at such performances, he will in this respect possess means of enjoyment far superior to those of any civilized monarch.

The display will be still more brilliant if we suppose the arrival of a company of amateurs, making their tours, as they will constantly do in the Combined Order, where travellers will organize large caravans of Knights and Ladies Errant, seeking adventures, and representing in each case some particular branch of artistic talent.

To-day, for instance, will arrive the Bands of the Rose coming from Persia, and representing the dramatic and lyric character. Some days after will come the Bands of the Lilac from Japan, representing the poetic and literary character ; and the successive arrival of these caravans will furnish, in the course of the year, brilliant fêtes and varied delights to every lover of the arts and sciences. There will be Bands representing every department of art. They will admit into their Corporations only the persons of each sex capable of sustaining the reputation of the corps.

Suppose the Bands of the Rose of Persia to arrive in the environs of Paris. They are composed of six hundred Knights and Ladies Errant, all chosen from among the Persians most distinguished in dramatic and lyric art. The Bands station themselves at the Phalanx of St. Cloud. They arrive there in great pomp, displaying the banners which have been presented to them during their excursions, and on which are inscribed the achievements of the Persian Bands of the Rose.

Arriving at St. Cloud, they are received by the Knights Local, composed of the rich amateurs of the drama and of music, and forming a corporation for the reception and entertainment of the Bands of their favorite art.

As the Bands of the Rose are composed of the élite of Persia, every member is one of the artistic celebrities of his country. The corps is thus composed of the first singers, the first dancers, the first musicians of Persia, who give performances of an excellence beyond description. The region which they visit exhibits to them, an array of its most distinguished performers who are brought together for the occasion.

Meanwhile arrive the Bands of the Hortensia from Mexico, which come to measure their skill with the Rose Bands of Persia, and the Tournament of Talent between the two bands takes place at the opera-houses of the Phalanxes of St. Cloud, Neuilly, Marly, etc. If the pre-eminence is decided in favor of the Bands of the Rose, they will receive from the Phalanx a Banner which they will display among their trophies, and on which will be inscribed: — *Triumph of the Persian Bands of the Rose at the Phalanx of St. Cloud.*

In the course of their travels, Bands of the same character will cross each other in every direction, in order to meet their rivals and engage in Tournaments of Talent, which will be the delight of the regions where these artistic encounters take place. In making their tour, instead of travelling in a body, like our regiments, they disperse along the road. If the Bands of the Rose have chosen for their next station the Phalanx of Loiret, near Orleans, they will find at St. Cloud, deputations from the Phalanxes bordering on the route to Orleans. These deputations are composed of men and women of the most enticing manners, whose mission it is to allure and fascinate the Knights and Ladies of the Persian Bands, who will be invited to the Associations at a distance from the great thoroughfares; the Phalanxes will vie with each other in securing their presence for a day, and each Knight and Lady will find in the Phalanx which they have preferred, the same politeness and attention which the entire band found at St. Cloud. The Staff of the Band only will follow the main road, and on a given day all the members will meet in Orleans, and prepare for a triumphal entrance into the Phalanx of Loiret. In this way will travel the corps of amateurs, organized in caravans of Knight-errantry, leading everywhere a joyous life, and availing themselves of the hospitality of the whole human race, without incurring the least expense, since the whole cost is defrayed by the corps of Knights Local.

We may judge from the above, that in respect to dramatic and artistic displays, the poorest man in the Combined Order will enjoy, and enjoy gratuitously, delights a hundred-fold greater than those of our richest sovereigns; for he will frequently see contests between thousands of famous actors, singers, dancers, and musicians, one of whom, at the present day, suffices to enrapture a court or a capital, while the country towns, and cities even of hundred thousand inhabitants, which can not support an opera, are entirely deprived of them.

What pettiness, what pitiful insipidity in the pleasures of Civilization, compared with those which even the poorest Association will enjoy in the Combined Order!

IX.

GALLANT POLICY FOR THE LEVYING OF INDUSTRIAL ARMIES.

As the prediction of amorous liberty in the future will be sure to excite the great choler of sober citizens and philosophers, it is well, in order to calm them, to give a glimpse of this liberty in its relation to pecuniary interest, which is their only god.

Love, which in Civilization is a source of disorder, idleness, and expense, becomes in the Combined Order a source of vast wealth and of industrial prodigies. I shall give an illustration of this, taken from what among us is one of the most difficult branches of administration, namely, the levying of Armies, which in the Combined Order will be effected through the agency of gallantry.

In every Phalanx, the passion of Love produces two great Series, called the *semi character*, and the *full character*. The latter is divided into nine groups or branches, the first of which is the VESTALIC GROUP, of which I shall now speak.

In each Phalanx, the choir of youths, composed of both sexes, elect every year two Vestalic Groups, each composed of two couples—one of parade to preside at ceremonials, the other of merit to preside over labors. The choice of the former is regulated by beauty, that of the latter by success in the arts and sciences, or devotedness in industrial works.

The Vestals will everywhere take rank among the superior officers. The poorest girl elected to the Vestalic Body will wear the jewelled insignia of her Phalanx, and ride in the state chariot drawn by six white horses. Every possible honor will be rendered to these youths, who will have command of the industrial groups of children. In fine, the system which encourages and upholds Vestality, instead of isolating young girls from the world, will tend to bring them out. Far from habituating them to act the part of automata, like our young women with their simpering morality, who pretend to know nothing of love, and to have no other will than that of papa and mamma, their natural inclinations will be developed as much as possible, and the Vestal youths of both sexes will have accepted lovers.

These brilliant youths will have the privilege of joining the Industrial Armies, which will be magnificent gatherings, and it is there that the young vestals will contract their first loves. At the close of each day, when its labors are terminated, the army will give fêtes which will be especially brilliant from the fact that they will bring together the élite of the youth of both sexes celebrated alike for their beauty and their talents. These fêtes will offer a vast field for the display of courtesy; the suitors will follow the vestal youths, who will make their choice in the course of the campaign. Those of the young lovers of either sex who are attached to but one person, will enter the groups of constancy, forming the second of the Love-Groups. Others who have a taste for variety, will join some one of the seven other groups.

The principal result of this system of gallantry will be that immense industrial armies may be formed without the least compulsion, and without any other artifice than that of bringing out and publicly honoring this vestality, which the philosophers would exclude from the world, and surround with duennas and prejudices.

To assemble an industrial army, it will be sufficient to publish a list of the vestals of both sexes to be furnished by each Phalanx; for the declared suitors will be irresistibly attracted to follow the objects of their attachment to the armies, where their union will be privately consummated, without any of that vulgar publicity which prevails among us at marriage festivals, when a whole city is notified that on such a day some libertine or scapegrace is about to deflower a young innocent.

One must needs be born in Civilization to bear the sight of these indecent customs, in which the priest and the magistrate join, and religion is mixed up with ribaldry and dissipation. And why? Because after vile intrigues, after a bargain got up by notaries and matchmakers, two individuals are about to be chained together for life, who perhaps at the end of a month will be insupportable to each other. And what is the object of it all? The hope of an heir? But who knows but the woman will prove sterile? The hope of conjugal happiness? But who knows that the parties will not detest each other the next year, and if their union will not bring misery upon them both. The family giving these fêtes on the strength of a vague hope, may be compared to a silly fellow who, on taking a ticket in a lottery, gives a sumptuous repast to his neighbors in celebration of the fact that he hopes to draw a prize. The guests would partake of his hospitality, but would ridicule him saying: "He has not yet drawn the prize."

Do you not imitate such a thoughtless fellow, when you give a fête on the occasion of a marriage which is not even a lottery but worse still, since the union may produce misery instead of happiness? The only case when there is any sense in such fêtes, is that when a man marries a rich wife; then there is some occasion for rejoicing; and yet, ordinarily, wives expend more than they bring, and if the rejoicing were postponed for a year, to the epoch when the husband has experienced the embarrassments of domestic life, the enormous expenses of the household, and the deception which sooner or later arrives, there would be found few husbands disposed to celebrate their wedding day. And how many of them are undeceived, even the next day, in not finding their union what they expected?

In the Combined Order, the fêtes on the occasion of first unions will not be given till after they have been consummated. Good care will be taken not to imitate the Civilizees, who call the public to witness a bargain concluded for the acquisition of a young girl. A vestal will see her suitors assembled together, exhibiting their prowess in public games and in the works of the industrial army; their number will diminish successively according to the hope she holds out to them. At last, when her choice is decided, the couple will forward a sealed declaration of their intentions to the office of the High Matron (the presiding officer in affairs of love, directing these affairs in the army so far as concerns the Vestalic Body) or to the Vice Matrons who govern each Division; suitable arrangements will be made every evening for the union of couples who wish to be privately united, and the union will not be divulged till the next day, when the vestal will resign her crown of lilies for a crown of roses, and present herself in the costume of her new position, in company with her accepted suitor.

When we come to know all the details of the mechanism of the Love-Series in the armies of the Combined Order, the loves of Civilization will be found so monotonous, so pitiful, that we shall no longer be able to read, with any interest, our novels and dramas. It will easily be conceived that, in the Combined Order, admission to the industrial armies will become a favor; that twice as many volunteers will offer as will be necessary; and that, by the mere stimulus of love, there could be assembled on the globe 120,000,000 of industrial soldiers, of the two sexes, who would execute works, the very idea of which would strike the Civilized mind dumb with astonishment. For example, the Combined Order will undertake the conquest of the Great Desert of Sahara;

it will be attacked at various points by ten or twenty million hands, if necessary, who, by transporting soil and planting trees from station to station, will succeed in moistening the atmosphere, arresting the sands, and transforming the whole desert into a fertile region. Canals navigable for large vessels will be cut where at present we can not even dig trenches for irrigation, and ships will navigate, not only the isthmuses like those of Suez and Panama, but the interior of continents, as for example from the Caspian sea to the seas of Aral and Azoff, and to the Persian gulf; they will sail from Quebec to the five great lakes, and, in fine, from the Ocean to all the great interior basins whose length is equal to a quarter of their distance from the sea.

The various legions of the two sexes will be divided, in each empire, into several armies, which will amalgamate with the armies of neighboring countries. The Combined Order will never leave the execution of an enterprise to a single army, but will combine three at least in order to call forth and develop emulation. If it be found necessary to fertilize the waste lands of Gascony, this work will be executed by three armies, French, Spanish, and English, and in return France will furnish two armies, one to Spain and the other to England, to coöperate in their national works. Thus will be associated all the Empires of the globe; and the principle of compensation will be the same in the armies of a province, and in the works of a single Phalanx.

Suppose that the Phalanx of Tivoli wishes to mow a field requiring the labor of three hundred men for two hours; if it has only sixty mowers at command, it will borrow four cohorts from the four neighboring Associations; it will negotiate this labor-loan through its official minister at the Industrial Exchange of each of the said Associations, and, at the time appointed, the four cohorts will arrive and join the Tivolians in the field. The mowing will be followed by a repast, where will be found the belles of the different Associations; and the Association of Tivoli will send cohorts of men and women, when wanted, in return for those they have borrowed.

This exchange of cohorts is one of the means which will be employed in the Combined Order for transforming into pleasures, labors the most repulsive. These labors will become attractive,

1. By the dispatch resulting from a large number of coöperators;

2. By the union of cohorts, which will be joined by amateurs of both sexes;

3. By the perfect mechanical arrangement and the general elegance afforded by large combinations.

I insist on this last point. We see in our manufactories and workshops so much disorder, monotony, and filth, that they inspire horror for Industry and disgust for the persons engaged in it. This is especially true in France, which would seem to be the adopted country of uncleanliness. What can be more repulsive than the washing-houses of Paris? In place of these sinks, you will see, in the Combined Order, an edifice fitted with marble basins, and furnished with pipes supplying water of different degrees of temperature, so that the women need not spoil their hands by plunging them in water either too cold or too hot. There will also be ample arrangements for expediting the work by machinery of all kinds, and also for giving a charm to the repasts which will follow the work of four or five cohorts of laundresses, assembled from the neighboring Associations.

However insipid these minor details may seem, I do not disdain stopping to explain them, in order to prove that all industrial obstacles have been anticipated. Convocations of Cohorts constitute but one of the numerous processes by which all difficulties will be overcome; and the Combined Order will furnish the means of accomplishing, by attraction and rivalry, labors now the most repugnant.

Gallantry, so useless in Civilization, will become one of the most brilliant instrumentalities in the Associative Mechanism. And while the Civilized Order levies with so much difficulty and so much coercion the destructive armies which ravage the globe periodically, the Combined Order, by means of Attraction and Gallantry, will levy productive armies which will vie with each other in executing the most magnificent works. Instead of devastating thirty provinces in a campaign, these armies will have spanned thirty rivers with bridges, rewooded thirty barren mountains, dug thirty trenches for irrigation, and drained thirty marshes; and still these industrial achievements will be but a portion of the prodigies we shall owe to liberty in the passion of love, and to the downfall of philosophy.

In these discussions, which may appear futile, we must not lose sight of the aim of the Combined Order, which is to create INDUS-TRIAL ATTRACTION. All the arrangements I communicate in re-spect to this Order, however fanciful they may appear, must inva-riably be subjected to two tests, namely, INDUSTRIAL ATTRACTION, and ECONOMY OF MEANS. I will give an illustration of this, drawn from the Corps of Knight Errantry.

This Corps, so attractive to the young, will admit no one to membership who has not made at least three campaigns in the Industrial Armies, besides possessing the necessary attainments for sustaining the particular branch of art or science to which it is devoted. Here then is another means for raising industrial armies. Besides the influence of love, which will lead both sexes to follow the vestalic groups, besides the curiosity excited by the great events which will take place in the army, besides the eager-ness to be present at its great festivals, to participate in its pleas-ures, and to share the glory of its achievements, there are still other motives, such as the hope of obtaining, after three campaigns, a brevet of Knight Errantry, giving the right to travel over the globe with the bands of this brilliant Corps. Other privileges will be the reward of six campaigns, and at the end of nine, ad-mission will be granted to the Corps of Knights Paladin, who, all over the earth, will be the officers of the Supreme Sovereign of the Unitary Government of the Globe. On the return from each campaign, the youths of both sexes will be entitled to wear a deco-ration, such as a cross or a star, which will have for its legend the chief industrial feat of the army; and the number of rays will indi-cate the various campaigns of the bearer, and his titles to distinc-tion. Women will wear this decoration as well as men, for there will always be a moiety of women in all the industrial armies.

By means of the various inducements which the industrial ar-mies will offer to youth, they will enlist voluntarily at the first call —admission, as I have said, being a privilege to be purchased by various services. Thus will be attained the two ends above indi-cated, namely, INDUSTRIAL ATTRACTION, and ECONOMY OF MEANS.

As the chance of being admitted to the Corps of Knights Er-rant, forms one of the inducements which allure youths to the army, observe that these corps are not mere parties of pleasure, conceived without object, and that all the arrangements of the

Combined Order must necessarily, like the Bands of Knight Errantry, coöperate toward the two ends required — INDUSTRIAL ATTRACTION, and ECONOMY OF MEANS; and the measures which lead to these two ends will consist in enjoyments, romantic and intense, like those of which I have just given a slight sketch.

Fearing to present these pleasures in all their variety, I have dwelt only upon those which relate to the passion of love.

In speaking of love, I have restricted myself to describing the least of its pleasures, namely, those of the Vestalic Body, admitting only of courtesy, or spiritual enjoyment, and not of material or sensual. The vestal functions are a privation not an exercise of love, which commences only from the time when the vestal yields to a first inclination.

Of the circumstances which give full development to gallantry, and which contrast so strongly with the vile intrigues of civilized marriage, and the odious calculations by which among us first loves are degraded, I have not spoken. I have therefore given no idea of the loves of the Combined Order; and yet the accessories upon which I have touched will already have sufficed to make it evident that this Order will open to the love-passion a career so brilliant and so varied that we shall look with contempt upon the gallant chronicles of Civilization.

If I had been treating of the Love Series, and of the relations of their various groups, I might have demonstrated this in a few lines. But as I desire to excite reflection rather than enthusiasm, I pass over these details, which would cause a more lively impression than I care to produce.

I have complied with the wishes of various persons who have asked of me a slight description of the Combined Order, by giving a few pages of details, which, however, are as incomplete as they could well have been. If any one is inclined to suspect me of exaggeration in these descriptions of future enjoyments, it must be borne in mind that I have been speaking of the eighth Social Period, which is immensely distant from the fifth, in which we now are. I might have accommodated myself to the feeble passions of the Civilizees by depicting to them only the tamer and more commonplace enjoyments of the sixth and seventh Periods, but these Periods we shall pass over, and thus arrive at once to the fullness of the Combined Order.

EPILOGUE.

ON THE DECLINE AND FALL OF MORAL PHILOSOPHY.

CIVILIZED Nations, you are about to take a giant's step in the social career. In rising at once to Universal Harmony, you will escape twenty revolutions, which would have deluged the Globe with blood for twenty centuries to come — till the discovery of the theory of Human Destinies. You will make two thousand years of social progress at a single leap. Learn to take another such leap in the conquest of your prejudices. Scorn the feeble desires, the low aspirations inculcated by an impotent philosophy. Now that you are about to enjoy the blessing of Divine Social Laws, conceive the hope of a happiness as immense as the wisdom of God who planned it. In beholding the Universe which he has so magnificently ordered, the millions of worlds which he has made to roll in harmony, acknowledge that a Being so omnipotent could never tolerate the littleness and mediocrity preached by philosophers, and that we should insult his greatness if we expected anything like moderate happiness from a Social Order of which he is the Author.

Theology extols poverty as the path to eternal riches; Political science extols the riches of this world, while waiting for those of the next. Both doctrines are adapted to the human heart, which can never be satisfied with mediocrity.

Moralists, in eulogizing mediocrity, you are guilty either of absurdity or of charlatanry. If the eulogy be sincere, your science is absurd. If you believe in good faith that mediocrity can satisfy the human heart, can appease its perpetual cravings, you do not know Man. Instead of giving lessons to others, you should yourselves be at school. If the eulogy is only an oratorical flourish, you are charlatans, since you extol a mediocrity which is unsatisfactory to those who have obtained it, and which you can not secure to those who have not. Choose between these two alternatives, either of which sink your dogmas below mediocrity.

Do you hope to be excused on the ground of your good intentions—to secure praise for your efforts on the plea that they give consolation? If you had the sincere intention to console the unfortunate, you should have sought other means than your dogmas, which you yourselves confess to be insufficient. Witness a modern moralist—Bernardin de St. Pierre—who, speaking of the masters of the art, of Seneca, of Marcus Aurelius, says:—

"To sustain myself in my misfortunes, you bid me lean on the staff of philosophy. You say to me;—'Take courage! Go through the world begging your bread; behold yourself then as happy as we in our palaces, with our women, and with the esteem of our neighbors.' But the first thing I lack is this philosophic reason by which you wish me to sustain myself. All your fine dialectics fail at the precise moment when I have need of them. They are no more than the rosary in the hands of an invalid."

Behold moral philosophy discredited by its own writers; but without waiting for their disavowal, are not their actions sufficient to disabuse us? Demand of the virtuous Seneca why, when boasting of the charms of poverty, he accumulated for his own little pleasures a fortune of millions? Doubtless he considered poverty and mediocrity more beautiful in prospect than in reality, like those rude statues which appear best at a distance. We are of the same opinion; and why may not we, like him, consign poverty and mediocrity to the dusty shelves of the libraries.

When, moralists, you attest by your actions and confessions the inefficacy of the succor promised by your science, what motive must we attribute to you for persisting in offering to us such useless consolation? Is it not irony on your part to seek to familiarize us with privations, when we demand of you riches and real enjoyments? For yourselves, moralists and philosophers, whose minds and senses, more cultivated and refined than those of the mass, render the charms of fortune more precious to you, are you not enchanted to learn that the fall of your systems is about to secure to you that fortune which, while feigning to disdain, you yet idolize in secret?

Do not hesitate to make a full confession of your errors. The disgrace of them will fall not upon any particular class, but upon the learned as a whole. Fancy you that the men of science and of letters can escape their part of the universal reproach ? Had they not, like you, reason and good sense to make them perceive and denounce the general absurdity ? Yes, the general absurdity, for the folly of men is universal, and will continue so till a remedy is found for that most scandalous of all social disorders —POVERTY. So long as this exists, your profound sciences are nothing for you but brevets of insanity, for with all your wisdom you are but a legion of lunatics.

You proclaim yourselves to be the oracles of reason. As long as Civilization lasts, then, be silent; for if it recommends both mediocrity and truth, it is incompatible with reason. In what parts of the world, has Civilization made the most progress? In Athens, in Paris, in London, where men have been in no sense the friends of mediocrity or of truth, but on the contrary have been the slaves of their passions, and devoted to intrigues, to wealth, and to luxury. And where has Civilization languished and remained stagnant? In Sparta, and in primitive Rome, where the voluptuous passions and the love of luxury had but a feeble development. After such precedents, can you doubt that the Civilized Order is irreconcilable with reason, which, according to you, should moderate the passions? Can you doubt that it is necessary to banish reason, if we wish the maintenance and the progress of the Civilized Order ?

Your science had some vogue in antiquity, because it flattered the passions. In fact, in those times, when literature and the positive sciences were in their infancy, imagination and curiosity had but little to sustain them. Men naturally and eagerly accepted doctrines which opened to them an immense career of controversy and speculation. Speculative philosophy was then sustained by its union with the positive sciences and religion. Pythagoras, the father of moral science, was at the same time a skilful geometer and a revered prelate. He had founded a kind of monastery where he pretended to work miracles, such as raising the dead, and other absurdities. His neophytes were subjected to the severest tests, like the Trappists of the present day.

Finally, if the moralists obtained the favor of the people, it was because in the mythological religion, they were colleagues of the priesthood, like the monks in the Catholic religion.

While the ascetics of the ancient philosophy seduced the people by the practice of austerities and the study of the useful sciences, other schools, more tractable, like that of Epicurus, enlisted the rich, and formed coteries which were favored by the cultivated classes, who had no other means of employing their time—just as in Paris we see the same classes becoming enthusiastic for a given theatre or actor. Thus we see that the vogue which the moral sciences obtained among the Greeks, was founded on the superstition of the common people and the indolence of the great, in a word on the opportunities they afforded for gratifying the passions, but not at all on the influence of reason. Other times, other customs. The moral coteries having fallen into disrepute among the Romans, Cato, on the occasion of a political intrigue in which figured certain Greek sophists, sought to have all the philosophers driven out of Rome—a proof that they no longer preserved the odor of sanctity.

As for the moderns, moral philosophy has reappeared among them only to die an inglorious death. At first, it followed servilely in the footsteps of the ancients; but in vain did it serve up their old diatribes against the passions and against riches; what was amusing enough in Athens, was no longer so in Paris or London. It is with the speculative sciences as with the fashions; their existence is ephemeral. The clique of moralists is nearly extinct. Isolated from religion and from the exact sciences, they ventured to reappear only to mutter a few current phrases about analysis, synthesis, etc., upon which they still lean, and to retail a mass of verbiage about the passions, against which they launched their feeble anathemas,—reminding us of those old men who, retired in their chimney-corners, have their say against the times which no longer recognise their existence.

If moral science accuses our age of perversity for being insensible to her charms, it is easy to prove that her abandonment is the only reasonable act of which the present century can boast. An anomaly connected with her doctrines is that the places where they have been most taught, are those where they have been the least followed. Sparta and Rome are cited as the headquarters of asceticism, but the number of moralists must have been very small in Sparta, when the people would hardly tolerate even Diogenes, the great apostle of poverty. And there were still fewer in Rome at the time Cincinnatus was planting his own turnips. Men were no better for being poor; their parade of austerity was only a fashion of the times. At Rome, as elsewhere, increase of wealth gave to ambition more refined forms; and in proportion as Civilization advanced, austerity and moderation became less and less in vogue. The efforts of philosophy to restore these political pruderies are only an indication of their absurdity. The more moral theories a nation accumulates, the less it is disposed to follow their precepts. Moral philosophy is an offspring of luxury; hence in declaiming against luxury it denies its paternity. Its volumes and systems augment in proportion to the increase of luxury; and when the latter declines, moral theories decline with it, without the ruined nation becoming any the better for it, for the Greeks of the present day, who have no philosophers, are no more moral than the Greeks of other times. The moral controversy, then, has no other source, no other support than luxury, under whose reign, if it conform itself to circumstances, it can obtain credit as something romantic and adapted to amuse the rich and the indolent. Far from being able to moderate the passions, it is reduced to the necessity of flattering dominant vices under penalty of being despised; hence it has greatly moderated its tone in treating with the moderns, among whom poverty is no longer in repute.

Moral philosophy strangely deceives itself, if it fancies it possesses any independent existence. It is evidently superfluous and powerless in the social mechanism, since on all questions within its domain, such as larceny, adultery, etc., religion and politics suffice to determine what is requisite in the established Order. As for any reforms to be attempted in morals, if politics and religion fail in them, moral science will be still more certain to. What is it in the scientific world but the fifth wheel to the coach; what but impotency in action! Whenever it combats single handed with any vice, it is sure to be defeated. It may be compared to a poor regiment which allows itself to be repulsed in every encounter, and which ought to be ignominiously disbanded. It is thus the scientific corps should treat the moralists for the services they have rendered them.

If, at times, politics and theology have accorded to you, moralists, a feigned respect, if they have admitted you as a third party in the struggle against vice, it is to cast upon you all the disgrace of defeat, and to keep to themselves all the advantages of political and religious influence. You are for them but

L'instrument servile,
Rejeté par dédain lorsqu'il est inutile,
Et brisé sans pitié s'il devient dangereux.

See in what estimation they have held you in all great emergencies, like the massacre of St. Bartholomew, and the French Revolution. If you doubt the contempt they have for your dogmas, venture to oppose them, and you will soon have the measure of your importance.

———

A fact which occurred in the course of the seventeenth century, has at last convinced you of these unpleasant truths. A schism took place in the philosophic corps, from which was born a new science — Political Economy. The rapid progress of this science should have led men to foresee the triumph of doctrines favorable to wealth and luxury, and the consequent downfall of the moralists. The latter perceived, late in the day, that political economy had invaded the whole domain of speculative controversy. By the middle of the eighteenth century, all parties rallied to the support of this new science, which proclaimed itself the dispenser of riches, and held out the promise of national wealth, in which all flattered themselves they should participate. The usurpation of the economists had already been consummated, when the moralists were still found extolling the charms of poverty. Finally, the French Revolution having dissipated all their moral chimeras, they wished to make a compromise ; to this end, they set forth certain ambiguous doctrines, such as " indifference to riches without either loving or despising them," doctrines truly entertaining, but which could not save the moral coterie, since the economists, become too strong to have need of allies, disdained all means of reconciliation, and did their best to glorify riches, proclaiming the necessity of great and still greater wealth, with — *un commerce immense et un immense commerce.* Thenceforth, the moralists fell into disgrace, and were ranked

without mercy in the class of rhapsodists. Their sect died out
with the eighteenth century. It is politically dead, no longer enjoying the least reputation, especially in France, where it has
ceased to have a place at the Institute.

I shall demonstrate in the Third Part of this work that political economy is also hastening to its ruin, and that the fall of
the moralists prepared the way for that of their rivals. We
may apply to these parties the remark of Danton, who being on
the scaffold and already bound with one cord, said to the executioner : "Keep the other for Robespierre, he will follow me
soon." So the moralists may say to their executioners, say to
public opinion which is about to sacrifice them : " Keep the other
cord for the economists, they will soon follow us."

If ever Civilization had occasion to blush for its scientific errors
and its credulity towards charlatans, it is now, when it is tramp-
ling under foot theories which it has reverenced for thousands
of years, now when we see the philosophic class cringing before
Passional Attraction, which they have always sought *to repress,
to correct, and to moderate.*

One of these sciences, political economy, excites to love of
riches ; the other, moral philosophy, permits us not to despise
them, and raises a dying voice to make its humble apology to the
passions. The human mind, then, it would seem, has the faculty
of feeding for thousands of years upon sophisms which it finally
comes to repudiate. And how know ye, Civilized Nations, that
your modern visions, your economic chimeras are not still more
absurd, and will not draw down upon the nineteenth century
more contempt than the moral delusions which you are ashamed
of to-day ?

Do you fancy yourselves nearer to the truth, nearer to Nature,
in deifying Commerce, which is a continual exercise of falsehood
and cunning ? Think you that God has conceived no more loyal
and equitable method for the exchange of products, which is the
chief function, the soul of the industrial mechanism ?

I shall consider this question in the Third Part.

Meantime I would remind you that it was not sufficient to
recognise the empire of Nature, whose supreme influence you at
last confess. It was very little to disavow a science which proposed to suppress the passions. It was necessary, in order to

regain the favor of Nature, to study her decrees as revealed by her sole interpreter — PASSIONAL ATTRACTION.

You make a parade of your metaphysical theories; but of what use are they, if you disdain to study Attraction, which is the guiding principle of the soul? Your metaphysicians lose themselves in the mazes of ideology. And of what importance is all their scientific trumpery? I, who am ignorant of the pretended origin and mechanism of ideas, I who have never read Locke nor Condillac, have I not had ideas enough to discover the complete system of Universal Movement, of which you have only discovered the fourth branch, the sidereal, after twenty-five hundred years of scientific effort? I do not pretend that my ideas are vast because they extend to regions which yours have never reached. I have done no more than a thousand others might have done before me; but I have worked my own way, without the aid of acquired means or of beaten paths. I, alone and unaided, shall have confounded twenty centuries of political imbecility; it is to me that present and future generations will owe the initiative of their immense happiness. Before me, Humanity lost thousands of years struggling foolishly against Nature. I, the first, have bowed before her by studying Attraction, the organ of her eternal decrees. She has deigned to smile on the only mortal who has offered incense to her, and has given me the key to all her treasures. Possessor of the book of Destinies, I come to dispel the night of moral and political ignorance, and upon the ruins of the speculative sciences to erect the theory of Universal Harmony.

Exegi monumentum ære perennius.

END OF THE SECOND PART.

PART III.

CONFIRMATION

DRAWN FROM

THE INCOMPETENCY OF THE SPECULATIVE SCIENCES

ON ALL

PROBLEMS RELATING TO THE CIVILIZED MECHANISM.

PREAMBLE.

SYSTEMATIC NEGLECT OF ALL FUNDAMENTAL QUESTIONS.

THE speculative sciences have all fallen into an absurd error; they have neglected the fundamental problem of every science of which they treat—the problem which was the pivot of the science itself.

For example:—

If they treat of *Industrial Economy*, they neglect the subject of *Association*, which is the basis of all economy.

If they treat of *Politics*, they neglect the question of *Equilibrium of Population*, which is the basis of the wealth of nations.

If they treat of *Government*, they neglect to consider the means for establishing *Unity in the Government of the Globe*, without which there can exist no permanent order, no guarantee of the stability of empires.

If they treat of *Industry*, they neglect to propose measures for the *Suppression of Fraud, Monopoly, and Spoliations*, which fall upon both producers and consumers, and are a direct obstacle to the circulation and exchanges of products.

If they treat of *Morals*, they neglect to recognise and insist upon the *Rights of Woman*, the denial of which is a fundamental violation of the laws of justice.

If they treat of the *Rights of Man*, they neglect to lay down the principle of the *Right to Employment*, a right which is not admissible in Civilization, though without it all others are useless.

If they treat of *Metaphysics*, they neglect to study the *Relations between God and Man*, and to seek the means of permanent communication which he has established with the human race.

The philosophers, then, have the singular habit of neglecting the fundamental problems of every science ; it is systematic neglect, since it exists universally in respect to all primary questions ; I might indicate the cause of this oversight, but if the philosophers are as skilful as they pretend to be in the use of analysis, let them discover it.

ARGUMENT.

UNTIL the publication of the laws of Social Movement, I can accompany my announcement only with negative proofs, such as the incompetency of our learned men in respect to all the problems of the Civilized Social Mechanism. This Third Part, therefore, will be occupied exclusively with criticisms.

To expose the incompetency of modern science, I will give two illustrations relating to questions the most intelligible to the present generation.

These illustrations will be drawn from,

1. *The Commercial System.*
2. *Free-Masonry.*

This second subject, Free-Masonry, will be presented in its relation to the chances it offered to the philosophers for achieving something really useful. It will be seen that this institution offered them a stepping stone by which they might have risen to consideration and fortune, and thus repaired their defeat of 1793; but they lacked the tact to profit by it. Now, since they were so blind to the opportunities offered their personal ambition, were they likely to be any less so, as to the means of serving the human race? Far from this, they have turned to the detriment of humanity, opportunities which might have opened to it ways of social amelioration.

In demonstrating this assertion, I shall have occasion to contradict all the systems admitted in modern politics, and especially the prevalent ideas respecting Commercial Liberty, which can not be other than injurious, since it is preached up by the philosophers. It is in this connection that their blindness will be made evident, and that we shall be convinced that the human race, by confiding itself to men so rebellious against the most evident truths, exposed itself to new calamities.

FIRST ILLUSTRATION.

COMMERCIAL LICENSE,

ITS KNOWN EVILS AND UNKNOWN DANGERS.

INTRODUCTION.

WE are about to probe Civilization in its most sensitive part: to raise one's voice against the dominant folly of the day, against chimeras in full vogue, is always a painful task.

To speak at the present day against commercial follies and blunders, is to expose one's self to anathema, as if one had spoken in the twelfth century against the tyranny of Popes and Barons. Were it necessary to choose between the two dangerous alternatives, I consider there would be less risk in offending a sovereign by the announcement of disagreeable truths, than in offending the mercantile power, which reigns as a despot over Civilization and even over sovereigns themselves.

It is never at the height of an infatuation that men form sound opinions on social questions. Witness the supremacy of the commercial theories now in vogue; we shall show by a brief analysis that they tend to deprave and disorganize Civilization in every sense, and that in the matter of Commerce, as in everything else, society is led more and more astray under the auspices of the speculative sciences.

The commercial controversy dates back hardly half a century, and its writers have already published hundreds of volumes, without discovering that the mechanism of commerce is organized in opposition to common sense. It subordinates the whole social body to a class of parasitic and unproductive agents, called Merchants. All the essential classes — the land-owner, the cultivator, the manufacturer, and even the government itself — are under the control of a secondary and accessory class, namely, the Merchants, who should be their subordinates, their commissioned agents, removable and responsible, whereas at present they direct and obstruct at will the whole s stem of exchange and circulation.

Such is the thesis on which I shall dissert; I shall show that in sound politics the commercial body should be *collectively responsible for all its acts*, and that the social body should be *guaranteed* against bankruptcy, stock-jobbing, monopoly, speculation, usury, deterioration and waste, and all other evils resulting from the present system—a system which would have long since aroused the indignation of political writers, if they had had a shadow of the respect for good morals which they pretend. In this first Memoir, I wish only to introduce the question, and point out the evils and abuses which attest our ignorance, and which should have led to researches for a mode of commercial exchanges much less defective and pernicious than the present, which we call Free Competition.

For the exchange of products, as for all other relations, there is a method especially adapted to each Social Period. For example : —

In the fourth Period or Barbarism, compulsory sales, limitation of prices, tariffs, etc., determined by the government.

In the fifth Period or Civilization, free competition, and irresponsibility of the merchant to the social body.

In the sixth Period or Guarantism, collective competition, joint responsibility, and the subordination of the commercial body to the interests of the producers, manufacturers, cultivators, and land-owners.

There are other methods for the succeeding Periods, of which I shall not here give the Table, as I wish to speak only of the method of the sixth Period, Collective Competition, which is compatible with existing usages, and which is preferable to free competition, as the latter is preferable to the system of forced sales, maximum prices, tariffs, etc., of the fourth Period or Barbarism.

In this discussion I shall speak as a Civilizee, in other words, as if the laws of Movement had not been discovered; let us forget their discovery then for the moment, and reason as if the question were simply to find a remedy for the Commercial disorders of Civilization. Let us see what steps should have been taken under existing circumstances by the political economists, the men who consider themselves the most competent in mercantile questions.

In the course of the discussion, I shall have occasion to express opinions but little flattering to the Commercial system in general; for I have already observed that in criticising a profession, I do not criticise the individuals who exercise it. Those who declaim against the manœuvres of monopolists, speculators, etc., would perhaps, if in their place, surpass them in rapacity. We should blame, not the passions of individuals, but Civilization only, which, opening to the passions no career but that of vice, compels men to practise vice in order to attain to fortune, without which the passions can not be satisfied.

The subject will be divided under the following heads:—

1. *Origin of Political Economy and of the Mercantile Controversy.*

2. *Spoliation of the social body by Bankruptcy.*

3.   "   "   "   "   " *Monopoly and Forestalling.*

4.   "   "   "   "   " *Agiotage.*

5.   "   "   "   "   " *Commercial Parasitism.*

6. *Decline of Civilization through the Commercial policy, which is leading to the fourth Phase of this Order.*

I.

ORIGIN OF POLITICAL ECONOMY AND OF THE MERCANTILE CONTROVERSY.

THIS is a subject well worthy of an epic. Muse, recount to us the exploits of the audacious innovators who have vanquished our old and time-honored philosophy — of this new sect, the Economists, which, springing suddenly into existence, has dared to attack the revered dogmas of Greece and Rome. The true models of virtue — the Cynics, the Stoics, all the illustrious lovers of poverty and mediocrity — have been discomfited, and now cringe before the Economists, who combat in the cause of Wealth and Luxury. The divine Plato, the divine Seneca, are driven from their thrones. The black broth of the Spartans, the turnips of Cincinnatus, the rags of Diogenes, in fine all the

panaceas of the moralists have become powerless, have all van-
ished before these impious innovators who permit the love of
splendor, luxury, and the vile metals.

In vain have the Rousseaus and the Mablys courageously
defended the honor of Greece and Rome. In vain have they
preached to the nations the eternal truths of morality—that
" poverty is a blessing," that " we must renounce riches and give
ourselves up to philosophy without delay."* Useless appeal!
Nothing has been able to resist the onset of the new doctrines.
Our corrupted age breathes only of commercial treaties and bal-
ances of trade, dreams of nothing but dollars and cents. The
Porch and the Lyceum are deserted for Chambers of Commerce
and " Associations of the Friends of Commerce." In a word,
the irruption of the Economists has been for the moral sciences
but another day of Pharsalia, by which the wisdom of Athens
and Rome, and of all classic antiquity, has suffered an irreparable
defeat.

Humanly speaking, Civilization has changed Phase. It has
passed from the second to the third Phase, in which the Commercial spirit reigns in Politics, exclusively. This change has
grown out of the progress of the Nautical Art and of Colonial
Monopolies. The philosophers, who always support a social
movement after it is accomplished, chimed in with the spirit of
the age, and as soon as they saw the commercial policy dominant,
commenced to extol it; thus originated the sect of Political
Economists, and with it, the mercantile controversy.

How happens it that the philosophers have changed their
opinions after so many centuries, and now come to meddle in
questions of Commerce, which was the object of their ancient disdain ? In classic antiquity they never ceased to ridicule it.
Then, all writers treated tradesmen with derision and repeated

---

* These are the very words of Seneca, the man of millions ; he would have us give
up riches at once. He allows no delay. " Why do you wait ?" he says, " do not
put it off till to-morrow ; abandon your wealth to day, and give yourselves up to philosophy." Such is the nonsense which has prevailed in Civilization for two thousand
years ; and this folly passes for wisdom. At the present day, we see the absurdity of
these wiseacres who counsel us to " cast perfidious riches into the bosom of the sea."
[*J. B. Rousseau.*] But there are phrase-mongers still more ridiculous, charlatans still
more silly and culpable ; these are the political economists, who disguise themselves
under the mask of reason.

after the fashion of Horace, that the science of trade consisted in knowing that

A hundred francs at five per cent. yield just five francs!

Still it might have been seen, by the nfluence of Tyre and Carthage, that the Commercial Power would one day overmaster the Agricultural Power, and control the political policy of the world. *But the event not having occurred, it therefore never could occur!* Such is the logic of Civilized politics; it sees nothing but the past. Hence future generations will represent Civilization by a head reversed and looking backward.

Up to the middle of the eighteenth century, the speculative sciences fostered the old prejudice which treated commerce with contempt; witness the spirit that reigned in France in 1788. Then the Collegians in their debates often sneered at an adversary, calling him the son of a tradesman, and it was a cruel insult. Such was the feeling in the provinces; the mercantile spirit was confined to the seaports and large capitals where resided the great merchants, bankers, and stock-jobbers. It was not till some years after that the merchants were transformed into demi-gods, when the philosophic cabal enlisted openly on their side and exalted them to the skies, because they were useful in carrying out their designs.

Thus, in its origin, Commerce was misunderstood and despised by the philosophers, who know so little about it, even at the present day, as to confound it with the useful profession of manufactures. It failed to secure their homage till it had completely triumphed ; then their orators celebrated the virtue of the merchants and partook of their fine dinners. In a word, the philosophers began to flatter commerce only when it had obtained the vogue ; before, they did not think it worthy their attention. Spain, Portugal, Holland, and England, carried on their commercial monopolies for a long time, without the philosophers dreaming of either praising or blaming them. Holland had succeeded in accumulating its immense wealth without asking any aid of the Political Economists, whose sect in fact had not been born when the Dutch had already piled up tons of gold.

The philosophers at that epoch were still employed in rummaging classic antiquity, and mixing themselves up in religious quarrels. At last they saw that the new commercial policy might furnish matter for new volumes of controversy, and bring into vogue a new coterie; then it was that philosophy gave birth to the sects of Political Economists, who, despite their recent origin, have already brought forth a goodly number of volumes and promise to be more fecund than their predecessors.

According to the custom of the sophists, these new-comers have embroiled the subject as much as possible. Far from having discovered anything, they do not yet know what they are treating of; for in the most important questions of political economy, such as the *limit to be assigned to population*, they confess that their science has no fixed principles. It gives no positive results, and it is difficult to see of what use it is. But that is of no importance. Theories multiply, the presses groan, the books sell, and the philosophic end is accomplished.

We might ask of the Economists, whether it is their intention to diminish or to multiply social scourges—such, for instance, as increase of taxes, the augmentation of armies, the encroachments of the parasitic classes, national debts, bankruptcies, etc. It is certain that none of these scourges ever increased so rapidly as since the birth of Political Economy. Would it not have been better if the science, as well as the evil, had made less progress?

What motives could have decided the philosophers, those vehement apostles of truth and honesty, to rally in the eighteenth century to the support of duplicity and fraud—that is, of Commerce? For what is Commerce? It is nothing but fraud and duplicity, with all their paraphernalia of monopoly, speculation, usury, bankruptcy, and roguery of every description; but modern philosophy passes a sponge over all these scandalous abuses. Let us point out the causes of this effrontery, applying to these savants the analytic methods they pretend to apply to everything.

In deciding to preach up Commerce, they were swayed only by the influence of wealth. They were allured by the enormity and rapid accumulation of mercantile fortunes; the independence attached to the mercantile profession, which is at once the most free, and the most favorable to personal ambition; the air of grand speculation given to vile manœuvres which the merest dolt could conceive and direct at the end of a month; and, finally, by the luxury and display of wealthy speculators and stock-jobbers, who often vie in magnificence with the grandees of the state. All this *éclat* dazzles the philosophers, who after sleepless nights and countless schemes, succeed only in earning a few francs and obtaining a little humiliating patronage. At the sight of these commercial and financial Plutuses, they became bewildered and hesitated between sycophancy and censure. At last, the weight of gold turned the scale, and they became, finally, the very humble servants of the mercantile class, and the warm admirers of the commercial policy they had so much ridiculed. But how could one help admiring these great operators, speculators, and stockjobbers, these men who, according to Boileau,

Have for their only secret this refrain,
That five and four make nine, take two, and seven remain,

and succeed with such a science in acquiring palaces in cities which they entered barefoot. We see them in our large capitals living in luxury and splendor by the side of literary men, living in poverty and obscurity. A philosopher admitted to the mansion of a stockjobber, finds himself seated at table between a countess and an ambassador. What course is one to take under such circumstances but to worship the saints of the day? For nobody makes his way in Civilization by proclaiming truths; and hence we see why the philosophers, while nourishing a secret hatred against Commerce, have nevertheless bowed before the golden calf, not daring to write a page without sounding the praises of—"*le Commerce immense et l'immense Commerce.*" And yet they had everything to gain by attacking it; for by denouncing the frauds and spoliations of Commerce, which they secretly despise as much as Commerce despises them, they might have regained their lost position, and repaired their defeats. An analysis of Commerce will show that the mercantile body (care must be taken not to confound it with the manufacturing class) is in Civilization but a horde of confederated pirates—a flock of vultures, preying upon agriculture and manufactures, and plundering the social body in every possible way. This, be it understood, without criticising them individually. They are ignorant themselves of the pernicious character of their profession, and even were they aware of it, how can one be blamed for being a spoliator in Civilization, when this Society is but a game between rogues and dupes ?—a truth already too well known, but which will be made still more evident in the following chapters.

II.

SPOLIATION OF THE SOCIAL BODY BY BANKRUPTCY.

WHEN a crime becomes common in society, it is looked upon with indifference. In Italy and Spain a hired assassin poignards his victim with impunity and retires for protection to the nearest church. In Germany and France, where the national character is opposed to treachery, such an assassin would be looked upon with so much abhorrence that he would perhaps be torn in pieces by the populace before the authorities had time to arrest him. And how many other crimes we see dominant in one nation and abhorred by its next neighbor! In Italy, parents mutilate their children in order to perfect the voice, and the ministers of a God of Peace patronize the custom by devoting these unfortunate victims of paternal avarice to the service of his altars. This, again, is an abomination which would excite horror in any other Civilized nation. In the same way, you will find among the French, the Germans, the Russians, and the English, other revolting customs which would arouse the indignation of the Italians and Spaniards.

If the customs and opinions prevailing in Civilization vary so much in different nations, how much must they vary in different Orders of society, and how odious would appear the vices tolerated in the Civilized Order to less imperfect societies. In the sixth, Guarantism, which will still be far from perfection, it will be difficult to believe that nations calling themselves polite, and having theories of property and justice, could have tolerated for an instant such abominations as Bankruptcy.

Bankruptcy is the most ingenious and the most impudent form of roguery which has ever existed. It insures to every tradesman the privilege of plundering the public of a sum proportioned to his fortune or credit, so that a rich man may say to himself: " I establish myself as a merchant this year: two years hence, on such a day, I shall plunder the community of so many thousands."

The new French Code which promises to suppress bankruptcy, we will not here consider. As opinions differ in respect to the working of this Code, and as means for eluding it have already been indicated, let us wait till experience has decided the matter (that is, if Civilization is to be prolonged long enough for the trial) and meanwhile reason upon what we know—upon the disorders which result from the philosophic doctrine of *leaving the merchants entirely free, without requiring of them any guarantee of their prudence, probity, or solvency.*

From this doctrine has sprung, among other abuses, Bankruptcy—a kind of robbery much more odious than that of the highway. We are nevertheless accustomed to tolerate it, even to the extent of recognising honest bankruptcies, or those in which the speculator makes way with only one half; here is an example:

The banker Dorante possesses a fortune of half a million, and wishes to increase it by some means to a million. On the strength of his known property, he obtains credit in bills of exchange, 'produce, etc., to the amount of two millions. He can then operate with a capital of two millions and a half. He engages in vast commercial and financial speculations. Perhaps at the end of a year, instead of having doubled his original half-million, he will have lost it. You would think him ruined. Not at all. He will yet come out with a million, just as if he had succeeded ; for he has remaining on hand the two millions obtained on credit, and by means of an "honest bankruptcy" he compromises with his creditors and pays fifty per cent. on time. Thus, after having lost his original fortune, he finds himself possessor of a million robbed from the public. A fine thing this commercial liberty! And do we not understand now, why we hear it said every day of some merchant: " Since his failure he is very well off ?" Here is another game for the bankrupt:—Dorante, after his robbery of half a million, preserves his honor and the esteem of the public, not as being a fortunate rogue, but as being an unfortunate merchant. Let us explain. While premeditating his failure, Dorante takes pains to forestall public opinion. His fêtes in town and country have procured him warm partisans. The great and fashionable are all on his side. The ladies sympathize with his " misfortune" (at present, the synonyme of bankruptcy), and his noble character is spoken of as worthy of a better fate. It would seem, to hear the apologies made for a bankrupt, that he is even more unfortunate than those he has ruined. All the fault is attributed to political events, to disastrous circumstances, etc.—excuses with which notaries, who are so skilful in arranging matters and pacifying creditors, are all familiar. After the first shock, Dorante employs certain agents, who by means of suitable bribes soon suborn public opinion to such an extent that the man who should speak against Dorante would be called a monster. Moreover, those from whom the bankrupt has robbed the largest sums are one or two hundred leagues off, say in London or Amsterdam, and in time these will become quiet. But that is of little importance ; their distant complaints are not heard in Paris. Besides, Dorante makes no one lose more than half, and custom has decided that the bankrupt who pays half is more unfortunate than guilty. Thus Dorante is washed clean in public opinion at once. Then, again, at the end of a month, a new bankruptcy takes place, which produces a greater sensation and which pays only a third or a fourth. A new triumph for Dorante, who paid half ! Moreover his is an old affair and is forgotten. Gradually the saloons of Dorante are reopened ; his splendid entertainments, once more the vogue, drown the cries of certain splenetic creditors, who are accused of having no respect for misfortune, none of the politeness belonging to good society.

It is thus that in less than six months terminates an operation by which Dorante and his kind rob millions from the public, ruin families which have confided in them, and drag honest tradesmen into a bankruptcy which confounds them with rogues. Bankruptcy is the only moral crime which is propagated epidemically, and which covers the honest man with the same opprobrium as the rogue. The upright merchant who suffers from the failure of twenty rogues, is at last forced to go into bankruptcy himself. Hence dishonest bankrupts, who compose nine tenths of the whole number, give themselves out as honest men who have met with " misfortunes," and chant in chorus—" We are more to be pitied than to be blamed." To listen to them, one would suppose they were all little saints, reminding one of convicts, who always pretend to have done nothing wrong.

The partisans of Commercial Liberty talk about repressive

laws, tribunals, etc. Oh yes, tribunals against men who have robbed millions at a single stroke! The proverb which says that "petty thieves are punished while great ones only escape," is found false when applied to Commerce, for even the smallest bankruptcies escape the pursuit of justice, being favored by the merchants themselves. For example:—

Scapin, a small shopkeeper, fails for only forty thousand francs. He pockets thirty thousand, the profits of the operation, and gives to his creditors the remaining ten thousand. If called upon to give an account of the thirty thousand deficit, he replies that he does not know how to keep books, like the large dealers, and that he has met with misfortunes. You fancy that Scapin will be punished because he is only a petty thief who has pocketed but thirty thousand francs; yet the creditors know full well that if they go to law it will eat up the ten thousand balance, which would only be a mouthful for it. The ten thousand swallowed up, there would still be nothing decided, and if you wish to have Scapin hung, it will be necessary perhaps to spend another ten thousand, without being quite sure of success after all. It is better, then, to take the small sum of ten thousand, than to expend as much more. Scapin takes advantage of this argument through the medium of his attorney, so that in fact it is the creditor, instead of the bankrupt, who is threatened with the law. And why should the creditors of Scapin be severe with him? Some of them think of following his noble example, and others have preceded him in it. Now, as wolves never devour each other, Scapin soon finds a certain number of signers who accept his proposition; others sign for fear the matter will get into court and leave nothing to be divided, while a third party, more stubborn, talks of sacrificing all for the sake of sending a rascal to the galleys. To the latter, Scapin sends his wife and child, who, with studied appeals, solicit his pardon. Thus Scapin and his lawyer obtain, in a few days, a majority of signers, after which those who refuse to come in are jeered at, since there is no longer any need of them. Their anger provokes nothing but mirth. Scapin replies to it by soft words and profound salutations, and, seeing the success of his first bankruptcy, already meditates a second.

It is useless to cite certain fraudulent bankrupts who have been punished, for out of a hundred, ninety-nine escape, while if the hundredth is foiled, he is without doubt a simpleton who has not known how to manage his game, for the operation is so certain at the present day, that the ordinary precautions which were once taken are now neglected. Formerly, the bankrupt fled to Trente, to Liege, to Carouge; but since the political regeneration of 1789, this practice has fallen into disuse. The operation is now quietly prepared beforehand, and when it comes out, the bankrupt goes and spends a month in the country with his relatives and friends, while in the interim everything is arranged by the notary. The bankrupt reappears after some weeks, and the public is so much accustomed to this manœuvre, that it is considered as a smart thing. It is called "lying in," and we hear it said very coolly:—"Mr. Such-a-one is just out from his confinement."

I have said that Bankruptcy is the only social crime which is epidemic, and which forces the upright merchant to imitate the rogue. I shall illustrate this by an example of bankruptcies *en feu de file*—one involving another.

The Jew, Iscariot, arrives in France with a capital of a hundred thousand francs, which he has gained by his first bankruptcy. He establishes himself as a tradesman in a city where he has for rivals six respectable houses in good credit. To get the advantage of these, he begins by offering his goods at cost, this being a sure means of attracting the crowd. Soon, the rivals of Iscariot cry out against him; he laughs at their lamentations and continues more than ever to offer his goods at cost. Then the people begin to exclaim:—"Hurrah for opposition! Competition is the life of trade! Long life to the Jews! Since the arrival of Iscariot, everything has fallen in price!" And the public say to the rival houses:—"It is you, gentlemen, who are the real Jews; you wish to make too much profit. Iscariot only is an honest man. He is satisfied with a moderate price, because his store is less splendid than yours." Vainly the old firms represent that Iscariot is a rogue in disguise, who will sooner or later become a bankrupt; people accuse them of jealousy and run more and more after the Israelite.

See the calculation of the rogue:—By selling at cost price, he makes no other loss than the interest on his capital, say 10,000 francs a year, but he finds a good market, gets the reputation in

26

the commercial towns of doing an extensive business, and if he is somewhat exact in his first payments, obtains a large credit. This artifice is continued for two years, at the end of which time Iscariot has made nothing, though he has done an immense trade. His scheme is not divulged, because the Jews employ nobody but Jews—a people secretly hostile to all others, and who never betray any knavery concocted among themselves.

When everything is ready for the crisis, Iscariot uses all his credit, and sends orders to the principal cities, to the amount of five or six hundred thousand francs, purchased on time. He then exports the goods to a foreign country, and sells his stock on hand at the lowest price. Finally, when he has turned everything into cash, honest Iscariot disappears with his money, and goes to Germany, where he has sent the goods bought on credit. He sells these at once, and finds that he left France four times richer than when he went there. He is now worth four hundred thousand francs, and goes to Leghorn or London to prepare for a third bankruptcy. It is then that the veil falls, and the people among whom he has played his game, come to their senses. The danger of dealing with Jews, with vagabonds who hold to nothing, is at last recognised. But this bankruptcy of Iscariot is only the first act of the farce; let us follow it to the end.

There were six houses in competition with the Israelite; let us name them A., B., C., D., E., F.

A. had been in difficulties for a long time. He kept up without capital on the strength of his good reputation; but the arrival of Iscariot having taken away all his customers, he struggles on but a year longer, after which he loses courage, and not understanding the new economical systems which protect vagabonds, is forced to yield before the tactics of Iscariot, and go into bankruptcy.

B. stands the shock longer. He saw the failure of Iscariot in the distance, and waited till the storm had passed, in order to get back his customers taken from him by the knavish Israelite. But in the interval, B. suffers from a bankruptcy in another town; this is sufficient to hasten his fall. He hoped to hold out two years, but at the end of fifteen months, he too is obliged to go into bankruptcy.

C. is in partnership with a firm elsewhere, which is ruined

by another Iscariot (for the tribe is found everywhere); he is dragged down by the fall of his partner, and after making sacrifices for eighteen months to sustain a competition against the Hebrew thief, C. too is forced into bankruptcy.

D. has a kind of probity, but it is more apparent than real. Though he suffers for twenty months from competition with the Jew, he has means enough left to keep up; but irritated by the losses he has sustained, he follows the example he sees everywhere about him. Finding that three of his colleagues have led the way, he concludes that he, the fourth, will pass with the rest under the pretext of real or fictitious "misfortunes." Moreover, he is disgusted with a struggle of twenty months against the Israelite, and finds no course more prudent than to go into bankruptcy.

E. had loaned large sums to the four others who failed. He believed them to be solvent, as, in fact, before the manœuvres of Iscariot had undermined their trade, they were. These four failures subject him to great losses. Moreover, he has no more customers; everybody goes to Iscariot, who sells at cost. E. thus finds his resources exhausted, and his credit shaken. He is pressed by his creditors, and being unable to fulfill his engagements, finishes, with the rest, by going into bankruptcy.

F., though not wanting in means, finds his credit shaken in all the large cities, owing to the failure of his five predecessors, which leads to the suspicion that he will not be long in following their example. Besides, some of them who have made a compromise with their creditors, sell at very low prices to be able to meet their first notes under the new arrangement. The latter, to expedite their sales, sacrifice a tenth, and still make a profit of four tenths, since they have settled up at fifty per cent. F. finds himself crushed by these circumstances and is compelled, like the rest, to go into bankruptcy.

It is thus that a single vagabond may disorganize the entire body of tradesmen in a large town, and drag the most honest persons into crime; for every bankruptcy is more or less criminal, though colored by specious pretexts, like those above described, in which there is rarely anything of truth.

If to bankruptcy, we add the numerous other commercial abuses, such as monopoly, speculation, usury, etc., growing out of our economic systems, we shall see the force of the opinion already expressed, namely, that the Civilizees have never committed more blunders than since they gave in to the commercial spirit, and adopted the theory that all mercantile enterprises must result in the general good, and therefore that the merchants should be left in entire liberty, without being required to give any guarantee as to the result of their operations.

And how is it that the Economists, who talk of nothing but checks and guarantees, have never secured to the social body those which governments have had the good sense to require of their fiscal agents? A government makes sure of the fidelity of its collectors and receivers by requiring them to give bonds, and by exposing them to inevitable punishment if they dare to risk or squander the public funds with which they are intrusted. Why do we not see half of the receivers of public moneys appropriating them to their own use, and saying to the government in a whining letter :—"The misfortunes of the times, critical circumstances, deplorable reverses—in a word, I have failed. The amount of public funds deposited with me amounts to two millions. I offer to reimburse one half, a million, payable in five years. Have compassion on an unfortunate receiver, continue me in your confidence and in the management of your funds, without which I can not pay you even the half I now offer. Only retain me in my place, and I will try to honor my engagements"— (in other words, will regale you with a second failure as soon as the treasury shall be filled anew.)

Such, in substance, are the contents of all letters from bankrupts. If the receivers of the public moneys do not follow their example, it is because they are certain that no philosophical theory will save them from the punishment from which bankrupts escape, on the principle of leaving merchants entire liberty without requiring from them any guarantee against malpractices.

To sum up; the mercantile body being the depositary of a portion of the public wealth, and every merchant using his trust for the purpose of engaging in hazardous speculations which have no rule but his individual caprice, there must result numerous evils, bankruptcy among others, in consequence of which the producers and depositors of capital must support the loss of foolish enterprises to which they have not consented. To repair this injustice, the commercial body should be subjected to a guarantee of such a character that no merchant, and no company of contractors, can lose or even risk what is intrusted to them.

There is a measure by which this end might be accomplished, and which would render the mercantile class collectively responsible for all its transactions, and thus insure the social body against the frauds of commerce. This measure once adopted, bankruptcies, speculations, monopolies, and commercial revulsions would cease to occur; commercial relations would then employ, at most, a fourth part of the agents and the capital they now divert from productive labor. It is not important to explain this measure here; suffice it to say, it is a method belonging to the sixth Period, and is in every sense opposed to the absurd method called Free Competition.

Let us continue our analysis of these mercantile abuses, which should lead us to suspect the whole existing system of commerce, and to seek some method for the exchange of products, less false than Free Competition, which would be better named *Anarchical Competition.*

III.

SPOLIATION OF THE SOCIAL BODY BY MONOPOLY AND FORESTALLING.

NEVER was the maxim,

Deformity itself is beautified by gold,

better verified, than by the favor and consideration which the monopolists and forestallers have obtained under the ægis of the Political Economists, who, influenced in the formation of their judgments only by the power of gold, flatter dominant vices in order to conceal their ignorance how to remedy them.

Monopoly is the most odious of commercial crimes, in that it affects the poorest class of producers. If there occurs a scarcity in any article of food, or in produce of any kind, the monopolists are on the look-out to aggravate the evil. They buy up the stock on hand, make advances on the supplies expected, take the article out of the market, and double or treble the price by circulating exaggerated reports of scarcity, and thus exciting fears which are discovered, too late, to be unfounded. They are a band of disorganizers—vultures let loose against honest Industry. They are, nevertheless, upheld by a class of savants—the

Economists—and nothing is more respectable at the present time· than forestalling and stock-jobbing, which are called, in the language of the day, speculating and financiering, because it would be rude to call them by their right names.

A singular result of the Civilized Order is, that if the classes evidently pernicious—the monopolists and forestallers, for instance—were *directly* suppressed, the evil would become so much the greater; we had sufficient proof of this under the Reign of Terror.

It is this fact which has led the philosophers to conclude that the merchants should not be interfered with, should be left free. A curious remedy, this, for an evil—to maintain it, because we have failed to discover its antidote! One should have been sought, and till it had been discovered, the schemes of the monopolists and forestallers, instead of being extolled, should have been denounced; we should have encouraged researches for some method competent for their suppression, and this would have been found in Collective Competition.

And why do the philosophers seek to palliate such calamities as bankruptcy, monopoly, forestalling, stock-jobbing, usury, etc.? It is because public opinion says to them:—"We know all these abuses which you so much regret, but since you are men of science, and more enlightened than we, apply yourselves to seeking for their remedies; till then, your sciences and your rhetoric are as useless as the verbiage of a doctor who talks Greek and Latin to a patient, without procuring him any relief." The philosophers, anticipating this reproach, blind themselves to the evil instead of exposing it, and pretend that monopoly and forestalling, usury and stock-jobbing, are the perfection of commercial wisdom. With their jargon about analytic methods, with all their metaphysical abstractions about "the perception of sensations which give birth to ideas," they plunge the world into a scientific lethargy, and endeavor to persuade it that all is for the best in the present social Order. They find it much more easy to praise or to palliate permanent abuses than to occupy themselves with correctives, in seeking for which they would run the risk of losing their time and labor without arriving at any result. Hence we find the philosophers defending monopoly and forestalling as being useful to the public interest.

Let us analyze the achievements of these monopolists. I shall cite two examples; one, of the monopoly in grains, which is the most pernicious; the other, of the monopoly in raw materials, which appears more excusable since it embarrasses Industry only, without starving the people.

1. MONOPOLY OF GRAINS.—The fundamental principle of the existing commercial systems, the principle of *non-interference with commerce*, gives to the merchants the absolute proprietorship of the produce in which they traffic. They are allowed the right of taking it out of the market, concealing it, and even of burning it, as the Dutch East India Company have done more than once, publicly burning whole warehouses of cinnamon to raise the price of that article. And what they have done with cinnamon, they would do with wheat but for the fear of being stoned by the people. They would have destroyed half the grain in store, or left it to rot, in order to sell the other half at four times its value. Indeed, do we not in our ports constantly see grain thrown into the docks, grain which merchants have left to decay while waiting for a rise in the market?

I myself, in my capacity as clerk, have presided over these infamous operations, and have, in one day, caused twenty thousand quintals of rice to be thrown into the sea, rice which might have been sold, before it was allowed to decay, at a fair price, if the holder had been less greedy of gain. It is the social body which supports the loss of this waste, which is constantly going on under the principle of non-interference with commerce.

Suppose, carrying out this principle, that a rich company of merchants should, in a year of famine such as 1709, monopolize all the grain in a small state like Ireland, at a time when the general scarcity, and the prohibition in neighboring states against exportation rendered supplies from abroad almost impossible? Suppose that the company, after having bought up all the grain in the market, should refuse to sell it except at three or four times its value, saying:—"This grain is our property; it pleases us to sell it at three or four times the original cost; if you refuse to buy it on these terms, get your supplies elsewhere, import them from abroad. Meanwhile, if a fourth of the population die of famine, what matters that to us? We shall persist in our speculation, and are only carrying out the principle of commercial liberty, sanctioned by Political Economy."

I ask wherein the proceedings of such a company would differ from those of a band of highway robbers? For their monopoly would compel the whole nation, under penalty of starvation, to pay them a ransom equal to triple or quadruple the value of their whole stock of grain. And when we consider that such a company, according to the rule of commercial liberty, would have the right to refuse to sell at any price, to leave the grain to rot in the warehouses while the people were perishing, think you that the famished nation would be bound in conscience to die of starvation for the honor of the vaunted principle of non-interference with commerce? Certainly not. Confess, then, that commercial freedom should be subjected to restrictions, according to the wants of the social body; that a merchant holding a surplus of any article of food of which he is neither the producer nor the consumer, should be considered as the *conditional depositary*, and not as the absolute owner. Confess that the merchants—the intermediate agents for the exchange of products—ought in their operations to be subordinated to the good of the mass, and not be left free to embarrass business relations by those disastrous manœuvres so much admired by the Economists.

Are merchants alone to be free from the social obligations imposed upon other and more deserving classes? If a *carte blanche* is given to a general, to a judge, to a doctor, they are not authorized for that reason to betray the army, to condemn the innocent, to kill the patient. When such men prevaricate, we see them punished; the treacherous general is shot, the corrupt judge is impeached. Merchants alone are held inviolable, alone are sure of impunity. Political Economy would forbid any interference with their machinations. If they famish a whole nation, if they embarrass its Industry by monopolies and bankruptcies, everything is justified by the simple title of Merchant, just as the quack in the play, who kills everybody with his pills, justifies himself by the single phrase, *Medicus sum*—I am a Doctor. And so in this age of social regeneration, we are to be persuaded that one of the least enlightened classes in the community can never, in any of its schemes, operate against the public good; formerly it was the Infallibility of the Pope, to-day it is the Infallibility of the Merchant.

2. MONOPOLY OF RAW MATERIALS.—I shall demonstrate the evils of this by an event which is taking place as I write, namely, the enormous rise in the price of foreign produce—sugar, coffee, cotton, etc. I shall speak particularly of cotton, because it is this which has advanced the most, and because it is an article of first necessity for our rising manufactures ; but my remarks will be applicable to monopolies of all kinds.

In the course of the Autumn of 1806, it was perceived that the importations of colonial products, and especially of cotton, would be small, and that the supplies would arrive too late in the season ; still there was no fear that the manufacturers would suffer, as there was stock enough in market to suffice for a year's consumption. The government, by ordering an inventory, could have established this fact, and meanwhile there would have been time to adopt the necessary precautions for the future. But the monopolists intervened, bought up and stored all the cotton in the market, and convinced the public, by false reports, that the manufacturers would be out of stock in less than three months. A rise in the market followed, which increased the price of cottons to double their usual rate, and threatened to ruin most of the French manufacturers, who could not advance the price of their fabrics to meet the advance in the raw material, and many of whom had, in consequence, to close their establishments and dismiss their operatives.

Meanwhile there was in fact no real scarcity ; on the contrary, the rich manufacturers, themselves become monopolists, had purchased cotton on speculation, and after reserving supplies for their own mills, were selling the surplus at the advanced rates.

In a word, the stock which was wanted by the regular consumers got into the hands of the speculators, and it was discovered, in the end, that France was neither devoid of supplies nor threatened with a scarcity.

In this conjuncture, what advantages did the community derive from commercial license—from free competition ? Simply these :—

1. The doubling in price of a staple material of which there was no real scarcity, and the price of which should have been advanced little if any.

2. The closing up of manufactories which had been slowly and with difficulty established.

3. The enriching of a coalition of monopolists and forestallers to the detriment of productive industry.

These are simple facts. It will be replied to my argument, that if the government had interfered with free competition and the right of monopoly, matters would have been made worse. I admit it; but you only prove by this, that the Economists know no remedy for monopoly. Is that a reason for not seeking one? And does it follow that monopoly is right? When you know no antidote for a social disease, have courage enough to confess that it is a calamity. Do not listen to the philosophers, who extol the evil only to excuse themselves for their ignorance how to correct it. When they counsel you to tolerate monopoly and forestalling for fear of a greater evil, they resemble the ignoramus who advises you to let a fever take its course because he knows no means of arresting it. Because men are ignorant of the means of preventing monopoly, is it prudent, therefore, to tolerate it without limit? No; and I shall show that the government might often have prevented such calamities as I have mentioned, without either resorting to force, or exercising any arbitrary power. Let us give an illustration applicable to the present case.

Suppose that the government, in order to save its cotton manufactures, had wished to restrain the monopolists, and had sent an agent to a given dealer in Paris, who in January, 1807, had a stock of cotton on hand which cost 5,000,000 francs, and for which he refused 8,000,000, because he calculated, in his moderation, to double his capital in three months. The agent might have said to such a man:—" The hoarding up of cotton by you and your accomplices threatens the ruin of our manufacturers, to whom you refuse to sell at fair prices. You are therefore ordered to deliver up your stock at 20 or 25 per cent. profit, instead of 100 per cent. which you demand. Your cottons shall be distributed among the small manufacturers, and not among the large, who are themselves monopolists leagued together for the spoliation of the small."

What would have been the result of such a measure? Let us observe, first, that it would not have been at all unjust, for the speculator would, at the end of three months, have received

6,000,000 for a stock which cost him 5,000,000, and would thus have made in that time 20 per cent. which is four times as much as a farmer makes in a whole year, after the most assiduous labor.

In consequence of this summons, all the monopolists who had calculated on doubling their capital, would have decided to sell their cotton at twenty per cent. profit, while the manufacturers would have suffered little if any, and would not have been compelled to close their establishments and dismiss their hands. This measure would have saved them and brought down a blessing upon the government. It would in no way have hindered importation from abroad, for if America in 1806 sent us cottons in the hope to sell them at twenty cents, she would have sent us still more with the prospect of getting twenty-five ; whence it will be seen that the government ought to interfere to prevent monopoly, not after the manner of the Jacobins who despoiled the holders by paying them with worthless paper, but by setting a limit to profits in order to prevent their degenerating into extortion.

It is right then, in Civilized Politics, when a short supply of any staple product is foreseen, and when its scarcity is likely to lead speculators to forestall the market, that the government should declare it to be *hors de commerce* (out of the regular market) by setting a maximum price upon it fixed at a rate high enough to encourage importations, say at twenty or twenty-five per cent. above the average market price, interdicting traffic in it, even indirectly, on the part of speculators who have no legitimate demand or consumption for it, and limiting the stock of each merchant to the amount of his usual operations, as shown by an average of his sales for several previous years.

I will not stop to indicate the other provisional measures which might be adopted against monopoly — measures it would be useless to make known, since Collective Competition or the commercial method of the sixth Period, instead of suppressing monopoly, speculation, and other such abuses, prevents them. In their ignorance of preventive measures, men are inexcusable for not, at least, having tried palliative measures, such as declaring products *hors de commerce* — a measure which France should have adopted in the winter of 1807, especially in regard to cottons.

And because the price of foreign products was allowed to

advance to double the usual rates, did that augment the supplies? No; the prices might have been quadrupled, without this advance removing the obstacles which the war interposed against importations; the rise in the price of raw materials, then, ends only in spoliating the manufacturers and consumers for the benefit of the speculators. Now during a crisis, when it is permissible to set aside ordinary rules and customs, who should be protected, the consumers and manufacturers, or a few birds of prey leagued together to derange Industry by unfounded alarms, and to monopolize products of which they are not consumers, and for which, before the crisis, they had no demand?

How easy it would be to confound these speculators by retorting upon them their own arguments! If they may be believed, there is a scarcity of everything; soon it will be impossible to obtain any product, even for its weight in gold. To which the government might reply:—" Either you believe that there will be supplies for the manufacturer and for general consumption, or you do not believe it. In either case you should be compelled to give up your stock; for if importations are to cease, if there is to be a positive deficiency, it becomes useless to protect your machinations, since they accelerate the ruin of Industry by subjecting it to a heavy ransom, and embarrassing it in a time of scarcity; but if there are means of securing supplies, by importation or otherwise, you are disturbers, alarmists who aggravate a temporary evil. Thus whatever be your opinion as to the continuation or cessation of supplies, you deserve punishment, and should consider yourselves fortunate that we go no further than to declare your goods *hors de commerce*, and to compel you to sell them, especially when we leave you the enormous profit of twenty-five per cent. above the usual rates.

By prolonging this discussion, it would be easy for me to prove that, without embarassing commercial relations, and without leaving the circle of Civilized politics, it would still be practicable to put a curb on the license of monopolists. The necessity of so doing in regard to bread and the trade in grain has been recognised by nearly all the governments of Europe. It is known that if the speculators in bread-stuffs enjoyed entire liberty, if they could form companies for buying up the harvest in the field—storing the grain and thus keeping it out of the market—

we should have periodical famines, extending even to years of plenty. How often, in fact, have the speculators succeeded in famishing a country, despite the danger of being stoned by the people and prosecuted by the government, which in times of distress would force them to open their warehouses rather than allow the people to become desperate. If, even now, we see the monopolists braving all perils, what would they not do in case they possessed entire liberty, and the certainty of protection?

You, political writers, who compose theories on the Duties of Man, do you not recognise the Duties of Society? And is not the first of these to suppress the parasites who spoliate Industry and grow rich on the sufferings of the people? If you had possessed the courage to denounce such abuses, you would before now have discovered their remedy—Collective Competition. Despite all its absurdities, how much wiser was Antiquity than we, in Commercial politics! It openly despised and scouted commercial abuses, while as for these industrial vultures, these monopolists who receive the incense of modern philosophy, which is the shameless apologist of every measure however infamous, that leads to the amassing of gold, it devoted them to infamy.

IV.

SPOLIATION OF THE SOCIAL BODY BY AGIOTAGE.[*]

AGIOTAGE is the brother of Monopoly; they have each in turn subjugated public opinion to the extent of making even sovereigns submit, and of openly opposing the operations of princes, who, deceived by certain sophisms, dare not even contemplate resistance, nor propose the discovery of any other commercial system. The following is an example of the tyranny which Agiotage exercises over sovereigns. I select a recent fact—the last manœuvre of the French Agioteurs.

During the late war with Austria, an obscure financial conspiracy counterbalanced the victories of Ulm and of Austerlitz. At

---

[*] We retain this term because there is no one word in the English language sufficiently comprehensive to be substituted for it; it signifies the manœuvres of speculators to raise or lower the price of public funds, stocks of all kinds, and the products of industry; it consequently comprises stock-gambling, speculation by means of monopoly and forestalling, and in general all plots and schemes for producing a factitious rise or fall in the market. — *Translator.*

the moment when France manifested the blindest confidence in the operations of the Chief of the Empire, the Agioteurs caused to break out the symptoms of a universal distrust. One would have said that it was Varron who commanded our armies. In two months the Agioteurs of Paris committed unparalleled ravages upon the Industry of France; it required the flood of sudden and miraculous victories which followed, to finally silence these Agioteurs, whose schemes threatened to destroy public credit and made one shudder to think into what financial distress France would have fallen, if she had made only a neutral campaign, without either successes or reverses.

The pretexts of the alarmists were based on the advance which, they said, had been made by the Bank of France for the opening of the campaign; this advance was estimated at fifty millions of francs, which was only a hundredth part of the territorial revenue of the country. And even if this advance had not been guaranteed by the whole capital of the Bank and by the public deposites, was it not amply guaranteed in the eyes of the French, by the confidence reposed in their sovereign? And how could they who laughed at the combined powers of heaven and hell when they saw Napoleon at the head of their armies, take alarm at an advance which did not amount to a hundredth part of the national revenue? Far from having any fears at the opening of a campaign, the French would have voluntarily pledged a portion of their capital that their Emperor would be victorious; they had not, then, the least doubt as to the reïmbursement of the small loan in question. Nevertheless, the Agioteurs caused to break out the symptoms of a universal distrust, and brought the Bank into discredit because it had responded to the wishes of the whole people, in seconding the efforts of their great Chief.

There is a Power, then, which exercises ascendance over heroes, as over the public opinion of nations; this Power is Agiotage, which controls at will the whole industrial mechanism; it places empires at the mercy of a class of parasites, who being neither land-owners nor manufacturers, caring for nothing but their strong-box, and being able to change their country from one day to another, are interested in spoliating all, and preying alternately upon every branch of Industry. And though we see our economical theories upholding such scourges as Agiotage, Monopoly,

Bankruptcy, etc., which constantly derange the whole industrial system, which baffle sovereigns even, and weaken the confidence that they inspire in their people,—though we see these infamies, and so many others engendered by the system of commercial license, no writer has the courage to denounce this absurd science called Political Economy, to condemn the existing commercial mechanism, or to propose any new method of industrial relations. They all cringe basely before commercial vices at which they are secretly indignant, and sound the praises of commerce, without devising any means for throwing off its yoke—so frightened are the Civilizees at the idea of reforms requiring a degree of inventive genius of which they believe themselves incapable.

Doubtless the political economists are secretly ashamed of their mercantile system; but to save their theories, they allow the evil to increase. They flatter these political pigmies, these Agioteurs and Monopolists whom they have not the art to restrain, and accustom the public mind to truckle and bow at the very name of Commerce. How completely do such scandals give the lie to modern science, which makes so great a boast of its achievements. In what a quagmire has this science plunged modern empires! Were we not less degraded, and was not Civilization less contemptible, when mercantile philosophy and the economic sciences were yet unborn?

Let us demonstrate by a few details that these commercial gamblers, so much revered under the name of speculators, are nothing more than a band of mitigated Clubists—of Industrial Jacobins. They have, like the Clubists, the custom of affiliation, and a tacit understanding to aggravate every scourge which befalls Industry. As the Clubists had the tact to interfere between the Government and the People, and to get the mastery of both, so the mercantile speculators know how to render themselves mediators between the Government and Industry, to subordinate them both to their intrigues, and to circumvent and mislead the public by a feigned solicitude for the interests of agriculture and manufactures. Without legal authority like the Clubs, they succeed in managing everything to suit their own interests.

The commercial Agioteurs, like the Jacobins, possess in an eminent degree the art of dividing their opponents and conquering them in detail. They both have secret conclaves for preparing their grand schemes of spoliation, and both disguise themselves under the mask of good intentions. On the one hand, it is to aid in the diffusion of political light, on the other to facilitate the circulation of products and of capital, but in reality their motives are the exact opposite of their pretensions. In their bold strokes, we find again the same tactics. With the political operators, it is the pretext of a great conspiracy, of which there exists in fact only the shadow, and on the strength of which thousands of victims are arrested and sent to prison, until a new conspiracy is pretended, which serves as an excuse for sacrificing still other victims. With the Agioteurs, it is the pretext of a great scarcity, the danger of famine, of which they manage to get up the appearance by buying up and monopolizing the product in which they would operate ; they suddenly raise the price of this product to an exorbitant rate, and thus subject all the manufacturers and others who employ or consume it, to an enormous ransom, after which they forestal some other product and spoliate another class of manufacturers and consumers.

Thus the political and commercial operators have one and the same tactics, namely, that of disorganizing and spoliating, under the cover of pretended calamities. In a word, the revolutionary clubs, or leagues of poor agitators for the spoliation of the rich, and the forestallers, or league of rich agitators, for the spoliation of the poor, present in all their manœuvres the most complete analogy. They are two classes of Jacobins ; the one rude and harsh in form, the other refined and polite. The reader will be better convinced of these facts, when I shall have explained the extent and the regularity of development which these disorders will assume in the fourth Phase of Civilization, to which we are tending. The land-holders will then become the mere slaves of Commerce, which I consider to differ but little from Agiotage, since most of the wealthier merchants are more or less implicated in its manœuvres, despite their affected lamentations over such scourges, of which they are secretly abettors and joint-partners.

But I have already said that the inherent vices of a profession are not individual vices ; that a lawyer in fleecing his client, an Agioteur in spoliating the public, are not to be blamed ; that the fault is attributable exclusively to Civilization, which engenders

so many branches of parasitic and pernicious Industry, and to
the philosophic sciences, which would persuade us that this infamous Civilization is the social destiny of Man, and that God has
invented nothing better for the organization of human relations.

V.

SPOLIATION OF THE SOCIAL BODY BY COMMERCIAL PARASITISM.

THE abuse of which I shall now speak, though not so scandalous as those just described, is none the less prejudicial to the social body.

In an age which has carried economy even into the minutest
details, substituting chickory for coffee, and making other savings
which serve only to favor the impositicns of tradesmen and to
annoy consumers, who can hardly obtain pure and good articles
at any price—in an age so mean and parsimonious, how is it
that no one has remarked that the chief economy should be
economy of hands, economy of intermediate agents, who might be
dispensed with, but who are so abundant in unproductive departments like that of commerce.

I have already observed that it is frequently our custom to
employ a hundred persons in functions which, in Association,
would require but two or three, and that after the seventh social
Period, twenty men will suffice to supply the markets of a city to
which we now send a thousand. In respect to industrial organization, we are as unenlightened as nations ignorant of the use
of the mill, and which employ fifty laborers to crush the grain
which is ground among us by a single machine. Everywhere
the superfluity of agents is frightful; in all commercial operations
the number is at least four times larger than is requisite. Since
the reign of free competition, we see tradesmen swarming even in
our villages. Peasants renounce agriculture to become peddlers;
if they have only a calf to sell, they go and spend days in town,
idling about markets and public houses.

In cities like Paris, there are as many as three thousand gro-
cers, where three hundred would amply suffice. The profusion
of agents is the same in the smallest towns; those which are visited now in course of the year by a hundred commercial travel-

lers and a hundred peddlers, were not visited, perhaps, in 1788 by more than ten ; yet at that period there was no lack of either provisions or clothing, and at very moderate prices, though trades men were less numerous by a third than at the present day.

This multiplicity of rival tradesmen drives them constantly to the adoption of measures the most foolish, and the most ruinous to the community ; for superfluous agents, like monks, being consumers and not producers, are spoliators of the social body. It is now admitted that the monks of Spain, the number of whom is estimated at 500,000, might produce enough, if they were employed in agriculture, for the subsistence of 2,000,000 of persons. It is the same with superfluous tradesmen, the number of whom is incalculable ; and when we come to explain the commercial method of the sixth Period, Collective Competition, we shall be convinced that Commerce might be carried on with a fourth as many agents as it now employs, and that there are, in France alone, a million of inhabitants withdrawn from agriculture and manufactures by the superabundance of agents created by free competition. France alone, then, in consequence of the error of the Economists, suffers an annual loss of products sufficient for the subsistence of 4,000,000 inhabitants.

Besides the waste of human labor, the present Order causes also a waste of capital and of products. I shall cite as an illustration of this, one of the most common abuses of the present day, namely, *the breaking down of commercial rivals.*

Since the Revolution, we hear of nothing in the commercial world but the breaking down of rival tradesmen. Become too numerous, they compete furiously with each other for sales, which owing to the excess of competition are more and more difficult every day. A city which consumed a thousand tons of sugar when it had but ten tradesmen, still consumes but a thousand tons when the number is increased to forty ; this is seen all over the world. Now we hear these swarms of merchants complaining of the dullness of trade, when they ought rather to complain of the superabundance of tradesmen. They exhaust themselves in making useless displays to attract customers, and run into the most foolish extravagance for the purpose of crushing their rivals.

It is an error to suppose that the merchant is a slave to interest alone ; he is equally a slave to jealousy and pride. Some of them ruin themselves for the sterile honor of " doing a big business," others from a desire to break down a rival whose success enrages them. Commercial ambition, however low it may be, is still violent, and if the achievements of Miltiades disturbed the sleep of Themistocles, it may also be said that the sales of one tradesman disturb the sleep of another. Hence comes this insane competition by which so many merchants ruin each other, and exhaust themselves in expenses the burden of which falls ultimately upon the consumer ; for, in the last analysis, all loss is supported by the community at large. Now if the new commercial order (Collective Competition) would reduce by three fourths the number of commercial agents and the amount of commercial expenses, the price of products would be diminished in a like proportion ; then we should see production increase in proportion to the demand occasioned by the reduction in price, and to the amount of labor and capital restored to agriculture by the diminution in the number of commercial agents.

One abuse leads to another ; this is as true in Commerce as in Government. For example, multiplicity of commercial agents leads to speculation and bankruptcy. We see a striking proof of this in the rivalry of stage-coach companies, which for the sake of ruining each other would often be willing to carry travellers gratis. In seeing them lower their prices, in order to break each other down, people say : " Soon they will pay us a premium to go in their conveyances."

It is important to dwell on these details, in order to prove that the Economists, in assuming gain to be the only motive of tradesmen, have grossly deceived themselves. What sensible man would have conceived the idea of carrying passengers from Paris to Rennes for eighteen francs ? Yet such are the follies produced by the mania for breaking down rivals. The result of these industrial conflicts, so agreeable to travellers, is the bankruptcy of the various parties engaged in them, who, at some months apart, are ruined by each other. The loss occasioned by their bankruptcy is borne, in the end, by the public who always take an interest in the most foolish enterprises which, notwithstanding their non-success, yield a profit to the bankrupts by the spoliation of their co-associates whose funds are never reimbursed. Hence it is that the merchants, certain to

save themselves, in case of reverses, by a bankruptcy, hazard
everything in order to ruin a rival and rejoice over the downfall
of a neighbor, like those Japanese who put out one eye at the
door of an enemy that they may cause him, according to their law,
to lose both. The old established commercial houses, discon-
certed by these destructive rivalries, renounce a profession become so hazardous and corrupt through the intrigues of the new-
comers, who, in order to obtain the vogue, commence by selling
at a loss. The old houses not caring to lose in this way, find
themselves deserted, deprived of custom, and unable to meet their
engagements. Soon, the two parties fall into difficulties and are
obliged to recur to the money-lender, whose usurious aid increases
their embarrassment and hastens the fall of both.

It is thus that *Free Competition*, by engendering bankruptcies,
encourages the system of usury, and gives to it the colossal importance it now possesses. At the present day, usurers are
found in our smallest towns ;* everywhere we see men who, under
the name of bankers and brokers, have no other trade than that
of lending on usury, and thus stimulating the strife of competition. By their advances they encourage a host of superfluous
tradesmen, who plunge into the most absurd speculations and
who, when they are in difficulties, have recourse to the bankers
by whom they are " shaved." The latter, from their favorable
position in the commercial arena, aggravate the evil, and resem-

* The number of usurers in France at the present day is incredible. It is beginning
to be appreciated on the borders of the Rhine, where the Jews have got possession of
a large portion of the landed property ; the evil is less perceptible in the interior,
because usury is practised there by the native inhabitants. The most lucrative calling
at the present time, after monopoly and stock-jobbing, is lending money on security,
on bonds and mortgages, and discounting notes and drafts. Shrewd merchants retire
from commerce to engage in this pretty business, which the Revolution has favored by
the changes it has effected in the ownership of the soil.

I do not pretend to blame the usurers ; all political vices are imputable to circumstances, and not at all to the persons who profit by them. It is fortunate in such a
conjuncture that the Jews have not become very numerous in France, for being a people especially given to usury, they would by this time have become possessed of most
of the landed property, and have acquired that political weight which everywhere attaches to their sect. France would have become nothing but a vast synagogue ; for
if the Jews held only a fourth of its landed property, they would still have immense influence on account of their secret and indissoluble league. This danger is one of the
thousand symptoms which attest our social degradation, the defective character of our
industrial system, and the necessity of reconstructing it, throughout, on an entirely
new plan — that is, in case Civilization is to be prolonged, which God forbid !

ble those hordes of Arabs who hover about an army, waiting to despoil the vanquished, whether enemies or friends.

In view of so many rapines and absurdities engendered by Commerce, can it be doubted that the ancients were right in treating it with contempt? As for the philosophers, who in their theories of Political Economy extol and defend it, are they not a set of shameless charlatans? And can we hope to see the reign of truth, of justice, or of order, in industrial relations till we have condemned the present commercial system, and invented a method for the Exchange of Products, less degrading to the social body?

VI.

CONCLUDING REMARKS ON COMMERCE.

I HAVE shown in the preceding chapters that Commerce, while appearing to serve Industry, tends in every way to spoliate it, and have given four illustrations of this, drawn from Bankruptcy, Monopoly, Agiotage, and Parasitism.

I. Bankruptcy spoliates the social body for the benefit of the merchants, who never support its losses; for if the merchant is prudent, he has calculated the chances of the bankruptcy of his customers, and fixed his profits at a rate which will cover the presumed risk. If he is imprudent or dishonest (qualities very similar in commercial affairs), he will not be long in becoming a bankrupt himself, and will then indemnify himself for the losses he has experienced by the bankruptcies of others; whence it follows, that the loss falls upon society at large, and not upon the merchant.

II. Monopoly spoliates the social body, because the advance in price of a monopolized product falls ultimately upon the consumer, and, before that, upon the manufacturer, who, obliged to keep up his establishment, makes pecuniary sacrifices and manufactures at a very small profit; in the hope of better times, he sustains the business upon which he bases his calculations for support, but does not succeed for some time in establishing his prices at rates to meet the advanced price of raw materials forced upon him by the monopolists.

III. Agiotage spoliates the social body by withdrawing capital from productive enterprises for the purpose of operating with it in public funds, of speculating in the rise and fall of stocks—a game which, in the hands of skilful players, yields enormous profits. The result is, that agriculturists and manufacturers can not obtain the capital necessary for their business, except at an enormous interest; and useful enterprises, yielding only moderate profits, are disdained for financial speculations which absorb the principal part of the floating capital.

IV. Parasitism, or superfluity of intermediate agents, spoliates the social body in two ways: first, by withdrawing an immense number of hands, which it employs in unproductive labors; second, by the immorality and disorders which are engendered by the desperate struggle between innumerable competitors, whose fraudulent manœuvres put obstacles in the way of the exchange of products, amounting frequently to prohibition.*

This digression will suffice, I think, to show that Free Competition has produced new disorders, not only in Commerce, but in all the trades and professions to which it has been extended. For example, it has more or less disorganized the learned professions; witness those of Medicine and Law. During the period when these were left wholly free, quacks were seen traversing the country and killing off the credulous peasants by the thousand, on the principle of unrestricted competition. The lawyers, on the other hand, imitating the noble example of Com-

---

* I will cite only one proof from among a thousand. We have seen the knavery of the Russian and Chinese merchants operate even to the extent of nearly suspending all business between the entrepots of Kiatka and Zuruchaitu.

"The Russians," says Raynal, "had given to the Chinese spurious furs, and the Chinese had given to the Russians spurious gold." (Behold your true merchants and Civilizees!) "The distrust between them increased to such an extent that business came nearly to a stand, and was for some time reduced to little or nothing"—though the demand had not ceased, and the respective sovereigns did not interrupt but rather facilitated the caravans.

The embarrassment of which I speak was perceived only because it affected a large mass of business relations. We have here an example of a whole branch of commerce declining, while in a state of full liberty, by the simple effect of fraud. And to how many other hindrances does this general system of knavery and fraud give rise in all industrial relations! How much expense, management, anxiety, and time, it costs to purchase an article the value of which is unknown to us! And if, after every precaution, after journeys, etc., we are still constantly deceived in our purchases, how great would be the economy of time, trouble, and expense, in case the exchange of products were effected all over the earth without the least dishonesty! This result will take place in the seventh Period; even in the sixth it will be rare to experience any deception in commercial affairs.

merce, were accustomed to drum up clients, stopping peasants in the public places and at the doors of the courts, and soliciting their patronage. This prostitution of a profession up to that time honorable, excited public indignation, and led to the adoption of repressive laws, to reforming the rules of matriculation, etc., in opposition to the principle of free competition.

In respect to professional liberty, as in respect to political liberty, men have acted blindly, not knowing where their fine philosophic theories might lead them. Now people begin to see the error, and in seeking to remedy it, commit greater errors still, such as that of confounding the interests of Commerce with those of Manufactures of which it is the natural enemy.

Let us establish a comparison showing the inutility of the Merchants, and the importance of the Manufacturers, the interests of which two classes are so often confounded.

The Manufacturer can easily supply the place and perform the functions of the Merchant: he can purchase his raw material of first hands, and either consign his manufactured products directly, or send his clerks over the country to sell them ; but the Merchant can in no case supply the place or perform the functions of the Manufacturer.

If a city loses its Merchants, as happened in Marseilles in the time of the plague, their place is at once supplied with new-comers, if the locality is at all favorable to commerce. If a city loses its Manufacturers, as happened in the case of Louvain, we do not find other Manufacturers transporting their machines and business there. Merchants abound wherever there are the means of trading freely and advantageously ; but Manufacturers are not always established, even in places where everything favors their success. The departure of the Manufacturers from a country would reduce all the Merchants dealing in raw materials, and all their agents for buying or selling, to inactivity ; while the departure of the Merchants would cause no stoppage of Manufactories, whose directors and clerks, as I have said, could supply the place of the Merchants.

For example, the protestant Manufacturers of France, when they emigrated to Germany, were not replaced by catholic Manufacturers ; their business was expatriated with them ; but if Louis XIV had proscribed only the Merchants and the Bankers, making an exception of the Manufacturers, the protestant Merchants would have been replaced the following year by catholic Merchants, and France would have experienced only the loss of men and of money, which would have been easily repaired, instead of a loss of manufacturing Industry, which was irreparable. We find all governments anxious to send their Merchants to establish themselves in the East, but no government would like to see its Manufacturers establish themselves there. On the contrary, every nation is eager to attract Manufacturers from China and India, though there is little desire to attract their Merchants or Navigators.

The further we extend this comparison, the more we shall be convinced that the Merchants and Bankers should be rigorously watched, and be restricted to the useful functions of which I have spoken. If we grant them full license, according to the advice of the economists, they turn their capital against Industry; they imitate undisciplined soldiers who, the moment they are free from the fear of punishment, commence pillaging the country in which they should preserve order.

It was a long time before the moderns came to suspect their idol, or to admit that the entire commercial system, which is a tissue of abuses, must be changed. It may be replied, that it would be better to propose a remedy for these abuses than to declaim against them, and that I should hasten to present the theory of Collective Competition, which is to extirpate all commercial disorders.

To this I answer, that my object is not to ameliorate Civilization, but to expose it, and to create a desire for a better social mechanism, by showing that the present Order, both as a whole and in all its parts, is absurd, and that far from making any real progress we are falling more and more into political errors; witness the late theories on the subject of political liberty and commercial freedom — theories against which Nature and reason alike protest.

The collective impulses which Nature gives to the human race are never deceptive. When the great majority of mankind despise a given profession, like that of Commerce for instance, and when this feeling is dictated by natural instinct, be sure that the object of it contains some latent and odious evil. Which of the two have been the more sensible, the moderns who honor commerce, or the ancients who despised it? *Vendentes et latrones*, says the Gospel, which makes no distinction between the two classes. Thus thought Jesus Christ, who "cast out all them that sold and bought in the temple," and said to them with evangelic frankness:—" Ye have made my house a den of thieves."

Fecistis cum speluncam latronum.

In accordance with Christ, classic Antiquity coupled traffickers and thieves in the same category, and placed them under the patronage of Mercury, the god of thieves. It appears that at that epoch the mercantile calling was considered as little less than infamous, for St. Chrysostom assures us that "a tradesman can not be acceptable to God;" hence tradesmen have been excluded from the honor of canonization, though the elect of all other professions have been admitted to it, even a lawyer, to wit, St. Yves.

I mention these incidents to show the opinion of the ancients, which I would compare with that of the moderns. I am far from approving the exaggeration of the former; it was as ridiculous to proscribe and sneer at tradesmen, as it is at the present day to exalt them to the clouds. But which of the two extremes is the least absurd? In my opinion that of the ancients. Despite the commercial abuses which everywhere prevail and which should excite the indignation of all honorable minds, despite the testimony of sound reason which shows by the analysis of Commerce that it is a parasitic, subordinate, and disorganizing function, we see Commerce at the present day usurping the throne of public opinion. This was natural, since Civilization is essentially favorable to corruption, and tends by the influence of Commerce to the establishment of an industrial system which will be more odious and perfidious than the present, and of which I will point out the germ. For the rest, till I have made known the Mechanism which is to replace the present system of Commerce, and cause the reign of truth and justice to succeed to that of commercial perfidy and folly, I can understand how my criticisms may seem out of place and even revolting. Meanwhile, I denounce the cowardice of the philosophers who have not dared to engage in researches for such a system, but who have dared to call themselves the friends of truth while acting as the apologists of Commerce.

VII.

DECLINE OF THE CIVILIZED ORDER THROUGH THE INFLUENCE OF
JOINT-STOCK CORPORATIONS, WHICH ARE LEADING TO THE FOURTH
PHASE.

I SHALL merely allude to a subject here which should be treated
in full, namely, The Right of Man to Labor, in other words, the
right to regular, congenial, and remunerative employment.* I
shall take good care not to renew the old political controversy
upon the rights of man. After the revolutions to which this controversy has given rise, will it be believed that we are running
the risk of new political convulsions for having overlooked the
first and most important of these rights, namely, the Right to Labor?—a Right of which our politicians have never made the
least mention, according to their uniform habit of omitting the
most important questions in every branch of science.

Among the influences tending to restrict this right, I shall cite
the formation of privileged corporations which, conducting a
given branch of Industry, monopolize it, and arbitrarily close the
doors of labor against whomever they please.

These corporations will become dangerous, and lead to new
outbreaks and convulsions, only by being extended to the whole
commercial and industrial system. This event is not far distant,
and it will be brought about all the more easily from the fact
that it is not apprehended. The greatest evils have often sprung
from imperceptible germs, as for instance Jacobinism. And if
Civilization has engendered this and so many similar calamities,
may it not engender others which we do not now foresee? The
most imminent of these is the birth of a Commercial Feudalism,
or the Monopoly of Commerce and Industry by large joint-stock
companies, leagued together for the purpose of usurping and controlling all branches of industrial relations. Extremes meet;
and the greater the extent to which anarchical competition is car-

---

* The two primary rights of man, rights which have always been overlooked, are,
1st, the RIGHT TO EDUCATION, that is, the right of every individual to the development of the faculties and capacities given to him by Nature ; 2d, the RIGHT TO LABOR,
that is, the right of every individual to take part in those branches of Industry, Art,
and Science for which his education has fitted him.—*A. B.*

ried, the nearer is the approach to the reign of *universal Monopoly*, which is the opposite excess. It is the fate of Civilization to be always balancing between extremes. Circumstances are tending toward the organization of the commercial classes into federal companies or affiliated monopolies, which, operating in conjunction with the great landed interest, will reduce the middle and laboring classes to a state of commercial vassalage, and, by the influence of combined action, will become master of the productive industry of entire nations. The small operators will be forced, indirectly, to dispose of their products according to the wishes of these monopolists ; they will become mere agents, working for the mercantile coalition. We shall thus see the reappearance of Feudalism in an inverse order, founded on mercantile leagues and answering to the Baronial leagues of the middle ages.

Everything is concurring to produce this result. The spirit of commercial monopoly and financial speculation has extended even to the great ; the old nobility, ruined and dispossessed, seek distraction in financial speculations. The descendants of the old Knights excel in the mysteries of the Ready Reckoner and in the manœuvres of the stock-market, as their chivalrous ancestors excelled at the tournaments. Public opinion prostrates itself before the bankers and financiers, who in the capitals share authority with the government, and devise every day new means for the monopoly and control of Industry.

We are marching with rapid strides toward a Commercial Feudalism, and to the fourth Phase of Civilization. The philosophers, accustomed to reverence everything which comes in the name and under the sanction of commerce, will see this new Order spring up without alarm, and will consecrate their servile pens to celebrating its praises. Its debut will be one of brilliant promise, but the result will be an Industrial Inquisition, subordinating the whole people to the interests of the affiliated monopolists. Thus, the philosophers, within a brief period, will have permitted the social Movement to retrograde in two ways, first, by the violent Revolution which in 1793 conducted Europe rapidly toward Barbarism, and second, by the commercial anarchy and license which at the present day are causing a rapid decline toward the Feudal Order. Such are the melancholy results of our confidence in social guides who have no other object than to raise themselves by political intrigues to position and fortune. Philosophy needed some new subject to replace the old theological controversies, which it had completely exhausted; it was therefore to the Golden Calf, to Commerce, that it turned its eyes, making it an object of social idolatry and scholastic dispute.

It is no longer to the Muses nor to their votaries, but to Traffic and its heroes that Fame now consecrates her hundred voices. We hear no longer of Wisdom, of Virtue, of Morality; all that has fallen into contempt, and incense is now burnt only on the altar of Commerce. The true grandeur of a nation, its only glory, according to the economists, is to sell to neighboring nations more cloths and calicoes than we purchase of them. France, always infatuated with novelties, inclines before the folly of the day, so that, now, no one can think or write except in praise of august Commerce. Even the great are slaves to this mania; a minister who wishes to become popular must promise to every village —"*un Commerce immense et un immense Commerce ;*" a nobleman journeying through the provinces must announce himself in every town as a friend of Commerce, travelling for the good of Commerce. The savants of the nineteenth century are those who explain to us the mysteries of the stock-market. Poesy and the fine arts are disdained, and the Temple of Fame is open no longer except to those who tell us why sugars are "feeble," why soap is "firm." Since philosophy has conceived a passion for Commerce, Polyhymnia decks the new science with flowers. The tenderest expressions have replaced the old language of the merchants, and it is now said, in elegant phrase, that "sugars are languid"—that is, are falling; that "soaps are looking up"— that is, have advanced. Formerly, pernicious manœuvres like monopoly and speculation excited the indignation of writers; but now, these schemes are a title to distinction, and France announces them in a Pindaric strain, saying: "A rapid and unexpected movement has suddenly taken place in Soaps"—at which words we seem to see bars of soap leap from their boxes and wing their way to the clouds, while the speculators in soap hear their names resound through the whole land. Whatever Commerce touches, were it only a stock-certificate or a quintal of fish, the philosophers speak of in sublime style and in accents of delight. Under their pens, a cask of rum becomes a flask of rose-water, cheese exhales the perfume of the violet, and soap rivals the whiteness of the lily. All these flowers of rhetoric contribute, doubtless, to the success of Industry, which has found in the support of the Philosophers the same kind of assistance they have extended to the people, namely—fine phrases, but no results.

When were there so many abuses, so much anarchy in the industrial world as now, when the mercantile policy is in the ascendant. Because an insular nation, favored by the commercial indolence of France, has enriched itself by monopoly and maritime spoliation, behold all the old doctrines of philosophy disdained, Commerce extolled as the only road to truth, to wisdom, and to happiness, and the merchants become the pillars of the state, while all the continental Cabinets vie with each other in their submission to a Power which suborns them with the profits she has levied upon their people. One is ready to believe in magic on seeing kings and empires thus circumvented by a few commercial sophisms, and exalting to the skies the race of monopolists, stock-jobbers, agioteurs, and other industrial corsairs, who employ their influence in concentrating masses of capital, in producing fluctuations in the price of products, in ruining alternately all branches of industry, and in impoverishing the producing classes, who are spoliated *en masse* by vast monopolies, as we see herrings engulfed in the jaws of a whale.

To sum up:—I have already stated, in course of the discussion, what would be the effect of Collective Competition, which is the antidote of the present system.

I. It would lead, without compulsion and without the concession of exclusive privileges, to the formation of large Associations, which are the basis of all economy.

II. It would make the commercial body responsible to the community for all its operations, and allow to it only the conditional ownership of industrial products.

III. It would restore to productive Industry the capital now employed in Commerce; for the social body being fully insured against all malpractices on the part of merchants, they would everywhere have accorded to them entire confidence; they would have no occasion for employing large sums of money in their business, and the whole capital of the country would be invested in agriculture and manufactures.

IV. It would restore to productive Industry three fourths of the hands now employed in the unproductive functions of Commerce.

V. It would compel the commercial body, by a system of equitable taxation, to support its share of public expenses, which it now has the skill to avoid.

VI. Finally, it would establish in commercial relations a degree of probity and good faith, which, though less than will exist in the Combined Order, would still be immense as compared with the frauds and spoliations of the present system.

The above synopsis will create a desire for an entire chapter on Collective Competition, but I have already said that the object of this Prospectus is only to expose the ignorance of our social and political guides, and to explain the ends they should have had in view in their investigations. For the rest, of what use would it be to stop to explain the means of perfecting Civilization by measures, such as Collective Competition, borrowed from the sixth Period? What signifies to us the ameliorations of the sixth or seventh Periods, since we can overleap them both and pass immediately to the eighth, which therefore alone merits our attention?

When we shall have reached this Period, when we shall enjoy fully the happiness of the Combined Order, we can reason on the abuses of Civilization and their correctives at our ease. It is then that we may amuse ourselves with an analysis of the Civilized mechanism, which is the most curious of all, since it is that in which there is the greatest complication and confusion of elements. As for the present, the question is not to study, not to improve Civilization, but to quit it; it is for this reason that I shall not cease to fix the mind on the necessity of rejecting all half-measures, and of going straight to the proposed end by founding, without delay, an Association based upon the Serial order—an Association which, by furnishing a demonstration of Passional Harmony, will remove the philosophic cataract from the eyes of the human race, and raise all the nations of the globe—Civilized, Barbaric, and Savage—to their social destiny, —to Universal Unity.

INTERLUDE.

ON THE COURSE AND DEVELOPMENT OF CIVILIZATION.

I HAVE already notified the reader that I should, in the course of this work, insert several chapters of pure theory. The present one will be of that character; though anything but entertaining, it will be well to study it carefully, in order to get a clear idea of the course and development of Civilization, of which I shall point out the different stages of progress and decline, in the Table on the following page.

In indicating the social improvements to which various institutions in Civilization might have led, I have shown the ignorance of our social and political guides, who have not known how to take advantage of these means of escape from the Civilized Order.

The age is more ignorant still on the subject of the commercial mechanism, our analysis of which has exposed the persistence of the philosophers in error, and their blindness to the most positive proofs of the reigning ignorance in social science.

The supremacy of the commercial spirit will here be considered as a sign of the degeneration or decline of the Civilized Order; with this view, I shall show in the following Table, that the alternate decline and progress of this Society are accomplished by the sole impulse of Nature, and not by the speculative sciences, which have never been of the least assistance.

PHASES OF ASCENSION AND DECLENSION.

THE two Phases of Ascending Vibration operate a diminution of Direct or Personal Servitude.

The two Phases of Descending Vibration operate an increase of Collective or Indirect Servitude.

The APOGEE is the epoch at which Civilization presents a complete development of its sixteen characteristics, and assumes the forms the *least ignoble*. I do not say the *most noble*, because this Society is uniformly odious, and varies in its four Phases only by shades of perfidy and iniquity, which are always predominant.

TABLE

OF THE

ASCENDING AND DESCENDING PHASES OF CIVILIZATION.

Pivots of the Period	Individual Characteristic.	REIGN OF SELF-INTEREST; EGOISM.
	Collective Characteristic.	DUPLICITY OF SOCIAL ACTION.

ASCENDING VIBRATION.

INFANCY, OR FIRST PHASE.

Simple Germ.	Exclusive Marriage, or Monogamy.
Compound Germ.	Patriarchal and Military Feudalism.
PIVOT.	CIVIL RIGHTS OF THE WIFE.
Counterpoise.	Federation of the Great Barons.
Tone.	Illusions in Chivalry.

ADOLESCENCE, OR SECOND PHASE.

Simple Germ.	Commercial Privileges.
Compound Germ.	Cultivation of the Arts and Sciences.
PIVOT.	EMANCIPATION OF THE INDUSTRIAL CLASSES.
Counterpoise.	Representative System.
Tone.	Illusions in Liberty.

APOGEE, OR MATURITY.

Germs.	NAUTICAL ART. EXPERIMENTAL CHEMISTRY.
Characteristics.	DESTRUCTION OF FORESTS. FISCAL LOANS.

DESCENDING VIBRATION.

VIRILITY, OR THIRD PHASE.

Simple Germ.	Mercantile and Fiscal Spirit.
Compound Germ.	Joint-stock Companies.
PIVOT.	MARITIME MONOPOLY.
Counterpoise.	Free Competition.
Tone.	Illusions in Political Economy.

CADUCITY, OR FOURTH PHASE.

Simple Germ.	Agricultural Loan and Trust Companies.
Compound Germ.	Privileged Corporations, limited in number.
PIVOT.	INDUSTRIAL FEUDALISM.
Counterpoise.	Chiefs of the Industrial Feudalism.
Tone.	Illusions in Association.

N. B. We have replaced the original Table by the above taken from one of Fourier's later works.

In the preceding Table there will be observed an apparent contradiction, namely, that Civilization *falls into decline* by the birth of the Nautical Art, which is nevertheless the soul of social progress. [For the meaning of the word Decline, see page 88, where I explain how a social Period may decline through the progress of its institutions.]

By the term Nautical Art, I mean Navigation in its most extended sense, embracing the whole globe and bringing its seas and oceans under the empire of man. This Art, which is the finest trophy of the human mind, is not adapted to Civilization, but only to the sixth and following Periods. If Civilization has made such achievements in science, it is for its misfortune; it is laden with more than it can carry. In fact, the Nautical Art has produced the maritime monopoly of England and other calamities which could not take place in the sixth Period. Hence we see that excess of scientific discoveries may become detrimental to a Society, in the same way that the most wholesome food may become detrimental when taken in excess. Now the limit adapted to the capacity of the Civilized mechanism is partial navigation only —that is, coast and inland. It was necessary to pass to the sixth Period before organizing universal or ocean navigation, since this engenders among us numerous social and political convulsions, leading to the third and fourth phases of Civilization— to its decline and fall.

Each of the four Phases of Civilization, as well as the entire Period, has its term of Plenitude or APOGEE. It is evident that the third Phase has passed this point, since we see the reign of Maritime Monopoly, and also of other evils, such as bankruptcy, forestalling, agiotage, etc., engendered by the mercantile spirit.

[The abridged Table we have given of the Progressive Movement has no relation to the Mechanical Movement, which would present the *System of Passional Counter-march* in compound order—that is to say, would give the sixteen manœuvres of human character, or developments of the passions, in inverse order. It would indicate, first, their points of encounter and systematic strife, by collision, conflict, and divergence; then, the diffraction of the seven primitive passions and their formation in recurrent Series; and, finally, the grand *Pitched Battle of the Passions.* I

23

say *Pitched Battle*, because, although the passions are always in
collision and conflict in the five Societies organized in isolated
families, still their encounter in Civilization presents manœuvres
more curious and complicated than in any other Period. Thus it
is that the Civilized Mechanism is *the most brilliant Complication
of Horrors* that can be found on any globe; for it is a complete
inversion of the Combined Order, which is the wisest combination
of the Divine Mind.]

Let us remark, that in the three Phases of Civilization already
passed through, the philosophic sciences have never coöperated
in any way in the cause of social progress, though they arrogate
to themselves this trifling honor. They have always been *passive* in respect to the social Movement. I have already given
some proofs of this, which I will now sum up.

FIRST PHASE. — This Phase was engendered by the concession
of Civil Rights to the Wife, rights which the ancient philosophers, such as Confucius and those of Egypt and India, never
troubled themselves about. They never manifested even a desire
to ameliorate the condition of woman. The women of those times
possessed still less liberty than ours; they were refused partici-
pation in various amatory rights, such as the right of divorce, and
the moralists were indifferent, as at present, to their welfare.

SECOND PHASE. — Civilization entered upon this Phase through
a modification of the system of Slavery. It has been seen that
the amelioration of this system was the result of the Feudal Order,
which provided the laboring classes with the means of *collective
and gradual* affranchisement. By attaching the serfs to the soil,
and not to the individual, it turned to their advantage the weak-
nesses of every feudal lord; and the community being able to
obtain one concession from the avarice of a father, another from
the benevolence of a son, advanced step by step to liberty. This
was a process of which the ancient philosophers had no conception.

THIRD PHASE. — This Phase was developed by the influence
of the commercial policy which grew out of colonial monopolies.
This influence was not foreseen by the philosophers, and accordingly they have discovered no means of counterbalancing it, nor
even of attacking it in its most vexatory branch, which is Maritime Monopoly. They intermeddled with commercial politics,

not to combat its vices but to extol them, as I have shown in another Chapter.

Fourth Phase.—Civilization is tending to this Phase by the influence of *Joint-stock Corporations*, which, under cover of certain legal privileges, dictate terms and conditions to Labor, and arbitrarily exclude from it whomever they please. These corporations contain the germ of a vast Feudal Coalition, which is destined soon to invade the whole industrial and financial system, and give birth to a Commercial Feudalism. This the philosophers were far from foreseeing; and while they are wholly infatuated with the mercantile policy, the influence of which they so little anticipate, events are already in preparation which are to change this policy, and cause Society to decline to the fourth Phase of Civilization.*

But the philosophers do not trouble themselves about providing against future storms; they see the social Movement only in a retrospective sense, and are concerned but with the past and the present. At the present day, when the mercantile spirit is predominant, they decide, according to their custom, that the existing state of things is the perfection of human reason. They restrict themselves, therefore, to declaiming about what they see, without presuming that the Civilized Order may take new forms. And when Civilization shall have arrived, in due course, at its fourth Phase, when the Commercial Feudalism shall have become fully established, we shall see the philosophers come in, after the event, to make of it a new subject of speculation; we shall find them preaching up the vices of the fourth Phase, and writing scores of volumes on this new Order, in which they will again see the perfection of reason, as they see it now in the reign of Commerce.

---

* While engaged in the translation of this chapter, we find the following passage in a letter from the London correspondent of the *New York Tribune;* it is so illustrative that we deem it worthy of being inserted here as a note.—*Translator.*

"The immense success of the Credit Mobilier at Paris—which tends to monopolize the pawnbroking and banking business of the country, and to concentrate all the great companies of trade, public works, and even manufacturing enterprises, into one society—has given rise to the establishment of a similar institution in Austria, and Spain may soon likewise get the benefit of a Credit Mobilier. Swallowing up, by and by, all individual enterprise, and killing competition by an always-expanding capital, the Credits Mobiliers must soon either absorb the Government or be absorbed by it. In either case, they lead to a complete bankocracy, where the State is transformed from a political into an industrial, trading, and swindling Society."—*January* 14, '56.

SECOND ILLUSTRATION.

ON FREE MASONRY

AND

THE DEVELOPMENTS OF WHICH IT WAS SUSCEPTIBLE.

God is the enemy of uniformity; it is his will that the social Movement should perpetually vary, should always be either ascending or descending. To this end, he causes to spring up in our Societies, periodically, the germs of new institutions, sometimes beneficent, sometimes pernicious. It is for human reason to judge what use may be made of these germs—how to stifle the bad, like the Jacobin clubs, and how to develop the good, like Free Masonry, of which I am about to speak.

Of what useful developments was Free Masonry susceptible? Here was an entirely new question for the age, which has failed to discover the resources offered by this institution. It is a diamond which we have cast aside without knowing its value, just as the Savages of Guanahani did gold, until European cupidity had taught them its value.

While in the pursuit of pleasure, we are often effecting social innovations of the highest importance; of this nature are the Clubs and Casinos which are established in various parts of Europe, and which contain the germs of the Combined Household.

This little innovation, if it had taken a broader range, if the Clubs had gone to the extent of organizing *Permanent Households for single persons of various ages and fortunes*, might have overthrown the Civilized Order. The members of such a Household would soon have perceived that the passions tend to subdivide every Society into several unequal and rivalized parties or groups; after a few experiments of this kind, we should have arrived by degrees to the Combined Household, or *Series of Nine Groups*, in which the rivalries would have been regularly balanced and harmonized. On witnessing the delights and conveniences of such a Household, single women would have hastened to imitate it, and soon the Civilized Order would have disappeared, without the least convulsion, and to the amazement of the whole world.

A revolution less brilliant, less prompt, but still very fortunate, might have been effected by the aid of Free Masonry. If the philosophers have not perceived this, it is because their proud reason is forever losing itself in the clouds, without stopping in the middle region of common sense ; they thus become incapable of appreciating the processes of Nature, which are always of an extreme simplicity.

From the middle of the eighteenth century, they sought to effect some kind of a Revolution, by which they might mount to distinction and fortune ; but as there were several ways for accomplishing this, it is well to make known what other they might have adopted, both for their own good and that of the human race.

Previous to 1789, the public mind was eager for innovations ; any religious sect founded at that period would have had more chances of success than had Mohammed or Luther. To conform to the spirit of the age, the new sect should have been favorable to splendor, luxury, and pleasure ; but the philosophers had no idea of any such basis, even in 1795, when every one was at full liberty to found new religions, however vapid or superficial.

After the defeat they experienced in 1793, no other course remained for them than to abandon a career which was no longer practicable, cast aside their old dogmas, and rally frankly to the support of Nature—to the support of the passions, which, after all, must be tolerated, since it is useless to combat or oppose them.

It would have been a mortifying thing to the philosophers to offer incense to the passions, which they had so long defamed, and accordingly they faltered and hesitated, and at last proposed as a middle course, " indifference to riches and pleasures without either loving or despising them." But desperate diseases require desperate remedies ; the philosophers had nothing to hope from any course but an extreme one. Borne down by Civilization, they should have attacked Civilization on its weak side—attacked its system of Amatory Servitude; and to destroy this, it was necessary to institute a religion of love and pleasure—a religion of which they might at once have established themselves the priests and pontiffs. The Masonic Society offered them the means for this, if they had only known how to apply and direct them.

In entering upon the sacerdotal order, the philosophers would only have gone back to the point from which they started, for in antiquity they were the acolytes of the mythological religion. I have already said that the ancient moralists were only Pagan monks. The Cynics and Epicureans were but antitypes of the Capucin and Bernardin friars—so true is it, that in every phase of society the passions exhibit the same developments, differing only in form.

There was wanting to the Philosophers, to enable them to re-enter upon a religious career, some apostate from the dominant religion, some one like Mirabeau to put himself at their head and destroy his own sect. They could not have undertaken such an enterprise by themselves, for they are simple word-mongers, possessing neither boldness nor invention. They had need of a chief, to take the lead and furnish them with a plan of warfare, which they themselves could never have conceived; for the want of such guidance, they commenced their attack upon the Catholic religion without having any other to propose as a substitute.

For a long time, they had under their eyes an instrument which might have insured their victory; this was no other than the Society of Free Masons. This corporation, founded ostensibly for charitable objects, had already overcome the chief obstacles in the way of forming a religion based upon love and pleasure.

I. It had succeeded in establishing its lodges throughout all Civilized countries, and in constituting them exclusively of the middle and upper classes, under the patronage of the Great, who were at its head.

II. It had accustomed the people to look without jealousy upon its mysterious assemblies, held in secret and away from the profane vulgar.

III. It had given a religious tone to material pleasures; for what are the meetings of the Free Masons but convivial gatherings, accompanied by certain rites and ceremonies, which are useful as a substitute for cards, and for making the time pass economically. These continual festivals were a polite means of excluding the avaricious, who in such matters are always more injurious than useful.

Here, then, was a Society the arrangements of which were marvellously adapted for the foundation of a new religion. It only needed an able chief at its head, having the tact to introduce women and refined pleasures to make it become the dominant sect of the rich in all Civilized countries, while Christianity, which on account of its austerity is better suited to the poor, would have been imperceptibly restricted to them, like the worship of Fô in China, which exists only among the lower classes.

The details as to the statutes which would have been adapted to such a sect, and the means it would have possessed for attracting to it all the most prominent members of society, without separating them from the reigning religion, I abstain from entering upon.

Having enjoyed for a long period so enviable a position, the Free Masons must have been very blind not to have known how to profit by it. After this, if they have a secret, as they pretend, it is certainly not the secret of going ahead. The state of political nullity in which they have remained, despite their numerous means of advancement, gives one so poor an idea of their pretended secret, that if they should offer to divulge it, many persons would refuse to listen. Will they say that they have never desired to rise above political mediocrity? Will they succeed in persuading any one, that the chiefs of an extensive affiliated corporation can guarantee themselves against that love of power which is the essence of all corporate bodies, from the Janizaries to the Jesuits?

Meanwhile, it is well to communicate to them a truth which will console them for their political blindness, to wit, that they share the disgrace of not comprehending an iota of the affairs of social Movement, with the most learned bodies in Civilization.

A religion of love and pleasure would have been an admirable offset to modern philosophy, whose theories of political economy, too bald and meagre, and preaching the love of money too crudely, had need to be allied with a religious sect in order to give some soul to their dry precepts. Political economy needed a fine mask to conceal its ugly face. It is a science which appeals only to the pocket; it should have sought an ally which made its appeals to the heart, a sect which, giving to the pleasures of the senses a religious sanction, would have proved that the love of wealth and luxury is perfectly compatible with probity, charity, and all the generous passions. Alas, this love of money against which men declaim so vainly, would it not have been better to cover it with flowers than with slime, since it is to reign in Civilization as long as this Order exists, without it being within the power of any reasoning to deaden it for a single instant.

Let it be well understood that in speaking of a religion of love and pleasure, I consider it applicable in principle only to the polite and opulent classes; then, to a few adepts taken from among the people for the service of the sect, which would not admit of the initiation of the middle and lower classes, till it had been firmly established among the great. The progress of such a religion would have taken a direction opposite to that of the austere religions, which take root first among the people and thence extend to the upper classes, who find themselves at the present day *subordinated to the masses in religious matters*—this being another of the absurdities of modern Civilization.

In making the new religion attractive to the great, the Free Masons would have enlisted the whole opulent class at once. The great are eager after everything which tends to sanction voluptuous enjoyments; how much then they would have appreciated a refined exercise of love and pleasure in polite religious sects, composed exclusively of persons of their own rank.

As soon as the middle classes had seen the new religion welcomed by the great, they would have rushed into it blindfold as they now do into Free Masonry, influenced by the *spirit of sect and of proselytism*, which is natural to all men. This spirit of sect and of proselytism, *combined with the attraction of love and pleasure*, would have been certain, then, to seduce them; and such should have been the policy of the new sect.

It will be useless to raise any objections against the above plan, till I shall have explained the means of realizing it. Some of these means would have been infallible for enlisting the elite of society, and especially all women of fortune, who are the most liberal supporters of every religion. The religion in quest on would have enlisted in its favor, among others, all the aged, who in the exercise of the new worship would have found themselves in favor with the young, by whom they are at present avoided on all occasions of pleasure. Civilization which has been rightfully defined *a war of the Rich against the Poor*, is also *a war of the Old against the Young*, and I shall show that both ages are alike losers by this discord, which would have disappeared among the initiates of the new sect.

Instead of adopting the plan I have suggested, what has been the course of the philosophers in their attack upon the Catholic Religion? They have had the folly to declare open war against it, without knowing its means of resistance, and without offering any adequate substitute for it.

It is in religious matters that the philosophers proved themselves to be worthy lovers of mediocrity, for never did the human mind conceive anything more insipid than the two religions to which philosophy gave birth at the close of the eighteenth century; I allude to the worship of Reason, and to Theophilanthropy — religions really pitiable, dead before born.

Telum imbelle sine ictu.

Never did a religion make its debut under more favorable auspices than the worship of Reason. There was not a single obstacle for it to vanquish. France, all terrified as she was, would have accepted blindfold, any religion or any constitution which had been offered her. Was not this an unprecedented advantage for a new religion — the advantage of being able to instal itself at once throughout a whole empire, and compel friends and foes to practice its ritual? Had the new religion been at all adapted to the spirit of the people, or of the great, it would have succeeded from the mere fact that it had a chance of *temporary trial* — a chance no legislator, civil or religious, has had since the days of Lycurgus. The theories of the philosophers must be little compatible with the human heart, not to have succeeded in so fine a field.

Give to other innovators the same chance, and you would have invented for you a religion for which the people, after enjoying its delights for a year, would be willing to lay down their lives ; but it would have to be an impassioned, not a tame religion.

Theophilanthropy presented itself also under the best auspices, but preaching always the same mediocrity and moderation, which had only changed color, and which could not in any way accord with the passions of the human heart. It may be said of these two religions, that the one was a body without a soul, and the other a soul without a body. In the first, there were forms without doctrines ; in the second, doctrines without forms. The former was perhaps more politic in its conception, since it hoodwinked the people by a burlesque mixture of the sacred and profane. It had its gods, like Marat and Chalier—its devils, like Pitt and Coburg. It pleased the senses by civic parades and solemn hymns, mixed up with political diatribes. It was a religion for the eye and ear ; such a religion may have been adapted to the populace, for the mass of men, who are guided by the senses, want something to revere which is tangible.

The Theophilanthropists announced an invisible God of whom there existed no symbol. The more reasonable their doctrines, the more absurd they became in religious politics. What the multitude want is not to be enlightened but to be dazzled. To all your oracles of reason, they prefer the visions of the Apocalypse—the miracles, the mysteries, which offer sustenance and support to their feeble intelligence. In a word, they want a religion which appeals to the imagination and excites enthusiasm— a religion to silence the voice of reason, which comes only to discourage and dishearten them by revealing the extent of their social and domestic miseries.

An oversight entirely new in these two religions was that of their having no priests. The people wish to see men directly commissioned from Heaven. But the Theophilanthropists often chose a lawyer or a tradesman to proclaim the word of God, and one does not like to hear such men preaching virtue. Besides, how can the ministers of religion serve in the church and at the counter at the same time ? And how can we conceive of a worship being sustained without priests supported by the altar ?

While the philosophers were showing themselves so barren of conception by inventing these two tame religions, a rude Arab Mohammed, founded one with the greatest success, because he was in every sense immoderate and extravagant—because he relied only on excesses, marvels, and exaggerations. What a blow for the friends of moderation! If they wished to attack the Catholic religion, they should have' opposed it by a religion going to the opposite extreme; while that deified privation, it should have deified pleasure. This was an entirely new career of which Mohammed had no conception. His religion is in no sense a voluptuous religion. It promises certain delights, but to man only, without extending them to woman; nor does it elevate them to the dignity of religious acts; in a word, it restricts them to the lowest degree of development by instituting the harem, which is the tomb of love, and which can be enjoyed only by the rich.

I repeat it, there was a great thing to be done in the matter of religious innovation; but it is not by moderation that great things are achieved.* For the rest, the philosophers ought not to be surprised that I enter into no details as to the religious career which opened before them but which they failed to perceive, my intention being, not to expose their science, which is about to finish with Civilization, but to make them see that it has not known what course to pursue, nor how to save itself by creating a new religion. They possessed some influence in antiquity, owing to their alliance with the priesthood; but in proportion as the sacerdotal body isolated itself from them, owing to the birth of Catholicism, which was too austere a religion to be associated with any literary body, their credit began to decline. They ought, then, to have returned to the only road of advancement open to them, either by reuniting themselves to the priesthood, or supplanting it by the institution of a new religion of their own invention.

---

* There exist on the globe but three or four moderate sects, as, for instance, the Quakers, Anabaptists, etc. And what part do they play in the world? Are they not social nullities? Besides, what is the result of all this moderation? It is said that the Quakers, who are so moderate in the matter of dress, are not all so in the pleasures of the table, nor in the love of wealth—especially in Philadelphia. After this, it may be said on seeing their sober raiment:—" Chase the passions out of the door and they will return by the window." And, after all, may not this mummery of plain attire be a mere matter of interest? Hold it for certain that there is always some deviltry concealed under a show of moderation. The Quakers, for the trouble of wearing drab coats and plain hats, are exempted from military service, conscriptions, etc. At this price, how many of the inhabitants of France would gladly become Quakers—the fathers not to pay, the sons not to enlist! Where, then, is the merit in a moderation which secures such advantages?

This is what they attempted, without knowing how to accomplish it, without seeing that what was wanted was a religion of love and pleasure, of which Free-Masonry had already laid the foundation. Such a religion would have prepared society for entering the sixth and seventh Periods, for it would have led to freedom in the passion of love, which would soon have extended itself from the Masonic body throughout Civilization.

The question was to find the means of bringing the world to tolerate the idea of amatory freedom, to ascertain what social Order would result from it, and to point out the future benefits of such an innovation, which it would have been well, at first, to limit to a few corporations, isolated from the people, like the Masonic body. This institution, then, is one of the germs which Providence has sown in our midst, to offer the human race a means of escape from Civilization and an entrance to the Combined Order; and if this affiliated corporation has been able to exist for so long a period, without its nature or true destiny being perceived either by its chiefs or by the philosophers, it deserves to be ranked among the numerous monuments which will attest in the future to the blindness of Civilized politics.

EPILOGUE.

ON THE SOCIAL CHAOS OF THE GLOBE.

APOSTLES of the uncertain sciences, who pretend to labor for the good of Mankind, think you that six hundred millions of Barbarians and Savages form no part of the human race? Do they not suffer like other mortals? Yet what have you done for them? Nothing. Your systems are applicable only to Civilization, and even here, when put to the proof, they only aggravate the evil. And though you possessed the secret of human happiness, think you to fulfil the designs of God in restricting it to the Civilized nations, which occupy the smallest portion of the Globe? God sees in the Human Race but one great Family, all the members of which have an equal right to his bounty; it is his will that all nations be happy together, or that happiness shall be possessed by none.

To second the designs of God, you should have sought for a Social Order applicable to the whole Globe, and not to a few nations. The immense preponderance of the Barbarians and Savages should have taught you that they are to be elevated, not by Coercion but by Attraction. And can you hope to allure them by the spectacle of your institutions, which are sustained only by the aid of the scaffold and the bayonet —institutions odious to your own people even, who in all countries would rebel against them at once, if they were not restrained by fear of punishment?

Far from having succeeded in enlightening and establishing unity in the Human Race, your theories excite in Barbarians nothing but profound contempt, and your customs provoke the irony even of the Savage. The strongest imprecation of the latter against an enemy is: — "May you be reduced to labor in the fields!" — words which should be regarded as a malediction uttered by Nature herself. Yes, Civilized Industry is condemned by Nature, since it is abhorred by all free races, who would embrace it at once, if it accorded with the passions of Man.

Hence God has not permitted Civilized Industry to make great progress—has forbidden that a system so oppressive to those who bear its burdens, should be extended over the entire Globe. He has restricted it to a few regions—to China, India, Europe —where are amassed swarms of indigent laborers, forming a reserved corps to be employed in the organization of the Combined Order, so that, at its commencement, this Order may be provided with a disposable industrial force ; these wretched masses will be disgorged from the regions which they now cumber, and will be distributed by the Supreme Head of the Unitary Government at points suitable for commencing the regular cultivation of the Globe.

But it is in vain that you have sought to extend Civilized Industry, and to establish your system of incoherent cultivation over the entire earth. God (for various reasons which I can not here explain) would never have suffered that an Order so contrary to his designs should be extended over all cultivable regions, and he has adopted precautions for restricting its progress, either by intestine wars or the irruption of Barbarians.

If Industry has made some progress in Europe, has it not lost immense regions in Asia? If Civilization has founded colonies in America, has it not lost vast empires at the gates of Europe— lost Egypt, Greece, Asia Minor, Carthage, Chaldea, and a portion of Western Asia. Industry has been stifled in extensive and beautiful countries like Balk, where it began to be introduced, and the empire of Samaracand, formerly celebrated in the East, with all the regions which extend from the river Jihon to the mouths of the Indus, have retrograded politically and gone back to the Horde. The vast empire of Hindostan is marching rapidly to its ruin through the oppression of the English, who have created among the people a disgust for Industry, and caused them to assimilate to the Mahrattas, the Hordes of which already constitute a powerful group of Tartars in the centre of Mogul. These may in time encamp in the eastern and western chains of the Gauts, amalgamating with the tribes of Malabar and Coromandel, and by their nomadic life disgusting them also with Industry.

The Horde is daily encroaching upon the cultivated regions of Asia, passing more and more its natural boundary, which is the mountain chain of Imaus, extending from Bukaria into China. At our own doors even, the Horde is springing up in every part of Turkey; fifty years more of persecution, of Ottoman anarchy, and we shall see the whole of that fine empire gone back to the No-madic or Tartar life, which is making frightful progress in every part of the Turkish dominions. Other empires, once flourishing, such as Pegu and Siam, have sunk to the lowest degree of weak-ness and debasement, and their Industry, like that of Turkey, would seem to have hardly more than a century to exist. If the present disorder of the Globe were prolonged, Asia, immense Asia, throughout all her vast regions, would finally abandon In-dustry. China even, that Colossus of cupidity and corruption, is on the evident decline; recent accounts of travellers have fully undeceived us as to her pretended splendor. The character of the people has degenerated more and more since the mixture of the Tartars. The Horde now occupies immense territories in China; and in this Empire, so much vaunted for its Industry, we find at four leagues from Pekin fine lands uncultivated and all but unknown, while in the provinces of the south the priests call the people in vain to Agriculture; they leave large tracts to run to waste, and incline more and more to the formation of the Horde.

The Horde is for Civilization, a volcano always ready to over-whelm it; it is an inveterate humor which, subdued at one point, breaks out at another, and reappears the moment we cease to treat it. Finally, this tendency on the part of the laboring masses to go back to the Horde, should concentrate all the cal-culations of Political Science on this one problem: *To discover a new Social Order which will enable the poorest of the laboring classes to find in Industry a degree of comfort and prosperity suf-ficient to attract them constantly and passionately to their work, and make them prefer labor to the life of inertia and marauding to which they now aspire.*

Until you have resolved this problem, Nature will expose you to perpetual assaults. You erect Empires which serve only as sport for her, and which she delights to submerge in the abyss of revolutions. You are but a burden to her—a prey devoted to her vengeance. Your scientific prodigies result only in poverty and bloodshed. Your Heroes, your Legislators, build only upon the sand; all the foresight of the wisest Sovereign can not prevent feeble successors from destroying the most brilliant trophies of his reign. Civilization gives birth to the Heroes of the present only to humiliate the Heroes of the past; it eclipses, one by the other, those to whom it owes all its éclat. What a subject of anxiety for our Great Men, who, in their turn, will have feeble successors! Must they not suffer from fear of the revolutions of the future more than they enjoy in the triumphs of the present; and must they not abhor this perfidious Civilization, which only awaits their death to undermine and overthrow their proudest works?

Yes, the Civilized Order is becoming more and more unstable. The volcano opened by the Philosophers in 1789 is only at its first eruption; others will follow in proportion as the agitators are favored by feeble governments. The war of the Poor against the Rich has succeeded so well, that the demagogues of all countries aim only to revive it. All attempts at prevention will be vain. Nature, who mocks at our wisdom and our foresight, will cause revolutions to spring even from the measures we adopt to insure tranquillity.

I should not dare to present this frightful perspective, if I did not bring the calculation which is about to guide Political Science through the maze of the Passions, and deliver the World from Civilization, now more revolutionary and odious than ever.

Civilized Nations! while the Barbarians, deprived of your light, know how to maintain their Societies and their Institutions for thousands of years, how is it that yours are overthrown so rapidly, and often in the same century which gives them birth? We hear you continually deploring the fragility of your works, and the cruelty of Nature, who causes the prodigies of your genius to be so speedily destroyed. Cease to attribute these disasters to time or to chance; they are the result of the gross incompetency of your social systems, which fail to insure to the destitute Masses the means of labor and subsistence. It is to bring you to confess your ignorance, that Nature holds the glaive over your Empires and exults over their ruin.

I would be for a moment the echo of your political lamentations. What has become of the monuments of Civilized pride? Thebes and Babylon, Athens and Carthage, have crumbled into ruins. What an augury for Paris and London, and for those modern Empires whose mercantile follies weigh already upon Reason and upon Nature. Weary of our Societies, she overthrows them turn by turn, and derides alike our virtues and our crimes. Laws reputed as oracles of wisdom conduct equally with the ephemeral codes of demagogues to political shipwreck and ruin. To fill the measure of your disgrace, we have seen the rude legislation of China and of India brave the scythe of Time for four thousand years, while the prodigies of Civilized Philosophy have passed away like shadows. Our Political Sciences, after so many efforts for the consolidation of Empires, seem to have labored only to prepare a field for Vandalism, which constantly reappears to destroy in a day the work of centuries.

A few monuments have survived, but for the disgrace of Civilized Politics. Rome and Byzantium, formerly capitals of the greatest of Empires, have become two Centres of fanaticism and folly. At Rome, the temples of the Cæsars are invaded by the gods of obscure Judea; on the shores of the Bosphorus, the cathedrals of Christianity are polluted by the gods of ignorance; here, Jesus is raised on the pedestal of Jupiter; there, Mohammed plants himself at the shrine of Jesus. Rome and Byzantium! Nature has preserved you, to devote you to the contempt of the nations you had enslaved. You have become two arenas of political abominations;—two boxes of Pandora which have spread over the East, vandalism and the plague, over the West, superstition and fanaticism. Nature insults by your debasement the great Empire she has destroyed; you are two mummies preserved to decorate her car of triumph, and to give to modern capitals a foretaste of the lot prepared for the monuments and works of Civilization.

It seems as if Nature had permitted this odious Society to rise for the pleasure of overthrowing it, of proving to it, by disasters a hundred times repeated, the absurdity of our moral and political sciences. An image of the criminal Sysiphus, climbing toward a summit and falling back at the moment of attaining it, Civilization seems condemned to mount toward an ideal happiness, and to fall back just as it sees the end of its sufferings. Reforms the most wisely planned end only in the shedding of seas of blood. Meanwhile the ages roll on, and the people groan under their torments, while new revolutions threaten to demol-

ish our tottering Empires—Empires which, as long as they confide in Philosophy, in a Science inimical to Political Unity, in a
Science which is only a mask for party intrigues and serves but
to foment the elements of Revolution as fast as time develops
them, are destined, turn by turn, to overthrow and destroy each
other.

To the disgrace of our Sciences, we see multiplying every day
the germs of the disorganization which threatens our frail Societies. Yesterday, scholastic quarrels about Equality prostrated
thrones, altars, and the laws of property; Europe retrograded
toward Barbarism. To-morrow, Nature will array against us
other arms, and Civilization, put to new trials, will again succumb. We see it on the verge of destruction every century. It
was at its extremity when the Turks besieged Vienna, and if they
had adopted the European tactics, it would have been lost. In
our own day, again, it has been on the brink of ruin: the wars of
the Revolution might have led to the invasion and dismember-
ment of France, after which Austria and Russia would have divided Europe, and in the disputes which would have followed,
Russia (which has resources unknown to the world, and even to
herself) might have crushed Austria and Civilization. The fate
of this criminal Society is to shine for a few centuries, then disappear, to rise again once more to fall. If the Civilized Order
could have secured the happiness of the Human Race, God would
have been interested in its preservation, and would have taken
measures to establish it upon an immovable basis. Why, then,
does he permit your Societies, after having lasted for a brief period, to be engulfed in Revolutions? It is to confound your scientific guides who frame their social theories according to their
caprice, whereas God, less arbitrary than the Philosophers, does
not regulate the laws of the Universe according to his will alone,
but conforms in all his works to the eternal standard of justice
—to Mathematics, whose truth is independent of himself, but
whose laws he nevertheless rigorously follows.

Cease, then, to be astonished if your Societies destroy each other,
and hope for nothing stable under laws which come from man
alone—under Sciences hostile to the Divine Spirit, which tends
to establish Unity on the Globe as in the Firmament. A world
devoid of a Unitary Head, of a Central Government, would it not

resemble a Universe which had no God to direct it, a Universe in which the stars, gravitating without fixed order, would clash together perpetually like your discordant nations, which present to the eyes of the Sage but an arena of wild beasts infuriated to destroy each other?

In lamenting over the successive downfall of your Societies, you were ignorant that they were opposed to the designs of God; now that the discovery of his plans is announced to you, are you not disabused as to the value of Civilization? Will you not acknowledge that it has exhausted human patience; that to secure the happiness of Man, a new Social Order is necessary; that in order to conform to the designs of God, we must seek an Order applicable to the entire Globe, and not to a corner of the earth occupied by Civilized nations; in fine, *that we should study the vices and defects of all existing Societies, and not those of Civilization alone, which includes but a portion of the human race?*

Let us establish, on this basis, the thesis of the political infirmity of the Globe.

Three Societies exist upon the earth, namely, the Civilized, the Barbaric, and the Savage. One of the three is necessarily better than the two others. Now the two imperfect, which do not rise to or identify themselves with the best of the three, are affected with that chronic debility with which Montesquieu supposes, with reason, that the Human Race is stricken.

As for the third Society, which is supposed to be the best, and which can not bring the two others to imitate it, it is evidently insufficient to secure the happiness of the Human Race, since it leaves the major portion of it to languish in a state inferior to its own.

As a result, two of the three existing Societies are affected with paralysis, and the third with political impotency. Decide after this how these morbific characteristics with which the entire Globe is visibly affected, are distributed in the three Societies.

In discussing this thesis, you will perceive that the two paralytic Societies are the Savage and the Barbaric, which make no attempts at amelioration, but obstinately cling to their old customs whether good or bad. As for Civilization, it is this Society which is affected with political impotence, for we see it in a state of perpetual agitation, and constantly trying new experiments to deliver itself from its sufferings.

Mankind, in passing from the inertia of the Savage State to the industrial activity of Barbarism and Civilization, have passed from a state of apathy to a state of active suffering; for the Savage and

Barbarian do not complain of their lot, and make no effort to change it, whereas Civilized Man is always discontented, and is gnawed by unsatisfied desires, even in the midst of opulence:—

> He burns
> With inextinguishable fires,
> Less rich with what of wealth he has,
> Than poor from what he still desires.
>
> J. B. ROUSSEAU.

Apostles of Error, Moralists and Politicians! after so many proofs of your blindness, do you still pretend to enlighten the Human Race? The Nations will reply to you:—"If your Sciences, dictated by Wisdom, have served only to perpetuate poverty and bloodshed, give us rather sciences dictated by Folly, provided that they calm the despair and assuage the miseries of the people."

Alas! far from securing the happiness you have promised, you have known only how to sink mankind below the condition of the brute. If the animal is at times deprived of food, he has no anxiety about providing for his wants till he feels them. The lion, well clad, well armed, takes his food wherever he can find it, and without troubling himself with cares for his young or with fears for the morrow. How preferable his condition to that of the wretched poor who swarm in your cities, to that of your destitute laborers, who, out of work and harassed by debt, sink, after all their trials and disappointments, into mendicancy, and exhibit their sores, their nakedness, and their famished children in the streets of your capitals, which they make resound with their piteous laments. Behold, Philosophers, the bitter fruit of your Sciences! Poverty—nothing but Poverty. Nevertheless, you pretend to have perfected Human Reason, while you, its oracles, have known only how to conduct mankind from one abyss of suffering to another. Yesterday, you reproached Religion with the massacre of St. Bartholomew; to-day, she reproaches you with the scaffolds of the Revolution. Yesterday, it was the Crusades which depopulated Europe; to-day, it is the doctrine of Equality which mows down three millions of our young men; and to-morrow, some new Fanaticism will bathe our Civilized Empires in blood. Perfidious Guides! to what an abject condition have you reduced Social Man, and how prudent have been the governments most extolled by you, in suspecting your theories! You were always a subject of alarm, even to the sovereigns you counted among your disciples. Sparta cast you from her midst, and Cato would have had you driven out of Rome. In our own days, again, Frederic the Great declared that had he wished to punish one of his provinces, he would have put it under the government of the Philosophers; and Napoleon excluded moral and political philosophy from the temple where preside the useful sciences. And are you not even more suspected among yourselves? Do you not confess that in operating upon the Passions, you resemble children playing with firebrands amid barrels of powder? The French Revolution has come to put the seal upon this truth, and to cover your sciences with an ineffaceable opprobrium. You foresaw that your absurd theories would be annihilated from the moment they were put to the proof, and hence you conspired together to stifle the voice of men inclined to be sincere — men like Hobbes and Rousseau, who perceived that Civilization was a subversion of the laws of Nature, a systematic development of all social vices and abominations. You have rejected these glimpses of light to repeat your boasts of Civilized progress and perfection.

The scene changes, and the truth which you feigned to seek is about to appear to confound your theories. It only remains for you, like the fallen gladiator, to die honorably. Prepare, yourselves, the hecatomb demanded by Truth; collect the fagots, apply the torch, and commit the rubbish of your philosophic systems to the flames.